PAG.

This is the Future of War

FX Holden

© 2021 FX Holden.

Independently Published
135,000 words
Typeset in 12pt Garamond
All rights reserved. No part of this publication may be reproduced, distributed, or transmitted in any form or by any means, including photocopying, recording, or other electronic or mechanical methods, without the prior written permission of the author, except in the case of brief quotations embodied in critical reviews and certain other noncommercial uses permitted by copyright law.

This novel is fiction. No resemblance to any person, government or corporate entity, extant or defunct, is intended.

Contact me:
fxholden@yandex.com
https://www.facebook.com/hardcorethrillers

All Future War novels are self-contained stories and can be read in any order. However, chronological order is as follows:
Kobani, Golan, Bering Strait, Okinawa, Orbital, Pagasa

Cover art by Diana Buidoso: dienel96@yahoo.com

Maps © OpenStreetMap

With huge thanks to my fantastic beta reading team for their encouragement and constructive critique:

Sim Alam
Bror Appelsin
Mike Ashworth
Nick Baker
Johnny Bunch
Frank Daugherity
Wayne Frenck
Randy Hardin
Dave Hedrick
Tom Hill
Martin Hirst
Greg Hollingsworth
Steve Panza
Barry Roberts
Rob
Therese Blakemore Saffery
Lee Steventon

And to copy editor, Brigitte Lee Messenger, for putting the cheese around the holes.

COMING SUMMER 2022,
DMZ: THIS IS THE FUTURE OF WAR

China's push for global power

In the South China Sea, Beijing will continue to intimidate rival claimants and will use growing numbers of air, naval, and maritime platforms to signal to Southeast Asian countries that China has effective control over contested areas.

Annual Threat Assessment,
Office of the US Director of National Intelligence, April 2021

China's leader, Xi Jinping, warns China will not be 'bullied' by foreign forces

"The Chinese people have never bullied, oppressed or enslaved the peoples of other countries, not in the past, not now, and not in the future," he said. "At the same time, the Chinese people will never allow foreign forces to bully, oppress or enslave us," he added. "Whoever nurses delusions of doing that will crack their heads and spill blood on the Great Wall of steel built from the flesh and blood of 1.4 billion Chinese people."

NY Times, 30 June 2021

China has won AI battle with U.S., Pentagon's ex-software chief says

LONDON - China has won the artificial intelligence battle with the United States and is heading towards global dominance because of its technological advances, the Pentagon's former software chief told the Financial Times. Nicolas Chaillan, the Pentagon's first chief software officer who resigned in protest against the slow pace of technological transformation in the U.S. military, said the failure to respond was putting the United States at risk. "We have no competing fighting chance against China in 15 to 20 years. Right now, it's already a done deal; it is already over in my opinion," he told the newspaper.

Reuters, 11 Oct 2021

Contents

Maps	9
Cast of Players	11
A little fish	13
Learning moments	16
Kinetic politics	57
A surplus of pirates	127
Dying time	218
Where the metal hits the meat	285
Epilogue: two weeks later	366
Author Notes	376
Preview: DMZ	382
Glossary	413

Maps

Area of Operations

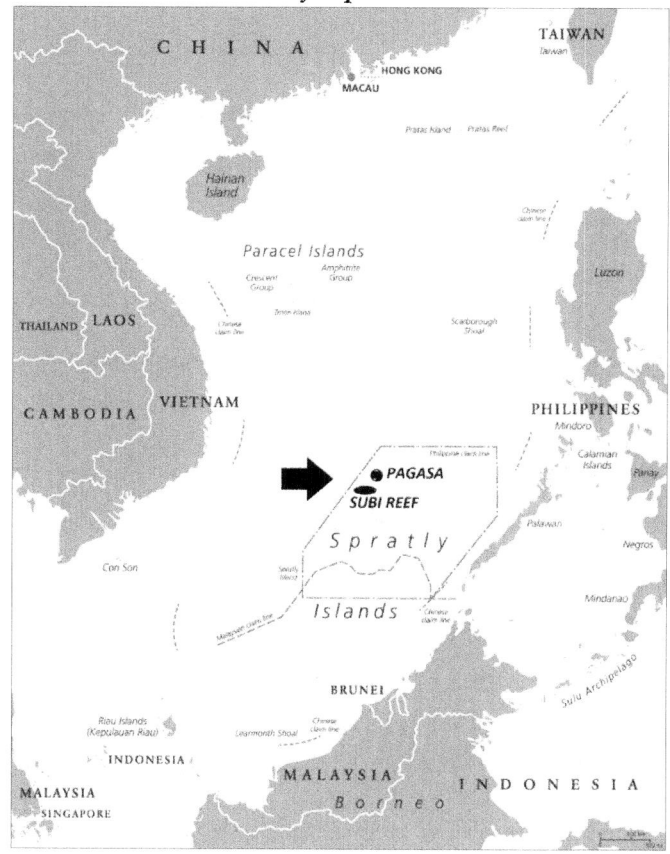

*Map of the Spratly Islands Archipelago,
showing (highlighted) Pagasa Island, Subi Reef*

Pagasa Island

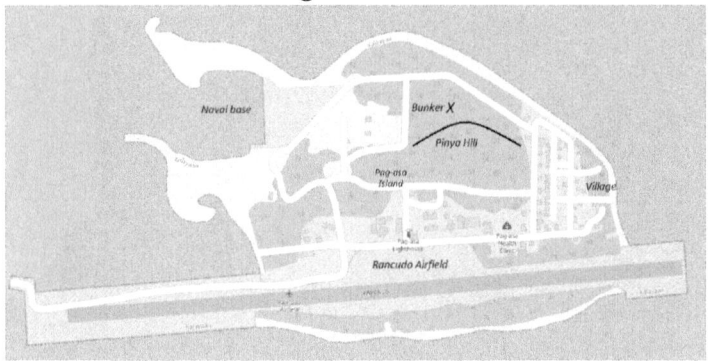

Map of Pagasa Island, showing Rancudo Airfield, Emilio Liwanag Naval Base, Pinya Hill, Japanese bunker

Subi Reef Chinese Military Installation

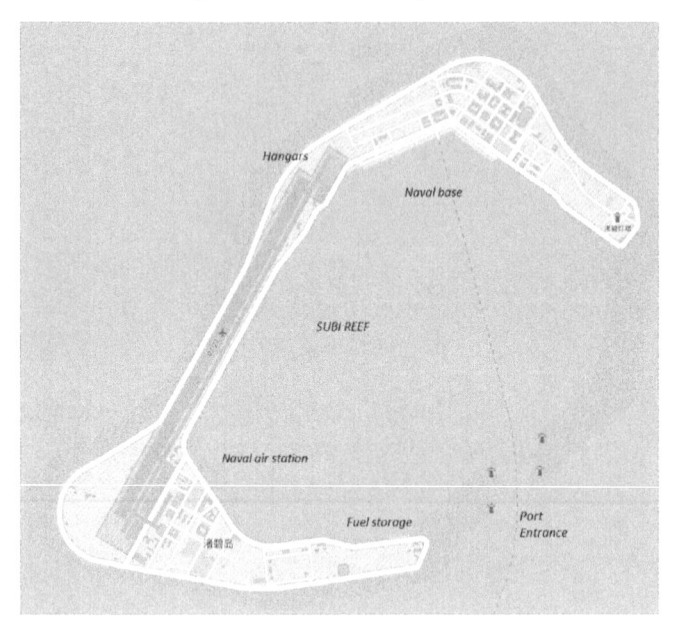

Cast of Players

by affiliation and order of appearance

White Star Lines
Karen 'Bunny' O'Hare, *pilot, Lieutenant (Retired)*
Sylvie Leclerc, *Head of Operations, White Star Risk Group*
Karl Sorensen, *founder and CEO*
Angus 'Ginger' McIntyre, *Communications Officer, White Star Andromeda*
Captain Jorgen Pedersen, *White Star Andromeda*
Kapil Bose, *Chief Mate, White Star Andromeda*

Pagasa Island, Philippines
Gonzales and Eugenio Maat, *civilians*
Captain Heraldo Bezerra, *Philippine Naval Combat Engineering Brigade, PN Seabees, 'Pagasa detachment'*
Conrado Reyes, *Mayor, Kalayaan municipality of Palawan province, Philippines*

Muara Container Terminal, Brunei
Abdul Ibrahim, *leader, Batu Bay militia*
Kamito, *boatmaster, Batu Bay militia*

Executive Committee (ExComm), US National Security Council
Carmine Lewis, *Director of National Intelligence, Lt. General (Retired)*
Chuck Abdor, *White House Chief of Staff*
Victoria Porter, *Secretary of State*
Phil Kahn, *Secretary of Defense*
Stuart Fenner, *President*
Jada Tyler, *Vice President*
General James Cavoli, *Chairman of the Joint Chiefs of Staff*
Kyle Sandiland, *Director, National Security Agency*

China
Lieutenant Baotian Liu, *Jiaolong (Sea Dragon) Commando team, PLA Navy*
Corporal An Ruan, *Jiaolong (Sea Dragon) Commando team, PLA Navy*
Lieutenant Commander Li Chen, *Ao Yin J-16 Squadron*
Admiral Li Bing, *Commander PLA Navy Southern Command*

US Navy
Commander Daniel Okafor, *Captain, frigate USS Congress*
Lieutenant Carlo 'Knuckles' Diavolo, *Executive Officer, USS Congress*

A little fish

Subi Reef, South China Sea, December 9, 2034

It was the most heavily fortified Chinese installation in the South China Sea. But Bobong Huerta knew it also had the best damn crab fishing anywhere for fifty miles.

His only crewman, Gonzales Maat, hadn't liked the idea of going anywhere near it. He had a scar from a tuna hook that ran down the right side of his face and it turned white when he was angry. It was white now. "Why we got to sail 20 miles to Subi? They never going to let you in man, the way our government been yelling about things lately. Chinese are not going let anyone even near Subi."

"I been fishing Subi fifty years," Bobong told him. "Best damn crabbing anywhere at the base of that reef and people too scared to go anywhere near it. Rich pickings, man."

"You been drinking your breakfast again, haven't you? It's like you *want* them to take your boat. How are we supposed to get home? Swim?" Gonzales pointed at their radio. "Probably been hailing you the last half hour."

"Radio don't work," Bobong grunted.

"I know that. They don't know that."

Watching the big white Chinese Coast Guard vessel motoring toward them from the mouth of Subi Reef's harbor, Bobong wasn't so sure; maybe Gonzales was right. It was pushing toward them at about ten knots, a half mile off but already dwarfing their little blue and white fishing boat. Gonzales recognized it, or at least the type. China used them to chase away any boat they didn't like. If they were in a good mood, they just yelled at you with bullhorns, or blasted you with high-pressure water hoses. If they were in a bad mood, they'd drive straight at you, try to capsize you with their bow wave. It made Bobong want to spit. Coast Guard? They were six hundred miles from the Chinese coast!

Bobong looked past the white ship to the reef, maybe a mile off. It had just been a coral atoll when he was a kid. His father would take him there and they'd fish the lagoon inside for jacks, largehead hairtail. Drop crab pots on the reefs around it, and every one came up filled with crab. It was an hour or more out of Pagasa Island, where they lived, but it had always delivered. Then the Chinese came. Started by chasing off the Philippine and Vietnamese fishermen, and then about twenty years ago they started building. First just pouring concrete over the reef so it wasn't submerged at high tide. Built a small dock. Then a big one. A runway for helicopters and jet fighters. Then they put in missile emplacements, barracks and warehouses and workshops. A lighthouse. Dredged the middle of the atoll and turned it into a deep-water port so they could anchor the big Coast Guard cutters like the one headed right for Bobong and Gonzales.

It wasn't a reef anymore; it was a Navy base. He wasn't dumb. He knew that. But Bobong had been stewing on it for years and he finally couldn't stand it anymore. These waters belonged to everybody. His family had been fishing here for a generation before the Chinese came. He had as much right to sail here as anyone. And he was sick of sailing past it knowing there was good fishing right here.

"He's coming straight for us. Gonna impound your boat," Gonzales said again. "Damn drunk old fool."

Standing up in his wheelhouse, Bobong spun the wheel clockwise, turning starboard to let the Coast Guard cutter know he'd seen it and was moving out the way. It corrected course too, kept coming straight at them.

"Maybe they will, maybe they won't," Bobong told Gonzales. "Was a time when you'd approach like this, the Chinese either waved you off, or waved you in. Sometimes they were friendly, let us drop some nets and pots. They didn't bother us; we didn't bother them."

"That was *ten years ago*, Bobong," Gonzales told him. He nodded at the cutter, a few hundred yards off now. There was a guy standing on the bow, filming them with a camera. Another one beside him with a rifle. Gonzales pointed at them. "You think they feeling friendly today?"

He'd barely finished speaking when they heard the engine note of the Chinese cutter change. Its bow lifted out of the water, the bow wave rising higher as it suddenly accelerated. Straight toward them!

"Get us out their damn way, Bobong!" Gonzales yelled.

Bobong already had the wheel hard starboard, turning his little boat the best he could, but all he was doing was putting it beam-on to the incoming cutter. He pushed the engine throttle full forward. It just coughed and choked at the flood of fuel.

The bow of the Coast Guard ship was like an ax, looming over them. Bobong whirled around, grabbed Gonzales and shoved him as hard as he could toward the door out to the stern. "Get out, man, jump for it!"

He just had time to see Gonzales dive clear, when the Chinese vessel was on him. He'd yelled so loud, pushed so hard, his lungs were empty when the cutter slammed into his boat just forward of the wheelhouse. His little boat folded like paper under the weight of the 2,400-ton warship. Bobong suddenly found himself twenty feet under the water in a welter of bubbles, wood and oil, his sinking boat dragging him down with it. He tried finding a way out of the wheelhouse – a broken window, the door, anything – but water was still pouring in, smashing him back against the wheel.

Sixty-year-old Bobong Huerta drowned scared and angry, screaming for his papa with empty lungs.

Learning moments

Hong Kong Harbor, January 7, 2035

Karen O'Hare had never been aboard a superyacht. In fact, now she thought of it, she'd never been aboard a yacht of any kind. She'd sailed on a destroyer – not her own choice – and piloted an unmanned submarine while sitting comfortably ashore, but that was the closest she'd ever wanted to come to actually being a sailor.

She was perfectly at ease pushing a stealth fighter through the sky at Mach 2.5 with a Russian K-77 missile on her tail, but put her on a deck at sea with nothing but the ocean deep and sharks and box jellyfish and stingrays and giant octopuses around her ... no thank you. Sure, it might have something to do with the fact Karen 'Bunny' O'Hare didn't have gills or webbed feet and couldn't swim to save her own life, but she didn't have feathers either and she wasn't afraid of flying.

"So how big is that thing?" Bunny asked the water limousine driver who had picked her up at 9 p.m. from a wharf near the ferry terminal and driven her to Repulse Bay on the other side of Hong Kong Island.

The ship that lay dead ahead of them had five decks that Bunny could see above the water, and probably two or three below. At the rear was a dock for a smaller boat that anyone else would probably call a luxury yacht in itself. Even sitting still, the behemoth looked fast.

"The *Sea Sirene*?" the limo driver replied, almost dismissively. "She is 62 meters long and 12 across the beam. Draft three and a half meters. Tonnage, about 1,280."

"Is it as sexy on the inside as it is on the outside?"

The man shrugged. "I've never been aboard it."

"Well, give me your cell number, I'll send you pictures of me at the swim-up bar with a daiquiri."

"I doubt that," he said with a smile. "I'm not taking you to the *Sirene*. Mr. Sorensen's new yacht is behind it."

By 'behind it' Bunny took him to mean 'smaller than'. Because as they approached the *Sea Sirene*, Bunny couldn't see any other ship.

As they swung around the bow of the superyacht, she got her first glimpse of the ship hiding behind it. It had only four decks above the water, which explained why it wasn't visible, but what it lacked in height it made up for in length. The area in front of the low, curved superstructure was at least two hundred feet long, and it had a newly arrived tiltrotor chopper parked on it, the blades still turning.

"The White Star *Warrior*," the man said, putting on his best tour guide voice. "A 120-meter aluminum and titanium trimaran hull, rotating master stateroom, indoor and outdoor dining for up to 30 guests, indoor cinema, gym and spa, jacuzzi, and a 25-meter lap pool."

"What, no roulette table?"

He ignored her. "The entire ship is designed for a zero-carbon footprint. The 70,000-kilowatt engines…"

"Kilowatts, that's like…"

"94,000 horsepower."

"Right."

"The engines are powered by hydrogen fuel distilled from seawater and can drive her at up to 20 knots…"

"I fly jets," Bunny told him. "So, 20 knots is kinda … not fast."

"Cruising."

"Ah."

"And 30 knots when aquaplaning."

Bunny turned her face away. "Still not fast," she said to herself, refusing to be impressed. But if an alien ship landed on earth and floated on the water, she was pretty sure the White Star *Warrior* is what it would look like.

Bunny was more interested in the tiltrotor. For a start, it had wings. Secondly, it had two turboprop engines turning rotors at the end of the wings. And lastly, it had two turbofan *jet* engines tucked in under V-shaped tail fins. But it disappeared from view as the limo driver swung his boat around to the back of the ship where there was a water-level fantail landing dock and two sailors – a man and a woman – in cream t-shirts, pants and spotless cream shoes to help her out.

There was also a woman in a red silk lounge suit with a cream blouse, leaning up against a bulkhead by a door and watching O'Hare negotiate the transfer with amusement. She was somewhere in her early 40s, tall, lithe, with long raven-black hair. Not exactly beautiful. Handsome was the word you'd probably use if describing how people look was your thing. Bunny preferred to judge people by how they handled themselves, by their range of creative swear words, and the variety and location of their tattoos and/or piercings.

"Ok, I got it," Bunny said, waving away one of the sailors. The tall woman kept her hands in her pockets and detached herself from the wall with a shrug of her shoulders, stepping down to greet O'Hare.

"Ms. O'Hare, I am Sylvie Leclerc. Would you like to come with me?" French accent. Of course she had a French accent.

She led the way, taking the steps up to the flight deck two at a time despite the three-inch heels she was wearing. They passed one deck level on the way up but didn't stop.

Damn show off. Bunny had already decided she didn't like her. Yet.

As they emerged into the cooler night air, Bunny's nostrils flared. She could still smell that heady alcohol-to-jet fuel smell coming off the aircraft crouched on the deck, see the shimmer of the heat over those turbofan engines. The thing was matt black, with the White Star Lines logo in plain white on the doors. It wasn't a copter, wasn't a plane. It reminded her a little of a Bell-Boeing Osprey special ops aircraft, but those jet engines at the rear … not an Osprey.

"You like?" Leclerc asked, pausing as they reached it.

"Can I touch?"

"Be my guest."

Bunny walked closer and ran her hand over the angular wheel housing and got her first surprise. It felt like rubber but buried in the skin were small irregularities.

"Stealth coating?"

Leclerc smiled and nodded, folding her arms and watching O'Hare with interest. "Oui."

She walked around the rear of the aircraft, Leclerc following. "Twin General Electric TF40 turbofan jet engines."

"Correct."

A sliding door to the interior was open and Bunny peered inside. It wasn't fitted out like an executive ride. The compartment inside was very spartan, with everything that might move either strapped down, locked in or stowed in netting-covered racks. "Modular payload bay," Bunny guessed. "This one is a personnel module. There are other modules?"

"There are," Leclerc confirmed.

Bunny walked around to the front of the machine. She was too short to hop up and see inside the cockpit and the door was locked (she tried it), but on the nose of the aircraft she spotted two round ports. They were barely visible to the eye, marked only by a circular break in the smooth metal of the aircraft's skin. She looked under the nose of the aircraft, at bulges in front of the forward wheels.

"These are gun ports," Bunny decided.

"They could simply be concealed landing lights."

"Yeah, they could. But they're not."

"Mr. Sorensen is waiting."

The French woman led them off the deck, past the lap pool and into a poolside salon with tiered birchwood benches around the jacuzzi, which thankfully was both empty and switched off. Bunny imagined the effect the designer was going for was 'Finnish sauna'. A trolley with iced water stood at the end of the pool and one of the sailors who had met her down at the waterline and followed them up poured Bunny a glass and set it down on a bench, which Bunny took as an invitation to sit.

19

"I'll be back," Leclerc said, disappearing deeper into the ship.

Leclerc found the elderly owner of White Star Lines standing in his oak-paneled office, flipping through mail on a tablet PC. She'd only been working for him for six months and still wasn't at ease in his presence. He'd never once engaged in small talk, even on a recent 10-hour direct flight from Hong Kong to Moscow in his executive jet. He'd sat across a coffee table from her and not said a single word except to reply politely if she asked him a question.

Karl Sorensen was 78 years old. He was the 25th richest man in the world and his White Star Lines was one of the leading mercantile shipping and port management companies on the planet. What made it a very sustainable company was that since the early 2000s it had been the cargo carrier of choice for the US military. Whenever the US went to war, it was White Star Lines that transported the Seabees, the dozers, tanks, trucks, and materials to make it happen. Containers bearing the White Star Lines starburst logo were almost as ubiquitous as the Stars and Stripes wherever the US was constructing its bases.

He looked over at her as she walked in. "She is here?"

"Yes."

"Let's make this quick. I don't like Australians. Noisy." He flipped the leather cover of the paper-thin tablet shut in his idiosyncratic way. It never left his side; in fact, it rarely left his hand.

Leclerc suppressed a smile and followed him aft, finding O'Hare standing on the deck with one foot up on a bench, looking back on the chopper on the flight deck.

Well, she was focused, Leclerc gave her that. About shoulder high to me, cropped, dyed platinum hair, pierced nose, eyebrow, lip and no doubt ... elsewhere. Tattoos on both arms where the black t-shirt stopped, also on her neck and ankle; the ankle tattoo just visible above combat boots. She had a pleasant face, but apparently an abrasive personality, which Sylvie had been warned she might need to 'manage' if the next few minutes were to go well.

Sylvie Leclerc was used to managing people. She'd managed billionaires, foreign intelligence officials and government ministers. So, she was sure she would be able to…

"Hey, you. Do you have anything other than water?" Bunny asked Sorensen as he approached her.

He frowned. "Yes. Of course. You wish for…" He snapped his fingers at the young sailor standing discreetly against a wall.

"Ginger ale, lots of ice," Bunny told the sailor. "Because what I really wish for…" she looked back at the chopper, "is to fly that thing."

Leclerc inserted herself between the smiling Bunny O'Hare and the billionaire with the embarrassed expression on his face. "Ms. O'Hare, this is Mr. Sorensen, the owner of White Star Lines."

Sorensen held out his hand tentatively, and O'Hare shook it. Leclerc breathed a sigh of relief. Alright, so she had some basic social skills, that was a plus.

"It looks like an Osprey, but it's not," Bunny continued. "What it really looks like is an A10 Warthog and an Osprey had sex and that is their ugly love child. You must have some kind of heavy-duty helo deck if you can land that thing on it."

Sorensen still looked confused, but Leclerc was glad to see he didn't dismiss O'Hare out of hand. "Sit, please," he said, as O'Hare took her drink from the sailor. "I have some questions."

"So do I," Bunny told him.

"I am sure. But this is my ship, I am the one looking for a pilot, so I get to ask my questions first."

"That's fair."

Leclerc took a glass of water and sat on a bench at a discreet distance. Far enough away so as not to intrude, close enough for another intervention if it was needed.

Sorensen opened his tablet cover and tapped the screen. "Why were you discharged from the Royal Australian Air Force without privileges?"

"Assaulting an officer."

"Insulting?"

"No, ass-aulting. With a flight helmet. To the jaw." She pointed at her face.

"What does it mean, a discharge without privileges?"

"No severance pay, no pension."

"I see." He flipped through some tablet screens. "Then Defense Advanced Research Projects Agency, DARPA, field-testing unmanned weapons systems in combat theatres: Syria, Alaska, Okinawa, Florida."

"Yes. Totally classified. And none of those jobs after Syria were supposed to be in combat theatres, by the way. The wars started after I got there."

"Yes. Do you love war, Ms. O'Hare?"

Leclerc saw O'Hare flinch. "I hate war. But it seems war loves me. And look, I love flying fast jets, I love testing new systems and making them work so that only the bad guys feel the pain when they are used, and they don't turn on their owners or innocent bystanders like some kind of robotic Armageddon death machines."

"Robotic, Armageddon…"

"Death machines, yeah. If it was up to the politicians and generals of most armies, including your customers, most wars would be fought in cyberspace, or space space, and if a war was forced out into the open, the skies and seas would be full of machines fighting each other with no soldiers, pilots or sailors getting killed, which sounds just dandy except it never works that way and the people who end up dying are old women, mothers with kids and young guys from Detroit who just signed up because they needed a job to pay their father's medical bills. But people like you don't need to worry about that because you can just get in your chopper with your ginger ale on ice and…"

Intervention time. "Mr. Sorensen and I would like to know, what is it you believe in, Ms. O'Hare?" Leclerc asked.

Bunny didn't hesitate, she didn't hum and haw. "I believe I am the best damn pilot of anything that can swim, crawl or fly. That's what I believe. And if I can put that to use in a way that lets me go to bed with my conscience and wake up in the morning still good friends, it's a good day."

"You are a mercenary," Sorensen said.

"My arse," Bunny replied.

"Sorry?" Sorensen frowned.

"She means no, Mr. Sorensen," Leclerc explained.

"I mean no. I was a combat pilot. Now I'm a test pilot. I am a computer coder, proficient in about six digital languages. *And*, on Okinawa, I learned Ikebana." Leclerc thought she caught O'Hare winking at her.

"That is some form of the martial arts, I assume," Sorensen said, nodding. "I learned karate, in Copenhagen in my youth."

"Well, it's a form of art, but not so martial," Bunny explained. "Japanese flower arranging. I rock it." She pointed at a spray of orchids on a table and fake-shuddered. "That, for example, is just vulgar."

Sorensen stood, flipping his tablet cover shut. "I do not believe in assertions of competence, Ms. O'Hare," he said. "I believe in demonstrations." He turned and walked off.

Bunny watched him go, then turned to Leclerc. "So, I take it I didn't get the job?"

Leclerc stood, motioned to the sailor who had been tending to them, and he disappeared out a side door. "That will depend," she said.

The sailor reappeared with a man who was clearly a pilot. He was carrying an extra flight suit and helmet.

Leclerc explained. "You will have one hour with the pilot to familiarize yourself with the machine out there on the flight deck. And then you will be given a mission to execute…"

Bunny's eyes narrowed. "What mission?"

Leclerc took the flight suit and handed it to Bunny. "Oh, I

think you'll enjoy it. We need a pilot who can get into, and out of, 'difficult' environments. So, you will take off from this ship, fly Mr. Sorensen's aircraft directly over the People's Liberation Army Guangzhou East Air Base at no more than 10,000 feet, and then return here."

"That's it?"

"That's it."

"No drug running, no picking up shady guys with wraparound sunglasses, no taking video of secret Chinese army weapons…"

"No. But I will be honest. The Chinese government does not allow civilian aircraft to overfly its bases. Guangzhou East is protected with Qianwei-2 vehicle-mounted infrared homing missiles and radar-guided 57mm anti-air cannons."

"OK."

"Plus, a Russian-made S-400 anti-air radar and missile system."

"Right. Not OK."

"No. But if you make it back here alive, we will check your flight data, and if you did indeed overfly Guangzhou East and make it back, you will get the contract."

Bunny sat, thinking about it. "You coming on this flight too?"

"No. Definitely not. Nor is Mr. Sorensen's pilot."

"I'll be alone."

"Yes."

"I could just steal Mr. Sorensen's nice stealth chopper and disappear."

"I doubt that. I mean, you could probably steal it, but you couldn't disappear. There is nowhere on the planet Mr. Sorensen couldn't find you."

"I was just joking. And I would do this, why?"

Leclerc sat again, close to O'Hare, lowering her voice.

"Because I have studied your background, examined your methods, and I know you can. I was the one who got Mr. Sorensen to agree to this little test, because I know you will ace it. And if you do, a new world will open to you that will quite simply blow your mind."

"I have a heavily-armored mind," Bunny told her. "It is not easily blown."

Leclerc leaned even closer. "Mr. Sorensen has been buying up military prototypes from all over the world for the last five years. Near-production systems that competed for weapons contracts and narrowly lost or were … how do you say … discontinued because of politics, or budget cuts."

"Systems … like that tiltrotor out there?"

"Oui. Aircraft, naval vessels, weapon systems, land, sea and underwater drones, Chinese, Israeli, American, Russian, Indian … and the technical crews to sustain them. You may even have worked on one or two…"

"Why? I thought he was a shipping magnate, not an arms dealer."

"Not to sell. To deploy, for the protection of his fleet. It is an uncertain world – Mr. Sorensen's very expensive ships and their cargoes sail dangerous waters."

Bunny O'Hare had a feeling that the big brown eyes, olive skin and sotto voce French accent of Sylvie Leclerc probably worked on 99.9 percent of people, male or female. Not to mention her perfume, which if Bunny were a perfume person, she would totally ask for the name of.

But Bunny was more a deodorant person than a perfume person, and sultry sotto voce voices were just annoyingly hard to hear, especially on the deck of a yacht out in the middle of Hong Kong's Repulse Bay. There were a million reasons why she should just ask to be driven back to the ferry terminal and only one reason why not.

It was sitting fifty yards away, still ticking as it cooled down in the heat, and it was calling to her: *come on, are you pilot enough?*

"I'll do it," she told Leclerc. "What happens if I get killed?"

"Then you won't get the contract."

"OK. Can't fault that logic."

The vertical takeoff aircraft crouched on the deck of the superyacht like a cougar waiting to leap into the air. Bunny had seen enough to recognize it now.

"This is a V-290 Vapor, right?" she asked Sorensen's pilot as she pulled on a flight suit.

He nodded. "A prototype. This one supplemented the two turboshaft tiltrotor engines driving the props with two GE turbofans for added speed. The props are only used for takeoff or landing. Once we go lateral, propulsion comes from the turbofans."

"More speed, but less range?"

"Not enough range for the US Army or Navy, apparently, because they didn't go with this version. But fine for operations off a ship deck. Mr. Sorensen has a private jet for longer trips." He had a Swedish accent. Former air force, she'd guess, the way he carried himself. He'd told her his name was Rolf.

Bunny pulled on the helmet he was holding out and adjusted it to fit, throwing the cable hanging off it over her shoulder as she walked toward the cockpit of the Vapor. As they walked around the dolphin-shaped nose, she patted it. "Mr. Sorensen's private jet fitted with Gatling cannons too?"

"You don't need to worry about those," he smiled. "You are going on a sightseeing trip. So, we only need to familiarize you with flight and navigation systems, not weapons."

"Righto."

The Vapor's instruments and nav systems were pretty standard, so most of her hour of instruction was spent doing takeoff and landing go-arounds so that she could get used to the transition between vertical and lateral flight. The flight computer handled most of the transition automatically, her helmet visor was constantly feeding her with handling and instrument cues, and the Vapor handled much more like an aircraft than a helicopter, so Bunny picked it up reasonably quickly.

After their final landing, the pilot looked at his watch.

"Time's up. I think you're good to go."

"Alright. Keep my ginger ale cold, will you?"

He had been about to climb out and paused. "I would not have accepted this dumb challenge. It is a one-way trip and when China shoots you down and examines the wreck, it could cause problems for Mr. Sorensen's business."

Bunny bristled. "Well, I guess that's why you are a glorified taxi driver and I am an ace combat pilot, Rolf."

He let the barb slide right past him without reacting. "The nav system will automatically log your position. We've filed a flight plan to Guangzhou civilian airport for you as cover. It's in the nav system. You don't need to fly right over the top of the air force base, just get within its physical perimeter and bug out."

"Any other special conditions or rules?"

"No. Good luck," he said, without feeling.

As she lifted off the deck and transitioned to horizontal flight, she reviewed the flight plan they'd filed and immediately decided to junk it. She didn't trust the wizened old shipping magnate or his svelte French sidekick for a moment, and wouldn't be at all surprised if they'd already tipped off the Chinese authorities to be on alert for an aerial incursion, just to make things interesting for her.

Pushing her sidestick forward, she took the Vapor down to wavetop height and started skimming across the harbor just over the masts of the sailboats and freighters that festooned the water. As the big turbofan jet engines kicked in, the broad-bladed propellers that helped her take off vertically folded back like the ears of a running rabbit, to reduce drag. She headed west, around Lantau Island, and swung out into the more open waters of the South China Sea. The ingress route they had plotted for her would have taken her straight up the Zhujiang River, which led directly from Hong Kong to the port and city of Guangzhou. Fifty miles out, fifty back, at the Vapor's cruising speed of 300 knots, it gave her a total flight time of twenty to thirty minutes.

Not including any time spent dodging Chinese ground-to-air missiles.

This Vapor had a top speed of about 600 knots, but Bunny wasn't interested in its top speed. She was interested in its stall speed. How slow could she go and still retain lateral flight control?

Circling an area of clear ocean, she gently pulled back the throttle. At around 100 knots, the flight computer started automatically engaging the turboshaft-driven rotors at the Vapor's wingtips to provide supplementary vertical lift, and it didn't like it when she canceled them.

Stall warning, engage tiltrotors. Stall warning, engage tiltrotors.

With landing flaps extended, the Vapor's handling started getting dangerously sloppy at 75 knots or about 85 miles an hour. She decided 90 would be manageable as long as she didn't try anything radical.

Pulling up the nav map, she replotted the waypoints for ingress to the People's Liberation Army Guangzhou East air base. It was basically a transport hub, not a fighter base, though a quick Google search told her there were also attack helicopters based there. She could probably outrun them but had no desire to even try.

The waypoints she laid in avoided the Zhujiang River entirely. It was too obvious. Instead, she would hit the Chinese mainland south of Guangzhou and fly up the S105 Nanshagang Toll Road at treetop height like she was some rich kid in a Ferrari burning up the expressway at a hundred miles an hour and not worried about speeding fines.

Infuriatingly slow for an aircraft, sure, but slow enough that a ground radar, if it could see her at all, might mistake her for a fast-moving ground vehicle.

She squinted at the map, talking out loud to herself. "So, ride the S105 all the way to Guangzhou city limits, turn right onto the S81, then take the S4 which … bloody beautiful." The final branch of the highway network was an expressway that actually went *across* the long runway at the PLA air base. She could fly right down the expressway, a hundred feet off the ground, and power right across the Chinese air base from south to north before doing a loop around a botanical garden and getting back over the expressway for the trip home.

Too easy, O'Hare.

Well, except for the fact she couldn't use the Vapor's otherwise capable radar, because it would give her position away. So she was limited to using the passive radar warning receiver, which could tell her if she was being tracked by Chinese air defense radar, or aircraft, or if someone fired a radar-guided missile at her, but forget evading a heat-seeking missile, because though she did have flares she could try to decoy it with, she would be going too slowly to evade anything. She would be putting a lot of faith in the Vapor's stealth characteristics.

Still, it was her plan, and she went with it.

Expecting to be hailed by Chinese air traffic control at any moment, she pointed the Vapor's nose at the huge container terminal on Longzue Island and sailed over the massive cranes with just feet to spare before picking up the expressway. It was a river of headlights, and traffic was flowing but didn't seem to be doing much more than about sixty.

Dammit, even crawling through the sky near stall speed she was thirty miles an hour faster than anything down there.

"Well, we're going to find out how good Chinese air defense radar is, Bunny my girl," she told herself aloud. "Whoa!"

A pedestrian crossover appeared right ahead of her and she just managed to get her nose up in time to lift the Vapor over it, stall warnings screaming in her helmet again, the faces of some very surprised late evening commuters burned into her retinas as she flashed past them and dropped the Vapor down above the traffic again. She wondered if the trailer truck drivers just below could see her matt black silhouette against the night sky as more than just a black on black shadow. She hoped not, because if they could, she would probably be leaving quite a few heart attacks in her wake.

She flipped one of the Vapor's view panels to show the radar warning receiver plot. Strong signal coming from Guangzhou Baiyun International Airport north of the city, as you'd expect, and an even stronger one from the military airfield to the east. But no lock on her aircraft, and no hail on the air traffic control frequency. Yet.

"S4 exit coming up. Damn you are good, O'Hare," she said, giving herself a little mental pat on the back as she swung the Vapor onto the turnoff that would take her along the expressway that crossed the air base runway.

On the lookout for the dangerous pedestrian crossovers she saw an object up ahead of her, right in her path. A sign of some sort? She squinted.

Oh, shit.

Sitting over the highway, right in her path, was a Harbin Z-9 attack chopper. It was the most common of China's copies of the deadly French Dauphin and it was hovering with its two 23mm cannon pods pointed straight at Bunny.

Not only had someone tipped the Chinese off that she was coming, they had also predicted exactly how she would attack the problem of getting herself into and out of the Chinese base. That damn Frenchwoman, it had to have been her. *I have studied your background, examined your methods…*

Was she that predictable? *Well, predict this.*

The need for stealth now irrelevant, O'Hare hit the toggle to retract her wing flaps, pushed the Vapor's throttle fully forward, and her machine leaped forward, pushing her back in her seat.

Straight at the Chinese attack chopper.

She was playing aerial chicken at a closing speed of 460 miles an hour, betting the Chinese pilot would get out of the way. It wouldn't open fire. Send her crashing down onto a busy highway below? Not a chance.

As if to prove her wrong, a stream of tracer fire started spitting from the cannon pods of the Z-9 and with a twitch of her stick Bunny rolled right, the 23mm shells flowing past her like a stream of laser light.

"Well that's just *reckless*, that is," Bunny muttered aloud. She rolled level again, blowing past the Z-9 as it spun on its vertical axis, trying to follow her with its cannon still spitting fire, but it couldn't rotate fast enough. Did it carry heat-seeking missiles? She was dead if it did ... her two turbofan engines pouring flame as she pulled away.

Guns, she needed bloody guns. She flicked the radar warning screen away and pulled up a systems menu. Of course, the guns weren't called guns. There was no 'weps' menu either. That would be too damn easy. Auxiliary systems? She punched the icon and saw menus for the sound system, emergency lighting ... ah, right. Countermeasures. Arm? *Hell yes.* Twin 20mm guns up. Chaff and flares up.

Her helmet view changed to show a targeting reticle that followed her head as it turned until it reached the limits of the gun's gimbals. But it also showed her something else. An ammunition counter. It showed 'RNDS: 0'. They hadn't loaded her guns. Of course they hadn't.

Craning her head around and looking over her shoulder, she put the Vapor into a skidding bank so that she could get a look behind her and saw the Chinese chopper falling behind. If it had missiles, she'd have been dead already, but she was out of reach of its cannons now.

Maybe this was going to work after all.

From the corner of her eye she saw a flash of light and reacted instantly, hauling the Vapor around in a stomach-wrenching turn as she pumped out a stream of flares. Heat-seeking ground-to-air missile, had to be! Sure enough, an arrow of fire lanced overhead and disappeared into the night.

Down, she had to get lower!

The expressway over the runway was raised on concrete

pillars and she dropped the Vapor down below the level of the expressway, so that as she pulled her machine around, she was looking back at the Chinese airfield through the expressway supports.

She saw an aircraft taxiing out for takeoff. There was another, already speeding down the runway.

"Oh, come on! That ain't fair!" she yelled, thumping the canopy beside her head with a gloved fist.

The air base Google entry had mentioned transport aircraft and choppers. It hadn't said anything about damn fighter aircraft. But that's what she was looking at. She only got a glimpse, but if she was guessing, she'd guess they were J-10 Vigorous Dragons. Light. Fast. Big guns. And they carried half a dozen missiles. They looked like small Eurofighter Typhoons.

They would reel her in and swat her from the sky within minutes of getting airborne.

"Screw this." She looked desperately around her. To her right was the cityscape of Guangzhou city. She could hide in among the skyscrapers maybe? For how long? And they'd be sure to send those damn Harbin helicopter gunships in after her. She was crossing over the river now and out of an instinctive desire to stay as low as humanly possible, she started following it southeast, away from the city, her jet wash kicking up twin furrows of water behind her.

Minutes, she probably had *minutes* before those fighters lit up their search radars and locked her up, stealth coating or not.

Ahead of her on the water was a huge freighter. She'd become a bit of an expert on merchant shipping after a few months spent watching shipping ply the lanes between Alaska and Russia, and she recognized this one immediately as a crewless autonomous container ship. It had a radio mast and radar dome where the wheelhouse superstructure would have been and could navigate itself between ports, only needing a human pilot – usually sitting in a control room hundreds of miles away – as it was entering or leaving harbor.

Bunny grinned as she recognized the large star on the flat

stern and the name; White Star *Magellan*. Well, wasn't that ironic?

Chopping her throttle and dropping her flaps, she circled around and lined up on the long deck, tightly packed with containers. This time she let the automatic landing system deploy the wingtip tiltrotors as she positioned herself right over the middle of the dark foredeck between two cranes, matched speed with the ship, and ever so gently dropped the Vapor down onto the containers on the deck of the *Magellan*.

On the observation deck of the White Star *Warrior*, Sylvie Leclerc glanced at her watch for about the 100th time and paced over to the starboard railing, looking out over the water toward the north.

"Will you please stop stalking around like that?" Sorensen asked her. He was sitting on a leather couch, looking through a contract. "Or at least take off those heels. She is dead. It should have taken her thirty minutes, and she's been gone two hours. You should be spending your time finding a new candidate."

Leclerc spread her hands on the railing, still staring into the night sky. "A shame. I really thought she…"

Really thought she … what? That she could pull off an impossible mission with all the odds stacked against her? No, of course not. But Sorensen had insisted on the unorthodox test.

So, the brash Australian had failed. At best, she was now languishing in a Chinese military prison or hospital. At worst, she was dead, and the test had cost Sorensen his expensive toy.

As she looked across the water, she saw a massive container ship gliding through the bay about five hundred yards away. It was dark except for the pilot lights on its bow and stern, and a few LED lights on its large onboard cargo cranes. A light on the bow showed it was one of Sorensen's ships. Nothing special in that, the chances of any particular container ship being one of his were about forty percent.

A sound reached across the water to her. Engines. Aircraft engines, spooling up. The sound seemed to be coming from near the container ship. Definitely an aircraft ... she could hear the *whap whap whap* of rotor blades. But where? A small darker-than-night shadow detached itself from the blackness of the ship's deck and rose into the air.

"*Le diable*!" she exclaimed. "I don't believe it."

Sorensen looked up. "What?"

Leclerc pointed. Within a minute, Sorensen's Vapor was hovering over the deck of the White Star *Warrior*, with O'Hare flipping them both a sardonic salute from the cockpit as it settled onto its landing gear.

Sorensen stood, not waiting for Bunny to climb out. "I still think you are making a mistake," he said, and walked into the cabin.

Leclerc waited by the railing as Bunny approached, pulling her helmet off as she walked and running a hand over her close-cropped hair to wipe off the sweat. Leclerc could see the faint outline of a tattoo under the stubble.

"I have a complaint," O'Hare said as she approached Leclerc.

"I'm sure you have many."

"Well, true, but one *big* one. It was impossible to connect my cell phone to the sound system in that thing," Bunny said. "I had to listen to Rolf's bloody Celine Dion playlist all the way back here."

Muara Container Terminal, Brunei, January 7

"You have a complaint?" the Chinese businessman standing opposite Abdul Ibrahim asked in a tone that implied he had no interest in hearing it.

"Yes, Mr. Lim, I do. You promised me five rib boats. I do

not see any."

They had just opened Lim's containers after Ibrahim had arranged for them to be delivered to a quiet corner of the terminal. His men were still going over the inventory and checking everything off, but Ibrahim didn't need an inventory to see that what he was looking at were *not* the inflatable rubber raiding craft known as rib boats.

Lim patted the hard-shell hull of one of the boats. "These are ex-US Navy Mark V special operations craft. There are three here, assembled, and two more, crated. You can assemble them yourself, or just use them for parts."

"I asked for rib boats," Ibrahim said, not ready to let go of his gripe yet. "Fast, light. Not these things."

"And rib boats I have delivered. Each of these 'motherships' can carry sixteen men, or ten men *and* a rib boat across its stern, which I have included in the shipment. They are powered by twin 12-cylinder diesel engines driving water jet propulsors that give them a top speed of 50 knots."

"We're not entering them in a race," Ibrahim scowled. "Where we're going, nothing moves faster than 30 knots anyway."

"But a little extra speed is useful to have up your sleeve, no?" Lim insisted. He was a large, round man, and it was hot inside the container. He dabbed his forehead with a stained rag. He rested a hand on a crate near the stern of the boat. "Not to mention these."

"They do not look like AK rifles," Ibrahim commented, bending down and reading the stenciled labels on the side. "We agreed AKs, and ammunition. *'Mark 19 40mm'* ... what is this?"

"Grenades, for the forward-mounted grenade launcher." He gestured further up the container. "*Those* crates hold a 7.62mm Gatling gun; you mount that behind the wheelhouse. Or a .50 cal machine gun, you have the choice, I included ammunition for both, and you have a set for each boat."

"We can't board a vessel with a mounted .50 caliber machine gun."

"No, your men will find your rifles are in one of the other containers." Lim ran his rag over his neck. "Not AKs. M16s. Do you have any other complaints?"

"I guess not. How did you get a hold of US surplus equipment?"

Lim started walking outside, toward the cooler air. "Not your concern." He pulled an envelope from his pocket and handed it to Ibrahim. "Here is the data on the target. Photographs, plans of the ship's construction. It will be leaving Singapore on the 9th at 0600 hours. That will put it off the coast of Brunei at about 0900 on the 10th. How do you plan to approach it?"

"Not your concern." Ibrahim repeated Lim's own words back at him. He looked over the information Lim had provided. "It has an escort."

"Yes, as we discussed. The White Star *Andromeda*. It controls the navigation of the *Orion* and has the usual defensive systems to defeat piracy, so you may need to incapacitate it to approach the *Orion* safely."

"What is the *Orion*'s cargo?"

"I have no idea."

Ibrahim blinked at him. "Why the hell would I hijack a ship if I don't even know what the cargo is worth?"

"Oh, you seem to have misunderstood my instructions," Lim said. "I said I wanted it 'intercepted'. Perhaps I should be clearer." He dabbed his face again and put the rag in a trouser pocket. "You will find a case of magnetic limpet mines in one of the containers. I want the White Star *Orion* and all its cargo *destroyed*. Put it on the bottom of the South China Sea."

Ibrahim considered this. "So, it's an insurance job."

"Sure. If you like. An insurance job."

"Alright, be mysterious, Mr. Lim. What about the crew?"

"As you know, the *Orion* is semi-autonomous. There will be the usual security party aboard, maybe a couple of engineers for any repairs needed while it's underway. That's all."

"I mean, what do you want us to do with the crew?"

"Do what you like, they are no concern of mine. Take them hostage, ransom them if you want to. Send them to the bottom with their ship if you don't." Lim looked at his watch. "Are we done here?"

"No. When we agreed our price, I assumed I would be able to offload the cargo and sell it. If I'm *sinking* this ship, I'm making a lot less than I thought. I have men to pay. That escort ship will be armed. Some of my people could be injured or killed and that means I have to pay their families compensation. I will need more."

Lim appeared unconcerned. "How much more?"

"Double," Ibrahim blurted, getting ready to haggle. "Half up front, half on completion."

"Very well. Anything else?"

Damn. He should have asked for more. Clearly, he was underselling his services. It was too late now. "Uh, no. I guess not."

Hong Kong Harbor, January 7

There's an old joke about a guy who dies in a car accident and finds himself in limbo. Saint Peter tells him he's lived a good life, but he's no saint, so it could go either way. Saint Pete has decided to let him choose for himself whether he goes to heaven or hell. An angel gives him the tour of heaven, showing him the soft clouds, harp-playing angels and manicured lawns full of nuns and priests playing croquet. Then he goes down to hell and is shown around by the Devil. He sees the casino, the bordello, the bars and restaurants, horse racing and dance parties full of people doing drugs, and it's a no-brainer. He chooses hell.

"Great!" the Devil says. "Go back to limbo, have a good night's sleep, come back here in the morning."

He does, and the next morning takes the elevator down to hell. As he emerges, the doors slam shut behind him and he finds himself in a torture chamber full of screaming people. The Devil is standing there, waiting to greet him with a glowing-hot branding iron. "Welcome to hell," he says.

"Wait, what happened to the casino, the bordello … the dance parties?!" the guy asks desperately.

The Devil steps forward. "Oh, that was yesterday, when we were recruiting you. Today you're staff."

The difference between the Devil and Sylvie Leclerc, as far as Bunny O'Hare could see, was that she put O'Hare through hell during the 'interview' and was now showing her heaven.

"I told you I would blow your mind," Leclerc was telling her. She was holding out a flight helmet for O'Hare to put on. It was large, with a wraparound visor, but with none of the usual cables … just connections for an oxygen mask.

"Don't consider it blown yet," O'Hare told her. "I used to fly F-35 Panther fighters. I've used Gen IV helmet-mounted display systems before."

"This," Leclerc said, handing it to O'Hare, "is not Gen IV. It is not even Gen V. It is Gen Z, and to call it a helmet is an insult. To obtain it, Mr. Sorensen had to buy the company that designed it."

"Yeah, yeah," O'Hare said, but the moment she pulled it on, she lost the ability to speak.

She was no longer sitting in a lounge chair on the deck of the White Star *Warrior*, she was back in the cockpit of the Vapor. In front of her were the multifunction display panels, on her right, the flight stick, on her left, the throttle. Looking down, she could not only see the aircraft's rudder pedals, she could see her own feet! She experimented by pushing her right foot down, and the image of the right foot in her visor pushed the rudder pedal down. "*Whoa.* Get out of town." She held her hands out in front of her and saw two gloved hands that flexed their fingers in synch with her flexing the fingers on her own hand. "How does it *do* that?"

"Millimeter radar, reading the environment," Leclerc told her. "It will be more precise once it is configured specifically for you."

Bunny tried to grab the flight stick and move it, but her 'virtual hands' passed right through it, as though she were a ghost.

"If you are trying to manipulate the controls, you will need VR gloves," Leclerc said, guessing what Bunny was trying to do. "The system can read your foot movement easily enough, but for the precision needed for flight controls, you need pressure simulation gloves which send signals to the unit accurate to a fraction of an inch and enable you to feel like you are touching the controls yourself."

"OK, nice toy," O'Hare said, looking around her. As she turned her head, she could see out of the Vapor's cockpit windows and, turning her head over her shoulder, the view continued as though she had a 360-degree panoramic window behind her. "Kind of like the distributed aperture camera system on an F-35 Panther."

"More than that," Leclerc told her. "Much more. Please sit back, watch and listen. The Vapor out on the deck is currently keyed to recognize my voice commands."

Bunny leaned back expectantly.

"Vapor, start all engines please," Leclerc said.

Inside the helmet, a deep male voice began speaking. *Ensuring all personnel are at minimum safe distance. Starting turboshaft and turbofan engines. Engines to idle. Park brakes, on. Do you wish to power up navigation and avionics?*

"Yes, initiate navigation system."

Initiating. Engine startup complete. Navigation system, online. Avionics, nominal. Vapor is ready for takeoff.

"No freaking way," Bunny said. "You're flying it remotely via the mike in this helmet?" Looking out the virtual windows, she could see the tiltrotor propellers on the tips of the aircraft's wings spinning up. Over the sound being piped into the helmet, she could hear the physical sound of the rotors beginning to thump from the aircraft out on the deck, feel the blast from the props on her own body through the open entrance to the top deck lounge.

"Oui. Vapor, engage trail protocol five."

Engaging trail protocol five. All systems nominal for launch. Confirm launch."

"Launch confirmed."

A hundred points of data began flowing across the virtual screens on the instrument panels 'in front of' Bunny, showing nearby aircraft, shipping, relative altitudes and speeds, instrument readouts and system states. The noise from the deck outside rose to a crescendo. With a jerk, the view in Bunny's helmet began moving as the Vapor lifted off the deck and rose to a position 500 feet above and a hundred feet behind the White Star *Warrior* and hovered there.

Bunny couldn't stand the suspense; she ripped the helmet off her head and looked out of the top deck lounge to where the Vapor was standing. *Had been* standing. It was gone. Standing to look out a side window, Bunny could see the aircraft hovering patiently behind the ship, its blinking nav lights just about the only thing visible against the skyline.

Bunny stared at the helmet in wonder. "OK. Mind, blown."

Leclerc smiled. "That's a station-keeping protocol. It orders the aircraft to trail its host ship at a safe distance and adjustable altitude, to extend the range of the ship's sensors, and so that it is ready for … other commands." She took the helmet back and spoke in the same neutral tone. "Vapor, return to base and shut down."

Without her head inside the helmet, Bunny couldn't hear the aircraft's verbal response, but she saw it easily enough. The thud of rotors grew louder as the aircraft circled around to the front of the ship and, after a somewhat painstakingly slow approach, dropped onto the helipad and cut its engines.

Leclerc put the helmet on the sofa between them. "You are familiar with the concept of data fusion, yes?"

"From my time in air force and space force, sure," O'Hare

told her. "Helps pilots with situational awareness, threat identification. Don't tell me that helmet can also access US military data sources?"

Leclerc shook her head. "Not without permission," she answered, somewhat obliquely. "White Star Lines has its own security and intelligence Risk Group that has access to the most advanced civilian satellite and open source intelligence databases. The helmet gives you 24/7 real-time access to that intel with a simple verbal request. Also, you can pull up the radar and communications feed from any of several hundred White Star Lines ships globally, so that you can see what their radars are seeing and communicate with their comms officers, again, in real time. Most White Star ships are fitted with all-aspect radar systems that enable them to monitor both surface *and* airborne contacts. For safety reasons, of course."

"Of course. You had better stop now, or you are going to need to put plastic covers on these seats," Bunny told her with a dead-pan expression. "So, if *you* can fly that aircraft with a voice command, what does Mr. Sorensen need a pilot like me for?"

"Mr. Sorensen does not," Leclerc told her. Reaching out to a table beside her, she lifted a tablet PC up, turned it on and handed it to O'Hare. "I do. Please read this carefully. If you agree to the terms, just apply your thumbprint to the end of the document."

Bunny took the tablet from her. The first part of the document was a standard employment contract, like she'd signed a dozen times, both in the air force and outside it. She looked at the salary, sign-on, and sign-off bonus and saw nothing she didn't like, until she scrolled to the final page.

SECRECY AND INDEMNITY
The undersigned agrees that they will not disclose any information obtained in the course of their employment to any person or agency outside of White Star Lines, unless authorized in writing by a senior executive of White Star Lines (Executive Vice President or above). This agreement does not

prevent the undersigned from cooperating fully with an officer of the law of a recognized police or security force engaged in official duties, or an officer of a recognized military service. Failure to respect this agreement will result in forfeiture of all salary and bonuses owed and civil action for damages related to theft of intellectual property.

The undersigned further agrees to indemnify White Star Lines against any legal proceedings for property damage, injury or death caused by or occurring to the undersigned during the execution of their duties.

The indemnity agreement Bunny could live with, even though it sounded rather extreme, but the secrecy agreement had her attention. "Uh, this," Bunny said, showing Leclerc the screen. "I had to sign something like this when I worked with DARPA on top-secret military projects. Why all the secrecy if I'm just going to be flying for a civilian shipping company?"

"Well, that is, how you say, a 'Catch 22', Ms. O'Hare," Leclerc shrugged. "I can't tell you that until you sign your contract, including the secrecy agreement."

Ah, what the hell, I'm already in at the deep end. Bunny scrolled to the bottom of the document where a green square said, "Apply thumb here." The tablet beeped and the document flashed, then disappeared from the screen. Bunny handed the tablet back to the French woman.

"Merci. You are now a member of White Star Risk Group, Ms. O'Hare," Leclerc said. "It is a pleasure to have you on my team."

Bunny narrowed her eyes, looking at the woman in the red silk lounge suit and high heels dubiously. "Uh-huh. You work for this Risk Group?"

"Non. I run it. Before joining White Star Lines I was a section head in the DGSE, the Direction Générale de la…"

"French CIA, yeah, I know it."

"I was head of the department of Irregular Warfare, Naval Intelligence. And before that, I served in the French Navy. But that is old news." Leclerc held out her hand. "Welcome to *Operation Fencepost*, Bunny O'Hare."

Pagasa Island, Spratly Islands Archipelago, January 7

In the Filipino Tagalog language, 12-year-old Eugenio Maat's home was called *Pulo-ng Pag-asa*: Island of Hope.

Eugenio didn't see a whole lot of hope in the faces of the people around him. Mayor Reyes had called everyone in for a meeting in the school hall, and the Philippine Marine Lieutenant was there sitting up front next to him. He had introduced himself as Captain Heraldo Bezerra, but Eugenio and his friend Diwa called the guy 'Cat Hair' because his spiky black hair stuck out from under his baseball-style cap like a cat that had exploded. He was rarely seen without his cap on, even inside. He was standing beside Mayor Reyes, who had sweat rolling down his chubby cheeks.

It was stuffy in the school hall because it had been empty all day and so the air conditioning hadn't been turned on. So stuffy only half the people on the island, maybe fifty, were inside the hall. The rest were sitting on chairs outside where a loudspeaker had been set up.

"You know that hair?" Eugenio whispered to his friend Diwa. "You think it's actually a wig and the hat is sewn on? Maybe he takes the hat off, and he's completely bald." Diwa giggled, covering her mouth so the troops at the front of the hall couldn't see her laughing.

His Ma bent down and pinched his arm. "Be quiet, you." Eugenio's Ma was a big lady, and she wasn't happy. The mayor and the Lieutenant were still getting their microphone set up, but she wasn't in a mood to wait. She stood, and suddenly everyone in the hall stopped talking.

"Mayor! Hey, Conrado."

The man looked over and winced.

"Conrado, what are you doing to get my Gonzales back?"

Eugenio sat up, waiting for the answer. His Dad, Gonzales, and Bobong Huerta had not come back from their last fishing trip. His father had made one call to tell them Mr. Huerta was dead, but that he himself was OK and being held in jail on Subi Reef by the Chinese, and then the call had been cut off.

Reyes fidgeted uncomfortably. "Now, Maja, you know it's complicated. I've been on the phone with Puerto Princesa, they got to go to Manila…"

Eugenio's Ma scoffed and turned her face to the naval officer, who was fixing a microphone to a stand and trying to make out he wasn't involved. Not yet anyway. Eugenio's Ma involved him. "You, Lieutenant. The Navy is supposed to protect our fishing boats. But Bobong Huerta is dead and my husband is a prisoner, what kind of protection is that?"

"Yeah, Navy," someone up the back of the hall said in support. "What you going to do?"

The Philippine Seabee Lieutenant, Heraldo, straightened and tapped the microphone, then switched it on and tapped it again. He leaned in to put his mouth closer to it. "Ma'am, we don't know what happened on Subi Reef, but we have a situation here now…"

"You're damn right we have a situation," Eugenio's Ma said quickly. "The situation is my husband, Gonzales, is a Chinese prisoner and you are doing sweet nothing about it."

People behind Eugenio started calling out. Most were agreeing with his Ma. Others were yelling other stuff they were unhappy with. Mayor Reyes was waving his hands like he wanted people to calm down, but that just made them yell more. The Lieutenant stepped back from the microphone and put his hands behind his back.

It was all too strange to Eugenio. His father a Chinese prisoner? His father was probably the one guy on Pagasa who was most China-friendly. Gonzales Maat had once saved a Chinese fishing crew when its boat was in trouble and towed them back to Mischief Reef. The Chinese military there gave him a thankyou letter in Chinese, which he framed and put on his living room wall. Gonzales would get in arguments with other fishermen when they complained about Chinese fleets overfishing the sea around Pagasa. He'd say there was no way to beat them, so maybe it was time to join them. "Those Chinese fleets, Eugenio," his father told him, "that's the future of fishing." His opinions didn't make him popular, even Eugenio could see that. Eugenio never actually heard him say Pagasa should be a part of China, but he never said it shouldn't either.

When people calmed down a little, the Lieutenant stepped back up to the microphone. The Filipino Seabees had come to the island about six months ago. There had always been a small squad of Marines on the island, like about twenty, but in the middle of last year the Seabees had arrived. They'd come to fix the air strip and the harbor, but to Eugenio it looked like they mostly just lay around in the shade unless the Lieutenant was shouting at them.

"I understand you're all upset, but it's not just a matter of asking China to give Gonzales Maat back. He's been charged by the Chinese with terrorism."

"That's a lie and you know it. You got a boat in the harbor," Eugenio's Ma said. "You go over there, and you get him. Or what is the Navy good for?"

Not much of a boat, Eugenio was thinking. It held about four sailors and had one little machine gun on it. He couldn't see the Chinese being too worried about it.

"Ma'am, that boat wouldn't make it a hundred yards out of the harbor. China has two Coast Guard frigates anchored offshore. You've all seen them, some of you have tangled with them. You can't even get your fishing boats out of the harbor – they aren't going to let our patrol boat out, and they've warned they'll shoot down any aircraft flying in."

"We don't fish, we starve!" Someone up back called out. "We don't get supplies from Puerto Princesa, we starve. And that includes you, Navy man."

At least we have water now, Eugenio was thinking. One of the

45

good things the Seabees had done was fix the pipes to the underground tanks that caught the monsoon rains, and hook up some new solar cells and batteries so that they had power to the water plant that made fresh water out of sea water in the dry season.

Speaking of rain, Eugenio thought he heard thunder off to the south, high up. He looked out a window, but the sky was clear. Not a cloud. *OK, that was weird.*

The US Navy MQ-25 Stingray had started life as a refueling drone which the US Navy could launch off carriers to extend the strike range of their short-legged F-35C Panthers and F/A-18 Hornets. But the failure of Navy's unmanned combat drone program to deliver a carrier-launched long-range reconnaissance platform had seen the Stingray fitted with a reconnaissance module to enable it to perform that role as well. Carrying 15,000 lbs. of fuel, it had a range of nearly 18,000 nautical miles and could stay aloft for more than 40 hours.

The Stingray currently approaching Pagasa Island had launched from the carrier *USS Doris Miller* 700 miles west of the US naval base at Guam and had completed its 1,300-mile journey to Pagasa in just under three hours. The next ten minutes would decide if it would survive to complete the journey back to its mothership.

It had been tasked to secure optical/infrared imagery of every inch of the 70-acre island and the nearby Chinese base at Subi Reef. On approach to the island, it had engaged its radar detection suite, to assure itself there were no missile-targeting radars in the Operations Area capable of locking and tracking it. It was not a stealth design, so any halfway decent ground or air-based radar would be able to see it, and that meant a missile or aircraft could be sent to kill it. It had detected low-powered surface radar, probably from China Coast Guard vessels, but nothing else, and was in any case flying too high for them to intercept it.

It was a clear evening, with good visibility from 40,000 feet to the surface, and as it neared the small rocky outcrops, it began streaming vision and data back to the *Doris Miller*. From that moment, it was doomed.

On Subi Reef, 20 miles away, the Commander of Subi's Red Banner 9 anti-air missile battery had been patiently waiting, like a spider waiting for a fly, for the US aircraft to enter the airspace near his military facility. He had kept his radar array in passive mode, tracking the aircraft only by the radio signals it had been transmitting to the satellite controlling it – because he had known for some time by the pattern of the transmissions exactly what it was: a US MQ-25 Stingray. Chinese signals intelligence ships trailing US carrier groups had long ago developed the algorithms needed to identify US surveillance drones based on the pattern of their radio communication with the satellites to which they sent data and from which they received their commands.

The Red Banner unit had conflicting orders. China had declared a state of emergency in the region due to the contrived 'terrorist attack' on its naval base at Subi Reef by Bobong Huerta and Gonzales Maat, and any Philippine aircraft entering its self-declared air defense perimeter – which now included Pagasa Island – was to be shot down. So as not to inflame international tensions further, the order did not apply to other foreign aircraft, but if the aircraft was an unmanned surveillance drone, like the one he was tracking, he could track it and ask for permission to engage. As the US Stingray started streaming data via satellite back to the *Doris Miller*, the signal was detected by the Red Banner array, its position was confirmed and a missile oriented on the bearing of the signal. Bringing his phased-array radar online, the Red Banner commander sent a brief pulse of energy down the bearing of the Stingray's radio signal, got a solid return, locked the US drone up and called his superiors.

Who called theirs.

When the order to engage was finally relayed, the drone was

almost directly overhead. The Red Banner commander acknowledged the order and fired his missile, all inside a second.

The unit's HQ-9C missile was never going to miss. At *four times the speed of sound* the Chinese missile covered the distance to the Stingray inside fifteen seconds, homed on the drone using its own radar, and erased it from existence.

While the Chinese anti-air missile crew was celebrating, so was the naval intelligence analyst aboard the *USS Doris Miller*. They'd lost a Stingray to a Chinese missile attack, sure. It was a loss they would have to learn from. But they had taken beautiful high-resolution images of every square inch of both Subi Reef and Pagasa Island, not to mention the seas around them and the ships upon those seas.

The analyst got started on the task of making sense of them.

Liberty Crossing Intelligence Campus, Virginia, January 7

Carmine Lewis was trying to make sense of the situation on the screen in front of her.

As Director of National Intelligence (DNI), she had a hundred intelligence analysts and their support AIs to 'context' the intel she was looking at, but she'd asked for it raw so that she could try to make sense of it herself before she called the President.

There was no doubt, though. Carmine was looking at the most profound cyber-attack on US interests since ... well, since the last one. But this one was *sophisticated*. And it had an angle that perturbed her greatly as she sat staring out the window of her apartment at the slow-flowing Little Patuxent River outside.

Since the US had adopted a public policy of 'retaliation in kind' for State-led cyber-attacks on its institutions or infrastructure, most of the big players in cyber warfare – China, Russia, North Korea, Israel and Iran – were more cautious in the 2030s than they had been during the gold rush years of cyber warfare in the 2020s. China and Russia had learned that they could try to hide their activities behind criminal hacker collectives and disavow knowledge or involvement, but it made no difference to the nature or strength of the US retaliation. An attack traced to China or Russia would result in an even more damaging counterattack in kind. You tried to penetrate the network of one of our defense contractors and steal designs for our next generation frigate? Fine. How about we shut down your stock exchange for a few hours?

Mutually assured destruction was a language the superpowers understood, and the US had started applying it to cyberspace in the late 2020s with good effect. While it didn't *stop* cyber warfare, it made the activity as high risk as all other forms of espionage, causing State actors to think hard before they committed an attack because the benefits had to far outweigh the risks.

Which made this latest attack all the more worrying.

China's People's Liberation Army (PLA) had six cyber warfare hubs, and Strategic Support Force Base 32 Guangzhou was a well-known, well-studied and, luckily for Carmine, well-penetrated adversary. Base 32 had its focus on supporting PLA operations against Taiwan and in the South China Sea.

The CIA had managed to recruit sufficient human sources within the ranks of Base 32 that the US National Security Agency (NSA) had its work delivered to it on a plate. No sooner was a cyber offensive planned than CIA agents within Guangzhou had leaked intelligence on the attack, and if the Advanced Persistent Threat teams of Base 32 found a new attack vector, NSA or CYBERCOM were usually forewarned and forearmed. Any attacks that got through in the last couple of years were those that were allowed to 'succeed' so as not to raise suspicions among the commanders of Base 32.

It seems we got complacent, Carmine mused.

An Advanced Persistent Threat Team traced to Base 32 had been scooping up communications between the US State

Department and the Philippines government, in an operation that had not once come up on Carmine Lewis's radar. Communications between the US Embassy and other US government agencies were heavily protected and regularly audited for vulnerabilities. But those of allies such as the Philippines were less so, so Base 32 had focused its energy on exploiting the fact that China ComTech had won a huge telecoms contract serving both the Philippines Departments of Foreign Affairs and Defense.

Exactly as the US had warned the Philippines in advance of their signing the deal.

According to the intel Carmine was reviewing, China had been intercepting the US Embassy's unencrypted mail and phone calls to their Philippines counterparts for close to two years. Top secret data exchanged between intelligence agencies hadn't been compromised, but the hundreds of daily emails and phone calls between Embassy staff and Philippine government officials had been.

Carmine had reviewed the intel personally to make sure it was solid. She'd looked up reports on similar attacks against other allies. She'd cross-referenced with human source reports from within Base 32 trying to understand how this had slipped under CIA and NSA's radar. She'd done a keyword search of the minutes of National Security Council briefing documents to pull out anything related to the Philippines, Taiwan or the South China Sea over the last two years, to give her an idea of just what topics Embassy staffers in Manila might have been asked to feed in to.

And only then, after a shot of coffee to sharpen her mind, had she made the video call to President Fenner.

"Please hold for the President," the White House operator said, forcing Lewis to sit through a mixtape of jazz standards chosen to be so inoffensive they made her teeth grind.

"Hey Carmine, what's up?" a voice broke in over the muzak. It was his Chief of Staff, Chuck Abdor, not Fenner. His two-term veteran right hand was often delegated to take his calls, and Carmine was used to incoming calls being vetted by Abdor first. She and Fenner were ... close. Brother–sister close. If she'd wanted to, she could reach him directly on his cell, and he'd have picked up straight away. Everyone in the West Wing knew that, but she always observed protocol if she was calling the President in her role as DNI.

Carmine didn't sugarcoat what she had to say. "Chuck, I think our Embassy in Manila has given our entire game plan on the Spratly Islands to China."

Abdor remained calm, as usual. "By entire game plan, you mean..."

"Timetable, diplomatic strategy, command structure, force strength and composition..."

"But the Embassy staff are not across all the detail. Only the broad strokes."

"Except State has been sloppy. The Embassy has been asked very specific questions to help feed into briefings for Cabinet meetings and Secretary of State interactions with our *Fencepost* allies. Any competent AI can take those questions and the answers they got to reverse engineer the detail."

"Dammit. You're sure? Of course you are, or you wouldn't be calling."

"We're sure. I checked the raw intel myself. We recently learned China has been siphoning up Embassy comms with the Philippine government for the best part of two years. We ran the Embassy email and voice traffic through an AI, looking for everything related to the Spratly Archipelago, and then analyzed it to see what actionable intel China could have milked from it..."

"Phase one of *Fencepost* has already been initiated," Abdor said, sounding less calm now. "The White Star convoy will sail from Singapore in two days."

"I know. And I'm sorry, Chuck, but according to our analysis, China knows what we are planning."

"The President is in a meeting with the Secretary of Commerce. I'm going to pull him out, and we should probably dial in the Secretary of Defense. State too, since they'll end up carrying the can for this. Can you hold?"

"Of course."

Carmine had been playing the Washington game long enough to know her information would not be welcomed, either by Defense Secretary Phil Kahn, who would now need to gather his staff to reconsider every single element of what was opaquely known as *Operation Fencepost*, or by Secretary of State Victoria Porter, who Carmine knew would devote the coming days, weeks or even months to trying to prove Carmine wrong and avoid taking any blame for the leak of intelligence on her watch.

That thought had Carmine reaching for the coffee pot again, wishing it was a bottle of bourbon instead. Victoria Porter was a DC politics cage fighter, but Carmine had done her due diligence. She'd faced her down before, which didn't make it something she ever enjoyed, but she was ready for her.

Bring your best game, Madam Secretary.

An eternity of jazz standards flowed by until finally the music was broken again, and three screens opened up on the laptop in front of her. In the feed from the Oval Office she saw Abdor and Fenner. The rest of her screen showed Kahn, in a dark suit, white shirt, and red tie with a US flag background, and underneath him, Porter, in a white blouse and blue blazer, glasses down over her nose as she continued working on some papers while the meeting got started. Nothing Porter did in view of the President was an accident; this particular pose was intended to signal that whatever Lewis had to tell them, it couldn't possibly be as important as what Porter was currently doing. She only deigned to look up once Abdor started speaking.

"Thank you for joining Mr. President, Cabinet colleagues … Carmine, why don't you tell these good people what you told me?"

Carmine laid it out, in more detail this time. She only got as far as the Chinese telco hack before Porter started in.

"Why wasn't NSA able to protect against this?" she asked. "We've known about this vulnerability since China ComTech won that contract."

"Yes, Madam Secretary, and I understand NSA Cyber Security repeatedly warned State Department Manila staff about sharing sensitive information in the clear with our Philippine allies…"

Secretary of Defense Phil Kahn – a bullish but competent former four-star General – was used to Porter's tendency to target the person and not the ball, and he interrupted impatiently. "We can play the blame game later, Victoria; right now I'd like to hear what we think China knows about *Operation Fencepost*."

Lewis laid it out in plain English. "Mr. Secretary, they know we have decided to help the Philippine government fortify its outpost on Pagasa Island in the Spratly Archipelago."

"Exactly what do they know?" he asked.

"We are completely confident they know we are sending building materials to enable the Philippine government to rebuild its air and naval base there." Lewis paused. "We suspect, but we aren't sure, they also know the plan includes anti-air, anti-ship missile batteries and a detachment of US Marines."

Porter went on the attack again, unable to contain herself. "You 'suspect'?"

"Yes, Madam Secretary. We fed our AI everything that had been passed over the infected Philippine network infrastructure by Embassy staff, either text or voice, and had it prepare a report on likely US intervention in the Spratly Archipelago. It was basically able to reconstruct *Fencepost* Operations Orders at Strategic, Operations and Tactical level."

"But this is an AI *we* programmed, analyzing data *we* fed it. You have no guarantee, whatsoever, that China has reached the same conclusions."

"I am confident they could have."

Porter scoffed. "We can't rewrite our entire strategy for the

South China Sea based on 'could have'." And to reinforce her disdain for Lewis's interruption, she pushed her glasses back up her nose and looked down at her papers again.

Lewis knew better than to wade into a game of hypotheticals with Porter and remained quiet.

"I don't like it," Kahn said. "This might explain why China has put Pagasa into lockdown now, and why there have been other ... developments."

That got Secretary Porter's attention. She took off her reading glasses. "What 'other developments', Phil?"

He looked annoyed, though Kahn really only had two settings, annoyed and about-to-be-annoyed. "Space Force is monitoring a Chinese task force nearing readiness at Dalian Naval Base and multiple-source intel indicates it is headed for Pagasa Island."

"The phrase 'task force' worries me," Abdor said, apprehensively.

Kahn consulted a tablet in front of him. "It's relatively small. A *Yushen* class helicopter landing ship with an escort of two *Luyang* class missile destroyers," he said. "But it had just come off exercises and was supposed to be going into maintenance, not cycling up again for deployment."

"Small, but potent," Lewis pointed out. "The *Yushen* is an assault ship equivalent to our *America* class. It can field two dozen helos, two thousand Marines. And the *Luyang* destroyer is their version of our *Arleigh Burke*, a multirole platform with advanced anti-air and anti-ship capabilities. Two of those would give China anti-air area denial capability over hundreds of square miles."

Abdor tried to sum up the conversation. "Whether or not our people in Manila have given away anything material, China appears to have decided to force our hand. It's a flat-out footrace to see who can put boots on Pagasa Island first."

"China already has several hundred Marines on Subi Reef," Kahn pointed out. "Sixteen miles away. They already have frigates offshore, air cover. If they put their Marines on choppers, they could fly them in tomorrow."

"The troops they have on Subi Reef are not combat troops, except for a small detachment of Commandos. There are a hundred armed Philippine Navy and Air Force personnel on Pagasa," Lewis pointed out. "Chinese troops would have to roll in hot and take the island by force. They wouldn't want the humiliation of failure, so they'll wait for the *Yushen* to get in range and do the job properly."

Fenner had risen from his chair and Carmine could see him pacing in front of his desk, as he often did when agitated. He'd been quiet until now. He had a pinched, narrow face and long nose, atop which sat small round rimless glasses of a type that had been fashionable several years ago. His bushy silver hair was swept across his forehead and he ran a hand through it now. "What is the status on our convoy?"

Kahn looked at some notes. "Two civilian ships loaded and at berth in Singapore, waiting for our frigate, USS *Congress*, to meet them and escort them into the South China Sea. *Congress* is also carrying a detachment from 1st Battalion, 10th Marines, to help site the new missile batteries."

"Why can't the damned convoy just sail now, if it's ready? The *Congress* can meet it closer to the island and escort it past those frigates before the Chinese task force gets there," Fenner said. "What am I missing?"

"The quickest route between Singapore and Pagasa is straight up the west coast of Borneo, Mr. President," Kahn told him. "Those waters are infested with heavily armed pirates and an unescorted convoy would be a juicy prize."

Abdor broke in. "If we stick to the current time schedule for *Fencepost*, when would the *Congress* and that convoy reach Pagasa?"

Kahn consulted his notes. "Three days."

"And our estimate of when the Chinese task force could be within helicopter transport range and start landing troops on Pagasa?"

"Three days."

Fenner stopped pacing. "Well, it's pretty damn obvious to me. We need to get that convoy there first. It needs to sail, at risk, right now. *USS Congress* can meet it halfway."

"Yes, Mr. President. Since we are advancing *Fencepost* Phase One, I suggest we also advance Phase Two."

"Are the assets in place?"

Kahn nodded. "The *USS Doris Miller* Strike Group is currently 1,300 miles east; the *USS Idaho* is one day out…"

Lewis hated the necessity but had already agreed to the logic. When she and others in the Cabinet Security Committee had recommended Fenner sign off on the 'military intervention' that was *Operation Fencepost*, they had foreseen it would provoke a kinetic reaction from China. Apart from the inevitable diplomatic howling, everything from missile or air strikes against Philippine and US forces in the South China Sea, to cyber and space-based warfare was possible. In the event the Chinese Navy or Naval Air Force was deployed, *Fencepost* Phase Two envisaged unmanned aircraft from the *Doris Miller* being forward deployed to the former US Clark Air Base on Luzon, 500 miles away. Their Fantom and Sentinel drone pilots would remain safely aboard the *Doris Miller* and fly anti-ship or anti-air missions remotely from a thousand miles away, as needed.

Low-level targets – small Chinese military bases on reefs and atolls within a hundred miles of Pagasa Island – had already been identified, and the conditions under which they would be attacked agreed. They included Subi Reef, just 16 miles from Pagasa, but also the air and naval bases at Mischief Reef and Fiery Cross Reef.

The *Virginia* class submarine *USS Idaho* was their weapon of last resort if China moved significant naval assets into the Spratlys – such as one of its three new carrier strike groups. *Idaho*'s Long-Range Hypersonic Weapons (LRHW) were the most potent ship killers in the US Navy arsenal. Hiding deep under the waves until needed, *Idaho* was their guarantee the Chinese Navy would pay dearly if it tried to escalate, but sinking a Chinese capital ship would almost certainly provoke an all-out war with China.

Fenner nodded. "Makes sense. But I sincerely hope China backs off and we never need to use them." He clapped his hands briskly. "To work, people, I am sure you all have plenty to do."

Kinetic politics

Pagasa Island, Spratly Islands Archipelago, 1201 a.m. January 8, 2035

A half a world away on Pagasa Island, Captain Heraldo Bezerra of the Philippine Navy (PN) Seabees had more than enough to do too.

He'd just hung up from a late-night call with the Lieutenant Commander who was his CO, who had warned him Brigade Intelligence had received indications Chinese forces were planning to insert troops to take Pagasa Island, possibly inside the next 48 to 72 hours.

That news had not surprised him. Heraldo was a pessimist by nature and he knew China regularly rotated a rapid-reaction Jiaolong Commando force of 100 special operations troops through Subi Reef who could be choppered over to Pagasa within 30 minutes. Offshore, China had the two *Jiangwei* class multirole Coast Guard frigates Heraldo had warned the islanders about, which Chinese troops could use to call in indirect fire support. On Subi, Mischief and Fiery Cross reefs, China had built landing strips and naval air bases which could host up to 70 aircraft.

To defend Pagasa, he had around a hundred combat engineers, armed with rifles, a few squad automatic weapons, grenades, some shoulder-launched anti-armor missiles, but mostly ... shovels. In the harbor, he had a patrol boat with a .50 cal machine gun on it, barely even suited to the job of scaring away Chinese fishing boats. Air support? None. The Philippines Air Force consisted of a handful of light attack aircraft it used for counter-insurgency operations, none of which had the range to even reach Pagasa, let alone defend it.

But Heraldo was not so worried about the risk of Chinese troops landing on Pagasa. He wasn't even worried about the Chinese blockade of Pagasa and the risk they could eventually run out of everything except whatever fish they could catch from the shoreline.

He was much more worried about the fact he had been told a month ago that he needed to urgently complete a deep-sea pier extending out from the harbor, to allow ships with a deep draft to dock. What about the repairs to the air strip? They could wait. What about completing the repairs to the harbor itself? Also, a lower priority. The missile emplacement he had his men digging on the summit of the low hill? Yeah, keep going with that, but the pier was the priority. With only a month to get it done, the only option was to build a half-mile-long floating pier, capable of bearing a 30-ton load. They wouldn't have time to drive supports into the sea floor, and he had to allow for the 15-foot difference between high and low tide, so he'd opted for a cable-tie design, anchored to the coral and sand below with one-ton concrete blocks.

They'd started a half-mile out and built inwards, so at least his men weren't out there too long in boats where they'd probably attract the ire of those frigates. But they still had to complete the last twenty yards between the pier and the concrete dock to which it was going to be fixed. A week ago, he'd been told about the convoy that was coming their way. Suddenly the mysterious orders made sense. An auxiliary feeder ship and a US frigate would be tying up at his pier! A massive freighter would be anchored offshore as its cargo was ferried to the island.

That was why he wasn't too worried about the food situation. The convoy would be bringing everything they needed, from food, to building materials. Nor was he too worried about Chinese commandos or PLA Navy frigates. They wouldn't dare invade with a US Navy frigate tied up at *his* pier.

But now he'd been advised that rather than three days to complete the last stage of the pier, he would only have two, and they still had to lay and fix in place the last wooden beams that formed the ramp up onto the shore.

He looked at his watch. Midnight. Four hours' sleep. He'd just close his eyes for a few hours.

Eugenio and Diwa could have made their way across Pagasa blindfolded. They knew every track, rock and tree on the island and had their own names for some of them. In the south of the island was the Rancudo Airfield, its packed red dirt strip running west to east, with a few military buildings and a barracks alongside it, and the old lighthouse in the middle which doubled as a control tower. To the west, the runway had crumbled into the sea, and to the east, it was only above the waterline at low tide. In the middle was a large square the size of a football field, covered in sea grass. Eugenio had never seen anything more than a light plane land on it, or helicopters; both ends of the runway had fallen into the sea and never been repaired.

The villagers' houses were all on the eastern shore of the island, and on the opposite shore in the west was the Naval Station Emilio Liwanag, which if you asked Eugenio was a pretty grand name for a few slabs of rust-stained concrete and a rotting pier. But it was where the Philippines Marines docked when they were rotating troops onto the island, and it was where their parents said the action was now, with Chinese ships coming and going from Subi. Eugenio and Diwa hadn't been over there since the Seabees arrived, and tonight they were going to check it out. Eugenio fumed impatiently, waiting for his mom to go to bed so he could sneak out, but it was not until just before midnight she finished watching TV, checked to see he was asleep, and went in to her room. He had to give it another fifteen minutes so that she was settled, then shoved his pillow under his sheet to cover his absence and dropped out of his bedroom window to the ground below.

In the middle of the island was the tree-covered hill Eugenio and Diwa called 'Pinya' or Pineapple Hill, because the trees growing on its low slopes didn't grow straight, they stuck out at all angles, like the leaves on the top of a pineapple. The Seabees had put up big halogen lights on top of the hill and Eugenio could hear the sound of machines working up there. They were building something. North of Pinya was just scrub, with only one track, and no one ever went that way if they were going to the docks because it took longer and you had to climb the slope of Pinya on the way up, which no one wanted to do on a hot day.

And it was always a hot day on Pagasa.

Eugenio went to Diwa's house and tapped on her window, then waited in the shadow of a tree for her to join him. As she came running up, she started complaining about it being so late, but he spun on his heel and started walking fast, sticking to a track in the shadows so they weren't likely to run into a random Filipino Marine. "Come on, we'll go to the base first and get our binoculars, then you can moan all you like."

Eugenio and Diwa's 'secret base' was a concrete bunker and radio listening post, built by the Japanese in the mid-1940s to monitor shipping to the north because the Japanese Navy was worried about a US invasion of the Philippines through the Spratly Archipelago. It was also marked on the maps of Japanese pilots in case their aircraft were damaged, and they had to ditch in the sea. But when a US reconnaissance force checked Pagasa Island in November 1945, they found no Japanese troops on the island and their cursory search failed to find the well-disguised bunker.

It remained deserted until 1956 when a Philippine businessman established a colony on the island, calling it 'Freedomland'. The fishermen he paid to relocate there found the bunker and stripped it of anything useful – some furniture, wiring, empty filing cabinets and a typewriter with Japanese keys – and then forgot all about it. The vegetation reclaimed it until Eugenio and Diwa, out exploring one day, saw a sea bird fly out of a hole in the hillside and decided to investigate. It was *big*, going deep under the hill. Over the next few months, they cleaned out the birds' nests and guano and made it their 'secret base', moving in an old mattress, two folding chairs, some 'borrowed' solar-powered lamps, a crate for a table and, slowly, more of their more precious possessions – like a pair of binoculars with one lens that still worked – and their most prized possession, a battery-powered radio a pilot had given them so they could listen to aircraft flying around overhead, though a lot of it was in languages they didn't understand.

"I want some peaches," Diwa said as they pulled aside the green curtain covering the entrance. She went in first, looking for the battery-powered lamp they kept on a hook on the wall, but Eugenio didn't follow her in. He'd seen something strange. Out to sea, to the north. The eyes often played tricks around nightfall; he'd learned that from being out at sea on fishing boats. Especially on nights like tonight on a new moon when all there was to see by was the light of the stars. But that's what had stopped him, because out to sea, he'd seen a string of lights. Tiny blue lights, like bulbs on a wire, bobbing up and down.

Diwa found the lamp and turned it on, and the blue lights vanished as Eugenio's pupils slammed shut. "Turn that off!" he told her.

"What?" She was holding the lamp, looking at him with a frown.

"Turn it *off!*" he said as loudly as he could, without yelling.

"Alright, wow." Diwa switched the lamp off.

There they were again. But larger now? He watched for a full ten seconds as the small blue lights grew slowly and the distance between them grew too. They spread out left and right.

Totally. Weird.

And that was all the thought he managed before the lights suddenly disappeared, turning into arrowhead shadows that streaked *right over their heads.*

They never heard the cruise missiles' sonic booms, because before they could even reach Eugenio's ears, their warheads were detonating with a thunderous roar.

Three hours earlier, the three Chinese H-20 stealth bombers had taken off from their base in China's Northern Command opposite Taiwan, and fifty miles out of Pagasa they radioed their PLA Navy contact.

"Sword, this is Scimitar, approaching release point."

As Eugenio and Diwa had been approaching their secret hideout in the forgotten Japanese bunker, the Jiaolong Commando unit waiting on underwater delivery vehicles, or UDVs, off the coast of Pagasa, radioed back.

"Scimitar, Sword, we are in position and awaiting strike."

They had not waited long. At thirty miles, the Chinese stealth bombers released six Sky Thunder cruise missiles and then banked, turning back to their base in the north.

The six dark cylinders swept over Eugenio and Diwa's heads on tails of blue fire and then fanned left and right. From the bellies of each of the cruise missiles, 260 anti-personnel bomblets were flung into the sky, scattering indiscriminately in the missiles' wake. Within seconds, the 92 acres of Pagasa Island were covered with 1,500 bombs.

Eugenio paddled backward into the bunker as the dark shadows blasted overhead, crashing into Diwa and knocking her down. Neither had time to even draw breath before a ripple of thunderous blasts rolled over their heads. Diwa screamed, holding her ears. Eugenio continued scrabbling backward, trying to reach the darkest, furthest corner from the bunker entrance that he could find.

No sooner had the first ripple of explosions died than a second rolling wave of thunder swept over the island as each of the six Chinese missiles finished delivering its load and buried itself in targets across the island.

Eugenio put his hands over his head, and he started screaming too.

As the barrage of missiles ended, six hundred feet downhill from the bunker, 12 commandos of the Jiaolong assault team came ashore. The planners of *Operation Fencepost* would have been surprised to see that they were so few, but then they had grossly overestimated the number of Chinese combat troops based at Subi Reef. It had been a long time since China had rotated a company of the valuable troops through the base. More recently, only platoon-sized detachments had been deployed.

The rapid escalation of the conflict over the island had also taken Chinese planners by surprise.

So, when the Jiaolong Commando had been ordered to prepare a lightning strike on the Philippine island, their commander had decided his best idea was to split his small force into two waves. One force of 12 commandos to sneak ashore under the cover of a cruise missile bombardment using their fleet of underwater delivery vehicles, the other to be airlifted in as soon as the local Philippine garrison had been suppressed. A much lower chance that way of losing a chopper and its payload of elite troops to a Filipino shoulder-launched missile.

So far, the plan appeared to be working. To their east, south and west, dozens of Philippine combat engineers lay dead, shredded by the cluster bombs dropped by the Sky Thunder missiles. Dozens more lay wounded, or simply stunned by the horrific force of the attack.

But not all.

Pulling himself to his feet in the wreckage of one of the barracks buildings by the airfield, Captain Heraldo Bezerra jammed his service cap back on his head and looked about. Around him, among the bodies of the dead and the cries of the wounded, the surviving men of his detachment were dragging themselves and their comrades out from under blasted timber and shattered glass. One was sobbing, head buried in his knees, blood trickling from his ears. As he surveyed the carnage, Heraldo realized two things.

They had either been attacked from the air, or by naval artillery. It made no sense unless China planned to land ground forces. So, whatever he did next, he had to do it *fast*.

As if to hammer the thought home, from the direction of the harbor Heraldo heard shouting, then the staccato rattle of automatic rifle fire. Ignoring the cries of his wounded, he scrabbled in the wreckage of the hut, lifting aside debris, looking for his rifle. *Or any damn weapon, dammit.*

No, he told himself. *You're not thinking clearly, Heraldo.* He turned to a man two feet away from him, trying to pull the strips of cloth that had been his shirt together to cover his bloodied torso. "You!" he said, grabbing the man's arm. "Help me move this debris. We need to find the radio!"

Heraldo Bezerra had never thought of himself as a military officer. Not really. He was an engineer, commanding construction workers. But the Philippine Marines had given him weapons and trained him and his men to fight, and without even realizing it, as he reached for the radio to contact his troops at the summit of Pinya Hill, Heraldo Bezerra was about to become a combat commander.

It was 1209 hours on Pagasa Island, January 8, 2035.

And the dying had just begun.

Hong Kong Harbor, January 8

After being told by Sylvie Leclerc that she would be inducted into *Operation Fencepost* in the morning, Bunny had been left alone and made the most of the facilities aboard the superyacht. She'd taken a run around the flight deck of the White Star *Warrior*, followed by a swim, followed by a ridiculously OTT buffet of wonton soup, stir-fried noodles, Chinese dumplings, fresh fruit, and fried ice cream.

Stomach full, after celebrating the end of another day above ground with a post-meal prosecco watching the lights of the city slowly wink out, she retired to the cabin she'd been given, read an interesting moral philosophy article about the challenges to international law posed by autonomous weapon systems (no, not really), and around midnight fell quickly asleep.

It felt like seconds later that Leclerc was leaning over her, shaking her awake. The French woman was dressed in a khaki jumpsuit and sneakers, a leather portfolio in one hand and a steaming mug of coffee in the other. Was it already morning? Bunny looked out the porthole of her cabin with bleary eyes. Dark.

Leclerc held out the mug to O'Hare. "I asked a steward to make you a strong Americano. I did not think you were the espresso type."

Bunny sat up, pulling her sheets up with her and tucking them under her armpits. "Good call. What the hell time of night is it?"

Leclerc looked at her watch. "Three a.m." She watched on as O'Hare took a long slug of coffee. "Is there a story behind all those tattoos?"

"Every one," Bunny told her. "Paid for in blood. Some of it mine."

"I would like to hear your stories one day. But not now. There have been ... developments." Leclerc sat at the foot of O'Hare's bunk, unzipping the portfolio and pulling out a tablet PC. "The timetable for *Operation Fencepost* has moved up," she said. "Consider this your strategic briefing. I will give you the tactical briefing afterward." She handed the tablet to Bunny.

Bunny leaned forward, seeing a news report about a clash between Chinese and Philippine forces somewhere. She rested the tablet on her thighs, hit play and listened. When it was done, she drained the rest of her coffee in a single gulp.

"Pagasa Island?"

"Oui. Claimed and settled by the Philippines. But also claimed by Vietnam."

"Confusing."

"And Taiwan."

"What a mess."

"And China."

"How *big* is this island?"

"Tiny, less than a hundred acres. But it is the only settled island in the Spratly Archipelago and it is currently controlled by the Philippines." She continued. "Control of that island means territorial, fishing and resource rights."

O'Hare pulled up a map on the tablet, used her thumb to get a measure from the scale at the bottom of the map, and then thumbed her way across from the Spratly Islands to the Philippines coast. "That's about 200 miles?"

"One eighty, I believe," Leclerc confirmed.

She did the same to the nearest point on the Chinese mainland. "And *six hundred and fifty* miles from China?"

"Six forty-five, yes."

"But China claims it's theirs?"

"The US claims Hawaii and it is 2,300 miles from San Francisco."

"Alright. Fair point. So, the Philippines has troops there and China attacked them?"

"Is attacking them. While you slept, Chinese commandos were landed on Pagasa by submarine and went ashore, supported by a cruise missile attack on Philippine positions."

"Where do we come in?" Bunny asked. "That little stunt over Guangzhou tells me *Operation Fencepost* has been planned for some time, so someone was expecting this?"

"Yes and no. *Fencepost* is part of a US plan to help the Philippines fortify Pagasa against Chinese aggression. The Philippines government has hired White Star to transport the materials and equipment needed to do so, and the US Navy will escort the White Star ships. But China has moved first. The battle for the island is already underway."

"Well, that sucks for the Philippines and the Pagasians. And for me, I guess."

Leclerc blinked at her. "For you, why?"

"Well, White Star won't be sailing its very expensive ships into a war zone, so I guess you are here to tell me I'm already out of a job."

Leclerc leaned back and crossed her legs, smiling. "Oh, you really did not read your contract, did you?"

"I might have skimmed a little. Why?"

"White Star is the world's biggest ocean carrier both by tonnage shipped and by revenue. Its most important client, by far, is the United States Defense Department. It has been able to hold onto that client against all bidders because Mr. Sorensen is willing to send his ships *wherever* the US Defense Department wants them, *whenever* they are wanted, and under *any* conditions, including war."

"Which has what to do with my contract?" Bunny asked.

"Your contract provides for a 50 percent 'risk' loading if you are asked to enter a conflict zone. This voyage qualifies, if you agree." She tilted her head. "But you don't care about that."

Bunny looked into the bottom of her empty coffee cup. "I don't?"

"No. I am pretty sure you could not give a fig about the money. Am I right?"

"Partly. A girl has to pay her bills. But I could pay them by giving flying lessons. I agreed to this job because…" *Yeah, why exactly, Bunny? Because it was something different? Because working for various governments has got you nothing but grief? Or because of that big black semi-autonomous beast up there on that flight deck? Are you really that superficial?*

"You will take this contract, because you will see this was about more than White Star Lines. This is about what is right, and what is wrong…"

Bunny pulled her sheets higher. "Oh, ouch. Major fail there, Sylvie. Your whole 'good empire versus evil empire' thing is water off this duck's back. I'm more of a…"

Leclerc leaned toward O'Hare and Bunny held her ground, frowning, as a wave of musky perfume washed over her, but the woman was just reaching for a picture in her back pocket.

She sat back again and held it out. "This little boy is Eugenio Maat, son of a fisherman of Pagasa Island. Please look."

Bunny took the picture. It showed a boy in a bright red t-shirt and shorts, with a huge smile, standing on the deck of a fishing boat holding a fish by the tail that was nearly as long as he was tall. Bunny handed it back. "And?"

"A couple of weeks ago, a Chinese Coast Guard corvette rammed his father's fishing boat, killing the Captain, Bobong Huerta. China rescued his father, Gonzales Maat, arrested him for terrorism, and then put Pagasa Island under blockade. They will attempt to use the incident to justify their action on Pagasa today."

Bunny tried her best steely gaze. "Which sucks for Gonzales Maat."

"And his wife. And his boy, Eugenio. Who are probably going through hell on Pagasa Island, right now." Leclerc put a hand on Bunny's thigh, over the sheet. "You will not stay here in bed and do nothing, I think."

Bunny took Leclerc's hand and put it back on her own thigh. "Yeah, yeah. You are very good at the whole motivational thing, you know that?"

"Yes, I do."

"So, what do you need me to do?"

"I need you to take the Vapor and land it on a ship that gets underway in four hours," Leclerc told her simply. "You will be flying convoy support for the two White Star Lines ships sailing for Pagasa Island. The convoy will be met underway by a US Navy frigate, the *USS Congress*."

"Four hours? Cool, I'll just have a quick shower and breakfast, pre-flight the Vapor, then…"

"No. The ship you are meeting is not in Hong Kong."

Bunny sighed. "Of course it's not. Where, then?"

"Singapore. You will need to leave in thirty minutes to make the rendezvous. I will brief you on the rest of the mission when we are airborne."

"*We?* You're coming on this voyage?" Bunny had trouble seeing Leclerc roughing it on a merchant ship in the middle of shark-infested Asian seas. But who was she to judge?

The French woman stood. "No. The White Star Risk Group has offices in Singapore and my team is running intelligence support for this mission. Now, we need to go."

Pagasa Island, Spratly Islands Archipelago, January 8, 2035

Eugenio and Diwa had stayed near the back wall of a side room just inside the mouth of the bunker, too scared to go deeper into the bunker while the ground around them was trembling with heavy explosions, and then too scared to go outside as the sound of gunfire started sounding all around them.

It had been close, then it had moved away. Finally, it had died down.

"Is it China?" Diwa had finally asked after a while went past where they didn't hear anything. "You think they're finally invading like everyone always said?"

"It must be," Eugenio decided. "What else could it be?"

They'd waited until the sound of gunfire died down. Diwa had taken a step toward the bunker entrance. "Maybe it's over. Should we try to get home?"

Then Eugenio heard the crack of a small explosion nearby, and gunfire started up again. A *lot* of gunfire, from down near the harbor, but also from the eastern side of the island, down near the village. "Or maybe we should stay right here," he'd said.

That had been a while ago. The shooting and explosions had continued, and worse, it sounded like it was getting *closer*.

Shit show. There was no other way to describe it, Lieutenant Baotian Liu of the Jiaolong Commando decided. He'd predicted it when the hurried operation had been put together and events had proven him right. He'd protested that the orders had caught them at a time when he only had two squads at Subi base. But urgency of action was of the essence, he was told. Air support had been hastily arranged.

And besides, their enemy were *construction* troops. Were his men not the Jiaolong Commando?

Oh, it had gone well enough in the first phase of the operation. His two six-man squads had secured their UDV mini-subs offshore north of Pagasa Island where satellite imagery had shown there was no Philippine troop presence. He'd taken team Alpha north around the small hill, toward the naval base where the largest concentration of Philippine troops had been seen; and he'd sent team Bravo south, toward the civilian village, which should have been left largely unscathed by the cruise missile attack.

As they'd advanced to contact, the smoke from the cruise missile explosions had settled eerily through the trees around them, and they'd heard shouting coming from the direction of the base. Liu knew the missiles had been targeted at the base periphery, as it hadn't been their intention to destroy the facility completely. So, they had to expect many of the estimated 100 Philippine troops had survived the barrage.

But not *so* many. Squatting up on the hillside looking down on the port, Liu and his men had counted at least twenty, twenty-five troops. He had landed with twelve in total, and Alpha team was six, including himself. The Philippine soldiers were still recovering from the attack though, dragging wounded to safety or waiting for someone to tell them what to do.

"Bravo, this is Alpha leader, report," he'd called to his other team.

"Alpha, Bravo leader," his Second Lieutenant, Siqin, had replied. "We're in the village. Some damage to civilian buildings, no Filipino troops here. People are all outside their houses though, panicking. We're trying to get them back inside. Zhang is scouting the airfield, says the barracks there took a direct hit, a lot of Filipino wounded, maybe ten troops combat-capable. Will engage when we're done here in five."

"Hustle," Liu told him. "We've got about twenty-five Philippine troops at the naval base. Engaging in five, Alpha leader out."

More enemy than they'd been told to expect. He'd turned to his radio operator, Corporal Ruan, next. He wanted to get word to the patrol boat serving as a mothership offshore, arrange an extraction in case the Philippine troops fought back, didn't surrender. "Send a text message to the Captain of the patrol boat…"

"He won't be expecting it," Ruan warned Liu. "We aren't supposed to check in until 0130."

He'd sighed. Ruan was good at his job but had a special talent for telling Liu what he already knew. "Right, but he'll probably have someone listening?"

"Yes, sir."

"So, send a message. Remaining enemy strength estimated 30 plus. Engaging 0030 hours."

He'd ordered his men into firing positions on the hillside overlooking the base and checked his flanks for movement. There was none. If there had been any Filipinos working on the hilltop above and behind him, the missile targeted on the crest had either taken them out or forced them to hide in place.

"Alpha team, choose your targets," he said quietly into his mike, looking at his watch. Three minutes. Four. *Five.* "Alpha, open fire."

With bloody precision, they lay the sights of their suppressed bullpup 5.8mm carbines on their targets and went about the business of cutting down the Filipino troops on the dock. Behind him, Liu trusted that Bravo team had started doing the same over at the airfield.

Heraldo had put in a panicked call to Puerto Princesa alerting them to the missile barrage. They couldn't do much for him, but maybe they could organize a med-evac flight. His men had been walking around dazed, so he'd organized for the wounded to be taken to the clinic in the village and got the rest of his men behind cover in the ruins of the airfield buildings.

His adjutant was dead. But the man who had found him the radio was still beside him, waiting for orders. Somewhere, he could hear a man calling for help. But Heraldo had no medics, not here anyway. His wasn't a rifle company, it was a damn construction unit. His only two medics were down at the docks, working alongside every other man down there, pouring concrete and manhandling rebar frames into place.

If they were still alive. He had to get over there to check. The wooden and concrete harbor was also the most defensible position on the island. He had to get his surviving men over there in case there was a follow-on strike. Also, it was possible the patrol boat there had survived the missile attack. If so, it was his ticket off this bloody island.

"Alright, listen up!" Heraldo shouted. "If you can walk, help someone who is wounded. We have to get to the harbor. Got it? Grab a man and get to the docks!" He looked around himself, saw a man nearby lying on the ground, clutching a bloodied thigh. He took the arm of the man who had found him the radio. "You, help me with that man there."

The soldier nodded, took a step toward his wounded comrade, and then staggered backward. He looked at Heraldo with a shocked look on his face and then crumpled to the ground.

What the hell?

To his right, another man shouted, and then his head snapped back, exploding in a cloud of blood.

"Enemy fire!" Heraldo yelled, diving for the cover of some building debris. He hadn't heard the shots, but it couldn't be anything else. Sticking his head up cautiously and scanning the vegetation at the perimeter of the airfield, he looked for the flash of firing gun muzzles, but saw nothing. One of his men had found a rifle and was firing it wildly toward the scrub on the perimeter of the airfield. He was silenced in seconds and went down clutching his chest. A man in front of him got up and ran straight at the treeline, firing a pistol. He zigged and zagged, and got nearly twenty yards without being hit, Heraldo willing him on. *Go, man!* Then he stumbled and fell onto his face, unmoving. Again, there was not a single sound from the treeline where the enemy must be hiding. Suppressors. *They are using suppressed weapons.*

Which told Heraldo they were not dealing with regular troops. *Damn, damn, damn.* He looked west. *Get to the harbor. You have to get to the harbor.*

Ignoring the cries and screams of the men around him, Heraldo lay down on his stomach behind cover and started crabbing backward, toward the landing strip and the sea behind it.

"Hold fire!" Liu ordered. They'd decimated the Filipino troops at the dock. Any still alive had managed to dive into the water and were hiding under the dock or had found other cover where Liu had no line on them. Eight, ten survivors maybe? It was good enough for now.

"Alpha leader, Bravo," Liu's earpiece had whispered. "No more resistance at the airfield. Estimate maybe four Filipinos still alive here, in cover. Don't appear to be armed. What you want us to do?"

"Pull south and engage again. Push them toward the harbor," Liu told Siqin. He had his orders. Neutralize any resistance, herd any surviving Filipino to the harbor and ask for their surrender or contain them there for a potential follow-up strike. "Send a man to the village to keep the civilians calm, but the rest of you keep pushing up and join us here at the port. Let's finish this."

It had gone so smoothly at first. Too smoothly. They'd pushed the surviving Filipino troops to the harbor, where about fifteen of them had taken shelter. A shot or two into the wood or concrete around them was enough to keep their heads down; there had been no return fire. Stumbling out of the darkness, some survivors from the airfield and barracks had also scuttled into cover at the port, a few rounds at their heels from team Bravo hurrying them along.

Bobbing at anchor in the small harbor was a patrol boat of some sort. It had a single .50 cal machine gun mounted on the foredeck, but none of the soldiers at the dock had made a move toward it, yet. It was only a hundred feet long, but more than big enough to take the Filipino survivors aboard.

Time to end this. "Alpha team, I'm moving forward, cover my front." Moving through the shadows from tree trunk to tree trunk, Liu got within fifty yards of the nearest Filipino soldiers, who were hiding behind a concrete road barrier and in the water by the dock. He leaned out from behind the tree, cupped his hand around his mouth and yelled in English, "Philippine troops! Your position is hopeless. But we will let you take your boat and leave Pagasa." There was no reaction from the dock. "Philippine troops! We will not fire on you if you board your boat now and leave!"

Nothing; no word, no movement. Did they even speak English? He tried again and got no reaction from the Philippine side. *Oh, well, I tried*, Liu decided. He started backing deeper into the trees. If the Filipinos wouldn't surrender, he would have to call in fire support from the frigates offshore. See how many were left after that, and try again.

Then he paused and whirled around. A shout. The hammer of a heavy automatic weapon, *behind* him. Tree branches and leaves around him exploding. He threw himself to the ground and pulled dirt around him as bullets chewed the ground. Then they stopped, as whoever was firing reloaded.

He stuck his head up. *Oh shit.* They were coming down from the top of the hill, a line of about 20 troops, advancing slowly behind the cover of a machine gun he couldn't see yet. It opened up again, somewhere uphill on his left. Encouraged by the counterattack, the troops down on the dock started shooting as well. A grenade cracked off to Liu's right. His squad was sandwiched. He threw himself at the base of a tree and huddled behind it as heavy-caliber bullets chewed the trunk above him.

His twelve men against maybe a dozen surviving construction troops, knocked flat by a surprise bombardment in the dead of night? Sure. His twelve men against a significant force of enemy combat troops who had apparently come through the bombardment unscathed? The mission was a bust, his only option now was to get his people back out to sea and radio for their boat to pick them up. "Pull out!" he'd barked into his mike. "All Alpha, Bravo troops. We're pulling out. Back to the UDVs, now!"

There had been more than 20 men working on the planned missile launch emplacement on the summit of Pinya Hill when the Chinese cruise missiles had struck. Not a single bomb had fallen on the crest.

Heraldo had waited in the surf south of the landing strip until he heard the fire front move off toward the harbor. Heading that way suddenly seemed like a bad idea. But from down at the waterline he could see the arc lights of the crew working up on Pinya Hill were still lit and thought he could see movement. It was only 500 yards to the summit, but it had taken him nearly twenty minutes, moving through the undergrowth, throwing himself flat every time he thought he saw a shadow move.

But he'd made it up there and found his men milling around, wondering what the hell had happened, and what they should do next. He solved that problem for them. In a moment of unusually clear-eyed prescience, he'd ordered an automatic squad weapon and ammunition hauled up to the summit 'just in damn case'. The troops on top of Pinya all had their personal carbines with them – Heraldo never let them go anywhere without their entrenching tool, a canteen of water and their carbines. He dedicated a few men as a heavy weapons squad, loaded the rest with ammunition and grenades, left a few behind to hold the hilltop, and then started creeping down the slope toward the harbor, where he could still hear sporadic shooting.

For good measure, he sent four men back to the village to make sure the islanders there stayed put.

"Contact!" Liu's man inside the village had called. Liu could hear the sound of rifle fire. "Filipino troops moving in. I'm cut off!" the man had said. That had been the last Liu had heard from him. The Filipino force moving down from the hill had joined with their comrades from the harbor and were pushing them east, away from their UDVs.

In the first five minutes of the Filipino counterattack, Liu had lost his second in command, Siqin. Trying to retreat, they'd also been cut off by the Filipino troops moving back out of the village and two more of his men had fallen in a vicious close-quarters firefight. The Filipinos had called in the contact to their comrades back at the harbor and soon Liu and his men were taking fire from three sides, being pushed slowly backward up Pinya Hill toward the still-smoking summit. Liu had looked up the slope behind him. He had a night vision lens over one eye and the smoke drifting from the summit was a ghostly green. He could see movement in the smoke. Filipino troops up there too. But if they could take it, they might be able to hold the hilltop long enough to get airlifted out. Over the sound of stuttering Filipino assault rifles, the crack of grenades and the suppressed cough of his men's bullpups returning fire, he made the call. "Everyone to me! Break contact!"

He turned then and stopped dead in his tracks.

Right in front of him, a mottled groundsheet covered a hole in an overgrown concrete wall in the hillside. Then he heard a voice from inside.

A child's voice.

Their bunker entrance was shrouded with a groundsheet, but on each side of the entrance were two mailbox-sized firing slits and Eugenio had been watching the firefight outside the bunker through them, his legs shaking, unable to pull himself away.

They'd killed their lamp. Downhill, he could see the flash of rifles firing. Every now and then a sharp explosion that must have been a grenade, and pretty soon he saw eight or nine shadows, crabbing backward from tree to tree, rifles to their shoulders, firing with a strange coughing noise, not like real guns. Then he saw one of the men stand and heard him call out.

In Chinese!

"It's not our guys!" Eugenio told Diwa in a terrified whisper. She was crouched down by his feet, back against the bunker wall. He bent down to her. "They're coming our way."

"Be quiet!" Diwa hissed. "They'll hear us."

Eugenio stood to look through the firing slit when someone pulled the groundsheet aside and peered inside. Seeing Eugenio, he instantly pinned him against the wall with the barrel of his rifle against the boy's throat.

Liu saw two kids, a boy and a girl, huddled near the entrance. Entrance to what? He spun the boy around, clamped a hand over his mouth and looked around with his light-intensifying lens. Another man grabbed the girl, put a glove over her mouth too before she could squeal. Liu saw a large dark room, rust-stained concrete. It smelled damp.

The boy was going to say something, but Liu put a finger over his own lips to warn him to be quiet. He indicated to two of his men to take up positions on either side of the door at what were clearly firing ports. A bunker? He was in a *bunker*. But there were no bunkers on the plans of the island he and his team had spent hours poring over.

He sent two men further in to clear the bunker of any other occupants. They were quickly back again. "Clear," one whispered.

"Enemy approaching," Liu heard Private Zhang say softly into his mike. "Should we engage?"

Thinking furiously, Liu weighed up their situation. "No," he whispered into his mike. "You and Gao watch outside. They might pass us. The rest of you, with me. Find a corner if you can." He still had a hand over the young boy's mouth. Nodding to the man holding the girl, they dragged them both back into the bunker with them.

His low-light night vision lens was near useless so deep into the bunker, but he vaguely sensed two more small rooms, one leading left, another off to the right. He pulled the children into the room on the left, and motioned to his men to take positions in the rear rooms that would let them cover the bunker entrance and fire from the cover of the corners.

Then he waited. He heard a faint shout from outside the bunker. Tagalog.

"Talk to me, Zhang," he whispered.

The man's voice was loud in his earpiece, but inaudible even from the six feet across the concrete room. "Movement left and right. Nothing in front."

"Gao?"

"I had two go past, I'm clear now, Lieutenant," the man at the other firing slit said. "I think they're moving uphill."

Liu leaned back against a wall, too worried about the boy

making a noise to let his hand fall from his face. He could hear the boy panting, blowing air through his nose.

After five minutes passed without a grenade being thrown into the bunker, and then ten, Liu bent down to whisper in the boy's ear in English. "I will take my hand away. If you yell, I will kill you."

He felt the boy nod and carefully lifted his glove from the boy's face. He stood stock-still, too terrified to even move.

"Tell the girl the same," Liu told him. "She makes a noise, we kill you both."

The boy tried talking, coughed, wet his lips with his tongue and tried again, speaking in Tagalog.

They huddled together in a corner by some shelves full of canned food. Liu kneeled in front of them. The boy was about twelve, the same age and build as his own son. He was chubby with a mop of tangled black hair. The girl was a little younger, maybe ten. Definitely not his sister, though. She was albino, he could see that even in the dark room. Pale hair, pale eyes.

"What is this place?" he asked softly.

"Our hideout," the girl said. She was scared, spoke in a high voice. Liu motioned to her to keep her voice down.

"An old war bunker," the boy said. "We found it."

Liu looked behind him to where the entrance to the bunker did a defensive dogleg and continued under the hill. "What's back there?"

"Just a big room," the boy said. "And a ladder up to an iron door. I got it open with a pry bar but there's just dirt on top, so I closed it again."

Liu pictured the bunker in his mind: entrance two men wide, a groundsheet where there probably used to be an iron door, two firing slits, small rooms either side, dogleg grenade trap, main room, ladder up … to an exit probably. He'd seen a fortification like this before, in Nanjing when he was a kid, touring the old Japanese bunkers with his father. The big room was probably a radio room, the two smaller rooms equipment, storage and bunks. The radio room would have had an antenna connection going up the same tunnel as the exit ladder, probably rusted away. Before the vegetation reclaimed it, it probably had a clear view out over the sea to the north-west, the main sea lane between Thailand, Malaysia and the Philippines – and if he remembered his history right, the main passage for ships of the British Eastern Fleet as they moved out from the Indian Ocean to attack the Japanese home islands.

"Zhang?" he asked into his mike.

"Still clear, Lieutenant," the man said.

"Clear my side too," Gao reported.

"Stay sharp. They'll keep searching."

Liu stood. The contact during the Filipino counterattack had been an intense, chaotic whirlwind of flying tracer, frag grenades, smoke and screams of pain. He'd automatically counted the number of Filipino troops they were engaged with during their fighting retreat: conservative estimate, twenty, high side, thirty. He was pretty sure he'd seen two of his men killed, two who might just have been wounded, probably captured by now. Six men left of the 12 who landed. Maybe Wu, down in the village, if he'd managed to evade.

They had the ammunition in their packs and, thanks to these kids, water and food by the look of it. A radio for contacting the support boat offshore and calling for an extraction if they could get back to their UDVs once things calmed down. He knew the PLA Navy sailors had been taking bets about whether *any* of the Jiaolong commandos would survive the operation. Well, screw them. Liu and half his men were still alive.

And maybe he was thinking about it wrong. He was thinking extraction. But there were still two frigates offshore he could use to call down fire support.

He looked around him at his men, crouched against the bunker walls, gathering their energy again. They didn't look beaten. They looked to him like they were still in a position to take the fight to the Filipinos.

Heraldo had a squad of men continue to scour the island for the Chinese soldiers. They'd found five bodies so far, but he had a feeling that far more had come ashore. "For Christ's sake take it easy out there in the dark," he told them. "Don't shoot our own men."

It wasn't the full-blown invasion his headquarters had warned him the Chinese were planning. In fact, apart from the damned cruise missile attack that had claimed nearly twenty of his own men, it had seemed a little half-assed. Rushed, perhaps. Maybe there was a clock ticking out there somewhere. That American convoy coming in? Could that be it?

Heraldo doubted the American ships would still be inbound Pagasa once the Philippine Navy passed on news of the attack to the Americans. This wasn't their fight, why would they send American ships into harm's way?

He had another group of soldiers moving among the ruins of airfield buildings, civilian houses and barracks, checking for signs of life. He heard one of them shout for a medic. He felt water running down his back, pulled the cap off his head and tipped seawater out of it, and then jammed it on his head again. He decided to head for the village clinic and check on the wounded there.

It was only a short walk to the southern end of the village and the clinic. A rifle squad was going house to house as Heraldo arrived, kicking in doors and searching for Chinese soldiers. When he reached the clinic, he helped a limping man inside and propped him against a wall. His medics were treating wounded soldiers and civilians as they were brought in. Heraldo walked around, satisfying himself no one seriously wounded was going unattended. Most of the men and women in the clinic had light injuries like the man Heraldo had brought in, if you could classify a shredded foot as a light injury. Heraldo knew a lot of the more seriously wounded would have died in the time it took for him to organize his men to counterattack and regain control of the island. The time he spent cowering in the surf next to the landing strip, listening to the firefight as it moved away, but too terrified to move? He wasn't too proud of that.

He walked up the road that went through the center of the village, looking for whoever was in command of the squad currently going house to house. He found a corporal standing at the end of the road with two of his men and, kneeling at their feet, head bowed, a single soldier in a night-black uniform. On the ground beside him was a black beret with a badge on the band Heraldo recognized instantly. A blue dragon, breathing fire. *Jiaolong.*

As Heraldo approached, the corporal whipped his pistol barrel across the man's temple and pulled his face up to snarl in it in Tagalog. "Where is your comrade!?"

The Chinese soldier's head lolled against his chest and he said nothing. The corporal drew his pistol back to strike again.

"Hold it, Raz," Heraldo called out to the corporal as he approached. He didn't admonish him. The hell the man had probably been through. "Who is this?" Heraldo nodded toward the commando.

"An enemy soldier, Lieutenant, we found him hiding under one of the houses. I was asking him where his buddies have gone."

"You saw others?"

"Not alive. But there were more."

"Hmm." Heraldo squatted in front of the commando. Blood was running from his temple, down the side of his face and dripping from his chin. Heraldo held a hand under the man's chin and tilted it up so he could look at him. The man looked at Heraldo, clearly having trouble trying to focus. There was no defiance in his eyes, only pain. The pistol-whipping was clearly not the only abuse that had been visited on him before Heraldo arrived.

Heraldo had some Chinese family on his mother's side and spoke passable Mandarin. He leaned closer to the man on the ground. "Listen. The man who hit you," Heraldo told the soldier, "is heartless. If you do not answer, he is going to shoot you. He will probably start by shooting you in a leg. Then he will shoot you in the groin. Finally, in the stomach. At that point, if you still do not talk, you will probably pray he shoots you in the head. But he won't. He will wait, letting you bleed slowly to death or fall into fever and delirium while he questions you. He can keep you alive for many, many hours before you die. And after what you did today, I will not stop him. Do you understand?"

The man looked back at Heraldo, eyes still unfocused. Heraldo wasn't sure what was getting through. He tried again. "I can have you taken to the clinic now and treated as a prisoner of war. But you have to tell me what we want to know."

The man's eyes seemed to focus for a second. "Gone," he said.

"What?"

His head dropped again. "My team, gone."

"Gone where? How?" Heraldo asked, pulling the man's face up again.

"Subs. Offshore."

It made sense. They had come in quietly, by submarine, and left the same way. God knows they couldn't just disappear on Pagasa – he'd studied every map of the island, walked it north, south, east and west. There was nowhere they could hide. He dropped the man's head and stood up.

Heraldo stood, addressing the corporal. "Find my radio operator, down at the harbor. Tell him to send this message to Puerto Princesa: *Chinese attack neutralized. Casualties high. Full report to follow. Urgent reinforcement requested.*"

The man nodded. "You think they can get reinforcements through to us, Lieutenant?"

"I sincerely hope so, Raz. I have a feeling the battle for this shitty island has only just begun," Heraldo said.

White Star *Andromeda*, 5 miles N-NE Riau Islands, South China Sea, January 8

Bunny's journey had gotten off to a good start. So she should have known it would soon go seriously sideways.

Piloting the Vapor from within the cockpit, while wearing the data-linked VR helmet, had taken some getting used to. Her first hour in the new unit was a head spin. Before spooling up the engines in Hong Kong, she'd sat in the cockpit and pulled the helmet over her head. It contained a form-fitting gel that adjusted to the shape of her head and as she pulled down the wraparound visor, the helmet synched to the aircraft's neural network, replacing the real world view with a virtual cockpit view so close to reality that she flipped her visor up and down a couple of times just to be sure. The main visible difference was that without her VR visor down, her view outside the cockpit was limited to what she could see through the windows, of course. With the visor down, the helmet pulled vision from cameras all around the fuselage of the Vapor, and she could not only see out the windows, she could see through the fuselage to the deck beneath her feet and the brightening Hong Kong skyline behind her.

Welcome, pilot. Beginning personalization routine. Do you want to continue with the settings you chose in your last session? She recognized the voice, because she'd chosen it herself before retiring for the night. It had the charming lilt of an Irish American actress Bunny was a fan of – one she was sure wouldn't start to grate in the many hours ahead. For simplicity, she had decided to keep the unimaginative but kind of superhero-sounding name of the AI given to it by its designers, 'Vapor'.

"Vapor, I want to review the cockpit layout," Bunny said.

Initializing V-290C Vapor cockpit configuration.

The virtual multifunction screens in front of her were a carbon copy of the physical screens in the cockpit. It meant with her sensory feedback gloves she could flip virtual switches and tap virtual buttons that for all intents and purposes looked like those she had in her physical cockpit, and if she flipped up her visor, the same view would be showing on the cockpit displays in the real.

"Can you remove all of the multifunction screens and just show me a through aircraft view?"

Yes, pilot.

The cockpit walls, floor and roof fell away. Now she was sitting suspended in space above the deck of the White Star *Warrior*, nothing at all obstructing her view. Another pilot might have gotten disabling vertigo. Bunny simply got a serious buzz out of it.

Turning her head to look over her shoulder, she saw the aircraft's stubby wings, tiltrotors deployed for takeoff, and by craning her neck she could look directly behind her over the back of the Vapor, no cockpit bulkhead obstructing her view as it would in real life.

"That will do nicely. You can bring up any screen I want when I call for it?"

Yes, it will appear in its standard position in the cockpit unless you ask for it to be repositioned.

"Alright, Vapor, start engines, prepare for takeoff."

Starting engines.

With that simple command, the AI took over the business of getting the Vapor ready to launch, saving Bunny from hitting about twenty different switches and buttons to kickstart the battery and auxiliary power unit, manage engine crank switches and spool the engines up, turn on heads-up displays and ground navigation instruments, flip her oxygen supply and radar on, set flaps for takeoff, trim her rudder, arm her ejection seat and slip the machine's parking brakes.

Instead, all she had to do was wait for the numbers in her visor to show the tiltrotors and rear turbines had reached takeoff power, slide her collective forward and push forward on the stick in her right hand – the real stick this time, not the ghostly VR one she would have to use if flying the Vapor remotely.

"Buckle up," she'd told Leclerc.

As she'd pushed the Vapor into the air above the *Warrior* and then out over the sea, she felt the acceleration push her back in her seat and her harnesses tighten to hold her in place as the Vapor pitched forward on its nose and started gaining both altitude and speed.

She had let out an uncontrolled whoop of delight and spent the first twenty minutes of the flight putting the drone through its paces and setting up her VR cockpit exactly the way she wanted it. Leclerc had the sense not to disturb her.

When she had settled in, and after engaging the Vapor's navigation autopilot, Bunny had turned to Leclerc in the shotgun seat and flashed her a fake 'in-flight service smile'. "Would madam like a beverage or snack?"

"You had time to make a thermos of coffee?" Leclerc asked hopefully. She'd brought a cup with her but it had no doubt gone cold.

"No, I did not," Bunny told her. "As you well know. So kindly tell me where you expect me to land this thing."

Leclerc had opened the leather folio in her lap and pulled out a photograph, handing it to Bunny. "This is the White Star *Andromeda*. Look carefully."

O'Hare pushed back the visor on her helmet and held the photo close to her face. It looked a little like the ship she had hitched a ride back from Guangzhou on, except someone had carved half of it away. At the front was a three-story superstructure that looked big enough to carry maybe a hundred crew or passengers, topped by the usual domes and radar dishes. At the rear, there was just a flat empty deck, with two cranes, one small, one large. A large 'H' was painted on the rear deck, inside a circle.

"Helo deck," Bunny said. "Don't tell me, it's just big enough to land a Vapor."

"More than sufficient," Leclerc nodded. She handed over another photo.

It was a ship slightly larger than the first, its long, empty deck at least 180 yards long and 40 across the beam. Like the *Andromeda*, it seemed it was able to land helicopters but, unlike the *Andromeda*, it could apparently land more than one. There were no fewer than three helipads on the long flat deck, and one helicopter – a civilian Bell 429 – lashed down on one of the pads, its main rotor blades locked in a stowed position. Bunny couldn't see any bridge or superstructure, not even a radar or satellite communication mast. Just the helo decks, what looked like handrails and barriers to stop people getting blown overboard, and some access hatches to the decks or holds below.

"The White Star *Orion*," Leclerc told her.

"I don't see a bridge. It's autonomous?"

"In a sense. It's what White Star is calling 'an Unmanned Trailing Utility Ship'. It's made to follow along behind another ship; in this case, the *Andromeda*."

"This *Orion* doesn't look like a normal freighter. If you painted it navy grey, I'd call it a small helicopter landing ship."

"You are not completely wrong. Each of *Orion*'s deck helipads is rated to support vertical takeoff and landing aircraft up to and including a weight of 33 tons."

"Thirty-three *tons*? That's the weight of a fully fueled and armed F-35 stealth fighter, loaded in 'beast mode'…"

"Is it really?" Leclerc said with a slight smile. "How interesting. But not relevant to this mission. *Orion* is a humanitarian relief vessel, capable of standing offshore from any disaster or conflict area to provide support. A ship like the *Andromeda* acts as a 'feeder ship', transporting cargo and passengers between the shore and the *Orion*." She handed O'Hare a cutaway diagram of *Orion*'s internal compartments, pointing to various elements. "Dock-level loading ramp, parking for up to ten heavy vehicles, freight compartment for building materials, food, water and medical supplies. Medical triage facility immediately beneath each helipad, surgeries and recovery wards on the mid-deck; fuel, propulsion, engineering, medical and security crew quarters in the lower decks."

"Why does a private shipping magnate have his own humanitarian relief ship?" Bunny asked, skeptically.

"White Star has two *Orion* class vessels," Leclerc explained. "They can be contracted by governments or relief organizations to provide emergency care facilities to regions hit by floods, cyclones or hurricanes. The US Navy uses them to supplement its fleet of Expeditionary Transfer Dock ships. Quite often, White Star loans them to client states on a non-profit basis. A little goodwill goes a long way in business."

"I'm sure it does. Sorensen didn't strike me as the humanitarian type," Bunny said drily. "I get why the medical crew quarters, but why a 'security crew'? Crowd control?"

"No, that's not an issue. The *Orion* has a 39-foot draft, it can't get close to shore in most disaster areas, so getting overrun by refugees is not the issue." Leclerc pointed to a list headed 'piracy countermeasures'. "The security crew is there to dissuade anyone who thinks an unmanned ship might be an easy target."

Bunny handed the photos back to Leclerc and pulled her helmet visor back down, running her eyes quickly over the Vapor's instrument display before turning to Leclerc again. "Alright, enough of the PR story. What is that mini-assault ship really carrying?"

"I'm sure I don't know what you mean," Leclerc said with feigned innocence.

"I mean, if the Philippines wanted to sail a few hundred tons of bulk concrete and rebar to its island, it could find a dozen ships to do it and they wouldn't require an escort by a US Navy missile frigate."

"I'm sorry, I have not looked into the detail of the cargo manifest…"

Bunny slammed her throttle forward and pulled her flight stick right, rolling the big machine inverted. She was ready for the maneuver, the straps holding her into her seat pulled tight. Leclerc was not. Everything on her lap fell to the top of the cockpit, including her coffee mug and the remains of her coffee. To her credit, she didn't scream, but she did let out a small surprised gasp, which turned to a moan as Bunny reversed the roll, bringing the Vapor back upright. Leclerc's belongings fell to the floor again and coffee started dripping on her head from the cockpit roof.

"What the…" Leclerc sputtered.

"Look, *Mademoiselle*. I'm not some jet-jock meathead. I talked to Sorensen's pilot, Rolf. This is the first time White Star has deployed an armed aerial escort on one of its ships. US Navy-guided missile frigates are not something you can just hire for protection. Which means there is more to this convoy than just transporting sacks of cement. So it's time to bring me into the circle of need-to-know."

Leclerc smoothed her hair and took a handkerchief from a pocket on her jumpsuit, wiping the cockpit glass overhead and then her hair. From the floor near her feet, she picked up her folio and its contents, before putting the coffee cup back. "This machine needs a better coffee cup holder," she said.

Bunny twitched her flight stick right again, as though starting another roll.

"*Merde!*" Leclerc yelled. "Alright, enough. Along with building materials and equipment, the *Orion* is transporting US-made weapons systems which are being leased to the Philippine government."

"Uh-huh. What kind of systems?"

Leclerc did not meet Bunny's eyes, staring straight ahead out the cockpit windscreen. "An MM104 Patriot Missile Battery including phased-array radar and 16-missile launcher trucks, 64 PAAC-4 missiles, and two networked Joint Medium Tactical Vehicle-mounted Naval Strike Missile launchers, with 20 missiles."

Bunny whistled. "They put that kind of hardware on that little island, it means they could strike just about any Chinese aircraft or ship in the entire Spratly Archipelago."

"Oui."

"And China knows about this? That's why they moved on Pagasa last night, to prevent the Philippines from fortifying it."

"We assume so."

"Which also makes your convoy a big fat target. China won't want to see those kind of weapons in the hands of the Philippines."

"*Operation Fencepost* planning has taken into account that threat scenario. Which is why a US Navy escort will be joining the convoy before it reaches Philippine waters and why you are sitting at the controls of this Vapor." Leclerc ran a hand across her hair and wiped it on her jumpsuit. "Though now I am seriously beginning to question that choice."

Bunny gestured out the cockpit window to the sea around them. "Philippine waters? There are a *lot* of nautical miles between Singapore and Philippine waters," she pointed out. "This part of the world is thick with pirates."

"Both *Orion* and *Andromeda* are fitted with the usual passive piracy deterrent systems, while the addition of this aircraft gives enhanced protection."

"You put a gunship on a merchant marine convoy, how will the pirates react?"

Leclerc gave O'Hare her own version of a sweet fake smile. "Let us hope we never find out."

Bunny had checked in with Singapore air traffic control, dropped Leclerc dockside at Singapore's Marine Bay Cruise Center, and barely waited for the French woman to pull her luggage out of the rear compartment before she lifted off again and lighted out for the White Star convoy, already at sea fifty miles to the north-east.

One of the capabilities the Vapor gave the White Star ships was a radar system that could track both air and sea targets and extend *Andromeda*'s own sensor range out to nearly a hundred miles. As she got about fifty miles out from the *Andromeda* she hailed the ship.

"*Andromeda*, this is Vapor pilot Karen O'Hare, heading in for a landing. Are you ready to receive?"

Leclerc had given her the name of the comms operator aboard the *Andromeda*, Angus McIntyre. The man had a Scots accent to match his name. "Aye, Vapor, we've got the kettle on. But we have a wee job for you first. We have a suspicious contact near your position, a group of small, fast-moving boats headed our way. Can't see how many. Sending you coordinates on text. Check them out, would you?"

Bunny checked her fuel and then plugged in the coordinates the radio operator had given her before bringing up her own radar. Ten miles north-west. "Roger that, *Andromeda*, will check and report. Suggest we synch radar, see if we can get you a clearer picture."

"Will do. Initiating handshake," the man said.

Bunny had been shown by the Vapor's pilot, Rolf, how to synchronize her own sensor data with that of any White Star Ship on the globe. It was just a matter of diving into a comms menu, selecting the ship she wanted to link with, establish a satellite connection and … "Got you, *Andromeda*. Moving in now."

Her radar screen populated with more maritime contacts as *Andromeda*'s powerful Marine radar data was added to her own. Including the group of small vessels along the bearing the radio operator had given her.

She laid in a course to the boats and was soon in visual range.

With a pinch gesture of her right hand, Bunny zoomed the surveillance camera mounted in a dome under the nose of the Vapor. The images being projected in a window on a virtual screen in front of her showed four needle-nosed boats, each about fifty feet long, eight to ten men in each, two big outboard motors at the back that were sending them flying across the glittering sea at what had to be thirty knots or more. They were on a heading that would put them right in front of the White Star convoy within about thirty minutes.

If that wasn't enough of a worry, on the Vapor's radar, she had picked up what had to be a surveillance drone or light aircraft, trailing the White Star ships. She couldn't tell if it was being controlled by someone in the boats, or someone on shore, but she'd seen one of the men in the boats speaking on a radio, so either was possible. Of course, it could just be a coincidence the drone and the cigarette boats seemed to be keeping company.

Uh-huh.

"*Andromeda*, you have four fast boats headed your way. About forty pax, and they don't look like they're on a fishing expedition to me."

"Uh, do you see weapons, Vapor?"

Bunny ran the camera across each of the boats, looking carefully. A guy on a radio, yeah, some duffel bags in the bottom of the boats, but no visible weapons.

"Negative, *Andromeda*. No weapons sighted." This time her machine had been loaded both with fuel and a 5,000-round belt of 20mm ammunition for each gun. "You want me to fire a warning burst ahead of them, scare them off?"

"I'll check with the Captain, Vapor, but I'm guessing that's a no. Until they directly threaten us, get within weapons range and you can see weapons, they are just a bunch of civilians out on a day trip, I'm afraid. But we'll be ready if they show malicious intent."

"Good copy. But I'd like to..." As she watched one of the cigarette boats on the screen, a man dragged a duffel bag from under his feet and unzipped it. It contained automatic rifles, which he started handing out.

"*Andromeda*, Vapor. Update to last report. The pax in those cigarette boats are carrying weapons. AKs by the look of it."

"Copy that, Vapor. Not fishermen then."

"Unless they're hunting Orcas the hard way. *Andromeda*, I'm going to try to image the aircraft trailing you. I'll copy it to White Star security for identification and advise."

"Roger, relaying your update and conferring with the

bridge."

Now was as good a time as any to test the analytical resources Leclerc had bragged were at Bunny's fingertips, supposedly available for her to task at any time of day or night.

Bunny locked the distant drone on her radar. "Vapor, queue a message to White Star Risk Group please, attention Sylvie Leclerc."

Message queued. What would you like to say?

"Will send image of an aircraft trailing White Star Pagasa convoy. Please analyze and report immediately."

Vapor repeated the text. *Message sent.*

"Thank you, Vapor, now put us on an intercept course for the locked target."

Yes, pilot. Intercepting marked contact.

As she closed on the unidentified aircraft, she let the AI do the flying as she worked the camera. The machine appeared first as a small dot, then an aircraft-shaped blob. When she was able to pick out wings and a tail, she took control of the stick, cut her throttle and pulled above it, guessing its own cameras, like its operator, would be focused on the sea below.

She knew it had to be a reasonable size, or her Vapor's radar wouldn't have been able to pick it up. But it was bigger than she expected. It was about 10 feet long with a 12-foot wingspan. Twin boom tail layout, pushed by a propeller, so probably electric. No cockpit, so, as she suspected, it was a drone. Too big to be hand-launched, so it must have been launched from the ground as those cigarette boats were getting ready to depart. Which indicated it had a ground operator, radio comms with the island, and probably a comms link to the boats out at sea. At least voice, maybe vision too.

Piracy is getting all grown up, Bunny reflected. Of course, it made sense that as the stakes got higher, and the shipping lines took more precautions, the pirates would too. Why go charging in to attack a ship if it was being escorted? Loiter above it, count how many crew, see what the security looked like. If the crew looked like they were on alert.

Bunny had enough imagery and quickly marked it for transmission. She matched the drone's course and speed and sat 500 feet above and behind it. "Vapor. Copy the data package to White Star Risk Group."

Uploading data to White Star Risk.

She figured that as she'd prewarned them, if they knew what they were doing, the analysts at the other end of the transmission should be able to get back to her inside ten minutes. This first interaction would be a good test.

They took less than five.

Message received, White Star Risk Group, Leclerc, S: message reads, aircraft identified Chinese CH-1 Rainbow drone. No longer in active service with PLA. Reported to be in use by African and East Asian militia. Recommend you treat as suspicious.

"Bingo. We have a winner," Bunny exclaimed out loud. "*Andromeda*, Vapor. Better put me through to your Captain. I confirm the drone is working with those boats. I predict you have less than thirty minutes before they intercept."

"Damn. We have to be their target, there's no other ship on their heading. Patching you through to the bridge, Vapor."

There were a few grey areas in the chain of command for this civilian operation that O'Hare did not like. Leclerc was her mission commander, but she could also be tasked by *Andromeda*'s Captain, Jorgen Pedersen, and Leclerc had made clear to O'Hare that in all matters regarding the physical safety of the convoy, Pedersen had the last word. He was a former Norwegian naval officer and, she was assured, a good man to be leading the White Star convoy.

Bunny hadn't even met the guy, and now she was asking him to work with her on a fast-developing crisis situation. Oh well, as long as he understood one thing. Leclerc might be mission commander, Pedersen might be commander of all things on water, but when she was airborne, she answered only to Bunny O'Hare.

"Vapor, this is Captain Pedersen of *Andromeda*. Welcome to the party, Ms. O'Hare." The man sounded calm enough, which

Bunny took as a good sign at this early stage in their relationship.

"Glad to be here, Captain. Let me update the situation for you," Bunny said. She gave Pedersen the relative positions of the trailing aircraft, the incoming cigarette boats and the time her nav computer predicted the tracks for the cigarette boats and the convoy would intersect. "So, Captain, what do you want me to do? I took off from Hong Kong loaded for bear, courtesy of your employer. I can send a few shots across the pirates' bows, let them know we are watching them. Might frighten them off."

"I doubt it, and you might get a nasty shock. It is not unknown for pirates in these waters to carry Flying Crossbow missiles, O'Hare."

"My machine has decoys for dealing with heat-seeking missiles. But who is *arming* these pirates?!"

"First lesson. Stop thinking of them as pirates and start thinking of them as militia. Armed by mafia, triads and drug warlords or even government officials in Africa, Indonesia, Vietnam or Brunei. Paid to do as they're asked, and free to keep the spoils or carry out some freelancing between jobs."

"In that case, why shouldn't I do the world a favor and just sink them? No warning shots. They won't know I'm coming until it's too late."

"That would not be proportionate, O'Hare. Second lesson. Law of the Sea: we can only take action to defend ourselves that is proportionate to the threat against our ships. Until those boats show hostile intent, there *is* no threat. But I think it would be a good idea to take out that surveillance drone. There is no point making the militia's job easy for them, agree?"

"I agree. O'Hare out."

The pirate ... militia ... drone was weaving a lazy s-track through the sky so that it could scan a broader arc of the sea ahead of it. Keeping an eye on its prey, looking for possible sources of interference. They were not in the busiest of shipping lanes ... most traffic was further north, halfway between Indonesia and Vietnam, on the route that went from the Malacca Straits to the South China Sea. One of the busiest sea lanes in the world, and there was safety in numbers. The White Star convoy was sailing a more easterly route, closer to Indonesia, ironically so as not to draw too much attention. Bunny had flown over several other ships on this patrol, so she couldn't be sure the White Star convoy was the target. But a big autonomous 'trailing utility ship' weighed down with cargo had to be a juicy target in any pirates' eyes. All they would have to do was separate it from its mothership, jam or hijack the signal controlling it, and sail it somewhere quiet to pillage, or to ransom.

Well, as the good Captain said, there was no point making it easy for them. Time to blind their eye in the sky.

She adjusted her trim to put the Vapor's nose down, sliding in behind the Chinese-made drone. It was bobbing up and down in the warm air, and snaking from side to side, so it wasn't exactly a fish in a barrel. But pretty close.

She realized this was her first live target interdiction in the Vapor. Until now she'd only tested the guns over water, on floating jetsam like drifting containers or islands of waste plastic.

"Vapor, guns up, lock aerial target," she said out loud.

Guns armed, rounds 4200, target locked, fire at will, pilot.

By habit her eyes flicked between instruments, head swiveling to check the sky around her, a quick spin of the surveillance camera to check she had clear air behind. Her finger closed on the gun trigger. OK, O'Hare, nice and ... *what?*

A shadow flickered across the camera screen. Reacting instinctively, Bunny pulled her throttle back, rolled the Vapor on its horizontal axis and pulled the nose toward the ground, firing decoy chaff and flares as she fell. Her radar warning receiver started screaming in her ears. *Fighter targeting radar!* Some swine had snuck up behind her while she was…

This is how you lose your life, O'Hare, she told herself as she flung the Vapor in a spiral at the sea below. Asleep at the damn stick.

She pulled the aircraft level about five hundred feet over the sea, scanning the sky around her, grateful she didn't have cockpit walls and instrument panels obscuring her view. But she couldn't see him! Her radar warning receiver was still urgently chiming, but it wasn't indicating a homing missile lock.

The voice that broke over the open Guard radio channel sounded almost amused. "Unidentified military aircraft, this is China People's Liberation Army Air Force, you are entering China self-defense airspace. Please identify."

Bunny looked over her shoulder and now she saw him, a delta-winged shape dropping in behind her. She had pushed her throttle forward to regain some speed, but pulled it back again, and deployed her air brakes. She was pitched forward in her seat inside the ovoid as the Vapor decelerated, and the tiltrotors began automatically spooling up. In seconds she had chopped a hundred knots from her airspeed.

She was nowhere near any of China's self-declared air defense zones in the South China Sea. So what the hell was this guy up to?

How about you identify yourself, buddy? Bunny thought grimly. To the fighter behind her it would have looked like she had stopped in midair, and sure enough, wobbling on the edge of a stall, the aircraft behind her overshot, pulling up and away and giving her a perfect view of its underside profile as it flashed overhead.

Chinese J-15 strike fighter.

Out here? Bunny quickly checked her nav screen. She was still 200 miles from China's disputed 'nine-dash line', the area of South China Sea it had repeatedly tried, and failed, to claim as its own. What in hell was a J-15 doing off the coast of Indonesia claiming she was violating Chinese airspace? Armed for bear, too. She'd seen missiles hanging from its wing pylons. The J-15 was a multirole fighter, like the American F-15. The latest versions were painted with a stealth coating – not sophisticated enough to defeat an advanced military phased-array radar but more than enough to hide it from Bunny's 'off the shelf' airborne radar. What worried her most was that while the J-15 could be used to engage hostile aircraft, it could also be loaded with air-to-ground, or air-to-*sea* missiles. Its sudden appearance near the White Star convoy did not bode well.

Bunny pushed her throttle forward again and keyed her mike. "Uh, that's negative, Chinese Air Force, I am a civilian aircraft, flying in international airspace in accordance with international law, and I will not be identifying myself to you today. You seem a little lost, pilot, do you need directions back to China?"

The Chinese pilot wasn't going to be deterred. She could no longer see him, either on visual or with her radar, but her radar warning receiver told her he was still out there. "Unidentified aircraft, your heading will take you into Chinese air defense airspace. Please turn south and exit the area to avoid misjudgment."

Misjudgment? She was about to say something smart but caught herself. Unfortunately, Bunny wasn't strapped into the cockpit of an F-35 Panther fighter. She was in the airborne equivalent of a militarized SUV. She was in no position to go mouthing off at the pilot of a Chinese strike fighter. She turned her machine east, toward the *Andromeda*.

"Chinese Air Force Pilot, I am ending communication, you have a nice day," Bunny said, cutting away from the Guard channel and opening her link to the *Andromeda*. Guard was an open channel; she knew anyone within range could have picked up the exchange.

"*Andromeda*, Vapor here, you copy that little discussion?"

"Roger, Vapor, you alright up there?"

"I left my virtual lunch up at 5,000 feet but, yeah, I'm alright." The beeping in her helmet ceased suddenly. "OK, he's switched off his targeting radar now, probably has me locked up on infrared still. I'm going to keep circling here for a moment to let him know he doesn't own the air."

"Appreciate the gesture, Vapor, but don't dally up there.

Captain wants your machine refueled and ready to dispatch again as needed. We just picked up a news report that the conflict in the Spratlys is heating up. Seems China isn't minded to back off."

"Well, that explains why the Chinese are getting a little overzealous up here," Bunny observed. "Uh, *Andromeda*. I have bad news. I wasn't able to take out that drone. It's still on your tail, along with those four cigarette boats."

"Acknowledged, Vapor, we're ready for the wee buggers. See you soon, alright?"

After circling for a while without picking up a return from the Chinese aircraft, Bunny pushed the throttle forward and her machine moved to cruising speed again, the tiltrotor engines and blades tucking themselves into their nacelles as she told Vapor to lay in a course for the *Andromeda*, the back of her neck still itching at the thought there was probably an invisible Chinese fighter still lurking nearby.

Had it actually been *escorting* that pirate drone? It certainly felt like it. That would be a level of State cooperation the planners for this little operation had not taken into account.

White House Oval Office Study, January 8

Director of National Intelligence, Carmine Lewis, and President Fenner were sitting, chewing over the day's developments over coffee. They kept the door open at times like this, not least because of the endless, unfounded rumors about her 'special relationship' with the widowed Fenner.

One thing Lewis allowed herself in one on ones with the President – that *would* definitely have raised eyebrows, though, with people seeing it for the first time – was that she kicked off her shoes and padded around the study in stockinged feet. Yes, she had that kind of relationship with Fenner. The freedom to be herself, speak her mind and call him out if she thought he needed calling out.

"If there is one thing I have learned in this job, it is that the other guy never plays by our rule book," Fenner was saying. He was sitting by the low telephone table against one wall of the small room. It was barely big enough for the table, an office chair and a single plush sofa-style armchair, which Lewis found so stuffy she preferred not to use. Usually, when they worked in the President's study, Lewis preferred to stand, or lean on a wall, as she was doing now. "Goddamn cruise missile strike."

"Actually, that *is* straight out of our own playbook," she pointed out. "We knew they had the capability; we just haven't seen China use it before."

"Those Philippine Seabees fought off one attack, we need to make sure there isn't another before the *USS Congress* can lend support." Fenner lifted his wire-rim glasses and pinched the bridge of his nose, something she knew he did when tired. "Joint Chiefs are recommending we stand up fighter patrols over Pagasa."

"That makes sense."

"Secretary of Defense and General Cavoli are also suggesting we take out China's base at Subi Reef, where those commandos came from. Stop it happening again."

"I thought we were told that would be a declaration of war," Lewis said. "You'd need Congress to…"

"Apparently not. We already have a mutual defense treaty with the Philippines. Congress re-ratified it just two years ago. It gives me all the authority I need for a 'military intervention' on behalf of the Philippines."

Lewis knew Fenner was no hawk. Not anymore. Several international crises during his term had taken his nation to the brink of nuclear war, even though the wider world did not know it. And he'd replaced his first Vice President over that man's constant push for more and more assertive action against Russia. *Operation Fencepost* was something Fenner had been nudged towards by the Joint Chiefs and members of his Cabinet over several years. Eventually, he had grown tired of being accused of impotence in the face of what they saw as growing Chinese belligerence. The tipping point had come when Defense Secretary Kahn had warned him about his legacy in a conversation Lewis had been party to.

"It's 1939 all over again, and Mr. President, you are British Prime Minister Chamberlain."

"What the hell, Phil?"

"The Munich Accord. Chamberlain let Hitler roll into the Czech Republic and take over Sudetenland. Poland and France were next, and you know what happened after that. We let China's expansion into the Spratly and Paracel Islands go completely unchallenged, with respect, you will be remembered as this generation's Chamberlain, Mr. President."

The barb had struck home, Carmine saw that. Within the month, Fenner had signed off on *Fencepost*, the plan to turn the Philippine island of Pagasa into a missile base that could command the seas and skies for hundreds of miles around. What he was now contemplating was the equivalent of Chamberlain not only refusing to sign the Munich Accord, but conducting a pre-emptive strike on a German Luftwaffe base to show he was serious.

"You're thinking about it," Carmine guessed.

"More than thinking," Fenner admitted. "I asked Chuck to have the Executive Order drawn up. It's on my desk. I wanted to talk to you before I sign it, because there's no way back if I do, Carmine."

Carmine leaned against the wall. They'd already considered and debated a hundred different scenarios with the Pentagon and Joint Chiefs. This was one. Right now, she was talking to him as a friend, not an adviser. "Stuart, no President goes to war without a heavy heart. If they did, they wouldn't be worthy of the position. But if we do this, we have to do it smart."

Fenner nodded. "Smart meaning…"

"Nearly every defense research and procurement program for the last 20 years has been geared to give us the ability to fight a major war without risking thousands of American lives.

It's time for us to unleash that capability and show China that they are *not* our equal."

"Cry 'havoc' and let slip the silicon dogs of war?" Fenner asked, standing and moving to leave. At the door he paused. "Thanks, Carmine. I'll let you know what I decide before I announce it to the world."

Carmine watched him walk out into the corridor. She had the feeling that the world already had a pretty good idea what Fenner and the USA was going to do. Her AI analytical support systems had pretty much nailed the *Fencepost* playbook just by reading the comms in and out of the Philippine Embassy, so she was sure China had also already anticipated their next move and was busily planning to thwart it.

Beach Road, Singapore, January 8

Sylvie Leclerc had been met at the container terminal by a White Star company limousine to take her into the city. It dropped her at the Raffles Hotel, where Sorensen kept a suite in the Bras Basah wing for use by himself and visiting executives.

After the porter had dropped her cases in the suite's parlor, she found the bar – which in no way could be described as 'mini' – and poured herself a mineral water, slice of lime. Then, kicking off her heels, she walked out to the balcony doors, which the porter had opened for her, and closed them. Pulling her tablet PC from her leather portfolio, she sat at the dark teak dining table, found the app she was looking for, and tapped to open it. Then she waited patiently as it scanned her face and asked for a thumbprint.

Satisfied, it flashed a simple black screen and the words 'No Surprises'. She smiled. It was the White Star Risk Group's motto.

So tired. One task, then she could sleep. She felt like she hadn't slept at all since … ever. She'd thought that leaving French Intelligence behind and going freelance would mean she got some control over her own life at last. But nothing in Sylvie Leclerc's life was ever that simple.

The problem for today was the *Andromeda*'s crew manifest. She had asked for an updated copy before leaving Hong Kong and had reviewed it on the flight, comparing it to the version she had been given a week earlier, just to be sure there were no changes. She was responsible for security vetting all members of the *Andromeda*'s and *Orion*'s crews, and had weeded out any whose bona fides she couldn't confirm.

What was preventing her from falling asleep right there and then was that there had been a last-minute change to the *Andromeda*'s crew. A communications technician, Sunil Mehotra, had been taken off the roster and another, Lawrence Winter, added in his place. Mehotra had been vetted by her. Winter had not, which annoyed her, though he had been vetted by one of her team.

Still, Sylvie Leclerc was the kind who believed trust was good, but certainty was even better.

Logging in to the White Star human resource directory, she did a search on both Mehotra and Winter. It seemed poor Sunil Mehotra was in hospital in Singapore, having been hit by a taxi while crossing the road in front of his hotel. Multiple fractures, possible internal bleeding; the police were still looking for the taxi driver.

Lawrence Winter was a new hire; a UK national. She reviewed his application letter and resume. He'd been employed by a rival South Korean shipping company and when his contract had expired while he was in Singapore, he'd approached White Star. Nothing unusual in that.

Except … Leclerc looked at the dates of Mehotra's accident and Winter's application.

They were both, coincidentally, dated January 6. Two days before the convoy sailed. White Star human resources had rushed through Winter's contract and failed to copy Risk

Group until the last minute. Laziness, human error ... or something else?

Dammit.

It was probably an oversight. She enlarged the picture of Lawrence Winter on her screen. Young, freckled skin, with light hair, a very prominent Adam's apple and jug ears. The kind of face only a mother could love.

You are being paranoid, Sylvie, she told herself. *You need to sleep.*

She thought back to O'Hare's report. A drone, shadowing their convoy? If China had an agent aboard the *Andromeda*, they'd hardly need a drone. Just give him a satellite telephone or GPS transmitter.

She turned off her tablet, walking to the bathroom to get ready for bed.

Sleep tonight. And tomorrow: run a background check on Lawrence Winter.

White Star *Andromeda*, Riau Islands, 600 miles S-SW of Pagasa Island, January 8

"Contacts are closing," *Andromeda*'s Captain was muttering. He was on the bridge of the *Andromeda*, watching the plot on the ship's radar of the approaching cigarette boats. "Regrettably."

Bunny had to agree. It seemed the gods had not heard Sylvie Leclerc hoping pirates would not be a problem.

She had put the Vapor down on the slowly moving ship and was now on the bridge looking at the radar screen over Pedersen's shoulder. It was a big ship, by Bunny's standards, but a rather small bridge crew. It comprised his Chief Mate, a large but light-footed Indian seaman called Kapil Bose, a second and third mate, also Indian, who looked after navigation and steering, and due to the automation of most of the ship's functions ... that was it.

What Bunny was wondering right now was why the pirates had been making an uninterrupted beeline for the *Andromeda* and *Orion* since the moment she landed, and kept coming on even though it was now broad daylight, and as though they were somehow invisible to the ship's radar.

Perhaps if *Andromeda*'s Captain hadn't been forewarned, and if the crew had been asleep, or the radar had been down ... but none of those were the case.

"This is going to be hairy," the Chief Comms Officer, Angus, whispered to her. A round, befreckled and bewhiskered auburn-haired giant of a man, he'd personally met her out on the helipad to escort her to the bridge and ensure the crew got started on refueling her kite. She'd reached a hand out to shake. "Bunny O'Hare."

"Just call me Ginger," he told her, his hand engulfing hers as he shook it enthusiastically. Even the hair on his knuckles was red.

"You're kidding," she replied.

"No. The other nicknames people come up with are worse."

He led her down a ramp from the helipad and toward a hatch leading into the ship's superstructure. "Been with White Star long, Ginger?" Bunny had asked as they took a corridor leading toward some stairs. He didn't look like he was long out of high school, let alone a merchant marine academy.

"Few years. I was Royal Navy for five years. Submarines actually. Served on *Dreadnought* class ballistic missile boats. Royal Navy pay sucks, so I went civilian..." He paused and scratched his stomach. "Happened to be in Singapore on another White Star ship when they posted the notice for this voyage. Pay was too good to pass up. Risk loading and all that." He stopped at the entrance to the stairwell. "Here we are, after you, ma'am."

"No, you go first," Bunny said, automatically.

"Alrighty," Ginger said, heading up the stairs ahead of her. "But if you're worried I'd be staring at your arse on the way up, don't be. I'm not into women."

Bunny smiled and started climbing the stairs behind him. How should she follow that little personal disclosure? "Ah, so you ... prefer men?"

"No, not at all. Not into either, really. Just not a people person, I guess. I like to call myself a friendly misanthrope." He shrugged. "I prefer the company of cats."

They'd reached the bridge level and he'd waited at the hatch for her. "And I had you picked for a dog person, Ginger," she'd said.

"Dogs? Nae. Too needy."

"We have clear seas for ten miles around. Mr. Gupta, ahead full, port twenty, put us between *Orion* and those cigarette boats please," Pedersen ordered his helmsman. He reached for his ship's intercom handset. "All hands on *Andromeda* and *Orion*, security stations. This is not an exercise, hostile boats approaching. Security teams, small arms issue authorized, security teams to action stations."

Bunny half expected him to say 'stand by to repel boarders' so she was disappointed when he dropped the handset back in its cradle and turned to his Chief Mate. "Tour *Andromeda*'s action stations please, Mr. Bose, and coordinate with *Orion*. Make sure passive systems are armed, the water cannons are ready and sonic disruptors are powered up. Active systems to deploy only on my order."

"Aye, sir," Bose replied, disappearing off the bridge at speed.

Now Bunny leaned across to Ginger and kept her voice low. "Sonic disruptors?"

"Aye," he nodded. "*Andromeda* and *Orion* have passive and active defenses. Passive; we've got anti-grip foam dispensers in the hull, electrified razor wire we can pull around the outer railings, deployable chain rakes at the waterline to foul outboard engine props, that kind of thing. Active, we've got your usual water cannons, sparklers..."

"Sparklers?"

"Lasers. Burn your retina out you look straight at them. And we've got sonic disruptors … Captain only likes using those as a last resort. They put out high-intensity ultrasound in a 30-degree arc that can give people fits and cook their intestines." He must have seen the look of surprise on Bunny's face. "Only if they insist on getting too close, ye ken."

Bunny had limited experience of life on a merchant ship, but right now, it didn't seem to her to be particularly different to life aboard a naval ship; if anything, it seemed more likely a merchant ship would use its weapons against pirates than would a navy ship against a foreign navy. Angus made a similar observation.

"I knew this would'nae be no pleasure cruise," he said. "But it feels like a combat zone already and we aren't even near Pagasa yet."

"You've been in a combat zone?" Bunny asked.

"Aye, briefly. I was aboard His Majesty's submarine *Agincourt* when she put two missiles into an Iranian frigate in 2030. That was our only action in that war."

Bunny smiled. "Yeah, I heard about that."

"Someone said you're ex air force?"

"Don't hold it against me."

Pedersen turned to Bunny. "O'Hare, I'd like you aloft during contacts like this, please. The usual strategy of militia in fast boats is for one or two to scoot in and out, harassing our defenses and trying to draw the escort vessel away from the primary cargo vessel, while the rest of the boats sneak around to what they hope is our blind side and try to disable the escort vessel's prop with nets. I need you to make sure we aren't blindsided."

"Yes, sir," Bunny said. She was about to head down to the helipad but stopped to ask Ginger, "Who is manning the comms if you are up here?"

He turned his head, showing her an in-ear transceiver. "Me. My 2IC is down in the comms room twiddling the dials, but he's a newbie, I wouldn't trust him to boil a cup of tea without burning himself. Forget leaving him to man a comms watch during a hostile contact."

"And that little gadget in your ear has what kind of links?"

"Satellite, 6G, wifi, and it's waterproof too, why?"

"Would you like to join me, Ginger? Would be valuable to have someone up there who's been through this kind of scenario before."

"Would I? You bet," Ginger said. Bunny had made sure Pedersen could overhear them, and Ginger addressed him directly. "Captain? Permission to…"

Pedersen waved a hand, distractedly peering at a navigation screen. "Yes, yes."

Ginger beamed at her. "We'll go past the radio room on the way down."

Ginger's comms center was a small compartment, not much larger than a portable toilet. Inside it sat a young, fresh-faced seaman, face covered with freckles and head covered with … *ginger hair*?

"This is Lawrence Winter," Ginger said. "Lawrence, this is our pilot, Karen O'Hare."

The boy stood, holding out his hand awkwardly. "Pleased to meet you, ma'am."

Bunny shook. "You're British too?"

"Welsh, ma'am," he said.

"Well, Lawrence, I am way too young for you to be calling me ma'am. The name is Bunny."

Winter frowned uncomprehendingly and Ginger clapped him on the shoulder. "Don't worry, son, you'll work it out sooner or later. Ms. O'Hare is taking me on a short joyride. I'll monitor comms on my earpiece, you keep the systems up and running and don't touch anything I haven't learned you about, alright?"

"Yes, sir."

As they walked away, the boy looked very nervous.

"He's not too bright but my usual 2IC got hit by a car in

Singapore and I had to find someone to replace him fast. Lawrence was the first one White Star sent me and with our departure being moved up and all…"

"You're telling me that hair color is just a *coincidence*?"

"Aye, no. Well, you know how it is." He gave her a guilty look. "Us gingers need to look out for each other."

Bunny started up her engines as soon as she had Ginger set up in the copilot-observer's chair with his own VR helmet. The whine of the tiltrotor turboshaft engines was loud inside the helmets, and though immersion was important for all-round awareness, Bunny dialed it down so they could speak.

As she looked around the Vapor using its 360-degree pan and tilt cameras, the flash of sunlight off metal surfaces was dazzling, and Bunny kicked in polarizing filters to cut the glare. On virtual screens floating in front of her where the Vapor's instrument panel would normally be, Bunny was streaming data from the radar aboard the Vapor, from the *Andromeda*'s more powerful surface radar, and near-real-time optical and infrared satellite imagery of the area pulled from the White Star Risk Management Group's feed which tapped into a commercial satellite surveillance network with close to military-spec resolution.

She checked the two radar displays. They were showing some large merchant ship contacts well off to the north in the main shipping lane between Singapore and Japan, and a few scattered ships in their lane, none close. The group of small fast boats on an intercept course for the convoy were a single glowing blob on her own radar at the moment. Altitude would give her a better return.

"Vapor, prepare us for takeoff, please."

Wing rotor performance nominal. Turbine engine performance nominal. Avionics nominal. Releasing parking brakes, you are clear for liftoff, pilot.

"Who is the sexy babe?" Ginger asked.

"Vapor," O'Hare explained. "Flight AI. Think of her as my

copilot."

"I feel like I'm floating, not sitting in the cockpit," Ginger marveled. "I can see through doors down to the deck. If ... if I turn my head, I can see *inside* the crew compartment. This is amazing."

"Buckled in?" Bunny asked.

"Good to go."

"Alrighty. I'm taking her up. I'll go out to meet the contacts and stand off out of small arms range. You can give the convoy a heads-up if they move within a mile of *Andromeda* or *Orion*."

"Roger that," Ginger said. "Anything inside that range, especially in our rear quarter, is a direct threat. The last voyage I was on that got attacked, a needle boat put a rocket-propelled grenade into our stern plates and buckled the shaft. We couldn't make more than five knots after that. Would have been dead meat if the fools chasing us hadn't closed inside sonic disruptor range."

"I hear you. You holler if you need me to lay anything other than eyes on these guys."

"I forgot this thing is armed," Ginger said. "Maybe I should have stayed down on deck."

"Twin 20mm Sky Viper chain guns in the nose, and that thing behind you."

Ginger turned to look more carefully at the personnel module 'behind' him. It couldn't be reached from the cockpit; there was a blast-proof bulkhead behind their seats, but he could see into it via the helmet display. The space was configurable for personnel or cargo transport, or as it was now, with a combined personnel and ground support module with a GAU 17, 7.62mm Gatling gun, on a pintle mount that could be swung out so it could be fired by a crew member from the portside door. It would have been ideal to have the gun on a swivel mount that dropped from below the fuselage and could be fired by Bunny remotely from her pilot position, but it was a prototype, you couldn't have everything.

"That's *legal?*"

111

"According to the White Star lawyers. As long as we only use it 'proportionately'."

"In what situation is the firing of a chain gun ever proportionate?" Ginger asked.

"I hope never to find out. You ever fired one?" Bunny asked Ginger.

"In His Majesty's Navy, once. Six, seven years ago. Since then, hell *no*."

"Let's keep it that way, then."

The Vapor had the combined controls of a helicopter and conventional aircraft, with a single stick and throttle like the fighters Bunny was used to. The AI managed the transition between vertical and horizontal flight and a collective slider under Bunny's thumb controlled altitude when she was in or near a hover. Pushing her throttle forward as she slid the collective up, the Vapor lifted smoothly off the helipad and, rotating into the wind, Bunny quickly gained height, moving the machine out and away from the *Andromeda*.

She swiped at the multifunction screen in front of her and flipped a copy to the observer's helmet. "Sending you a tactical map, the contact is painted on it by our radar, triangulated by the *Andromeda* and *Orion*'s surface radars. You can see the *Andromeda* here, the *Orion* … here." She painted boxes around the convoy. "The ship to the north is the nearest surface contact at the moment, a civilian merchant ship heading southeast toward Singapore. About ten miles out." She zoomed further out. "Looks like your militia pulled their drone back. It's no longer trailing anyway. And here, in the red box, are our friends. Sailing two by two so they don't lose contact with each other, I guess."

"They'll have radio and GPS," Ginger told her. "Unlikely to have radar."

"Heading straight into our path," Bunny observed. "How can they do that if they don't have radar or that drone to guide them?"

"Not easily. Every merchant ship is required to have an

automated identification system transponder – AIS - beeping out its position, speed and heading about every three minutes. But when we're in pirate waters we can turn it off so they can't track us. Could they be getting help?"

That had occurred to her. A small surface radar mounted on a militia boat wouldn't have the range to track the White Star ships, but a military radar – based, say, on China's Fiery Cross Reef, could. Or they could be getting satellite imagery. Bunny surveyed the tactical situation. The unarmed and unmanned trailing utility ship, *Orion*, was plodding along at 20 knots, north-north-east from the Riau Islands. *Andromeda* was coming around to put itself between *Orion* and the incoming cigarette boats. Bunny had a good return on the four cigarette boats and couldn't see any other threats.

Or any friendly naval vessels for that matter. "Can I ask a dumb question, Ginger?" Bunny said.

"I'm a sailor," Ginger replied. "Pretty sure I've heard them all."

"You know what is in *Orion*'s hold?"

"Concrete mix and construction equipment."

"Yeah. And that 'construction equipment'..."

"Is actually an advanced missile system bad enough to knock down anything that floats or flies for hundreds of miles around." He shrugged. "I read the manifest."

"Right. It's just, if that cargo is so valuable, why send one puny frigate to escort us. Why not half the US Indo-Pacific Fleet?"

Ginger scratched his beard. "Well, I guess they don't want to telegraph that," he said. "Or get China too riled up before we get there."

"You heard about the cruise missile strike on Pagasa, right? I call that pretty riled."

"Yeah, well. No plan ever survives contact with reality," he said. "But the *USS Congress* is no puny frigate. I looked it up. It's one of the new *Constellation* class multirole ships. Stealth hull, anti-submarine, anti-ship, anti-air capabilities, flight deck for launching and recovering helicopters or drones…"

Bunny reached out and wiped a finger across his chin. "You're drooling, Angus."

"Aye. Once Navy, always Navy, they say."

She nodded. Given what lay ahead of them, she was glad to hear they were getting some heavy-duty protection. She pointed at the screen. "Speaking of which, I think we'll put ourselves behind the pirates…"

"Militia."

"…militia, here, a mile or two back, and follow them in at 15,000 feet," she told Ginger. "That way we can react fast if *Andromeda* is threatened."

"How about you go low and buzz them, go right over their heads, and let them know you're shadowing them? Scare their pants off," he suggested.

"How about I don't," Bunny replied. "I don't want to take a heat-seeking missile in one of the engines. Fifteen thousand feet puts me above hand-held missile range. They'll see us if they aren't blind."

"Heat-seeking *missiles*? Starting to think coming along with you was not such a good idea."

"Sorry, I don't do refunds," Bunny told him.

It took only minutes to close the gap to the cigarette boats, and about two miles out, Bunny swung left and started circling, giving Ginger a good look at the small boats on her zoom camera and showing him how to manipulate it.

"I see them. Looks like the water is pretty choppy, they keep disappearing," he said.

"Good. I hope they're all sick to the stomach." Bunny did a couple of circuits. "That's enough circling, they should realize we're up here now. I'm going to set up behind them." She peeled away and cut her throttle, setting the Vapor up about a mile back and 15,000 feet over the sea. She couldn't match their 40-knot speed over the water without going into hover mode, but kept station at about 100 knots by weaving back and forth behind them. She was burning fuel like there was no tomorrow, but endurance wasn't a problem this close to the *Andromeda*.

The *Andromeda* had completed its screening maneuver now and was sailing parallel to the *Orion*, about 500 yards off its port side, enabling it to bring its anti-piracy water and sonic cannons to bear on the threat if needed. But the way Bunny looked at it, if the pirates got that close, she hadn't earned her paycheck. Her eyes flicked constantly from instruments to visor indicators, to the tactical display and back again as she kept her machine in level flight on the edge of a stall, right on the cigarette boats' tails. They were about two miles out from the *Andromeda* now, and...

Ginger put his hand to his ear and keyed his earpiece. "*Andromeda*, Vapor, the pursuers are splitting. Two are heading to your port, two to your starboard. The bridge seeing this, Lawrence?"

"Confirm that, sir, the bridge has them on radar," his comms second officer said.

"Alright, Vapor out." Ginger turned to Bunny. "It's a chain-trap. Damn."

"Chain-trap?"

"They're going to try to take out the *Andromeda* first. All four boats get in front of it, outside the range of water or sonic cannons, and drop magnetic buoys with long trailing chains that stick to the hulls while the chains foul our screws. Cripple *Andromeda*, and then they'll drop behind and try to cripple *Orion*."

"Leaving your security crew on the *Orion* to fend for themselves." Bunny whistled. "You know, it's almost like these guys know what they're doing."

"You think?" Ginger said, dryly. "We have to declare every weapon or anti-piracy system we mount on our ships; they can look it all up in the insurance register online. I've got to get onto the Captain."

He switched channels and got Pedersen up to speed on this thinking. Moments later, Pedersen's voice came over the radio.

"We can't let those cigarette boats get in front of us. They do, *Andromeda* is out of the fight and *Orion* is easy prey. O'Hare, I need you to put some warning shots across their noses, let them know we have armed air support."

"Copy that, *Andromeda*, going in hot. Warning shots only." She keyed her internal comms channel. "Vapor, arm forward guns, flares and chaff."

Nacelle ports open, decoy systems armed and nominal, guns armed and targeting system nominal.

"I thought you said you need to stay out of hand-held missile range," Ginger reminded her.

"I did."

"So how are you going to put a warning shot across their bows from 15,000 feet?"

"I'm not," Bunny said, orienting the Vapor on the ships below and putting its nose down as she pushed her throttle forward. "Let's see if we can spook them into showing us what they've got. You keep the camera zoomed on them, see what you can see."

"*Such* a bad idea."

She watched her altitude, keeping her wings level as the altimeter counted down, bringing her into Crossbow missile range. *Decoys up and ready to fire.* Her hand tightened on the stick, her thumb hovering over the infrared decoy flares release. If they launched on her she'd have less than a second to respond and only a fifty-fifty chance she'd bank the right way…

15,000 … 14,500 … 14,000 … 13,500 … 13,000 …

"OK, that's far enough," she said through gritted teeth, pulling back on her stick and zooming back out of missile range. "Either they didn't take the bait, or they're aren't packing missiles."

"I just saw them looking up at the sky, no sign they were getting ready to launch anything," Ginger said, with as much hope as conviction.

"Alright, let's do this." Bunny flipped a virtual screen to show her weapons system and checked the status of the two forward cannons. *Armed, 4,200 rounds per gun loaded.* At the same time, she pushed her throttle forward, accelerating to put herself ahead of the two pairs of cigarette boats, one of which was slightly ahead of the other because it had plowed straight ahead, where the other one had swung around behind the two ships and was accelerating now to overtake them from the other side.

"We'll take the nearside pair first," Bunny said.

"I should be down in my nice cozy radio room," Ginger muttered, almost to himself. "I didn't realize this was going to get so serious so quickly."

Bunny had no reply to that. She was busy with her flight controls. At 2,000 feet she leveled out, putting the Vapor into a nose-down attitude so that she could keep flying straight and level but spray the sea ahead of them with 20mm shells when the time came. Every tenth shell was a tracer round, so there was no chance the pirates could miss the fact they were being fired on.

But Bunny couldn't actually *see* the damn boats, even with her low-light optics. They were too small, too dark. She had them on radar, she was closing fast. *Where the hell…*

"There, two o'clock!" Ginger yelled.

Bunny saw them, kicked in some port rudder, yawed her nose so that her targeting reticle was about a hundred yards ahead of the two speeding boats, and with a tap of her thumb triggered the cannons for two seconds. Marked by the tracer rounds, she saw her fire smack the water just ahead of the fast boats, exploding as they hit the surface, sending gouts of spray into the air right in their path.

There was a sound like a pair of jeans ripping across the seam and the Vapor shook violently.

Bunny was ready for it, but Ginger grabbed the seat of his observer's chair. "*Crivvens…*"

The militia boats scattered like surfers in front of a Great White shark. As she pulled up and away to avoid any return fire, Bunny tried to imagine the contact from the point of view of someone in one of the boats. *The roar of a jet engine in the distance, aircraft dropping on you like a hawk, suddenly tracer coming at you and the water exploding in front of you…*

"They're breaking off," Ginger said, looking at the radar screen. "Slowing down maybe?"

"I'm betting they're on the radio to their buddies," Bunny said. She was swinging around in front of the *Andromeda* to approach the other two boats on the far side of the *Orion*. The radar showed they were almost level with it now, hammering across the water, trying to get ahead of the two big merchant ships so they could drop their 'chain-traps'.

Bunny didn't have time to finesse her run. She came around ahead of them, chopped her throttle and deployed her speed brakes so that she was hovering about a mile in front, right in their path. The maneuver caused the machine to jerk-stop, throwing them against their straps and then back against their seats, knocking the wind from their lungs.

Laying her targeting reticle on the water ahead of the other pair of boats, Bunny repeated her warning volley, tapping her right rudder gently so that the nose of the Vapor swayed, spraying the cannon rounds across the water, the Vapor bucking and shaking as the tracer sped downrange.

The effect was the same. One boat heeled over to the right, the other to the left.

But this time, they kept coming.

A sparkle of lights erupted from the boats plowing through the water toward them.

"They're *shooting*," Ginger pointed out.

Bunny pulled back her stick, sliding the Vapor backward through the air ahead of the pirates. "Well, that's just stupid. What are they going to hit from down there?"

Ginger was watching the tactical screen. "I think they just want to drive you off. The other boats have joined together and they're coming on again too. *Andromeda* and *Orion* are turning." Ginger keyed his radio transceiver. "*Andromeda*, Vapor. Our warning shots appear to have made no impression. The contacts have returned fire with small arms and are still moving to place themselves in your path. Orders, *Andromeda*?"

Pedersen's voice was pitched low and even. Apparently, it took a lot to get him excited. "We have tried hailing the contacts, but they don't respond. We have also radioed for help from any naval vessel in the area but there are none in range. We are bearing off to port, Vapor, but it may not be enough."

"You have about two minutes before they cross your bow, Captain," Bunny warned him. *Come on, man, make the call.*

Pedersen spoke as though his words were being recorded. Which, since merchant ships, like aircraft, carried a black box recorder, they were. "Vapor, the contacts have ignored your warning and shots have been fired at your aircraft – you are authorized to defend yourself and our vessels."

Alright then. Bunny heeled her machine into a tight banking turn, gathering speed away from the cigarette boats as she transitioned from a near hover to a fast-cruising speed. If the pirates were watching, they might assume she was bugging out and giving up the fight.

"Now I'm wishing someone was in the back there with that Gatling," Ginger remarked. "We could stand off and shoot back from outside the range of their rifles."

"You volunteering for next time, Ginger?"

"Hell nae. Just prattling out loud, to avoid peeing in me diaper."

Bunny firewalled her throttle and hauled the Vapor around in a tight banking turn. At 400 knots she wasn't exactly going to break the sound barrier, but it gave her the speed she needed to put guns on target and pull away before the boats below could react.

Ginger moaned at the G-force of the maneuver.

The four boats were forming up again, line abreast as they sped into the path of the *Andromeda*. It made the job of hitting just one of them no easy task, but Bunny had no appetite for a massacre. She kicked in some right rudder, skidding the Vapor a little to starboard so that she approached the line of speed boats diagonally, and lined her gun reticle up on the nearest. She could see men in the back of the boats getting ready to deploy their buoys ... looking up ... and then scrambling for their guns as she dropped lower.

One mile, *800 yards, 600* ... flashes from the boat below as the militia crew began desperately firing its automatic weapons at her ... then at 500 yards she tapped the gun trigger with her thumb, that chilling *brrrrrrrrrrt* sound hitting her ears through her helmet, fingers of fire reaching for the water below, the Vapor shaking as she pulled it into a high-g climbing turn, watching her altitude, watching her speed, making sure she was orienting herself to the ground and not the sky...

Ginger was craning his head to look behind him. "*Splash one militia boat,*" he yelled. "I think you smashed it in two."

"Let's haul off and see what happens," Bunny said, pulling them up to 10,000 feet. They should be out of range of the machine gun fire from the militia boats, but she needed to be sure. "Vapor, systems check. Report damage and fuel state."

All systems nominal. Fuel eighty-two percent.

On the tactical screen, the radar plot she was pulling both from her own aircraft and the *Andromeda* told the story. The three remaining cigarette boats scattered. After a couple of minutes, one of them detached from the others and seemed to be circling, probably around the wreckage of their destroyed buddy, fishing survivors from the water.

Andromeda and *Orion* were slowly swinging north, behind them now. The distance between the convoy and the cigarette boats slowly increased. After about ten minutes, the three remaining cigarette boats started moving off again, slower this time, back in the direction of the Riau Islands.

"*Andromeda*, Vapor: one boat disabled, the remaining three appear to be headed back to port. We'll shadow them at visual range to make sure they don't double back."

"Thanks, Vapor, we're seeing the same picture, nice work," Ginger's number two replied. "That could have gotten ugly. Captain sends his regards and says to tell you we're resuming our original course."

"Copy that, *Andromeda*, we'll see you shortly. Vapor out."

Bunny rolled her head, easing the tension in her neck. Why had the militia boats kept coming? They should have turned back after her warning salvos. She could have sent them *all* to the bottom, forty men. For what? Would they have gotten a share of the cargo, or just a lousy paycheck? But she already knew the answer. If you had nothing to live for, even a lousy paycheck could be worth dying for.

As she swung the Vapor around to start trailing the cigarette boats, she noticed Ginger had gone very quiet.

"You alright there, Angus?"

"Grand. Just a wee bit puggled."

"Puggled?"

"Something my old mum says. Like a combination of drunk, knackered and confused. Your joyrides always like this one?" Ginger asked.

"Couldn't say," Bunny admitted. "Yours is the first sightseeing trip I've ever given with guns hot. How do you rate the service, sir?"

"Outstanding," Ginger told her. "But I think I threw up in my helmet a little bit."

"You just sit back and relax," Bunny told him. "I'll take it from here."

Celebes Sea, 720 miles E-SE of Pagasa Island, January 8

"Thank you for leading the way, *Alvarez*, we'll take it from here."

"Received, *Congress*. *Congress*, can we give you a bit of Filipino wisdom to take with you?"

Captain of the *USS Congress*, Commander Daniel Okafor, smiled broadly. "We'll take all the wisdom we can get, *Alvarez*." The US guided-missile frigate *Congress* had been led through the tight channels in the Celebes Sea between Philippine islands and atolls by the *Alvarez* for the best part of the last day and night, a very welcome service considering it was one of the most treacherous backwaters on the planet.

Not just because it was a favorite playground for terrorist groups and pirates. Okafor was not worried about small swarming boats posing a risk to his brand spanking new ship – its twin High Energy Liquid Laser Area Defense System, HELLADS, was competent to take care of those. Okafor was more worried about the Celebes Sea's strong currents, noisy volcanic activity, deep trenches and near-surface seamounts, all of which could be used to hide an attack submarine from his sonar. The *General Mariano Alvarez* was a surplus littoral combat ship sold to the Philippines by the US, and as such had a decent, if very much older, acoustic detection suite. With *Alvarez* sailing ahead of *Congress* and using its crew's local knowledge to scan likely hiding places on the sea floor, *Congress* could focus on what was directly beneath it, and what might be trailing behind as they made their painstakingly slow passage through the waters of the Celebes Sea between the Philippines and Malaysia.

Okafor had had his crew on high alert since leaving the Pacific and entering Philippine waters, because their entry into the Celebes Sea had come a day after the Pentagon had moved the timetable for *Fencepost* up 24 hours and their escortees had sailed without them. Any half-competent military intelligence service would have been tracking the White Star ships and also quickly developed a list of the likely candidates for an escort, and found the *Congress* to be at the top of their list. Navy PR had already flagged it leaving Guam to conduct a 'freedom of navigation' transit of the South China Sea. And in fact, that had been what Okafor and his crew thought was their mission until they were inducted into *Fencepost*.

But once the orders for their part in *Fencepost* came through, he had been glad he already had his officers walking on the balls of their feet at the thought of potentially running the

Chinese gauntlet in the South China Sea, because he was absolutely certain that at some point in the next 12 hours, the *Congress* was going to be tested.

"And what little pearl would you like to share, *Alvarez*?" he continued.

"An old Pinoy saying, *Congress*," the Captain of the *Alvarez* said. "*Whatever you are planning, think seven times before you act.*"

Okafor laughed. "Only seven? I can promise we'll do that, *Alvarez*." The combat AI at the heart of the *USS Congress*'s command, control and intelligence systems could sift through a teraflop of data a second, weighing a million scenarios and their possible outcomes before presenting the best of these to its human operators. "*Congress* out."

Okafor watched carefully as the *Alvarez* peeled away to the north, headed back to Subic Bay. They were on their own again.

He was ready. The son of Nigerian immigrants, Okafor felt like he'd been preparing his whole life for exactly this moment. He'd learned leadership as the oldest of four boys in his family, his father dead at forty in a Nigerian gang gunfight in Chicago. His father's life insurance had paid for Daniel's degree, at his mother's insistence, but his application to officer training school at Newport had nearly been rejected because of his father's criminal record. The recruiter told him straight to his face he had only gotten through because of the Navy's 'diversity quota'. Since that day, he had been proving to Navy, and to himself, that he was more than just a quota hire.

Now, after getting to Exec Officer aboard an *Arleigh Burke* destroyer, he had been given one of the most prestigious commands in the whole Navy. The *USS Congress*, product of the fast-tracked US FFG(X) program, fresh out of sea trials and ready for anything America's opponents could throw at it – on, under or above the waves.

Still, he felt the need for a tour of the ship to reassure himself. Okafor's 'walkarounds' were legendary. There were plenty of warship Captains who never ventured down to the main engine room, let alone the auxiliary machine rooms, the central control station, number three generator room or after steering. But Okafor did. Some of his men loved him for it, others said it gave them the creeps, their CO suddenly climbing through a hatch behind them with a 'how you men doing?' Not all of his officers loved it either; said it showed a lack of trust. He didn't care. It served two functions – he got to know his crew and they got to know him. If they weren't happy, he could see it. Do something about it. As importantly, it taught him what kind of condition his ship was in. Like the time he walked into one of the comms rooms and saw a series of 'sticky notes' and some tape on the racks of equipment.

He'd talked briefly with one of the operators, then walked casually over to the racks, flicking at one of the notes. "What's this?"

"Voyage management system, sir," the operator replied. "Broke, only works intermittent, but we're out of parts. Have to wait until we get back to Guam so I can follow up."

"How can we be out of parts already? Can't you take them from the spare VMS in my cabin?"

"Already did that, sir. Been cannibalizing yours for like half a year now."

"Then order new."

"Order put in months ago, sir. Follow it up every couple weeks. Manufacturer issues, they tell us, which is typical on a new build." The operator shrugged. "So, I got one note to warn people it don't work, and another to remind me to follow up."

There was a piece of tape over a large button. "And this?"

"Server boot key for the Aegis radio comm system. Permission to speak freely, sir?"

"Go ahead, sailor."

"It's a piece of shit, sir. I seen it on more than one ship I served on. You tap the RCS boot key even a little bit hard, the thing snaps at the base. Some guys hold it on with gum, but you got to reboot in a hurry, like there's missiles flying, and the system goes down? You don't want to be scrabbling around on the deck looking for it because your gum dried out, am I right?"

"You are very right, Petty Officer Daly. And you can't replace that either?"

"You can, sir, but it will break again in a week. So, you might as well keep the old one." He reached behind him on a shelf and lifted something off it. "And a roll of tape."

Okafor had ordered his quartermaster to conduct a 'fatigued equipment audit' and when they got to port, he let Fleet know he wasn't going to be putting to sea again before critical equipment deficiencies had been remedied. Not everything was, of course, but he left Guam in better shape than he'd arrived.

He turned to his XO, a pugnacious five foot nothing Lieutenant by the name of Diavolo, but known to his men by the moniker 'Knuckles'. Like many short men, he also had a short fuse and, according to the stories, a right hook to match it. "Deck is yours, XO, I'm going for a walk around."

"Aye aye, Captain. XO has the deck," Diavolo repeated for the benefit of the watch officers.

As he stepped through into the gangway behind the bridge, a Nigerian saying came to Okafor. One his father had drilled into him and his brothers from a young age. "A man being short does not make him a boy – a boy being tall does not make him a man." His father had used it to illustrate several things. Firstly, don't judge a book by its cover. And secondly, don't think too highly of yourself. Possessing a gun doesn't make you gangsta. Okafor could imagine his father looking down on him now, smirking. *Look at you there, your shiny gold stripes on the nice white uniform someone else pressed for you. Really think you're something, don't you? Well, I thought I was something too, and it only took a quarter ounce of lead to prove I was nothing. Think about that as you walk around your big shiny ship, boy.*

He hadn't been able to brief his officers or crew fully about the upcoming mission for reasons of operational security. But they weren't fools. They'd seen on the media that Chinese bombers had fired cruise missiles at a Philippine island in the

South China Sea, and they were sailing at flank speed right into the eye of a storm.

Okafor slid down a stairwell, landing heavily at the bottom because he was thinking, not looking. He had other things to worry about than the dangers of hubris. Like, whether his 'big shiny ship' and its crew were prepared to survive a kinetic engagement with China's South Sea forces.

Brunei Navy Base, Muara Container Terminal, January 8

It had seemed like easy money. That's why Abdul Ibrahim had agreed to take the contract on the White Star convoy. A single civilian escort ship, an autonomous trailing utility ship packed with saleable cargo. All they had to do was cripple the escort, the *Andromeda*, and its autonomous trailing ship would be easy prey. Sure, it probably had a security team aboard, but he'd had a plan for them. With Lim's orders to just sink the *Orion*, the matter of the security crew became irrelevant.

Sure, his crew might come out of an engagement with a sophisticated target like this with a couple of injuries, but he had figured that into the fee he'd asked. Not to mention he'd end up with some nice new ordnance and equipment. It had seemed sweet.

Now, he was not so sure. He was sitting with his feet up on a desk in the rusted tin shed that was his operational base, in a corner of the naval base at Muara, on the radio to Riau Islands.

"Slow down, Ajij! Take it from the top…"

"From the top? I'll give you from the top," the Riau Islands gang boss told him. "From the top, you owe me a bloody boat and two men, including my best damn hacker, you mother."

"I owe you nothing, I gave you a friendly tip is all."

"Friendly tip? Easy prey, you said. Two unescorted freighters, you said. I asked why didn't you hit it yourself if it was so easy, what did you say?"

"I said by the time it gets to my hunting grounds, it could have picked up a navy escort. You ran into an escort?"

"Escort? It don't need no escort. It's got a bloody helicopter gunship."

"Helicopter what?"

"Black like night, jet-powered freaking helicopter gunship! You heard me."

Ibrahim had heard him. He knew the *Andromeda* carried a helicopter. Anyone could see that just by looking in the shipping register. But his Chinese client had told him the helicopter would be 'taken care of'. And Lim had neglected to mention it was *armed*.

The Riau Islands boss was still complaining. "…could have cut every one of my boats to pieces if my guys wasn't able to slip away."

Ibrahim sighed. "Look, Ajij, don't get so worked up. Because I'm a nice guy and we have history, I'll cover your boat. But you knew the risks, you pay off the families of those men yourself."

They argued some more but it was a fair offer and the Riau Islands boss took it, like Ibrahim knew he would. As he laid the radio handset down on his desk, his crew boss Kamito sat down opposite.

"I don't know about this contract, boss," Kamito said. "The client didn't say anything about any armed chopper."

The man was right. But this type of thing was exactly why he'd tipped off Ajij about the convoy. He knew the man well and he knew he'd screw up. He had no subtlety, and he didn't have the resources, or the connections, needed for a job like this. But the failed attack by Ajij had forced the White Star convoy to show its hand early. Helicopter *gunship*, eh?

"Map," Ibrahim said, clicking his fingers.

When Kamito laid it in front of him he quickly found the spot where Ajij said he'd intercepted the convoy. "OK, so those amateurs hit it here, northeast of the Riau Islands. And as we figured, they're sailing the lower eastern route, up the

Brunei coast, probably to avoid the Vietnamese gangs, right?"

"That's our guess. Takes them to the top of Sabah, they turn north for Manila, if the client's information is right."

"That's the question, isn't it," Ibrahim said bitterly. "Chinese businessman comes out of nowhere, asks us to sink a convoy, gives us five fast boats and two tons of small arms and ammunition? None of which, I'm betting, can be traced back to China. We look up the data on those ships; one is a floating relief base, the other just happens to be carrying a helicopter gunship. And a few hours ago, the Philippines and China go to war in the South China Sea. That's a lot of coincidences right there, Kamito."

"I know. It all stinks. But it's a truckload of money."

Ibrahim studied the map again. "Yeah, Kamito, it is. And that convoy will be sailing into *our* waters tomorrow." He had a hollow tooth at the back of his mouth, and he sucked on it thoughtfully. "We stick to the plan. Hit them in broad daylight, take away any advantage they have from night vision equipment." He jabbed his finger on a spot on the map, 137 miles west of their base in Brunei. "Right ... here."

"That's a long way out," Kamito observed. "Further than we've done before."

"Weather forecast the next two days is light winds and calm seas. And we didn't have American special operations boats before," Ibrahim pointed out.

"You think the guns on those boats can take down that chopper?" Kamito asked.

"No. But for this to work, we need something that will," Ibrahim told him, standing up. "Get me that a-hole, Lim."

Kamito pulled a burner phone out of a cabinet, turned it on and then pulled a piece of paper from his pocket, punching in a number. After listening to it ring, he handed it to Ibrahim. "Here you go."

Lim sounded like the call had woken him up. *Good.*

"Mr. Ibrahim. An unexpected pleasure. I am guessing by the hour that there has been some sort of development?" Lim asked.

"Yeah, there has been some sort of development," Ibrahim told him. "A freaking helicopter gunship kind of development." Ibrahim filled Lim in on the Riau Islands fiasco.

"And how did this Indonesian crew find out about the convoy?" Lim asked.

"What do you care how I do it, as long as the job gets done?" Ibrahim replied. "Now, a helicopter of any kind makes my job a lot harder. You told me you'd take care of it. And you didn't tell me it was *armed*."

"It should have been dealt with. It wasn't," Lim said, sounding genuinely chagrined. "I assume you are calling because you have a plan for dealing with it yourself."

"Yes, I have, but it's going to cost you," Ibrahim warned.

"I expected as much," Lim sighed. "What do you need?"

A surplus of pirates

Pagasa Island, Spratly Islands Archipelago, 0530, January 9

Baotian Liu figured it was a miracle. Nothing less. He'd said a prayer of thanks to his ancestors in heaven, because who else could have delivered him and his men to this spot on the island, surrounded on three sides by attacking Filipino soldiers, to tumble into a hole in the hillside that didn't exist on any map.

Not on any map of Pagasa, anyway.

They'd seen Filipino troops pass the entrance to the bunker again, maybe a hundred yards away, but in the grey morning light, the Filipinos had not seen the green drop sheet hidden by vegetation at the mouth of the bunker, and they'd moved on. Since then, maybe three hours ago, there had been no more patrols out combing the hillside that he could see.

It didn't mean the Filipinos had given up. But it seemed for now, they were safe. He'd tied the two kids up with their own rope and put them in a rear room of the bunker. He'd hated doing it, but he couldn't risk that they would escape and give away the Chinese commandos' location.

Liu had two men stay at the firing slits, keeping an eye on the ground out front. He had two checking food, water and ammunition stocks. The rest he sent to see whether the tunnel to the surface from the back of the bunker could be cleared of debris and dirt.

Zhang reported back. "Those kids look like they were preparing for the zombie apocalypse, Lieutenant," he said. He was a squat, lean son of a boxer who had thought about going the same way as his father for a while and had the mashed nose to prove it. "We got enough canned food to hold out here for months. Mostly spaghetti meatballs and canned fruit, but what do you expect from kids?"

"Ammunition?"

"Not so great. We got fifteen 20-round mags for the carbines; half a dozen frags. Filipino troops find us in here, I figure we can hold 'em maybe 30 minutes."

Liu shook his head. "Be more positive, man. We've got more than a few 9mm rounds. We've got a secure base of operations, and we've got a *radio*." He peered into the darkness. "Ruan!"

The radio operator ran over and slid to a halt beside Liu. "Lieutenant?"

"Can you get a signal out?"

"Well, we're inside a concrete bunker, sir. It would be better to go topside, like the top of the hill."

Liu counted to three. "I know that, Corporal. But the island is crawling with Filipino troops. That's why I'm asking if you can get a signal out to the patrol boat offshore *without* leaving the bunker."

Ruan nodded. "Yes, sir. I stripped the wire to the old Japanese antenna that runs up to the surface from the radio room. It's copper, good as new. The antenna up top has probably fallen over, but signal strength is just good enough to get an L band satellite lock." He looked at Liu earnestly through his wire-rimmed glasses. "Topside *would* be better."

"We'll play it safe for now, Ruan. Use that Japanese antenna to send a burst text to ops command from inside the bunker. Text reads, uh, 'Renewing attack with intent to suppress enemy troops and allow reinforcement. Request naval indirect fire support, earliest opportunity'."

The radio operator had taken out a notepad and was writing in it with his tongue sticking out the side of his mouth. He looked up. "Is that it?"

"For now. When you get confirmation, we can move out of here, get an updated fix on the Filipino positions…"

"Sir. And then…"

"And then we are going to rain hellfire down on them again, Corporal."

White Star *Andromeda*, off Kuala Belait, Brunei, 400 miles south of Pagasa Island, January 9

Bunny took the stairwell flying, grabbing the handrails and sliding without her feet touching a single step on the way down. She hit the bottom, hard, her ankles protesting as she pivoted into the gangway, but she turned the pain into added volume as she bellowed at a group of sailors shuffling down the gangway, "Make way!"

They put their backs to the wall and drew in their guts as she pushed past them, ignoring their cat calls. She reached the forward deck from her quarters in record time and ran up steel stairs to the flight deck to find Ginger already there, ruddy-faced and pacing. But his frown turned to a wide-eyed stare as he realized Bunny O'Hare was wearing little more than briefs and a singlet.

"Wow, that's a *lot* of tattoos…"

"Yeah, and that's just the ones you can see," Bunny told him, punching open the cockpit access door. "It's been a big life. Now, why did you disturb my beauty sleep?" She jumped into the cockpit, settling in her seat as she pulled on her helmet and got the Vapor AI to bring the machine's systems to life. "It better be important."

"I was monitoring radio traffic," he told her. "As we move up the coast, I can triangulate the stronger signals, tie them to known actors, like Malaysian Coast Guard, Brunei Navy…"

"You speak Malaysian?"

"No, just the strength of the signals, quantity, that kind of thing," he admitted. "Around four hours ago radio traffic from the Muara Container Terminal in Brunei really spiked, which made no sense because there were no big ships pulling into port and it was the middle of the night there so I…"

Bunny had pulled up her VR displays and was busy checking

Vapor's startup routine was flowing as it should. The cameras on the fuselage showed her the ship's crew busy pulling out chocks and removing tie-downs. "Short version, Ginger."

"I got onto White Star Risk Group, gave them the GPS coordinates for the radio signal. It's Batu Bay militia, some seriously heavy-duty pirates."

"Every damn port along this coast seems to hold a militia base. You woke me because…"

"I couldn't understand what they were saying but then I very clearly heard someone say '*Andromeda*'."

"So you told the Captain?"

"Pedersen said there was nothing on radar and I was probably imagining it," he said. "He said I should get some sleep. But he told Mr. Bose to double the watch."

"Mixed messages, then," Bunny said, looking at her watch. It was 0530. Sun up in about ten minutes. "So instead of going to bed, you woke me and told me we are about to come under attack."

He looked sheepish. "I think we are, but I couldn't convince the Captain. The radio traffic, ship's name … their location…"

Bunny didn't need to get Captain Pedersen's permission to get the Vapor airborne, but she didn't want to get on his bad side. "Can you tell Pedersen I'm taking the Vapor up to check out your intel, and 'intel', by the way, is my polite way of saying 'wild-arse guess'." Bunny touched the stud on the cockpit door to close it. "Send me the coordinates for this base. I'll call you when I'm at cruising altitude."

Ginger started moving for the door. "Uh, one other detail," he said.

Bunny stopped the door closing. "What?"

"Muara Container Terminal? It's also a Brunei navy base."

"Of course it is. Stand clear."

The last thing she saw before the door hissed shut and her virtual cockpit filled her senses was the gap between Ginger's drooping jeans and his shirt as he waddled quickly away. With the crack in his ass sticking out over the top.

133

"There are worse things than a violent death in war," Bunny muttered. "I did *not* need to see that."

Thirty minutes later she had the Vapor skimming across the waves, the lights from the container terminal on the horizon competing with the sky brightening behind it. The halogen dock lights were still winning that little fight.

"Coming up on Muara now," Bunny said. She pulled back on her stick and thumbed the collective control, putting the Vapor into a hover about two hundred feet over the sea. To her left, a bridge connected the mainland to what looked like an oil refinery and storage center. Ahead of her, a half dozen container ships were scattered across the sea, at anchor and waiting their turn to either load or unload. She saw two large cranes, at least five stories high, framing the container park. Between them, ships tied to wharves, and thousands of containers, stacked high. "Looks like a big facility, Ginger, can you give me a steer as to where this pirate base is supposed to be?"

"*Militia.* You see the container park?"

"Got it."

"Look along the port to the right, you see two small piers, and then some navy ships? There's usually two or three small corvettes anchored there, according to the satellite images."

She had the camera in forward-looking infrared vision mode which gave everything a ghostly green glow. Bunny turned the nose of the Vapor and used its pan and zoom camera to look at the port in more detail. "Alright, got it. Two corvettes, one with a helo on the deck."

"Right, that's it."

"The *navy* base is a militia base?!"

"Officially, no. But there's a pier to the right and a small harbor with some dry docks and boat sheds. Our intel says there is a militia crew operating out of one of those sheds and their boats have been seen putting into the water there or tied up by that pier."

"They couldn't be doing that without the navy turning a blind eye, though, right?"

"Navies have always had 'understandings' with pirates, back to the age of sail," Ginger said. "Why should it be any different now?"

Bunny enhanced the image and zeroed in on the small pier to the right of the two navy corvettes. It was too dark to see anything other than bright lights, dark buildings and, judging by the flickering of light and shadow, maybe some movement of vehicles or people. There was a lot of clutter. She was going to see nothing if she stayed high. She checked for air traffic. All clear.

"I'm going to have to make a low visual pass," she decided. "This navy base has air defenses?"

"Nothing on file. Their corvettes will have radar ... I guess they have guns."

"You guess..." She checked her radar warning receiver. It wasn't showing anything more powerful than standard merchant ship or port traffic control radar systems. "Looks quiet. Taking her in low and fast."

Spinning the Vapor on its vertical axis, Bunny turned it away from the port and built up speed and altitude. When she got to two thousand feet and 400 knots, she turned the Vapor around again, set her cameras to record the view ahead and beneath her, and made a beeline for the naval base.

She decided to give Ginger a running commentary. "Alright, I got what looks like three hulls tied to the small pier, maybe inshore patrol boats, deck guns, no sign of missile systems. Harbor behind, getting a good line into it now, two more patrol boats, I'm calling them a couple hundred tons displacement, not more. Alright, yeah ... *hello there.*" She'd spotted something as the Vapor passed over the harbor and she banked hard right, the port disappearing beneath her, then beach, and then sea again. "I saw some activity, going back for another pass."

Abdul Ibrahim heard shouting before he heard the roar of a jet engine, low overhead. *A jet engine?*

He walked quickly to the door of the boat shed. Kamito was there with a few of their men, and they were all staring up at the lightening sky.

"What was *that?*" Ibrahim asked.

"Dunno," Kamito told him. "Plane landing at the airport? Was real low though."

Brunei International was about 12 miles to the west, but its runways ran NE–SW. Planes approached from over the sea or from the mainland side. They didn't blow over Muara Container Terminal just a couple of hundred feet off the ground.

"How big was it?" he asked, a suspicion forming.

"Small. Like a private jet or something." Like Ibrahim, Kamito had been brought up a fisherman, west of Brunei in a small port town called Sipitang. People often mistook them for brothers as they were both slight of build, burned brown by sun and salt water, with dark hair and unsmiling features. The main thing setting them apart was Kamito's bushy mustache, which he was now tugging on thoughtfully. But being a fisherman, his aircraft recognition pretty much sucked. "I think it's coming back."

Ibrahim looked down to where the slipway from the boatshed led into the water of the harbor. His men had been had at work, putting the American attack boats one by one on the slipway and launching them into the water, ready for the upcoming attack. They were done with two, there were three more fully loaded and ready to go.

Kamito was right. Whatever it was, the aircraft was coming back around. "Quick, cut the lights!"

"Which lights?"

"All of them!" Ibrahim yelled, pushing him toward the side of the boat shed. "Pull the breaker switches!" Without waiting he started running down the ramp, yelling at the men down by the water. "Hold that boat! Close the boatshed doors!" They looked at Ibrahim like he'd lost his mind. He'd only just told them to *launch* the third boat. "Don't just stand there, close the damn doors!"

Bunny maneuvered the Vapor to approach the harbor from the north so that she would be flying along the length of the terminal, positioned to take an oblique look into the buildings lining the naval base where she had seen lights and activity.

As she blasted overhead, she caught a glimpse of faces staring up at her, some lights on the naval docks, and two small boats floating in the middle of the harbor, men on their decks. But that was it before she was over the main container terminal.

Was it just her vision playing tricks, or was it suddenly a *lot* darker back there? She panned the camera to look back behind the Vapor. There, right in the middle of a row of sheds which were all lit up to some degree or other, was one that was completely blacked out. She was *sure* it hadn't been like that before.

"You uncrated that shipment from the client yet?" Ibrahim asked Kamito. They were standing down at the waterline at the bottom of the slipway.

"Just the launcher. The ammo is still boxed."

Damn. He would have loved to have a Crossbow missile to put up this nosy bastard's ass if he was dumb enough to make another pass. Though perhaps it was a good idea not to show the enemy the ace up their sleeve just yet – because he was pretty sure there was only one aircraft it could be, even though he had no idea how it had managed to get onto Ibrahim and his crew so early. Ibrahim watched as the mysterious aircraft pulled away over the container terminal and disappeared into the dark sky. *A jet-powered helicopter gunship, black as night*, that was what

Ajij had said, wasn't it?

He looked at his boats out in the harbor, men on the decks staring up at the skies uselessly. They hadn't got their radios up yet, and they were too far away for him to yell orders. He looked back at the boatshed's sliding iron door. "Get that boat out of the shed and down here to the waterline," he told Kamito.

The man frowned. "You just said to hold it back."

"I know what I said. Now I'm saying get it down *there* and get the auxiliary power on. Fast. I want it powered up if that aircraft comes over again."

"One last pass," Bunny told Ginger over her radio.

"You don't have enough video yet?" he asked nervously. "That whole facility has to be wide awake by now, you buzzing them like that."

"I'm not worried about the workers at the terminal, just the navy corvettes, and I'm still not seeing any tracking radar. If they're awake, they're standing there scratching their nuts waiting for someone to tell them what to do," Bunny guessed. "There's something I want to check. Going lower."

She banked the Vapor left, coming around to point its nose directly at the dark shed at the back of the small harbor, dropping it down to 1,000 feet.

The rollers in the slipway screeched as Ibrahim's men pulled the surplus US Navy Mark V boat to a halt and jumped aboard, powering up the battery system.

The six-barrel, air-cooled, 7.62mm Gatling mini-gun was electrically powered, and they'd mounted it by the stern to allow a near 300-degree arc of fire. Each had been test-fired before it was mounted, and Ibrahim had been pleased with what he saw – the client had delivered on his promises. It could sweep the deck of a merchant ship clean of security in seconds, or just fill its thin-skinned hull with fist-sized holes.

Stepping up into the stern, he pulled the cover off the mini-gun and powered it up. The barrel rotated twice without firing to let him know it was active. Taking his cue from Ibrahim, Kamito stepped up beside him, ripped the lid off a crate of ammunition at the base of the weapon and fed the belt into the breech of the mini-gun the way Ibrahim had shown him, as his boss tilted his head, listening for the sound of a jet engine.

Abdul Ibrahim was not just a fisherman's son. He'd served four years in the Indonesian Navy including two years aboard a *Krait* class patrol boat. He'd learned a few things, one of which was this…

If you are firing a projectile weapon at a fast-moving aerial target, you aim your bullets where it is going to be, not where it is.

As he heard the jet aircraft approaching again, he relied on his ears as much as his eyes. He swung the barrel around toward the source of the noise, bent his knees and tilted the mini-gun barrel skyward.

The building up ahead of the Vapor was still dark. Bunny could see small figures moving around on the dock, but the detail was terrible, so she flipped the camera to light-intensification mode.

Better.

Rushing toward the darkened shed she could now clearly see two boats in the water in front of it, crew out on the decks, and one on a slipway leading up into the shed, two men in the rear with…

Oh, hell.

A deck-mounted gun. Before she could react, a line of tracer fire rose into the sky ahead of her, coming from the rear of the boat on the slip. Like all ground fire it started as a lazy arc, appearing to move slowly, but as she closed on it, it turned into a laser-like beam of continuous light and as she slammed the

Vapor into a tight banking turn, it intersected with her path and the sickening sound of system failure warnings started screaming in her ears.

"You hit it?" Kamito asked, as the mini-gun spun down and Ibrahim lowered the barrel.

"I don't know," Ibrahim admitted. "I think it turned at the last minute."

"Nah, I think you got it, boss."

Ibrahim wasn't so sure. He'd heard an approaching roar, seen a shadow in the sky that was darker than the darkness around it, tilted the barrel of the mini-gun higher and fired into the path of the aircraft, but it seemed to Ibrahim it was already overhead and then past them before his bullets could have reached it.

The sound of its engines was fading now. Whatever it was, maybe they had at least scared it off. For now. He kicked some shell casings aside and turned to Kamito. "Alright, before it comes back again, get all the bloody boats into the water and get everyone aboard. I want us out of here inside thirty minutes."

The calm Irish voice of the Vapor's AI was running through a list of system failures as Bunny vectored herself back toward the *Andromeda*. She still had full control of flight systems, she still had airspeed and altitude, but...

"*Andromeda*, Vapor. Remind me to listen to you next time, Ginger."

"Oh no, what..."

Bunny tried making sense of the warnings in her ears and on virtual screens in front of her eyes. "We took some small-caliber fire. I've got a fuel pump warning, a port fuel line pressure warning..." Using her VR view to look behind the Vapor as looking through the airframe, Bunny could see a thick line of actual vapor trailing behind her. "Yeah, we're losing fuel, port wing tank."

Warning, fuel tank venting. Fuel starvation to port jet turbine engine imminent.

"Thanks for stating the bloody obvious, Vapor. Transfer all fuel to the starboard tank."

Beginning fuel transfer. Shutting down port jet turbine. Initiating trim compensation.

The AI was powering the left rear turbine down to avoid damage and automatically adjusting rudder and elevator trim to allow the Vapor to continue to fly on a single turbine. Thinking fast, Bunny set *Andromeda* as the terminal waypoint in her nav system.

"Vapor, calculate fuel burn rate and optimize flight profile for maximum endurance. Do we have enough fuel to reach home base?" In the Vapor's nav system, the *Andromeda* was defined as 'home base', and if it wasn't able to pull a location from its AIS tracker, the AI projected its location according to its last known position, speed and heading.

No, pilot. Assuming the Andromeda continues with current heading and speed, the Vapor will exhaust fuel reserves five miles from home base.

Damn. Bunny ran some scenarios, checking her calculations with the AI.

Not good. "Vapor, upload the video from this mission to White Star Risk, attention Sylvie Leclerc. Mark it urgent."

Yes, pilot. Uploading video footage to White Star Risk Group.

Bunny opened a channel to the *Andromeda*.

"*Andromeda*, Vapor. Is Pedersen on the bridge?"

"Roger, O'Hare."

"Good. Ginger, you have to get the Captain to turn to meet me and slow speed all he can, I'm sending you my position; bear on that. I'll be coming straight in with empty tanks."

"Uh, he's not going to want to leave the *Orion* alone."

"Then he can bring the *Orion* with him."

"Yeah, right. *Orion* is doing twenty knots, O'Hare, heading *away* from your aircraft. That thing's a juggernaut. It would take twenty minutes and ten miles to make a turn like that. Plus, you're asking him to turn both ships *toward* whoever just fired at you!"

O'Hare had a dozen warning lights flashing in her peripheral vision. She felt like yelling at Ginger at the top of her lungs but counted slowly to three and spoke with false calm. "Ginger, can you patch me through to the bridge?"

"Sure. Wait one."

She waited more than one. She was about to pop a mental cog when the Captain's voice finally came over the radio. "O'Hare, Pedersen. Ginger filled me in. You took damage?"

"Yes, Captain," Bunny said. "Lost a lot of fuel, but I'm still flying and there doesn't appear to be any damage to flight control systems."

"You don't have enough fuel to make it back to the ship?"

"No. But if you adjust course toward me, cut the distance by about ten miles, I can get the Vapor down. It'll be with nothing but fumes in the tank, but…"

"Not happening, O'Hare. You're going to have to either ditch or try to find a friendly airstrip in Indonesia or Brunei where you can put it down. White Star Risk Group can organize a rescue."

"Captain, all I need…"

"I have a timetable to keep, O'Hare. That overrides my need to recover your aircraft."

Bunny clenched her gloved fists. "Captain, your radio operator reported intercepting traffic originating from a known pirate base. I confirmed activity at the base, and my aircraft was shot at and damaged. If there is another pirate attack inbound, without this aircraft you may not even make your damn rendezvous!"

"That radio intercept could have been the Brunei Navy discussing this convoy, which would make perfect sense, and for all we know, it was the Brunei Navy that engaged you, for flying too close to their facility. You'll have to account to our employer for the consequences of that decision, but I will not be ordering my ships to deviate one mile from their current course."

Bunny had broken knuckles before, punching the top or sides of her cockpit in moments of frustration, and had eventually learned. So, she made do with squeezing her gloved fists together so hard she felt like the bones would break. "Understood, Captain. I'll find another solution. Vapor out."

Not understood. Pedersen was up against pirates with their own air support, he had another couple hundred miles of high seas to sail before they met with their naval escort, and he was giving up his most potent defensive system? Maybe he had some 'plan B' Bunny didn't know about. Because his 'plan A' sucked and Bunny wasn't about to let it cost her her life.

She pulled up a theatre-level map and scanned for airfields. "Vapor, can you paint a ring around our Vapor on this map, and dynamically adjust it to show the projected range?"

Yes, pilot. Calculating and projecting.

A shaded circle drew itself around the Vapor, and Bunny scanned the area inside it for possible landing sites. Technically, she could put the Vapor down on any flat cleared area of land bigger than the aircraft itself, but if she did that, she would be at the mercy of whoever found her first. Fine if it was a friendly civilian with an aircraft repair business, not so much if it was a foreign military or police officer. In any case, there were no airports in range, and the only stretch of land currently inside the endurance circle was on the mouth of a river in northern Malaysia called the Baram River, right next to a crocodile farm. She didn't fancy the chances of surviving long if she landed there.

The circle showed the *Andromeda* outside the endurance circle and though she was still flying an intercept course toward it, the pace at which the circle was shrinking was greater than the speed at which she was closing the gap between the Vapor and the *Andromeda*. As the AI had already predicted, the new visual showed that even with its flight profile optimized for fuel efficiency, on current settings the Vapor would run out of fuel and drop into the sea about five miles short of the *Andromeda*.

Five lousy miles. If the Vapor had half-decent aerodynamic lift, she could perhaps have considered trading a little fuel for altitude and then tried to glide the aircraft some of the way back to the *Andromeda*. But with two big turbofan jet engines in its tail and tiltrotor turboshafts on its wings, it would…

Wait.

"Vapor, recalculate endurance assuming both turbofan engines are shut down."

That is a hypothetical scenario and out of compliance with manufacturer protocols.

"Whatever. Do it please."

Calculating. Onscreen.

The endurance circle jumped outward and showed *Andromeda* suddenly *inside* the circle.

Alright! It would take longer without jet power boosting her airspeed, but she could reach the *Andromeda* on good old-fashioned propeller power with fuel to spare. "Shut down rear starboard turbofan engine, Vapor. Adjust flight profile for tiltrotor-powered flight only."

Negative, I cannot comply.

"What do you mean, you cannot comply? Why?"

That flight configuration has not been tested except in a scenario of catastrophic engine damage resulting in failure of both turbofan engines.

"Yeah, so, shut the engine down and implement the emergency power failure scenario." Bunny couldn't see the problem.

Do you wish to land the aircraft on the water?

"What? No."

In the event of dual turbofan engine failure, the programmed response is to transition to vertical flight and rapidly descend to land the aircraft immediately. The aircraft is currently over water. That is the only response I am authorized to execute.

Ok, that was screwy. The predecessor to the Vapor, the V-22 Osprey, was a pure tiltrotor aircraft, it had no jet engines to accelerate it through the sky, just its big tiltrotor propellers.

Bunny was pretty sure that other prototypes of the Vapor she had seen were exactly the same. Sure, this version had two 1,500 lb. jet engines hanging off the tail, so without them firing to push it forward, its center of gravity would be all screwed up and flip the bird nose high, but couldn't the AI compensate for that?

Apparently, the designers had decided it couldn't. And neither could their test pilots.

Well, the alternative was losing the damn plane anyway, so what did she have to lose?

"Vapor, give me full manual on flight controls, avionics and engine systems."

Yes, pilot. You have full manual control. AI moving to backup support only.

Alright then. Bunny pulled back her throttle and played with the collective, putting the Vapor into a hover which effectively killed the thrust from the remaining turbofan engine and set it idling. Her plan was to kill the gas-guzzling jet engine completely, and then carefully adjust the tiltrotors and aircraft trim to give the machine forward airspeed. Play it by ear to see how much airspeed she could get before she started losing lift or stalling due to the extra weight in the aircraft's ass.

But even an idling jet engine used precious fuel. She pulled up the engine management screen and punched the controls to manually shut the engine down completely.

Unexpected engine shutdown, starboard engine. Initiating automatic restart.

"Vapor! Cancel engine restart."

Negative, I cannot comply.

"Oh, bloody hell."

She didn't ask why or try the same process over again. It would have given her the same result. She could see the machine logic at work.

>The aircraft risks crashing without sufficient airspeed.

>The aircraft has one perfectly good turbofan engine it can use to maintain powered flight.

>The pilot has cut turbofan engine power.
>The pilot is an idiot.
>Restart turbofan engine.

And so the logic loop would function, through any attempt by her to cut the power to the remaining rear turbofan engine.

There was only one way around it. She had to kill the AI before she could kill the remaining jet engine.

Bunny hadn't been joking when she told Sylvie Leclerc that she didn't trust AIs. Sure, they were good at pre-programmed situations, and they could be programmed for millions of potential scenarios. The best AIs could also learn from every single interaction, flight or combat engagement, getting continuously smarter and smarter. They could even craft poetry, paint original works of art and write action novels or movie screenplays.

But they sucked at wild-ass improvisation.

So, one of the first things Bunny did when getting certified on a new aircraft type was to dive into the control system computer code. Especially the maintenance and diagnostic routines. Looking for ways to shut down the unshutdownable or execute the 'never to be executed'. And for this particular aircraft, she'd studied how much of the Vapor AI she could cripple before the aircraft fell out of the sky.

She pulled up a new virtual screen display for the Enhanced DiagNostic Aid system – EDNA – and executed the exploit she'd created that gave her access to the system. EDNA had been designed to allow maintenance crews to isolate and test every single avionics sub-system on the Vapor. And the best way to test a system was to shut down all other non-dependent systems around it, so you could do your testing without 'confounders'. EDNA had *not* been designed to be operated by a pilot while the aircraft was airborne, because frankly, that would be an *insane* thing to allow a pilot to do.

"Hello EDNA," Bunny said with a grin, finding the software module she was looking for. "And goodbye Vapor."

As she hit a key to execute the kill, her hand was resting on her chair arm, gripping the sidestick, thumb hovering over the collective control that adjusted the tilt of the rotors on the Vapor's wingtips. The balls of her feet were hovering on the pedals at the base of the chair, and her left hand was ready to drop down to the throttle at the first sign the Vapor was going to fall out of the sky.

With that, she shut down the remaining turbofan engine.

"Oh, *shit*," she said, as the Vapor began to slip sideways, the million inputs a second from the AI flight assistant now absent, and the aircraft reacting only to the inputs from Bunny's fly-by-wire flight controllers. She corrected the sideslip, and the machine began nosing up, exactly as she'd feared it would, increasing the angle of attack on the wings to a point where the aircraft began sliding *backward* through the air. The automated stall warning alarm began sounding. "Down, boy!" she shouted out loud, shoving her sidestick forward, rolling the elevator trim wheel under her thumb and angling the tiltrotors ever so slightly to give herself a little more forward propulsion, and a little less vertical lift.

The tail came up, the Vapor stopped skidding and it started crabbing forward through the air at a blistering … *twenty knots*. Alright, not so blistering. But it *was* forward propulsion, the bite of air flowing over the wings now making up for the lift she'd lost from the angled tiltrotor, and she would take what she could get. She pulled up a nav screen and checked the position, speed and bearing of the *Andromeda*. It was moving at twenty-five knots. She needed at least double that if she was going to reel it in before she ran out of fuel. When she'd killed the Vapor AI she'd also lost its computational power, and her nav display no longer showed the all-important endurance ring around the Vapor; but she looked at her remaining fuel, her airspeed, her current fuel burn rate and did the math.

If she could tickle the Vapor up to 100 knots, she'd close the distance between her and the *Andromeda* inside an hour.

She adjusted the rotor tilt again … twenty-two knots … twenty-five …. side slipping again … rudder trim … less flap

… twenty-eight …

"O'Hare, this is Leclerc, what is the situation with your Vapor?" the radio said, of course breaking in at a perfectly inconvenient moment. Bunny could hear the thump of muted dance music in the background. She was imagining Leclerc standing outside a nightclub in Singapore somewhere, speaking on her cell phone, a million worlds away from her own reality.

"Just great, Mademoiselle," O'Hare said through gritted teeth. "Something you need?" Bunny had the Vapor up to nearly fifty knots now, but was getting stall warnings again because the damn machine kept getting nose high and she had her flight stick nearly all the way forward and her trim wheel maxed, so she was running out of options for getting the damn nose down.

"Oui, en effet. I am looking at the data stream from your aircraft," Leclerc said. "I am no aeronautical engineer, but it looks to me like that aircraft is in trouble."

Leclerc had an *app* that could see the data streaming from the Vapor? Of course she did. "Well, I made a little run over a pirate base," Bunny said bitterly. "I think they tagged me. And we think they are on their way to attack your convoy now."

"The Vapor is damaged?" Leclerc asked. She sounded keenly interested, naturally.

"Nothing some duct tape and spit can't fix," Bunny lied. "I'll get your precious aircraft back in one piece."

"I am not worried about the machine; I am worried about you. If you ditch in the sea while you still have control, I can send a helicopter rescue team from Brunei to retrieve you. But if you make an uncontrolled crash, you could *die*."

Bunny looked at her watch. Two hours until those militia boats reached the *Andromeda*, 0730 Zulu. Could she get down, get the Vapor patched up and get airborne in time to interdict them? She checked her nav screen.

Yes. Yes, she could. Or she could at least *try*.

"This Vapor will be down, refueled, rearmed and ready for operations again before those boats can make their intercept,"

Bunny assured her with false confidence. "Don't call air-sea rescue just yet."

There was a pause on the line. "I am responsible for your safety. I am *ordering* you to ditch that aircraft."

Bunny grimaced, looking at the sea below. It did not look particularly hospitable. Plus, sharks. She reached for the radio control panel. "Yes sir, ma'am," she said. "Order received; I will land the aircraft. O'Hare out."

She turned the radio off. Ditch/land, such easy words to get confused.

As Bunny went back to trying to tease more airspeed out of the Vapor without severely impacting her fuel burn rate, she felt warmed by the thought *someone* out there cared about her.

White House Situation Room, 1218 p.m. EST, January 9

So, we're actually doing this, Carmine Lewis was telling herself. Fifty years of talking about it, knowing the day would come, and now it's here.

Modern history had shown the world had really only room for one alpha dog, one true superpower. For one hundred and thirty years, that had been the USA. Russia had been a steadfast challenger, but in the middle of the twenty-first century lacked the economic muscle to back its ambition. China, however, was a different story. More and more headlines were predicting that the twenty-first century would belong to China, and certainly there were economic and industrial indicators that pointed that way.

Trend is not destiny, Lewis told herself. We are at the peak of our military and economic power. But so is China and they know they may never be stronger than they are today. The time to throw sand into the gears of China's outward advance was now. Fenner, Lewis, Kahn, Porter and the best minds at the Pentagon had crafted a plan they hoped would give China a reality check without sparking an all-out conflagration that would cost the lives of thousands of Americans and their allies.

It was a gamble. A *monumental* gamble.

Lewis was sitting in a packed White House Cabinet Room with the other members of the Principles Committee of the White House Security Council, the long table filled with Cabinet Secretaries and Cabinet-level officials like her, aides ranged on chairs along the walls behind them. The oil painting that hung over the fireplace during most meetings had been replaced by a large flat screen so they could follow the President's press briefing.

On the screen, she saw the door to the press room open and the President's press secretary walk through it. Back in the Situation Room, Carmine was at the President's side of the table, between his empty chair and Defense Secretary Phil Kahn. Opposite them sat the Vice President, Jada Tyler. He was the polar opposite of a cynical DC veteran; a relatively young, Harvard-educated former public defender, who could be the oil of calm on a sea of anxiety when needed. He appeared to sense Lewis's mood.

Without saying anything, he pushed a leather-bound book across the table to her. It appeared to be his appointments diary, and she raised her eyebrows at that, but he opened the cover so she could read what he'd written on the otherwise blank first page:

Remember: matter, how tiny your share of it. Time: how brief and fleeting your allotment of it. Fate: how small a role you play in it – Roman Emperor Marcus Aurelius.

In other words, 'Chill, Lewis'. She gave Tyler a wan smile and pushed the diary back to him, opening her mouth to ask him a question, but she was interrupted by the volume being turned up on the large flat panel screen as President Fenner walked into the Briefing Room to address the assembled press.

Stuart Fenner was a second-term President who history would, so far, not judge kindly. And Lewis knew he was keenly aware of that. He had inherited a troubled economy, which had spent most of his two terms in recession. He had no major social, economic or market reforms to his name. He had championed the transition of the US electricity grid from fossil fuels to renewables, and the transport sector from diesel and gas to renewable energy, but that had created as many enemies in Congress as it had won him friends. He was a President who had repeatedly claimed he abhorred war, and would not commit his country to long, drawn-out conflicts that would cost thousands of lives or trillions of dollars. Nevertheless, on his watch, the US and its allies had been involved in armed conflicts against nations ranging from Russia and Iran, to North Korea and even Japan. Short, sharp conflicts, to be sure. But for a President who abhorred war, he had spent a lot of time in the White House Situation Room with his generals, admirals and security advisers.

And now, he is about to start a small war in the hope of preventing a larger one. She knew it was a strategy that was fraught with risk, but she also firmly believed it was the right course of action. Or she would have resigned from Fenner's Cabinet.

Fenner was looking down at the speaker's podium as though gathering his thoughts. Uniquely among many modern Presidents, he did not like using a teleprompter for important announcements, though he kept notecards in front of him. He memorized such speeches, which also had the advantage of keeping them shorter, to the point. Carmine had the words of the statement on a page in front of her but wasn't reading either – she'd helped write them. He looked up.

"Thank you for coming. You would have seen in the news over the last few days that China has attacked the Philippine island of Pagasa in the South China Sea using cruise missiles. Chinese troops attempted to land on that island and were repulsed by Philippine Marines. The Philippine President called me yesterday and formally asked for our assistance in this matter, as provided for under the 1951 Mutual Defense Treaty between our nations. Specifically, he asked for US help to defend internationally recognized Philippine territories in the

South China Sea. And I assured him the US stands with the Philippines in this. Thirty minutes ago, US forces began an attack on Chinese military targets in the South China Sea which are a direct threat to Philippine lives and territory. These attacks continue as I speak. US ground forces are not engaged.

Ground forces, no... Carmine mused. *But a carrier strike group, a nuclear attack submarine, a guided-missile frigate – oh, and a chartered civilian 'relief' convoy loaded with missiles.*

"This military intervention regrettably follows years of constant and virtually endless diplomatic activity on the part of the United Nations, the United States, and many, many other countries intended to force China to respect international law in the South China Sea." Fenner looked down the barrel of the camera. "The USA will not allow Beijing to treat the South China Sea as its maritime empire. America stands with our Southeast Asian allies and partners in protecting their sovereign rights to offshore resources, consistent with their obligations under international law. We stand with the international community in defense of freedom of the seas and respect for sovereignty." Fenner paused and looked at a cue card on the podium in front of him.

Our objectives are clear... Lewis mouthed to herself. Come on, keep rolling.

"Our objectives are clear," Fenner continued to Lewis's relief. "Any Chinese military unit found on or within 12 miles of Pagasa Island will be destroyed. Let me repeat that with crystal clarity. Any Chinese military unit, whether in the air, on the ground, above the sea or under it, within the 12-mile territorial boundary of Pagasa Island, *will* be destroyed."

Lewis knew that the 12-mile exclusion zone was no accidental number. It was the internationally recognized definition of 'territorial waters'. And the distance from the outer reefs of Pagasa Island to the Chinese military base on Subi Reef was ... 12 miles.

The President paused, letting that statement sink in for a moment, before continuing. "Some may ask: Why act now?

Why not wait? The answer is clear: We have waited too long, and with too little effect. Years of diplomacy, of rulings against it in international courts of justice, have made no impact on China's inexorable and unlawful annexation of territory in the South China Sea. We have no recourse remaining but this."

Actually, some may ask 'why the hell a tiny island in the South China Sea?', Lewis reflected. Of all the places in the world to try to rein in Chinese ambition, why that place? The answer at the end of the day was, 'why not?'. If not Pagasa, then it would have been an island in the Paracels, or worse, Taiwan. Better now, at the time and place of their own choosing than of China's.

Lewis pulled her mind back to the here and now, as Fenner continued, trying to reassure the American people he did not intend for the US to be pulled into a protracted war. "Prior to ordering our forces into battle, I instructed our military commanders to take every necessary step to prevail quickly, and with the least involvement possible for American and allied service men and women. I'm hopeful that this fighting will not go on for long and that casualties will be held to an absolute minimum. We have no argument with the people of China. Our goal is *not* to seek a broader war with China, it is the defense of Philippine territory. It is my hope that somehow the Chinese people can, even now, convince their government that its attempted annexation of internationally recognized foreign territories should cease. Tonight, as our forces fight, they and their families are in our prayers. May God bless each and every one of them, and the allies at our side, and may He continue to bless our nation, the United States of America."

Fenner gathered up his papers, stepped down from the podium and walked out of the room, leaving his press secretary to face the inevitable barrage of questions from the press.

Minutes later, the President entered the Cabinet Room to applause from several members of his Cabinet and their aides. Lewis didn't feel that announcing the US was staging a military intervention aimed at China, even a hopefully limited conflict, was cause for applause. She noticed Vice President Tyler and Defense Secretary Kahn apparently felt the same way, both sitting still in their seats with hands folded in front of them.

Fenner sat and looked across the table at Tyler and Secretary of State Porter. "Jada, Victoria, it's good to see you here. How were your calls with our friends across the various ponds?"

Before joining the meeting, Tyler had been on the telephone with America's key 'five eyes' allies, the UK and Canada, while Victoria Porter had been making calls to the 'quad nations' of Japan, Australia and India. Courtesy calls to let them know what Fenner would be announcing, because with luck, the US would only need their diplomatic and not their military support. US diplomats, intelligence officials and military services had been laying the groundwork for this kind of scenario, but assurances of support given at a time of peace were one thing. The real test came in a time of war.

Porter nodded to the VP to go ahead. "In short, the UK is open to requests for support. Their Minister of Foreign Affairs went as far as to point out 'apropos of nothing' that their *Queen Elizabeth* carrier strike group was currently in the Mediterranean and could transit the Suez Canal and be in the Indian Ocean within three days. Theoretically, of course." Tyler checked the notes in front of him. "Canada is 'concerned' and hoping the conflict can be quickly resolved. Victoria?"

Porter nodded. "Similar picture in my interactions. Japan and India worried and hoping not to become involved. The Australian Prime Minister will issue a supporting statement and is open to requests for material support, including combat aircraft, troops or ships."

"Much as we expected, then," Fenner observed. "But with all we've invested in getting Japan onside again, I want to see them in our corner instead of on the fence. You'll work on that, Victoria?"

"Yes, Mr. President. I'll deliver Japan."

Carmine knew from the intel that had been coming across her desk that Japan was not 'on the fence' at all. It was firmly behind the notion of a small-scale US military challenge to China in the South China Sea, and in fact, it also had a statement prepared and ready for its Prime Minister to release, strongly condemning the Chinese attack on Pagasa. Porter had, typically, prepared Fenner for the worst, so that later she could claim to have won Japan over to the US side. Through sheer force of personality, no doubt.

Ah, the games we play, Lewis reflected. Except it isn't a game. Not anymore.

"Good. All good. We will need all the international support we can muster if, God forbid, this thing escalates."

Vice President Tyler had been listening to the discussion with a half smile on his face. Lewis knew his mild expression hid a rapier-sharp mind that often dropped a verbal bomb when a room least expected it.

"Have faith in our strategy, Mr. President," he said, speaking softly, but with the authority of a position that forced all but the President to button up and listen. "As we speak, the *USS Doris Miller* and her strike group is sending a host of drones and missiles to sweep the seas and skies around that island clean. Yes, China will respond with fury, but it will learn that a war fought with blood and bone, against machines, is one it cannot win. As fast as our aircraft are knocked down, more will be flown off the *Doris Miller*'s decks to Clark Base to replace them. Air and sea dominance re-established, the Philippine 3rd Marines will go ashore to reclaim their territory. Bleeding precious pilots, sailors, ships and aircraft, China will retire to its tiny reefs and atolls to rethink its blue water ambition, having learned that power springs not from the raw number of your soldiers in uniform, but from the strength of the economy, the technology and the political philosophy that produces them. And at that moment, *only then*, will Captain Okafor of the *USS Congress* and his convoy arrive triumphant at that humble island so that those brave Philippine Seabees can begin turning it from a bloodied battleground into a beacon of freedom." He sat back and swept his gaze around the room. "Pagasa Island will be the rock upon which China's Pacific ambition breaks its back. I have faith in our strategy, and so should all of you."

There was a moment of silence, and then Fenner spoke, without humor or irony. "Damn, Jada. Maybe *you* should give the next address to the nation."

Lieutenant Commander Li Chen of the People's Liberation Army Naval Air Force 9th Air Brigade didn't believe in fancy words.

Fancy words had been spoken when she had been given command of a People's Liberation Army Naval Air Force (PLANAF) FC-31 Gyrfalcon stealth aircraft squadron and assigned to the aircraft carrier *Liaoning* and its Special Aircraft division, certifying the new Gyrfalcon for carrier operations. But those fancy words had dissolved into blood when her unit had been sent into combat and she had watched her pilots die.

Despite her numerous and unforgivable failures, she had been presented with medals, and more fancy words were spoken when her Special Aircraft squadron assumed responsibility for operational testing of the new *Zhi Sheng* AI 'backseater' for the J-16 strike fighter. China had replaced the human weapons and systems operator in the fighter's back seat with a powerful AI, and more fancy words had been spoken by her commander on the *Liaoning* when she and her *Zhi Sheng* Squadron were sent to Subi Reef in the Spratly Islands in the hours after the Chinese cruise missile strike on the island.

Li Chen, unlike every other pilot in her unit, already knew the Tagalog Filipino name *Pag-asa:* Hope Island. She knew its Vietnamese name, *Dao Thi Tu:* Knife Island. And she knew its Chinese name: *Pehoeji*: Iron Shoal.

Li Chen had grown up in Shanghai, the daughter of a teacher and an engineer. But her family had not always been academics. Her mother had a family history that could be traced back to 111 BC under Emperor Wu Di of the Han Dynasty. Her ancestors had been merchants, trading goods from the South China Sea to the Indian Ocean and beyond, even before the Chinese invention of the mariner's compass, and two thousand years before any other nation sailed the South China Sea. As a child, her mother had taught her the names of every reef, shoal and rock in the Nansha Islands, the archipelago the rest of the world knew as the Spratlys.

Landing on the small airstrip at Subi Reef, now, at this time in her nation's history with her newly minted *Ao Yin*, or 'Bull Demon', squadron had not felt like coincidence: it had felt like … *destiny*.

She could understand, though, why the other fifteen pilots in the squadron did not necessarily feel the same as her. Circling the reef in the grey light of dawn, watching carefully from the circuit as they made their approach and prepared to land their aircraft, she let them vent some of their surprise. Taking off from Guangzhou, she had led them 800 miles south over the empty sea to a tiny atoll lost in the haze of the deep blue expanse until they were less than ten miles out. The voice of a Chinese PLAN air traffic controller had been a welcome sound so far from the land, but the sight of the Subi Reef air base when she saw it for the first time had not filled her with confidence, and she could understand her pilots' consternation.

"*Ma de* … there's nothing down there but a runway!" one of her pilots in the circuit observed.

"What did you expect *sha bi*, nightclubs and poker joints?" someone else replied. Li Chen smiled. But the first pilot was right. Subi air base had been built up from a semi-submerged reef, and it consisted of little more than a single runway running southwest–northeast, with five hangars and some Navy and Marine barracks and admin buildings, a radar installation and lighthouse, a few anti-air, anti-ship missile emplacements, and a harbor that right now held about twenty Chinese fishing boats because the two frigates based there were part of the blockade of Pagasa Island.

Another of the pilots had seen the fishing boats too. "Chill, comrades," he said. "There's a fishing fleet down there. Where there are fishermen, there are bars. Where there are bars, there is mahjong, and where there is mahjong, there are opportunities to relieve the locals of their cash and steal their women from them."

Enough. Chen reached forward and flipped her comms channel open. "Second Lieutenant Xhang, you have little to no chance of doing either. Concentrate on your landing, please."

Chen heard a chuckle or two, but then her pilots focused on the task at hand. After more than an hour and a half of flying they were about to put their machines down on one point eight miles of tarmac in the middle of thousands of square miles of empty ocean.

And they would do it perfectly, or Chen would make sure there were no bars, no mahjong, or anything else for any of them tonight.

"Ao Yin squadron leader, this is Subi Control," a voice broke in over the air traffic control channel. It had a note of panic.

"Go ahead, Subi," she replied.

"Ao Yin leader, we have an unidentified aircraft contact, possibly more than one, bearing east southeast, altitude two to five thousand, range, uh … a hundred ten to a hundred twelve miles. Synching contact data. You are ordered to investigate."

Chen quickly checked their fuel states. The J-16 had a 2,000-mile range, and they'd used nearly a third of their fuel on the trip over. But what they had was more than enough to investigate the 'contact'.

"Ao Yin squadron, abort landing, form up on me, squadron cruise formation," she said, banking her machine to vector it toward the contact that had just been thrown up on her screen by the Subi air base controller.

The contact was a single diamond, outlined in a dashed line. *Damn.* That immediately told her two things. The contact was already minutes old. And it had been a weak return, not a solid one. A passive sensor hit. Subi was equipped with the latest Chinese-made Red Banner 9 missile system, theoretically able to track anything from ballistic missiles in the upper atmosphere to hypersonic missiles or stealth aircraft. Its YLC-20 passive sensor was designed specifically to detect *stealth* aircraft. A series of transmitter beacons located on Chinese bases in the Spratlys sent pulses of energy into the sky and if the pulse was stopped by an otherwise 'invisible' aircraft, it would be delayed reaching the sensor on Subi. That delay could be used to get a bearing and altitude on the contact down which the Red Banner crew could search with their more powerful phased-array radar. Or despatch fighters.

If it was a passive sensor hit only, then the contact was probably stealth. Out here?

The Philippine Air Force had no stealth aircraft. At the pre-flight briefing led by a 7th Squadron PLAN intelligence officer, Chen had been warned that a US carrier strike group based on its carrier the *USS Doris Miller* had departed Guam a few days earlier and satellite intelligence indicated it was currently in the Philippine Sea a couple of hundred miles west of Guam, or nearly 1,200 miles from the Spratly Archipelago. Chen knew it carried piloted F-35 stealth aircraft and X-47B and Sentinel reconnaissance and refueling drones. Two days ago, a Sentinel drone had been shot down over Subi. She watched her pilots form up behind her, in loose 'finger four' elements, each five miles apart.

She didn't need an AI backseater to tell her the incoming aircraft were probably stealth aircraft flown off the *USS Doris Miller*.

Another surveillance aircraft, probably, given the fighting on Pagasa. Low-flying drones could gather a lot more intelligence than low-orbit satellites. But she could not be sure. Before scrambling for Subi, she had been warned to expect, and prepare for, the worst.

"Element Yi, stay with me, engage *Zhi Sheng* systems."

Chen reached toward a screen in front of her and punched the icon that engaged her own *Zhi Sheng* AI backseater in target prosecution mode, watching with satisfaction in her helmet visor as it linked with the Chinese BeiDou-3 satellite network and the ground control radar on Subi Reef, read the tactical environment instantly, engaged passive sensors, armed her air-to-air missiles and took control of her aircraft. All of this happened in the blink of an eye, and without her having to issue a single command.

One by one she saw all of the other aircraft in the squadron come online as their AI 'wizzos' took control of them and synched up with hers. Again, without having to issue any order, her machine began flying toward the unidentified contact, while to her left and right, the machines of her other pilots linked sensors and spread across the sky to maximize their chances of getting a lock on the incoming aircraft.

Although the J-16 had been in service in the PLAN air force for decades, the *Zhi Sheng* J-16 she was flying now was the culmination of China's efforts to take a global lead in Artificial Intelligence. It had sprung from a small paragraph in a Chinese planning document from 2017, committing State AI researchers to take the lead in 'brain-like perception, brain-like learning, brain-like memory mechanism and computing fusion, brain-like complex systems, and brain-like control'. Three years later, China was removing the backseat weapon systems officer or 'wizzo' from Li Chen's J-16 strike fighter, to replace it with an AI algorithm intended to handle all the wizzo's tasks: navigation, radar operation, target identification and selection, right up to the point of firing the aircraft's weapons.

Optimistically named 'Intelligence Victory' or *Zhi Sheng*, it had failed, miserably.

The computing power available at the time was insufficient, the learning algorithms employed were crude, and the data that individual aircraft could draw on was inadequate. But twin breakthroughs had made *Zhi Sheng* possible. The first was the advent of quantum-powered cloud computing, which could theoretically give every J-16 the 66 qubit superpowers of China's new Zuchongzhi quantum computers, if a way could be found to securely link the J-16 to the Zuchongzhi-powered cloud in flight. The second breakthrough was the system that did just that – the global BeiDou-3 satellite network.

In a matter of months after the two systems went live, Li Chen suddenly had a backseater with superhuman ability to observe, analyze, act and, more importantly, *learn*.

While the USA went down the route of developing more and more remotely piloted 'semi-autonomous' systems, with human operators located often hundreds of miles away calling every shot, China had decided to follow the path of human–AI *symbiosis*: man (or woman) and machine, melded together in a deadly combination.

They could have opted to take the human out of the cockpit entirely, but testing had shown that the strategic creativity of the human pilot combined with the tactical capabilities of the AI algorithms during combat gave superior performance versus AI alone. And the resources needed to maintain a continuous link to the BeiDou-3 satellite system were such that the pilot needed to be physically inside the cockpit, not sucking up bandwidth trying to pilot the aircraft from a trailer on the ground.

The product of these design choices was the J-16 *Zhi Sheng*.

From the moment it was engaged, the AI flew the aircraft and operated its critical systems. Li Chen moved from the role of pilot and squadron commander to tactical controller. She let her hands fall to the rests beside her throttle and stick, relaxed her feet on the gently moving rudder pedals, and concentrated on the data flowing across her helmet visor. In the other aircraft, every pilot was doing the same, staying ready to intervene if needed.

But Li Chen was tactical commander for this engagement. Her role was to issue orders to her AI that would guide how it handled the coming engagement. Centered in her vision was a tactical map screen showing all known air and ground contacts within 200 miles. On either side of this were two situationally dependent 'command wheels' that she could manipulate with eye-tracking technology that allowed her to select and execute commands simply by looking at them and blinking with a double-blink, like a double-click on a computer mouse. Once learned, the technique had proven faster and more reliable than voice recognition technology.

Chen's rules of engagement had been made very clear to her. The American declaration of a 12-mile no-fly zone around Pagasa Island was illegal. It was to be ignored. Any aircraft or ship refusing to identify itself in a 100-mile radius around Pagasa was to be engaged and ordered to turn away.

If it did not, it was to be destroyed.

The AI had already begun searching for the incoming aircraft on passive sensors. And it was not limited to using its own. It 'saw' exactly what the other aircraft in the formation saw. And it was able to pull data from the radar installations at Subi Reef, plus other radars at Fiery Cross and Mischief Reefs 150 miles to the south-east and south-west. She fine-tuned the search. The amount of data being fed to her would have been overwhelming if she'd also had to pilot the aircraft and operate its systems, but the AI took care of that, allowing her to concentrate on finding the needle in the haystack that was...

A chime in her ears announced a radar return from ground-based radars. Her AI immediately lit up the active phased-array radars on the two J-16s in the best position to get a solid lock.

Cao! Not one contact.

Ten!

"Contacts! Ao Yin Squadron, stay sharp, I am authorizing prosecution." Manipulating the appropriate command wheel with a couple of eyeblinks, Li Chen had her AI distribute the targets between her machines, allocate two PL-21 active homing radar missiles to each target, and flash her a question. *Launch missiles? YES/NO.*

The ten targets were now eighty miles out and closing on her sector. With another double-blink, she could send twenty missiles toward them.

But first...

She opened the international Guard radio channel.

"Unidentified aircraft approaching Pagasa Island. You are entering a Chinese air defense zone. Leave the area immediately or you may be fired upon."

The reply that came back was rather more insistent. "Chinese aircraft, you are within the 12-mile Philippines Pagasa Island territorial exclusion zone. Turn away *immediately*, or you *will* be fired upon."

It was not Li Chen's first rodeo. She did not continue with further banter. Her rules of engagement were clear.

She blinked. Twice.

There were not ten aircraft approaching Subi Reef and Li Chen's squadron. The *USS Doris Miller* had launched twenty-four unmanned X-47B Fantom stealth drones. One had comms issues and had returned to the carrier. A second had engine problems and had ditched five miles out from the carrier, deploying an airbag and GPS locator that meant it could be recovered if operational conditions allowed.

Twenty-two of the small Fantom drones had proceeded toward Subi Reef.

Each of the Fantoms carried 4,500 lbs. of ordnance on this mission, which included two Peregrine medium-range optical infrared air-to-air missiles for air engagements and two 2,000 lb. Joint Direct Attack Munition, JDAM, GPS guided bombs. Ten Fantoms were flying in close formation 25,000 feet above the sea, east of Pagasa Island. It was these the radar at Subi Reef and aboard Li Chen's fighters had detected. Twelve more Fantoms were spread over a twenty-mile front one thousand feet above the waves. At that moment, these were still invisible to Li Chen.

They were not semi-autonomous, but compared to the Chinese *Zhi Sheng* system, their AI was primitive. It could afford to be, because the US machines operated on a 'human in the loop' philosophy intended to minimize the risk of disastrous mistakes. The US Fantoms were being flown by pilots aboard the *Doris Miller*. The Chinese J-16s were larger and much more visible to optical infrared sensors than the deltoid-shaped American drones and the American pilots had been aware of their approach for some time. The moment Li Chen's aircraft locked up the low-flying Fantoms, their ship-borne pilots two hundred miles away reacted.

At almost exactly the same time as 20 Chinese PL-21 missiles leaped from the underwing pylons of Li Chen's squadron, 22 US Peregrine missiles speared towards the Chinese fighters both from down low over the sea and high up in the sky.

Flanked! Damn. Even worse, her AI had now identified the incoming aircraft based on their electronic signatures. X-47B Fantom drones. She had never before fought the American unmanned stealth fighters and China had nothing comparable in its arsenal against which it could have trained its pilots for this moment.

The Chinese PL-21 was a fire and forget missile that would use its own radar and optical-infrared seekers to fly itself to its target. That left the pilots who fired them to go about the business of trying to save themselves from the onslaught of missiles headed toward them. "Ao Yin pilots, evade!" Li Chen ordered, releasing their individual aircraft from central control so that the AI aboard each of them, including her own, could focus fully on surviving the next few minutes.

Li Chen's missile warning started warbling in her helmet and the visor was splashed with nearly two dozen red dots, tails behind them indicating their bearing, and boxes around those that were on a direct intercept course for her own aircraft. Two of the American missiles fired from more than fifty miles away were coming straight for her, one from down low, the other from up high, and about twenty miles laterally from each other. She quickly zoomed her tactical data screen to focus on the missiles targeting her. Her heart was pounding now. On the screen, her aircraft looked like a grain of rice at the tip of two chopsticks as the American missiles began tracking her.

A steering cue in her visor was showing her the escape vector calculated by her AI, and she felt a tightening in her gut as it pushed her throttle forward and centered the nose of her machine inside the steering cue. The AI was accelerating her aircraft to Mach 1.2 and aiming it at a point *right between* the incoming missiles. Of course, it made sense, with one approaching from down low on her right quarter, the other from up high on her left, the more she pushed forward, the more they would have to turn to keep a lock on her. But the maneuver went against every instinct in her body, which wanted her to turn tail and *run away* from the incoming missiles, not accelerate towards them!

With two missiles tracking her, she had to admit the limits of her own abilities. Without AI assistance she could concentrate on evading one missile, but in doing so, she would lose situational awareness about the other. In that moment of blindness, she could die. She zoomed the tactical screen out, saw the other aircraft in her squadron making radical maneuvers of their own as the American and Chinese missiles passed each other in the sky.

Would she still be alive, a minute from now?

Jiaolong Commando Corporal Ruan did not have faith in the strategy to retake Pagasa Island. The idea of landing just 12 Jiaolong Commandos to displace anywhere from 50 to 100 Filipino construction workers had sounded crazy, but just before they had been embarked on the patrol boat, they had been told the small island would be hammered with cruise missiles as they went ashore. "Shock and awe, men," Lieutenant Liu had told them. "Remember, you are Jiaolong! They are *construction workers*!" Still, Ruan had given himself a fifty percent chance of surviving the submarine deployment and making the beachhead at Pagasa. He gave himself a low

165

teens chance of surviving the first contact with Philippine forces. When they had been surrounded by the Philippine troops pouring down from the hilltop, he gave himself less than a five percent chance of making it through the next hour.

But like he'd been trained, he'd humped his radio around the hill on Pagasa, laid the sights of his carbine on anything in front of him that had moved, and he'd found himself still alive, in an old Japanese bunker with the remains of his team and a couple of fishermen's kids. He was still not convinced he wasn't going to die violently, and die soon.

Another soldier might have given up at that moment. But Ruan was not that kind of soldier. Ruan was the great grandson of Bao Ruan. No Chinese history book records the name of Bao Ruan, but he was Ruan's great-grandfather and the bugler in a platoon of Chinese People's Volunteer Army soldiers who gave their lives at Hell's Gates during the Korean War. Calling themselves 'human bullets', Bao and his men threw themselves at one imperialist gun emplacement after another, Bao always out front, his bugle signaling the platoon to charge.

He was captured in 1951 by imperialist troops. But that was not the end of Bao Ruan. Together with 4,000 North Koreans he was paraded through the streets of Inchon and incarcerated in a prisoner of war camp where he labored as a slave until the armistice was signed in 1953. Offered citizenship in South Korea or repatriation to the USA, Bao had refused, and had returned to China to become a union leader, communist party politician, and finally, a poet.

Bao was a hard act to follow, but Corporal Ruan had seen how he was revered in the Ruan family and decided at an early age he would try. So he had been the first member of his family to try out and qualify for the Jiaolong Commandos. And when the call came for volunteers to liberate Pagasa, he had been the first to step forward, as suicidal as the mission had seemed. Because his great-grandfather Bao had done the same, nearly a hundred years earlier, at Hell's Gates.

As he crouched at his radio inside the Japanese bunker on

Pagasa, he felt strangely close to his great-grandfather. Most Jiaolong Commandos carried pictures of their partners or kids. He had his great-grandfather Bao's picture in a locket around his neck. It felt weird, but also felt right, to think nearly a hundred years ago, Bao had been fighting against a foreign enemy determined to take his country from him. Because Ruan believed entirely what he had been taught at military college; namely that the Western Imperialists were rapacious beasts that would advance across the South China Sea toward the People's Republic – atoll by atoll, reef by reef – and they would not stop until *all* of Southeast Asia fell under their sway, from Taipei to Beijing.

Ruan didn't have the bandwidth to worry about the big picture, just as he knew Bao probably had not. Bao had by all accounts been a simple man, with simple values. Love of family, love of country, in that order. For both, he had been prepared to die, and so was Ruan.

So here he was, crawling through the undergrowth beside Lieutenant Commander Liu and the five remaining men of Jiaolong Commandos on Pinya Hill, Pagasa Island, still not dead, much to his own amazement.

Ruan had squirted his text message from deep inside the bunker to a satellite passing over the South China Sea, which had relayed it to Naval Computer and Telecommunications Area Master Station Southern Command, which relayed it to the two *Jiangwei* class Coast Guard frigates patrolling the waters offshore of Pagasa Island.

Though nearly 50 years old, they had been upgraded between 2015 and 2020 with new fire control and anti-air radar, anti-ship and anti-air missiles, and, for direct or indirect artillery fire, dual 100mm guns. A *Jiangwei* frigate's guns could put twenty-five 40 lb. high-explosive shells a minute on targets 10 miles away, with 10-yard accuracy. The Chinese Coast Guard vessels would put some nation's *navies* to shame.

"You got a link, Ruan?" Liu whispered. Ruan and the others had crawled out of the bunker in the pre-dawn darkness and made their way with nerve-sapping caution to the southern side of the hill overlooking the cratered air field and still smoking debris of the former barracks. Liu was hoping to see the Filipino troops re-establishing camp there, as it was the only real open ground on the island. Failing that, they would have to continue their hazardous circuit of Pinya Hill by scouting west, toward the small harbor.

They'd found their targets, but not out in the open, as Liu had hoped. On the hillside, under the cover of a stand of trees and just a hundred yards down from their vantage point, spread out two hundred yards in either direction, the remaining Filipino troops were industriously digging trenches and lining them with sandbags filled with wet sand hauled up from the shoreline. Using low-light binos to scan the slope below, he'd translated the Filipino trenches to coordinates on his map.

"Yes, Lieutenant," Ruan whispered back. "Frigates are in position and standing by."

Liu scanned the Chinese lines one more time and read some coordinates to Ruan. "Good. Tasking request, five rounds, ranging." Liu watched closely as the Philippine troops labored in near darkness, long lines of troops near them digging into the hillside as others filled and humped sandbags across the air strip to reinforce the trenches. He reflected with grim satisfaction that at least if they were digging, they weren't busy searching for him and his men. But the longer they were allowed to continue, the less chance a naval barrage would have of causing serious harm.

He watched as Ruan typed the request silently into his input device and hit 'send' to squirt it up to the satellite and down to the waiting frigates.

Five rounds. He had no idea how accurate the frigate's gunners were. "Incoming. Heads down, gentlemen," he warned his men.

He was beginning to wonder whether their message had

been received when he heard the sound of supersonic artillery rounds splitting the air, and the hillside in front of them exploded into dirt, smoke and fire. He waited for the smoke to clear, saw Philippine soldiers in their half-dug trenches, standing and yelling to each other.

"Long," he told Ruan. "Tell them to adjust fire fifty yards north and wait for my order to fire for effect." Liu wanted to fix the Filipino troops in place and, if possible, even draw more of them toward the Chinese position on the hillside, before the sky started raining high explosive on them.

Liu pulled his carbine off his back. He removed the suppressor from his barrel and pocketed it. Checking the carbine was loaded and set to fire a three-round burst, he pointed it downhill toward the Filipino positions. The enemy had run for their trenches as expected, but now they were shouting to each other, no doubt wondering if the few shells that had just fallen were all that were coming at them, or if there was more.

Liu looked up and down his line, checking his men's positions and then their line of retreat. Satisfied, he touched his throat mike. "Pick your targets. Short bursts. On my mark, open fire."

Down on his belly in the undergrowth beside Ruan, Liu laid his sights on the back of a soldier sixty yards away, lighting a cigarette. The way the man was lighting up, while others around him were panicking, told Liu he was an officer. An NCO at the very least. Liu tightened his finger on the trigger of his 9mm rifle. "Three ... two ... one ... *mark*!"

Across the line on either side of Ruan, rifles began stuttering loudly. Zhang and Gua, his heavy weapons specialists, had been placed at each end of the line and he could clearly hear the heavier drum of their squad weapons.

As his target was punched forward by the impact of his opening volley in his back, Ruan switched his sights to another man standing by the trench. Two times three shots in his direction until he disappeared. *Switch right. New target.* Someone bent double, trying to pick something up. One burst. Down. Grenades exploding now, Zhang and Gua again. He looked for his next target.

In a couple of minutes, the Filipinos had managed to identify where they were being attacked from, and bullets started zipping through the trees and leaves over his head. Wild, undirected fire for now, but the panic would soon subside and the Filipinos would locate them by the flash from their unsuppressed barrels. Liu had ordered his men to remove their suppressors, making their rifle fire audible and visible, to pull more Filipino troops toward them. *Well, it's working*, he thought grimly. He could see past the flash of Filipino rifles in the nearest trenches to the air strip and beach beyond, and saw dozens of troops running uphill from the air field, making straight for them.

Liu fired a volley of six shots and then rolled onto his back, changing his magazine. Over the sound of the firefight, Liu yelled at Ruan. "Contact the frigates. Five minutes, full barrage, fire for effect!"

Ruan had started tapping the fire support request into his transceiver's text panel, but then stopped with a frown. "Sir, a fifty-yard adjustment puts that artillery just fifty yards downhill from *us*, sir," he yelled over the sound of the firefight.

Liu spun around, sent three rounds downrange, and then turned back to Ruan. "That's because the closest enemy is fifty yards downhill, Corporal," he told Ruan firmly. "You send that command, we'll have a minute to pull out. We'll be fine." Ruan opened his mouth to speak again, but Liu reached out with gloved fingers and lifted his jaw to shut his mouth. A light on Ruan's transceiver started blinking green. "Data lock, Corporal. *Send. That. Tasking.*"

Shaking his head to free it of Liu's pinch grip, Ruan dropped his rifle and rolled onto his back beside Liu, holding his transceiver up in front of his face. The request for the strike was already cued up. He jammed his thumb on a key. Flashing lights confirmed his message had been received. "Strike incoming!" he yelled back at Liu.

Liu rolled onto his haunches and tapped Ruan on the helmet, reaching for his throat mike. "Team, disengage! Pull back!" If anything, the Filipino counter-fire seemed to have intensified.

Ruan swung his radio over his back, bent down to pick up his rifle, with bullets chewing the trees around his head, and gritted his teeth, knowing that in seconds several hundred high-explosive 100mm rounds would be spearing down through the night *right towards him*. The five percent chance of survival he'd given himself was suddenly looking wildly optimistic.

The gun crews on the two *Jiangwei* class Coast Guard frigates were, in fact, very good at their jobs. Patrolling largely unmanned atolls in the South China Sea left a lot of time for gunnery practice and the PLA Navy Southern Command was not stingy regarding the ammunition requisitions it received for conventional 100mm shells.

The Captain of the frigate *Xianyang* was on the bridge of his vessel, staring out to sea holding a mug of hot tea. A fifty-yard range adjustment had been necessary? Not acceptable. When this fire mission was over, he would be ordering his gun crew to recalibrate their fire control radar and conduct new drills. Of course, the error could have been the fault of those lazy bastards on the *Luoyang*, a half-mile off his port beam. They had opened fire a full five seconds later than the *Xianyang*, and had proven in exercises more than once they couldn't hit shit.

He'd supervised the relaying of the guns personally, and then returned to the bridge, waiting impatiently for the request to 'fire for effect'. When it came, he was pleased to see his men did not wait for him to formally order them into action, they jumped to it immediately. His twin 100mm barrels began a satisfying *thud thud thud*…

Then his radar watch officer shouted. "Contact! Vampires inbound! Bearing zero four two, altitude 20,000 descending, speed … speed 4,200 miles per hour!"

The Captain nearly spilled his tea. "Check your equipment, man. That speed is impossible."

"Targets confirmed!" the man replied, turning to stare at the Captain wild-eyed. "We have a bearing. I can't get a fire control lock."

Hypersonic missiles? They had to be. They'd wargamed defending themselves against a hypersonic missile attack. His ten-year-old Knife Rest anti-air radar would be useless, and he knew he had only seconds to react.

"Launch Red Banner missiles, full salvo, autonomous seeker mode!"

"Launching Red Banner, eight cells, aye!" The man punched a button on his fire control panel.

"Bring 37mm guns to bear," the *Xianyang*'s Captain continued. "Fire down the bearing, shield pattern!"

From the missile launch turret mounted about ten yards in front of the bridge, eight medium-range anti-air missiles leaped from their tubes and blasted into the night sky in the direction of the incoming hostile missiles. With radar and infrared seeker heads, if they picked up the body of the missile or the heat bloom from its nose cone, there was a chance they could get close enough to detonate and damage it. At the same time, his 37mm twin-barrel close-in weapons system began spewing out hundreds of shells in a circular pattern, trying to put a wall of lead between themselves and the threat.

Xianyang's Captain tightened his grip on his tea mug. He had followed procedure meticulously and his crew had jumped into action immediately. But he knew neither of these strategies had a hope in hell of stopping hypersonic missiles.

He shot a glance to port. The bloody *Luoyang* was still blazing away with its 100mm and hadn't got a single anti-air missile away. Those lucky bastards over there were going to die slow and ignorant.

Unfortunately, the designers at the Hudong–Zhonghua Shipyard had bet on the superiority of Chinese air defense weapons to defend against mere supersonic missiles. *Hypersonic* missiles had not even existed when the *Luoyang* and *Xianyang* were commissioned. Using optical image recognition software to pick out their targets, two long-range hypersonic missiles launched by the incoming X-47B Fantoms slammed into the Chinese Coast Guard frigates' aft helipads at a forty-degree angle that allowed them to smash through the steel helipads, through the light deck armor, and then detonate against the machined steel casings of the frigates' diesel engines, blasting molten metal fragments throughout the aft decks of the two ships.

The Captain of the *Luoyang* did indeed die ignorant to the threat, as his fuel and ammunition stores ignited simultaneously.

The Captain of the *Xianyang* lived long enough to see the gates of hell appear through the hole in his helipad, before a tower of flame shot up through the hole like a hundred-foot-high roman candle. He didn't have to call 'abandon ship' – men were already diving over the side when his missile store ignited and the entire aft section of the *Xianyang* was cleaved away as though a giant blowtorch had sliced through it, from the *inside*.

Her Captain stayed on his bridge, one hand clinging to his mug, the other to a safety rail, as her bow rose into the sky and she started sliding backward into the sea. Not because he believed any of that nonsense about a Captain going down with his ship. But because he knew that if he lived through the loss of his vessel, it would only be to face the indignity of a court-martial and the rest of his life in a labor camp.

He had long ago decided if this day ever came, he would take his dignity with him to a watery grave.

An unfortunate side effect of the destruction of the two *Jiangwei* frigates was that thanks to their autoloader systems, their 100mm guns kept firing, even as they were ripped apart.

Shells aimed with ten-yard accuracy started spraying wide. Most flew over the island's air strip and exploded harmlessly in the sea to the south. A half dozen arced toward the already battered village in the east of the island. Little of the barrage fell, as intended, on the Filipino troops moving up the hillside toward the source of the new Chinese commando attack.

With inexorable and fatal coincidence, though, ten shells plunged down through the air with supersonic screams, directly toward the retreating Lieutenant Baotian Liu, Comms Technician Corporal Ruan, and the remaining men of the Jiaolong Commandos.

Li Chen's head snapped to one side, then to the other, as her combat AI sent her machine into a wildly gyrating corkscrew through the sky. The J-16 used thrust vectoring and leading-edge canards to give it super-maneuverability, but she had no idea it was even *capable* of the maneuver that the *Zhi Sheng* pilot was putting it through right now.

It was as though the back of the aircraft down by the engines was fixed in place and the nose was spinning like a child's top as the American missiles homed on it from two directions, turning radically now to keep themselves pointed at her. As the missile warning warble in her ears turned to a screaming single high tone, the AI seemed to make up its mind at last, the nose of her aircraft stopped spinning as it transitioned to a jarring banking turn, and her flight suit inflated explosively as the aircraft started firing missile decoys and suddenly bunted into a desperate negative-G reverse that felt like it pushed every ounce of blood in her body into her head. Despite the best efforts of her flight suit, she started to red-out, her vision fogging and bile rising in her throat.

She vaguely heard two detonations nearby. Behind? Above?

She couldn't tell.

Her vision was starting to clear. Her machine had gone back into search and engage mode. It had dodged the American missiles, but it had also lost the targets. She focused on the tactical view in her visor. *Where the hell was she?* Her mad supersonic charge toward the American missiles had pulled her nearly fifty miles east of Subi and Pagasa. She had no US aircraft on her radar screen as the AI had shut it down to help her hide from enemy radar detectors and she had nothing on passive sensors, nothing on secondary radar sources. She zoomed out. Two of her pilots were still engaged and had locked up targets, but her AI had decided they could manage for themselves or it would have sent missiles their way to assist.

No Chinese aircraft destroyed. Eight American X-47s estimated destroyed or damaged. Two still engaged.

She felt a surge of primal joy and punched the plexiglass above her head. *Yes! Ao Yin!*

The US force of 22 Fantoms had been reduced to 14 by the Chinese fighter attack. Two Fantoms were still engaged with fighters of Chen's squadron, but 12 had swept through the Chinese fighter defense undetected and dropped down to wave height for their bombing run at Subi Reef.

Each Fantom had a radar cross-section smaller than a golf ball. Focused as they were on the furball high in the sky fifty miles to their east – hoping for a solid lock and a clear shot at one of the attackers – the Chinese Red Banner radar crew on Subi did not detect the threat coming at them from down low until the Fantoms popped up to 5,000 feet and opened their weapons bay doors. Their radar cross-sections briefly spiked as each Fantom released two precision-guided bombs, causing them to suddenly appear on Chinese radar. Before the Red Banner crew could get its missiles away, though, the Fantoms had closed their weapons bays and were diving for the wavetops again.

Their pilots were sitting comfortably aboard the *USS Doris Miller*, 1,200 miles to the east. Freed from the fear of dying in a ball of fire at the hands of a Chinese missile crew, they were able to focus entirely on the job of putting ordnance on target. Four of the bombs were aimed at the runway at Subi Reef and fitted with hardened penetrating warheads. They punched through the concrete of the runway to the earth below, and in four massive blasts, flung concrete and earth high into the air, leaving craters fifty feet wide and forty feet deep. Two more bombs activated two hundred feet above the runway, flinging out hundreds of proximity fused cluster munitions that would lie dormant on the runway and the area around it until a person or vehicle came near them. They were designed to make it too hazardous for combat engineers to repair the runway until the cluster munitions had been dealt with.

The rest of the Fantoms' payloads had been fed the latest GPS coordinates for the base's fixed radar and air traffic control tower, the most used locations of its Red Banner mobile command truck and launchers, the aircraft pens and maintenance hangars lining the runway, military barracks and administration buildings. The reef was shaped like a squared-off horseshoe, and the last of the hardened penetrating-warhead bombs had been reserved for two large underground naval and aviation fuel tanks out at the tip of one of the 'arms' of the horseshoe.

Punching through the 20-feet concrete caps on top of the fuel tanks, dedicated auditory sensors inside the bunker-buster bombs 'listened' to the noise made by the initial penetration and when they heard the sound of the bombs passing into liquid fuel, they detonated their 2,000 lb. high-explosive cores.

Four hundred and fifty miles to the east, over the Sulu Sea, the second wave of 24 Fantoms launched by the *Doris Miller* finished refueling from an orbiting Stingray drone tanker, and started forming up for a follow-up attack on Subi Reef. Half of them carried the same precision-guided gravity bombs in their internal weapons bays as the first strike had attacked with, but the remainder were each armed with six Peregrine medium-range air-to-air missiles.

Their twin mission objectives: eliminate Subi Reef as a base of operations for Chinese air or naval forces and achieve dominance of the airspace over Pagasa Island by destroying any Chinese aircraft entering a twenty-mile area around the island.

Ruan had no idea how many members of his Jiaolong Commando force were still alive. He wasn't even completely sure that *he* was. Crabbing backward up the slope of Pinya Hill, he had watched as the first shells fired by the two frigates had started erupting on the hill between himself and the airfield, turning the early morning into a blood-red and yellow hell of flying dirt and human bodies.

They had started running uphill. Then the ground around him began to heave, a blast wave picked him up and flung him into a nearby tree, and his world went black.

When he woke, he heard a man nearby crying out weakly for help.

His own body was numb from the waist down and he couldn't move his legs. He lay on his back looking up at the dark tree canopy, terrified to look down. What if his legs were no longer there? But if he'd been cut in half, shouldn't he be dead by now? *Maybe he was dead.* Maybe this was what happened. Your brain still alive, but your body unable to move as the last of your blood seeped out into the dirt, your eyes staring up into the sky as you…

No, he could feel his toes. He just couldn't move his feet. Gathering his courage, he lifted his head and looked down. *Ah, okay.* He was buried in loose soil and debris from the chest down. Looking around him he saw shapes moving in the smoke – staggering, crawling, stumbling. He heard them calling to each other in Tagalog. None were speaking Chinese. The other men from Jiaolong Commandos must have withdrawn while he was unconscious.

As quietly as he could he started pushing the dirt away from his chest, and then began wiggling his legs to free them. The effort wasn't helped by the radio backpack still wedged uncomfortably beneath his back, or his big combat boots, which seemed as though they were fixed in concrete. But he eventually got his boots loose too and, heaving until his shoulder muscles screamed, he slowly pulled himself out of the dirt and rolled onto his stomach.

He looked around. The trees were filled with smoke. Where was he? He needed to work out what was uphill, what was down. He needed to go up and east if he was to get back to the bunker. Most of the shouting and crying was coming from his left. So that should be downhill, where the bulk of the Filipino soldiers had been. That meant uphill was probably to his right. But which way was east or west? The sky looked like it might be getting a little more grey than black now. So dawn was approaching. But he couldn't wait for the sun to appear, he needed to be well gone by then.

Just move, Ruan! Yes. He should move. It was only a small hill, whether he went east or west, he'd eventually come around to the northern slope where the bunker was located. There would be clear air there, better visibility. Tightening the straps on his radio pack, he gathered himself to try to stand. His carbine. He should try to find his carbine. Liu would be pissed if he returned without it. He looked at the forest floor in every direction, seeing nothing but uprooted dirt, debris from smashed trees, smoke and shadows that could be low bushes, or Filipino soldiers. It was impossible to know in the shifting light, with his ears still ringing and his eyesight still blurred by concussion. *Seriously?* Forget that. He stood, took a step and then stumbled as his foot caught in something. A tree root? Looking down he saw a strap. His carbine maybe?

He reached down and pulled at the strap, but whatever it was attached to was stuck under the dirt. It seemed too narrow to be his rifle strap. Maybe a canteen? Water. Water would be good. He pulled on it again. Something moved under the dirt and then it came free.

A helmet. Filipino Marine helmet.

With the head of a Filipino soldier still strapped inside it. Severed at the neck.

He didn't fling it away in horror. He stared at it in fascination. The face was that of a boy his own age. He laid it gently back down on the ground and brushed the dirt away from his eyes. The boy's eyes were still open, but dulled by death. He tried to close the eyelids but they refused. There was congealed blood on the boy's cheek and Ruan wiped it gently off with his thumb. Without really thinking, he made the Sign of the Cross on his forehead in his own blood. He knew the Filipino boy was probably Catholic, which Ruan wasn't, but he hoped he did it right. *Sleep. You are with your ancestors now.*

Nearby, he heard a cough. *Move, Ruan!* What? Nearby, he saw the unmistakable shape of a man rise to his feet and then lean on a tree, trying to drag air into his lungs. As he backed away at a crouch, the Filipino boy's head fell to one side and his glazed eyes stayed on Ruan until he had faded into the smoke.

Within ten minutes he had reached the northwestern slope of Pinya Hill. He'd gone the wrong way, west, and had to evade two very jumpy Filipino patrols sent out from the harbor to the destruction by the airfield. Now he was looking for the entrance to their bunker, having a hard time finding it due to the grey pre-dawn light and the fact he hadn't approached it from this direction before.

He registered the flashes from the detonation of the massive bombs on Subi Reef, 16 miles away, before he heard the rolling thunder from the west that followed them, and turning around to look out past the harbor and over the sea, he saw two fireballs light the horizon and roiling black clouds of smoke rise into the air.

If he wasn't feeling like a chewed-up and spat-out dog's toy himself, he might have felt a little dismay. But all he could think about was how every single fiber in his body protested at every single jarring step he took. Finally, he recognized the ridge under which the bunker entrance lay concealed by brush and fallen trees and made for it, crawling the last few yards to pull aside the mottled, fungus-covered groundsheet and roll inside.

Except for the two children, it was empty.

White Star *Andromeda*, north Kuala Belait, Brunei, 350 miles south of Pagasa Island, January 9

Bunny O'Hare had put the V-290 Vapor down on the deck of the *Andromeda* with all but her emergency fuel reserve reading empty. True to his word, the *Andromeda*'s Captain had done nothing to make her return to the support ship any faster – if anything, he'd made it harder by altering course more to the north-east to increase the time it would take for the incoming militia boats to reach them.

Their new course shortened the time until the convoy would rendezvous with the *USS Congress* by about 30 minutes. It also had the advantage of taking them into shallower waters east of the southernmost Spratly reefs, most particularly a feature called Investigator Shoal, on which Malaysia had built a patrol boat refueling base. Not that Pedersen expected that to deter the militia chasing them, but the shallow water made it less likely they'd bump into a Chinese submarine.

An inspection of the damage from the heavy-caliber gun that had tagged her Vapor showed it had punched several holes in her starboard wing tank, too large for the self-sealing tank system to stop the tank from emptying itself before she could transfer the fuel to her other tanks. A bullet had also cut the fuel line from the starboard to port wing, so pumping the fuel would have been impossible anyway.

The *Andromeda*'s flight crew chief was a dour Norwegian. As he walked around the machine with Bunny inspecting the damage, he shook his head and muttered to himself, making Bunny despair that it would ever fly again. His crew certainly showed no indication that they would be needed any time soon. They had mooched over to the aircraft, thrown chocks under its wheels and then retired into the shade of its fuselage to sit on their haunches. Finally, the Norwegian stopped walking and muttering and pulled a rag from his pocket to wipe sweat from his brow. The sun had risen above the horizon and it was already getting warm out on the steel helipad. "Thirty minutes," he told her.

Bunny saw the comms assistant, Lawrence, walking across the flight deck toward them. "Can't you tell me now?" she said to the crew chief, thinking he meant it would take 30 minutes to thoroughly inspect the damage to the machine. "I need to give Captain Pedersen some idea of when…"

The man shook his head. "Captain Pedersen told me to get you airborne again, fast as we can. So, ten minutes to plug those holes, twenty to patch the fuel hose and test the system. We can't refuel until that's done, so add another fifteen after that. Forty-five minutes until you can take off."

"Wow," Bunny whistled.

"Forty-five minutes until what, ma'am?" Lawrence asked, arriving at the end of the conversation. Seeing him standing up for the first time, she saw he was quite tall and was hunched over as though afraid the Vapor's rotors might start up and take his head off.

"Until I can get my bird up again," she told him. "What are you doing out here?"

"Mr. McIntyre sent me to get you," he said. "Those militia boats are about an hour out now, the Captain is holding a briefing of the ship's officers."

"We'll get started," the crew chief told her, and twirled his finger to indicate to his men they should lift themselves from their butts and get to work.

Bunny grabbed her flight jacket from the cockpit and pulled it on. The indoor areas on *Andromeda* were air conditioned against the tropical heat and Bunny was constantly alternating between being boiled alive out on the deck or half frozen in the crew compartments. She trailed after Lawrence, tapping her helmet on her thigh as she walked. They climbed down from the helipad and headed for a side door on a low structure on the aft deck, about twenty yards from the main superstructure. "The briefing is not on the bridge level?"

The boy pointed down at the deck. "Below, in the secondary command room, ma'am."

"Secondary command room?"

He glanced over his shoulder at her as he stepped into a stairwell. "Yeah, you know, we call it the citadel. The Captain, First Mate, and watch crew move there when there is a piracy threat. All the ship's comms, sensor, engine and steering controls are duplicated there. It's like Fort Knox. Even if the pirates manage to board, they can't penetrate the citadel."

Bunny could see one problem. "And if they just decide to sink the *Andromeda*? You're down in the guts of the ship, locked behind steel bulkhead doors?"

Lawrence laughed, the first time she had seen him look other than embarrassed or confused. "Sink the ship? Where's the profit in that? And secondly, how? You'd need to blow a hole in the hull under the waterline, ma'am." He led her inside the small structure and down a flight of stairs. One level below the main deck, he took a tight corridor down the portside of the ship and stopped at what looked like an anonymous steel door. A wheel on the outside was used to secure it, and he spun the wheel, unlocking it. Pulling it open, he stepped aside with a flourish and an awkward smile. "Welcome to the citadel, ma'am…"

Ma'am again. Bunny would have to put a stop to that. It was bordering on ageist. She stepped through the door, expecting to see something like the command and control centers she was used to on ships of war. Banks of screens, men and women bent over them, headphones pressed to their ears, the air thick with tension. Or at least a small-scale copy of the bridge up above. Instead, she saw … nothing? The room was pretty much empty except for a large cabinet on one wall. She started to turn to Lawrence in confusion, then felt his hand on her back.

Before she could turn all the way around, she felt a hammer blow across the base of her skull and dropped to her knees. Dazed, she wasn't completely out, and she managed to turn her head to see Lawrence holding a pistol by the barrel, stepping into the room behind her.

What in the hell? He'd clubbed her with a *pistol*? He stepped inside the room, closed the bulkhead door behind him and spun the wheel to close it. She heard bolts click shut.

She fell forward, nauseous and dizzy, one hand trying to support herself, the other waving feebly at the air in front of her, instinctively trying to find something she could drag herself up with, but her world was starting to go grey.

He sighted the pistol on her back.

And fired.

What in the hell?

Heraldo Bezerra had been checking on his men at the harbor when the first salvo of the naval bombardment came down. It stopped as soon as it started, which he knew was a bad sign. *Ranging rounds.* He'd heard small arms fire next, but was on the western side of the hill, well away from the source of the firefight. More Chinese commandos? Or the same ones, come back to finish what they started?

Two strong points formed from concrete berms had been set up at either side of the harbor and he didn't need to tell his men twice – as soon as the firing started, they dropped what they were doing and sought cover. He was with them when the next artillery salvo came down. As soon as the explosions and small arms fire died away, he had a squad grab medical supplies and started running around the south of the island, toward the air base … then he heard thunder. It was like a monsoon had broken somewhere behind him, and spinning in his tracks he saw two mushroom clouds of smoke rising out of the sea.

Subi Reef. The Americans had hit Subi!

He turned back inland and saw there was no time to celebrate. Ugly black smoke was rising over the eastern side of the island where the village was.

Looking down at the devastation that less than 30 minutes earlier had been a functioning naval air base, Li Chen saw ugly black smoke rising too.

The naval air base which she had been ordered to defend was now a blackened ruin. She felt a hole in her heart where moments before her pride had been. They had killed every American machine they had detected. But the devastation below showed they had not detected them all. And those that had passed them unseen had wreaked this destruction.

She'd seen the twin mushroom clouds and smoke from secondary fires from twenty miles out. More worrying, Subi air traffic control was off the air. She could raise Mischief Reef Air Base one hundred and fifty miles to the south-east, but there was no reply from Subi on any channel.

With a blink, she retook control of her aircraft. "Ao Yin pilots, disengage *Zhi Sheng* and form up on me."

"Roger, leader. Damn Americans got through," one of her pilots said. "We failed."

"We killed a dozen of their machines," another protested. "It could have been much worse."

"No, we kicked their asses," a third said. "They sneaked a few through this time, they won't succeed next time."

"Quiet!" she ordered. "Eyes on the skies. This isn't over."

Chen was a combat veteran and experienced at assessing bomb damage from the air. She led the formation in a slow, sweeping circle of the Chinese base. *Cratered runway, shattered hangars, buildings.* Burning aircraft. Fire crews out at the southern arm of the reef, pouring foam into two massive fires that seemed to be erupting from the ground itself. *Fuel.* Their precious fuel. The challenge of operating small, widely spread bases nearly a thousand miles from the nearest Chinese port came suddenly home to her.

They would not be refueling at Subi Reef today. Hell, they would not even be landing here. But they had to put down *somewhere*, and soon.

She switched her radio to the Mischief Reef Air Traffic Control channel. "Mischief ATC, this is Ao Yin Squadron inbound Subi Reef. The base has been attacked. Runway destroyed. Fuel tanks burning. I can't raise them on radio. Requesting permission to refuel and rearm."

"Ao Yin leader, Mischief control copies. Report fuel and weapons state." The air controller on Mischief Reef did not have access to the same battle-net data that Li Chen in her *Zhi Sheng*-enabled aircraft did.

Chen could see the fuel reserves of each of the aircraft in her squadron. The highest was at sixty percent, the lowest – her own, thanks to the supersonic evasion maneuver her AI had executed – was forty-eight percent. Weapons? A few of her aircraft had not been engaged and were still carrying their full load of six missiles. She had used two. In total they had 67 missiles remaining. She read the figures out and looked at her watch. How long had it been since they left the carrier *Liaoning* in the East China Sea?

Less than two hours! It felt like a lifetime.

"Ao Yin leader, copy your report. I have new tasking for you. Enemy aircraft detected at bearing zero four zero, range two hundred fifty-nine, altitude unknown, speed unknown, strength estimate, ten plus … pushing data to you now. Patrol sector Juliet niner, prepare to engage any hostile aircraft or cruise missiles detected within one hundred miles of Pagasa Island. We are scrambling our J-10s to a position east of you."

Chen checked her map. Two fifty-nine miles … that was Philippine airspace. The American drones were probably coming off their carrier to the east, refueling at a base in

Philippine territory, and then rolling in to strike Subi and Pagasa. A challenge for another day. Right now she had a huge front to cover and only one truly capable squadron to cover it with.

The J-10 Firebirds scrambling from Mischief Reef to their south were what her pilots called 'meat shields'. They could fly missiles to the battlefield, but were not likely to survive long enough against an advanced enemy to be able to use them. Their main value was to soak up enemy missiles so that more advanced Chinese fighters like the FC-31 and *Zhi Sheng* J-16 could go to work.

"Orders received and understood, Mischief," she replied. "Ao Yin Squadron, patrolling sector Juliet niner." She sent the order on to her pilots. "Ao Yin Squadron, moving to sector Juliet niner, line abreast, five-mile separation, alternate high and low. Prepare to engage AI on my mark." As they checked in, she heard less than conviction in their voices. Of course she did. They'd handed out a beating, but the enemy had still gotten through and many of them, like her, had come within milliseconds of losing their lives.

They were scared.

"Ao Yin pilots," she said gently, "history will remember you this day. On this day, without provocation, our Main Enemy attacked Chinese territory for the first time in our history. This squadron drew first blood and kept a clean sheet. You have already made me proud. Now we will make our nation proud too."

Eugenio Maat was not plain and simple scared. He was scared out of his *wits*. As he and Diwa cowered at the back of their hideout, they'd fumbled about trying to untie each other, but their hands were tied behind their backs and their legs were bound at the ankles. Eugenio had tried moving, but he couldn't even *stand*. They'd wound their legs together for moral support.

"They're going to kill us," Diwa said whimpering.

"They would have already," Eugenio said.

Then the ground had shaken again, and dirt fell from cracks in the bunker roof. More missiles? Eugenio could only think of his Ma, alone in their house since everything started. She would be going crazy with worry.

If she was still alive.

The thought got him squirming around again, trying to loosen the ropes around his wrists and ankles. The squirming got him a couple of feet across the floor.

"What are you *doing*?" Diwa asked.

"I dunno. Shut up," Eugenio told her, on the verge of tears. But he had managed to get his butt a couple of feet away from Diwa, so maybe…

Ten minutes of concerted wriggling got him out in the corridor that led to the front of the bunker. Diwa was trying to copy him.

"I can't do like you," she told him. "I'm not moving anywhere."

"That's OK. I'm going to try to get to our larder. There's a knife there. I can…"

Before he finished the sentence, the groundsheet was swept aside and the Chinese soldier with the radio tumbled through and fell on the ground. When he saw Eugenio he pulled a pistol out of a harness on his thigh and pointed it at the boy, panting with exertion, squinting in the darkness.

He put the pistol down again. "Boy, I nearly kill you," he said in English.

Then he rolled onto his back and lay still.

"Ao Yin leader, Mischief control. Twenty J-10 fighters from Mischief base on station in sector alpha thirteen. Move to high cover, Ao Yin leader."

Li Chen saw the Chinese fighters on her radar, just as she was sure any incoming enemy fifth-generation aircraft would be able to see them too. She shook her head at the bravery of the men in those J-10 cockpits. They were not fools. They had been briefed on the first American attack on Subi. They knew they would be going up against American stealth aircraft, with about as much chance of surviving as a larva against a wasp.

And she was being ordered to stay behind them and attack only after the sacrificial J-10 pilots had given their lives to lift the veil of invisibility from the attacking American drones.

Li Chen felt sick to the stomach. Did it have to be this way? It was typical Chinese military doctrine, treating human lives as just another resource to be spent … like bullets or missiles.

But what if…

On a whim, she engaged her *Zhi Sheng* AI in 'decision assistant' mode. This brought its analytical power to bear, without giving it control of any of her aircraft systems. Instead, it simply analyzed the available data and presented her with prioritized battlefield options.

And it did so, literally, at the speed of light – pouring data up to a satellite above, down to a ground-based AI cloud system for analysis, and then back again.

She scanned the options it presented. There *was* a strategy that would give them a greater chance of destroying the incoming American aircraft and their missiles, and cost them fewer Chinese aircraft. But of course, it was one that was not in their rigid PLAN battle doctrines.

She keyed her mike, limiting her transmission to her own aircraft. "Ao Yin Squadron, close on me. Cruise formation. We are moving to sector alpha fifteen, altitude forty."

She expected a query, and it came less than a second later. "Uh, Ao Yin leader, that sector is *ahead* of the patrolling J-10s."

"Ah, well spotted, Li," she told the pilot.

He hesitated, but could not help himself. "But then the enemy will detect *us* first."

She smiled. "Good point. Shall we try and leave a few of them alive for the J-10 pilots to clean up?"

White House Situation Room, January 9

"Losses?" Secretary of Defense Kahn was asking Chairman of the Joint Chiefs of Staff, General James Cavoli. They were just getting a readout on the first-wave attack on the Chinese base at Subi Reef. Lewis was on the edge of her seat. A lot of the discussion in the room had centered around the belief that if they could deliver a decisive blow to China in the first 24 hours, it might persuade them that Pagasa was not worth the price.

"Two machines lost to technical issues, ten in combat," Cavoli said.

"Kills reported?"

Cavoli looked uncomfortable. "None in the air. Some ground kills; we laid some heavy damage on the Chinese base."

"We're batting ten for *zero*?" Kahn asked. "I thought China only had a handful of gen-three fighters on those damn reefs? How did we lose ten stealth airframes and claim none?"

"China has moved advanced fighters into the area, as we anticipated. Just earlier than we expected. Electronic intel indicates they are J-16s," Cavoli said.

"Still kites from the last century," Kahn insisted.

Lewis knew that wasn't entirely true. She'd read reports on China trialing AI upgrades on its old two-seater J-16s and she was willing to bet those were the birds the American drones had locked horns with. But Cavoli's intelligence team had read the same intel as her; they'd realize soon enough what they were up against so she didn't contradict him. In any case, they had known it would be a matter of hours, not days, before China reacted to the US ultimatum by sending its front-line hardware and best pilots into the theatre.

The American strategy depended on it.

"Dammit, we need to kill Chinese aircraft." Fenner's Chief of Staff, Chuck Abdor, said aloud what they were all thinking. "As fast as we knock each other's machines down, we can both keep pouring them in… but *our* advantage is that every time we lose an aircraft we only lose a machine, while the other guy is losing precious pilots with five to ten years' training, which they cannot afford."

Fenner looked up from reading a summary of the first hour of the operation. "We think they have a critical shortage of pilots, right?"

Lewis nodded. "Yes, sir. They can't train them fast enough to man their two new carriers, let alone the new squadrons they are raising in their central command opposite Taiwan. We estimate PLA Air Force and Navy Aviation are already at least 500 pilots short for their 3,000 aircraft. With their strategic ambition level, they can't afford significant attrition."

Fenner threw his papers down on the table in front of him. "General Cavoli, Secretary Kahn, I hope you have a plan for turning our kill–loss ratio around. Because zero kills in an hour of air combat is not going to scare anyone in Beijing."

Bunny O'Hare was dead.

She must be dead, right? Everything was white. That's what happened when you died. She'd seen the film *and* read the book it was based on. There was always a soft, blurry white light, like the one she could see, and you were supposed to go towards it. *No, wait.* You weren't supposed to go towards it. That way was the afterlife. If you wanted to stay alive, you were supposed to go *away* from it.

But she wasn't going anywhere. The light was just staying there, fuzzy, white, and neither close nor far. She blinked. Drew a breath.

And howled at the pain in her back.

Wait, if she was breathing, if she felt pain, didn't that mean she was alive?!

Without thinking, she lifted her arm and could see the outline of her hand against the white of the ceiling. It slowly swam into focus. Rolling her head sent a shot of blinding, nauseating pain down her spine, but she saw she was lying on the deck.

Phone. She needed to call for help. The ship had an internal wifi system. If she could just…

Her phone was in the Vapor. She'd finally worked out how to get her music app to work with the aircraft's sound system on the flight down and she'd left it plugged into the Vapor's instrument panel because … hey … who was she going to call out here in the middle of the South China Sea?

OK, O'Hare, you just going to lie here bleeding to death, or are you going to do something about it?

Yes. No. I am just going to lie here and die, she told the voice in her head. That seems like a perfectly good option, thank you.

Her head and neck were locked up, and she turned her eyes to look to the side. There was a big junction box on a wall, a panel with blinking lights and a large sign saying, "AUX POWER 32C. DO NOT POWER DOWN."

Alright, I won't do that, Bunny decided and laughed at herself. Underneath the panel, down on the deck up against the wall, was a bowling ball.

Well, isn't that weird? And ironic. My favorite sport, and no one in here to go bowling with. She chuckled, and then coughed in pain again. Her head throbbed like she'd been on an all-night tequila binge and her upper back felt like she'd been punched right between her shoulder blades. No. Not punched. *Speared.*

Then she remembered. That little bastard Lawrence had clubbed her, then shot her.

Not for the first time in her life, was O'Hare grateful for the flight jacket she'd inherited after testing it for DARPA. Insulated against heat and cold, it also had a carbon nanotube mesh sown into the lining to provide a measure of protection against projectile injury.

It had stopped Lawrence's bullet, but she still felt like someone had slammed her in the back with a sledgehammer.

If she got out of here, she was going to shoot *him*, then take that bowling ball and shove it so far up his…

Wait. Not a bowling ball. *Her flight helmet!*

Alright, O'Hare. Roll onto your stomach, try to get up on your knees. Attagirl. But just lifting her head nearly made her black out with pain. She lay it down again. Maybe she could roll over and crawl?

The rolling over went alright. The crawling went … not so well. Her legs didn't want to work. Had he damaged her damn spine?

No. It's just shock, O'Hare. Or muscle spasm. Worry about it later.

Reaching an arm out in front of her, fingers spread to give herself a hold on the painted steel deck, she pulled herself toward her helmet. Five inches. Then the other arm. Another five. She stopped, lay her head down on the deck and contemplated sleeping then, but anger kept her from closing her eyes.

Five inches. Attagirl. Five more.

Get that helmet. Sync with the Vapor out on the helipad. Get on the Vapor's radio and call the bridge.

Then get them to throw Lawrence Winter overboard, so she could use him for target practice.

Li Chen had spread her squadron out along a fifty-mile front, right in front of the orbiting J-10 Firebirds. With luck, her pilots and their *Zhi Sheng* AI backseaters would pick up the enemy aircraft or cruise missiles or at least attract their fire, so that the Firebirds would not get slaughtered. Once they located the bulk of the enemy force, she could vector the J-10s to them and they'd have a chance of getting their missiles away. Though they were more than two generations older than her J-16, they carried the same active radar seeker homing missiles. She just had to buy them enough time to get their missiles off, and with luck, the frigates below would also bring some firepower to play so that Subi Reef could dodge the incoming American bullet.

Suddenly, the sky ahead of her lit up with energy and her radar warning receiver started screaming.

The X-47B Fantom pilots coming at her were not all interested in Subi Reef, or the Chinese troops on Pagasa. All of them were armed with air-to-air missiles only, and their mission was to enter the Operations Area, destroy any enemy aircraft therein, and when weapons dry, return to Clark Base.

They were pulling targeting data from a Hawkeye Airborne Warning Aircraft patrolling over Luzon and could see every single one of the Chinese fighter aircraft that had been scrambled to defend Subi Reef.

In their weapons bays, each Fantom had six Peregrine missiles. As one, the pilots flying them lit their targeting radars and began locking up targets.

Bunny reached the wall, rolled onto her back and tried lifting the Vapor's flight helmet, but her hands were wet with sweat and she couldn't. She dried them on her thighs, then tried again. Better. Lifting her head painfully off the floor, she pulled the helmet on and powered it up with the stud at the side. It connected to *Andromeda*'s wifi network and the welcome menu pulsed in front of her eyes.

Scanning iris, please do not blink > Welcome pilot O'Hare > Building cockpit environment.

Even though she was lying on her back in an auxiliary generator room in the bowels of the White Star support vessel, within a minute the helmet built the cockpit of the Vapor around her and it was like she was once again sitting in the pilot seat.

About to die from head trauma in the real world, probably, yes. But for all intents and purposes, in the Vapor's cockpit.

Her arms felt heavy and her hands clumsy. She didn't have

her VR gloves with her, so she couldn't manipulate any of the unmanned aircraft's virtual instruments or controls using her hands.

But she had her voice. "Vapor, initiate engine start, prepare for emergency takeoff."

Emergency takeoff routine initiated. Refueling port emergency stop. Detaching rotor tie-downs. Engines spooling. Rotating. She wanted to get their attention up on the deck.

She saw one of the Norwegian's mechanics dive for the deck as the Vapor's rotors started to turn above his head. OK, mission accomplished. "Vapor, power up avionics, priority to comms system."

Powering up avionics, comms system ... online.

"O'Hare?" a French voice immediately said in her ears.

"Mademoiselle?" OK, she hadn't expected that.

"Yes. I heard you got your aircraft back to the ship. I suppose congratulations are in order. Are you taking it up again?" Sophie Leclerc sounded like she was in a car, driving somewhere. She was. "Wait, I will get my driver to pull over."

She was being put on *hold*? That would be kind of funny. If it wasn't literally life or death serious.

"Sylvie, just listen. A crewman called Winter from this all-balls crew shot me. I'm down in the..."

"*Merde*! I knew it!"

"Look, I'm ... you *what*?" O'Hare shook her head. Had she misheard?

"He was a late addition to the crew. I was in the process of running a background check. It takes time. He *shot* you?"

"Yes. I'm down in a generator room, I think. One deck down. I can see a number and a label ... Auxiliary Generator 32C. I was going to use the Vapor's comms to call the bridge and get them to send help."

"Of course," There was a pause. "No! He is a radio operator. If you send a message, it might alert Winter that you are still alive. He could get to you before help does. I will call Captain Pedersen directly."

Wait, what? Her mind raced. "OK, but get me medical help. Now. And warn them about him. Winter."

"Yes. Tout de suite. Do not die on me, Bunny O'Hare."

"Can't promise that; O'Hare out." She powered down the helmet and took it off, then fixed her blurred gaze on the access door into the generator room. There was nothing more she could do. Her fate was now entirely in the hands of a woman in a car in Singapore.

Sylvie Leclerc was acutely aware O'Hare's fate was in her hands. She should have worked faster. She had asked White Star Risk Group to run a background check on Lawrence Winter and accepted their standard timeline … three days. She'd also sent Winter's details to a friend from her French Intelligence days who worked in Interpol, and asked him to run a criminal background check. He'd obliged her over the telephone and the Interpol check had come back clean, so she had relaxed. A little. She'd also copied his details to the US Office of Naval Intelligence, which had also warned her a check of US intelligence databases would take a couple of days.

You fool, Leclerc! The man appears out of nowhere after one of the Andromeda's crew has an unfortunate 'accident' and he is a perfect clean-skin with not a blemish on his record?! She literally slapped herself, the sting of her palm on her thigh not helping her mood at all. *It should have set off every possible alarm in your thick head and instead, what have you been doing? Reviewing reports on the aerial drone capabilities of South China Sea militia groups.*

Her driver heard the slap of her palm on her thigh and looked at her in the mirror. She'd been on her way home from the Risk Group offices when the alert on her phone had been triggered by the Vapor powering up. "You alright, madam?" he asked with a worried frown.

"No, take me back to the office," she said.

She had *Andromeda*'s Captain, Pedersen, on speed dial and as she waited for the satellite link to connect, she started counting the ways in which this situation was bad.

China had managed to put an assassin aboard the *Andromeda*, on her watch. He had made an attempt on the life of *Andromeda*'s pilot, which was a straightforward way to put its aircraft out of action. Easier than sabotaging an aircraft, which could be repaired, whereas a combat pilot with a similar background to O'Hare's would not be easy to locate. Almost impossible, as Leclerc had learned during the search that had led her to O'Hare as a candidate. A US Navy or Marine pilot would have been ideal but Sorensen had already vigorously rejected that option. He was comfortable enough doing the US Department of Defense bidding. His largesse did not extend to allowing its personnel inside his operation or aboard his ships.

No, the easy and most effective way to take out the Vapor as a threat for the duration of the voyage was to kill the pilot and dump her body overboard when no one was looking.

Which, by the sound of it, he might succeed in doing, if O'Hare didn't make it through.

Not only that, China's security agents had gotten their man into the heart of the convoy's operations, in its communications center, where he could report on the convoy's every move.

"Pedersen."

Leclerc spoke quickly, knowing every minute could be vital.

O'Hare's muddled mind was running through her options in case her attacker decided to come back and check on his handiwork before help arrived, which tragically did not take long.

She looked at the wheel that operated the door lock. There was no latch or button on her side. So either it couldn't be locked or, more likely, it couldn't be locked from the inside and Winter had locked it from the outside.

She couldn't stop him from getting in.

She could pull on the helmet, try to contact the bridge, or

send out a mayday on Guard, but as Leclerc had pointed out, Winter would hear it and he'd be running forward again to finish his handiwork well before anyone else could react.

She could throw her helmet at him as he came in. Actually, that *was* an option. It weighed near 20 lbs., and she was feeling a little bit stronger now. Not strong enough to crash tackle him. Not strong enough to even stand, assuming her legs would cooperate at some point. But throw a helmet? She lifted the helmet and felt the weight, then had to put it down again, nearly throwing up with the effort. Alright, not an option after all.

Who was she kidding? There was simply no way to protect herself from…

Wait. She had an idea. But it was a long shot.

Literally.

Sylvie Leclerc had been right that Winter was listening in to radio comms and would have heard O'Hare's cry for help if she had tried to contact the bridge directly.

But what she had not counted on was that courtesy of software supplied by the Chinese Ministry of State Security, he was able to activate any one of the several microphones on the *Andromeda*'s bridge and eavesdrop on the officers' conversations.

As he listened to the woman from White Star Risk Group briefing *Andromeda*'s Captain, he realized two things. He had to get off the ship. He had a plan for that. But first, he had to finish the task he'd been given or he wouldn't live long enough to collect his promised fee. Which meant he had to take out that damned pilot.

Winter put down his headset while the woman from White Star was still talking, and quickly checked the magazine in his 9mm S&W Shield pistol. Still six rounds.

Bloody woman. Blow to the head and a bullet in the heart weren't enough to kill her? Well, he'd *aimed* for the heart. But hey, he'd been in a hurry to get back to his station before anyone noticed he was gone. Her damn hide must have been thicker than he expected.

He wouldn't make the same mistake twice. His next shot would be to the head.

He tucked the pistol into his waist in the small of his back and pulled his shirt over it. His comms alert buzzed. It was the bridge.

"Winter, this is the Chief Mate, is Mr. McIntyre with you?"

Bose. He would have been in on the call from White Star Security. "No sir, he said he wanted a moment of quiet before the contact with the militia, Mr. Bose."

"Very good, very good. We have an issue on the bridge, can you please come up here immediately?"

"Yes, sir."

An issue on the bridge? Sure you do, Winter smiled to himself. *Alright, Larry, order of events. Kill that bloody pilot. Head aft, get into the survival gear you stashed there and drop off the stern. Trigger your GPS emergency beacon and wait for a militia boat to pick you up.*

Easy bloody peasy.

He started for the door at a run.

Bunny had levered herself up against the wall. But in the virtual world wrapped around her throbbing head, she was aboard the Vapor and powering off the helipad.

"Vapor, take up station a hundred feet up and a hundred feet out from the portside beam of the *Andromeda*. Orient on gun reticle."

Roger, moving to hold station with Andromeda. Orienting on targeting reticle.

Slowly, too slowly, the Vapor moved into position, hovering off *Andromeda*'s center section, portside, with its nose and guns pointing back at the ship.

She looked gingerly around the aircraft. Clear skies. Her instruments showed the fuel leaks had been patched, but she had interrupted the fuel line repairs and refueling. She had ammunition. But she only had the fuel they'd managed to pump into the undamaged port wing tank. Enough for an hour of normal flight.

She only needed enough for the next ten minutes.

"Vapor, arm guns."

20mm guns armed.

A chime inside her helmet showed she had two incoming comms messages. One from the bridge of the *Andromeda*, the other from Leclerc, who had no doubt just seen that she'd powered up the Vapor. Or just wanted to check she was still breathing. She dismissed both callers.

Winter barreled down the stairs from the comms room to the exit to the main deck.

And listened.

Rotor blades. He could definitely hear the thump of rotor blades. That bloody gunship was lurking out there somewhere.

He stuck his head quickly out the door and saw it, hovering drunkenly off the port beam, about a hundred yards out, a hundred feet up.

Its gun ports were open.

So that's your game, bitch? Well, good luck w'that. Two-time winner of the Porthcawl Sprint, me.

He'd chosen the aft auxiliary generator housing because it was only accessible from the main deck, and the generator room was isolated two decks down among the crane support columns, so no one would hear the shots. It was only used to power the deck cranes or to provide emergency power if the main generator went offline, so while they were at sea, no one would go down there.

The problem. He had to cross twenty yards of open deck to reach the entrance to the housing. There was no way to reach it from any other deck because apart from the generator housing and crane supports, that area under the aft deck was used for bulk storage only. That's what had made it so damn perfect as a place to kill her and hide her body until he got a chance to dump it.

Not so perfect now.

He felt the hair on his neck rise, though. Just like it did when he had his feet jammed on the starter blocks for the sprint, waiting for the starter pistol. He ran his tongue across his lips.

Alright then, boyo.

Show yourself, Winter, you carrot-top fecker, Bunny muttered to herself. She'd already decided that if she so much as got a glimpse of the murderous red-head out on the open decks of the *Andromeda*, she was going to take him out.

She thought she saw a head poking out of the doorway at the bottom of the superstructure, but held her fire because shooting at her own mothership was bad enough. Killing one of her fellow crew – apart from Winter – might be a little awkward.

Now there was motion on one of the bridge wings, someone out there watching her machine with binos, others staring from inside the bridge. But no Winter. If that was him she'd seen sticking his head out the door, it seemed he wasn't inclined to show more of himself.

She decided to see if she could motivate him – trick him into thinking she was breaking away, perhaps to get a better position, perhaps to go after the militia boats.

"Vapor, rotate 360 degrees starboard, max yaw."

Executing fast rotation. Three sixty degrees.

The aircraft began to rotate on its vertical axis like a spinning top. And like a ballerina fixing her gaze in space during a pirouette, Bunny kept her vision, and her targeting reticle, lined up on the deck in front of the generator housing and the door leading out to it. As the Vapor's nose turned away from the ship, the targeting reticle went red to show she no longer had guns on the target. She was already nauseous and damn glad she wasn't physically up in that cockpit. Gyrating at dizzying speed, what the Vapor was doing could make even an experienced pilot like her puke.

Sure enough, at that moment there was the blur of motion at the door, and a figure that was all shirt tails, ginger hair and boots started sprinting for the housing on the aft deck. There were only two red-heads aboard *Andromeda*, and Bunny was pretty sure Ginger McIntyre wasn't a sprinter.

Winter.

Bunny let the nose of the Vapor come around, and as it slowed to a fast stop the gun reticle turned white, indicating she could lay guns on target once again. She turned her head to keep the gunsight reticle on the deck in front of Lawrence-dead-man-running-Winter and spoke softly into the helmet.

"Vapor, fire guns."

Firing.

Her first rounds hammered into the deck five yards ahead of Winter. He leaped away from them like a startled gazelle but she adjusted her sights, guiding the 20mm high-explosive shells into his path. One struck right in front of him and exploded, sending him backward.

The next struck right underneath him, and shredded him.

"Vapor, cease fire."

Standing at the starboard railing along with half a dozen other men, Ginger was watching events unfold as several things happened at once. He'd been trying to rest on his bunk when he'd heard the Vapor taking off and decided he should probably find out why.

As he emerged on deck he found the machine hovering off their beam and he could see from the clearly empty cockpit it was unmanned. Then suddenly it started spinning right, like it was turning to leave. But it kept turning until it was pointed back at the ship...

And it *opened fire* on them!

On the bridge comms feed in his ear he heard shouts of anger and alarm. Following the lines of tracer, he saw the bright sparks of high-explosive rounds punching into and probably *through* the aft deck plating. He saw a man running for his life as the shells seemed to zero in on him…

And turn him to red mist.

It happened so suddenly that Ginger didn't even have time to feel the bile rise up in his throat before he had his head over the side and was emptying his breakfast into the sea. He wasn't the only one. Wiping his mouth with one sleeve and his eyes with the other, with horror he returned his gaze to the scene.

The Vapor was just hovering there again, matching speed with the ship, its nose still menacingly oriented on the aft deck.

"Ginger, you there?" a voice said in his ear.

He spat on the deck to clear the vomit from his mouth. "O'Hare, is that *you*?"

"Yeah, Ginger, look I need…"

"O'Hare, are you at the controls of that gunship?! You just killed a man!"

"I know. Ginger, look, I need you to send a paramedic."

"Paramedic?! You mean a bucket crew. You bloody liquified him, O'Hare."

"Not for him, for me. I'm in a room…"

"Have you lost your *mind*?"

There was a tired sigh. "Just shut up and listen, Ginger, please. That man was your 2IC, Winter. He tried to kill me." Ginger heard her draw a ragged breath. "Clubbed me and then put a bullet in me, don't ask me how I'm alive, and I might not be for long. I'm in a room with a piece of equipment called, uh, aux generator 32C, you know it?"

"Wait." Ginger pulled out his cell phone and opened an app, trying to keep his shaking hands still enough to type, trying to process what he had just seen. He called up the ship's schematics. "Crane power plant, aft deck, got it."

"Good. Send a paramedic. Tell them to bring some tape to hold my skull together." She coughed, and then moaned. "And jumbo pain killers."

"O'Hare … there's a boggin' helicopter gunship hovering off our beam with its guns still pointing at us."

"Don't worry. It'll land itself if it … if there is no command input for ten minutes. So if it's okay, I'll just be … I'll be passing out now … if that's alright…"

Li Chen was learning that the problem with being a meatware accessory in an AI-controlled aircraft was that your silicon backseater apparently didn't care overly much whether you were conscious or not while it was going about its business.

She had greyed out twice in the past five minutes as they had traded missiles with the incoming swarm of American Fantom drones and her *Zhi Sheng* backseater flung her J-16 around the sky while dodging and dealing death.

The heads-up display in her visor told its own story. They had claimed eight Fantoms in the first flurry of missiles. Her Ao Yin Squadron had lost two pilots, one of whom managed to eject and make it to the sea below, his GPS locator flashing urgently. If he was lucky, a search and rescue helicopter from Mischief Reef might get to him before a shark did. The J-10 fighters she had tried to protect, however, had fared worse. Much, much worse. It had been as though the Fantom pilots had singled out the Firebirds deliberately, avoiding tangling with her J-16s unless necessary, as they detected and engaged the more visible Firebirds from thirty miles out – outside the reach of the Firebirds' own sensors – and swatted them from the sky. Of the twenty fighters Mischief Reef had vectored to them, only six remained in the fight.

Sixteen pilots down!

And what had they claimed in return? Eight lumps of silicon and aluminum.

Another one of the bat-winged hellhounds was coming for her right now! She was out of missiles, and out of altitude. The fight had taken her down to the wavetops as her AI had traded altitude for energy, twisting and turning to avoid American missiles while sniping away whenever it saw a chance. Twice, she had been driven by fear for her own life to contemplate taking control back from her *Zhi Sheng* AI, and twice she had resisted. In both cases, it had been the right choice: the AI had evaded the enemy attack and initiated counter-fire. She wasn't sure she would have been as successful.

As the enemy Fantom closed on her tail, trying to get a firing solution on her with its guns, she left the AI to do its work while she did hers. Eyes darting across the view in her visor, she searched for a free pilot from her own squadron on her tactical map.

There. And he had two missiles remaining! Only a senior *human* pilot could commandeer missiles from another fighter, as relieving them of a weapon could be a life or death choice, but Chen didn't hesitate. Her need, and her opportunity, was greatest right then.

With a blink of her eyes, she selected a missile from his payload and then allocated it to the Fantom weaving around behind her. She drew a target box around it and got a lock tone from her wingman's targeting radar.

Launch!

From fifteen miles away, the Chinese missile dropped and then accelerated toward her attacker. The pilot of the drone reacted immediately, breaking off his attack and spiraling into the sky to try to gain altitude with which to evade the incoming missile. Her own backseater seized the opportunity, hauling her J-16 around in yet another high-g turn that sent her to the edge of unconsciousness. Afterburner flame poured from her tail as she clawed into the sky behind the fleeing Fantom, trying to get into guns range as the Chinese missile closed on the American fighter.

Desperately spewing chaff and flare countermeasures, the Fantom rolled onto its back at the last second and accelerated vertically toward the earth, tricking the Chinese missile into overshooting – but sending it right into the gunsights of Li

Chen's rising J-16. With a sound like tearing cloth, her cannon sent a stream of 30mm shells right into the path of the Fantom and blasted it into a shower of metal and flame that continued past her, straight into the sea below.

Kill!

Her machine pulled itself wings level and started to climb for altitude.

A kill, yes, but was it really a kill, if all you were killing was a robot?

"I could have killed you!" Ruan was explaining to the boy who had been crouched at the entrance to the bunker. He had spent fifteen long minutes getting his breath, and his courage, back. What he desperately felt like doing was taking a long nap. But that could wait.

"I know! You already said that," the boy replied, hanging his head. "Like about five times."

Before heading out to call in the artillery barrage, carrying the heavy radio and his carbine, Ruan had stripped himself of everything not absolutely essential to the mission. Like reloads for the carbine and his water canteen, but not his pistol. Moving through the near darkness as he talked to the boy and waited for any other survivors from his team to return, he took stock. He had about ten loaded assault rifle magazines, but no rifle, a half dozen enhanced tactical multipurpose (ETMP) grenades, two smoke grenades and … his radio. Someone had left their beret behind, and Ruan had lost his, so he jammed it on his head. A bit small. It must have been Zhang's. That guy had a small head.

"Dead, with this," Ruan continued, holding out his suppressed Glock 17 pistol.

"I get it already," Eugenio said. "Thank you for not shooting me, okay?"

"Did anyone else come past here?" Ruan asked him.

"No." The boy wiped an arm across his nose. He looked

scared and lost. Kids weren't something Ruan had a lot of experience with. He had a six-year-old nephew in Foshan, but had hardly spent any time with him because, to be honest, Ruan found kids boring. Maybe when his nephew grew up he could take the kid fishing or something, but right now he was pretty useless. Like this little guy. He reached behind himself to a shelf and pulled a can off it. "Here, have a pineapple ring."

The kid looked at him like he was crazy, and Ruan frowned, then realized the little guy was still tied up. "Oh, right." Pulling a knife out of his boot, Ruan cut the cord that bound the kid's wrists and ankles. He put the knife back in his boot, watching as the kid massaged his wrists. "Don't think about running. You run, I kill your girlfriend. You shout out, I kill her. You try to untie her or do anything else dumb, I..."

"Kill her," Eugenio finished. "I get it."

"Good." Ruan shoved the can of pineapple rings at him. "Here, eat. Give your girlfriend some too."

Ruan walked quietly to the front of the bunker, looking out of the firing slits on the right and left of the door. The air was clear and the morning light was starting to filter through the trees. He gave it a good five minutes.

No movement.

The artillery barrage had come down on the other side of the hill, so the Filipinos were probably concentrated there, treating wounded and recovering their dead. Gently lifting the groundsheet in front of the bunker entrance aside, he stepped out on the balls of his feet and crouched low, making a half-circle to the right, uphill, so he could see the ground downhill from the bunker. Nothing. Going back inside, he walked past the boy, who looked like he was going to say something, but he put a finger on his lips and went past him to the ladder at the rear leading up to the surface. Several of the bolts holding it to the wall had rusted away, and it felt like it would come away or just drop off the wall at any moment, but it had held while Gao and Zhang had dug away the soil and old branches filling the upper exit earlier, and it held now.

He had a thought, and stuck a few twigs and branches through the cloth of the beret, but when he looked at it, he realized it didn't look so much like camouflage as deer antlers, so he rearranged it. Better.

The exit emerged inside a low bush, the iron trapdoor at the top having been destroyed by the two commandos pushing through its rusted paper-thin remains to clear the dirt and foliage covering it. He held his pistol by his cheek, working the slide gently and quietly to load it, clinging to the ladder with one hand and raising his eyes up to ground level. Turning his head slowly, he scanned the ground downhill to the north, then pivoted to look east and...

Froze.

Twenty yards away, a Filipino patrol was moving west to east across the hillside. They hadn't seen him, but if he moved again, even ducked back down into the vertical shaft, they couldn't possibly miss him again. They were spread out in a line, rifles ready, moving slowly like police looking for forensic evidence. Searching for him? Of course they were searching for him. Generally, not specifically. Someone had opened fire on them. Someone had called down that naval bombardment. Ironically, the tiny size of the island was proving to be his savior. A line of troops moving along the hillside through the sparse vegetation could see both up and down the slope, moving from the north coast to the south in a single 30-minute sweep. They were easily lulled into thinking they'd cleared the bunker side of the island, and from up the slope, there was no chance they would see the bunker entrance. Or the shaft he was standing in. They'd have to virtually walk right over it...

Like the guy at the end of the line was about to do.

He was wearing the mottled green uniform and baseball-style cap of a Filipino Seabee. It rankled with Ruan that they had been outplayed by a bunch of armed construction workers. But construction worker or not, he was making straight for the bunker exit, picking his way around shrubs and trees, scanning left and right nervously. Every time his head swung toward the bunker exit, Ruan held his breath.

Ten yards ... scan ... nine yards ... scan ...

Now the soldier was approaching the shrub covering the shaft. In front of it, between Ruan and the soldier, was a small bush. There was another on his left, nothing on his right. If he went left, around the bushes, he'd probably miss the shaft. But if he went right, then looked down and to his left ... Ruan would have to shoot him. The others in the line might not hear the suppressed shot, but they'd be sure to see the guy drop and Ruan would probably have a grenade following him down the shaft as he dropped back down the ladder.

Go left, he silently urged the man. *Downhill. It's easier. You're lazy. And that artillery ruined your breakfast. No, no, no, don't look down. Keep your eyes up! There could be a Jiaolong Commando behind every tree trunk, every rock. Go left, damn you!*

The man paused, and it felt like he looked directly at Ruan. Then he stepped to his left and moved past.

Ruan didn't turn his head to follow, he kept his eyes fixed straight ahead, listening to the sound of the soldier's footfall until he couldn't hear him any longer. With painful slowness, he went down two rungs, then turned, back against the ladder, and raised his head carefully again. The line of troops was moving away to the east. Resting his suppressor on the lip of the concrete-lined shaft, he sighted on the man nearest him, and kept his pistol on him until the squad had moved well away.

Alright.

Facing the ladder again he went down, not entirely sure that the ladder was shaking just because it was no longer secure. At the bottom, he put the pistol in its harness on his thigh and went back in to the boy.

The boy looked startled as Ruan walked in on him. The tin he'd given him was on the ground beside him, unopened. The girl was looking at him, wide-eyed.

Ruan squatted beside them. "You don't like pineapples?"

"I'm not hungry."

"Please," the girl said. "Our parents will be mad. Let us go."

"Eventually," Ruan said. He noticed the boy looking at the floor between his legs. "What?"

He pointed at the floor. "You're bleeding."

Ruan looked down. The problem with a black uniform, you couldn't see blood on it.

But there was blood dripping on the floor from the cuff of his trousers. He reached down and felt them. The inside of his left leg was wet, soaked in blood. Now he understood why he'd felt like taking a nap.

OK. Not good.

Bunny O'Hare was having a wonderful nap. Best damn nap *ever*. And dreaming a dream that was totally not suitable for minors. Then, suddenly, she was in a cold pool of water. Drowning. Something was holding her under, she couldn't *breathe...*

"Easy, tiger," a voice said. "I'm fitting a neck brace..."

Someone was holding her hands down by her side. She looked up and saw a beefy medico in blue overalls sitting astride her. With a knee in his backside and a twist of her hips, she forced him to lose his balance and topple to one side. *Alright, legs working again, that was good.*

"Hey, O'Hare, take it easy!" She heard Ginger's voice. He was kneeling on the floor beside her, getting ready to help roll her onto a stretcher. "The guy you just bronco bucked is the ship's surgeon."

Standing beside Ginger was the *Andromeda*'s Chief Mate, Kapil Bose. He was leaning against the wall with his arms crossed, saying nothing. She still felt woozy, but not as bad as before she passed out. "Sorry. How bad am I doc?"

The doctor was getting to one knee. "You're welcome. And not as bad as you probably feel. Blunt force trauma to the head, but no serious fracture as far as I can tell. The bullet didn't penetrate your body armor, but it may have broken a rib. Judging by your judo moves, we don't need the neck brace, but you should get an x-ray."

She didn't feel lucky. She felt like someone was still digging around inside her back with a hot poker.

"Any chance of some morphine?" she asked.

"No."

"Codeine?"

"No." He didn't look at all sympathetic.

With some difficulty she got up on one elbow. "Look, I'm sorry I shot up your ship. And your crew mate. But the situation…"

"Ms. O'Hare, the situation is, that you are under arrest," Bose told her, levering himself off the wall. "I don't know exactly what the crime is, but I'm pretty sure that using a helicopter gunship to fire on a civilian merchant vessel and kill one of its crewmen is against about a hundred laws."

"And if I hadn't, your crewman would have finished me."

"You say." Bose didn't look sympathetic either. He held up a small plastic bag with a flattened lead slug in it. "And we did find this embedded in your jacket. Unfortunately the man you killed can't give us his side of this story. But you can tell it all to the master at arms aboard the *USS Congress* after we rendezvous."

Ginger shot her a sympathetic look. "*Andromeda* is US-flagged. You commit murder aboard a ship in international waters, it gets investigated by the country the vessel is flagged in."

"That's BS," Bunny said, struggling to a sitting position. "I fly a defensive patrol for White Star, send a militia needle-boat to the bottom, that's not a crime?"

"No. That was proportionate use of force in self-defense," Bose said.

"I rest my case, your honor," Bunny said.

The doctor was picking up after himself and turned to Bose. "We won't need the stretcher. If she's going to be locked in her quarters, someone should check on her every 30 minutes for at least the next couple hours."

"Can she fly?"

"She has concussion, maybe a cracked rib. I wouldn't let her ride a bicycle, let alone fly an airplane. But it's her call, and yours…"

Bose nodded. "We have a swarm of militia boats twenty minutes out." With a nod of his head, he indicated to the doctor that he should help O'Hare to her feet. "Take Ms. O'Hare to her quarters to freshen up, then escort her to the bridge."

"*Freshen up*?" Bunny asked.

"If there is a chance you can still fly, we can't afford to have that aircraft sitting idle on our helipad, Ms. O'Hare. Our radar is not good enough to tell us how many boats we are facing, but according to White Star satellite intel from earlier today, there are at least five."

Bunny was lifted to her feet. Alright, she could stand. Maybe she could also walk. In which case, yeah, she could probably manage a remote flight in the Vapor, with AI help.

"How long was I out?"

The doctor looked at his watch. "About twenty minutes."

"Your aircraft landed itself. It has been repaired, refueled and rearmed. We don't have a lot of time," Bose said.

Yeah, maybe, but no. "I just got shot by one of your crewmen. I stopped him from finishing the job, no thanks to anyone else on this ship. Now you tell me I'm being put under arrest. But hey, could you please save our asses first, *before* we lock you away?!"

Bose was unfazed by the sarcasm dripping from her voice. "Yes, you have a good grip of your situation."

Bunny held out her middle finger. "Grip this." She staggered as *Andromeda* swayed on a wave. Her stomach lurched.

"You have thirty minutes to decide Ms. O'Hare. Are you mission capable, or should we just confine you to quarters?"

The doctor handed her a bandage and some tape. "If you plan to go up again, strap those ribs, tight. I'll check you again later. If you have trouble breathing, you'll be grounded. If you have nausea or dizziness, you'll be grounded."

Ginger stepped forward, taking her arm to steady her. "If it's alright, sir, I'll go with her, get her sorted."

"We need you on comms, McIntyre," Bose said. "Ms. O'Hare deleted your number two from the ship's complement."

Ginger winced at that, but tapped his ear to indicate he was wearing his earbud. "Comms goes wherever I do, sir. I'll manage."

Bose waved a weary hand at Ginger, who led Bunny out into the stairwell. They started up the stairs, one at a time, leaving Bose and the doctor to clean up and pack up the doctor's gear. Ginger was carrying her helmet in one hand, holding the stair rail in the other.

"Winter, eh? I'd never have picked that kid for a killer."

"Yeah, well, I guess that's what made him perfect for it."

They emerged onto the deck. A gang of four crewmen was mopping the deck between the generator housing and the main superstructure.

For the first time Bunny looked down and saw her t-shirt was bloodied. The cleanup crew stopped working as Bunny and Ginger appeared, and leaned on their mops with looks that ranged from contempt, through disdain, all the way to disgust. Not a lot of sympathy to be had there.

She hobbled past them, Ginger standing protectively between her and the *Andromeda* crewmen.

"Don't suppose any of you have any codeine?" she asked as she passed them. They gave her sullen, unresponsive glares. "No. I'll just ask the Captain then."

"Don't make it worse," Ginger told her.

"Guy only just signed on a couple of days ago, don't tell me he was that popular."

"No. Most wouldn't have met him. But they've all probably seen the video feed of you painting the deck with his insides. And they're the ones have to clean it up."

"Alright, alright."

They reached the crew level about five minutes later and Ginger led her into her cabin. As she collapsed on her bed next to her flight helmet, dumping the bandage and tape on the bed beside her, he pulled out a change of clothes, her VR gloves and boots.

"No time to shower," he told her. "But you cut your face when you fell on it, so it's a wee bit bloody. You probably want to wash?"

"No, I want the Captain to see me bloody," Bunny told him, stripping off her jacket, t-shirt and bra and reaching for the gauze and tape. "Should there be any doubt." Her back and the left side of her chest under her arm were already turning an ugly blue and yellow.

Ginger turned away, taking a sudden interest in the bullet hole in the jacket and the carbon nanotube mesh in the lining.

"Who sews *body armor* into an ordinary flight jacket?" he asked.

"Someone with a more than fair chance of being shot at some point in her future," she told him. She stood and breathed out, then started winding the bandage tightly around her chest before coughing experimentally, and wincing. Not good, but it felt more like bruising than a broken rib. "Can you tape it in place, in the back?" She held her hand up in front of her eyes. Vision was clear too now. Mostly.

She felt him pull the bandage tight and then rip off some tape, before gently taping the end of the bandage in place.

"What was it that turned you off mankind, Ginger McIntyre?" she asked, looking over her shoulder at him.

"Hold still, you're just making it harder." He put a hand on her back to steady her. "You're standing here with a cracked skull and a bullet hole in your jacket, and you're asking me that?" he asked.

She thought about that. "I'm a combat pilot. People try to kill me all the time, I don't take it personally."

"You should," he said. "If you weren't such a bampot fewer people might want to kill you."

213

"Touché. What I mean is, that Winter kid was just doing his job. He must have lived some kind of messed-up life to have found himself aboard the *Andromeda* pointing a gun at me."

Ginger checked the bandage was secured. "Your sympathy for the weasel feels kind of insincere, given you turned him into a red smear on the foredeck." He tore some more surgical tape off a roll with his teeth. "Will you not stand *still?*"

She crossed her arms over her chest and tried not to move, which was not in her nature. "I noticed you didn't answer my question, by the way. I'm guessing abusive father. Am I right?"

He paused. "Nae. That's you projecting, *I'm* guessing."

"Still didn't answer."

She saw him shake his head and smile. "These tattoos all over your back, it looks like each one marks a battle of one type or other. The evil Man does to his fellow Man is scarred into your skin with ink, so maybe you should just look in a mirror for your answer."

"Nope, and even if it were true, that's my answer, not yours."

He let out a big sigh. "*Alright*. If you must know, I served on submarines that had the power to destroy the planet, and realized I was surrounded by men who were actually willing to do it. If I had any faith in humanity going into the Navy, a few years of service on ballistic missile boats killed it dead."

"You were definitely overthinking it, Angus," she told him. "Try to worry less. Someone once told me superficiality is my superpower."

He finished taping her up and patted her shoulder gently. "That should hold you until the next time you annoy someone."

As she turned around to pull a new shirt over her head, he blushed and turned away again.

"You know, you are being positively *gentlemanly*." She decided to save herself some time and Ginger some discomfort and leave her jeans on. "I think there might be a humanitarian hiding deep inside you after all."

He opened the cabin door and turned back to her. "Don't get your hopes up. Self-interest temporarily trumps my overweening dislike of humanity," he smiled. "Because if you don't get that gunship airborne, I might end up held for ransom by pirates." He held the door open and extended a hand to her. "And then who would look after me cats?"

Abdul Ibrahim thought of himself neither as pirate, nor as militia-for-hire. If he were asked, he'd compare himself to the Chieftain of a seafaring tribe. He had more than a hundred men under his command – ex-naval ratings, hackers, mechanics, former soldiers, fishermen and more. Lifted out of poverty, living in hope for the first time in their lives. At least half had families living in his compound behind the naval base, in a village on Batu Bay. More than a hundred fifty grandparents, wives and children, whose welfare he was responsible for.

He paid his men subsistence wages when they weren't at sea, but they got a fair share of the bounty when they completed a job. If they were injured, he paid their medical bills. If they were killed, the dead man's share from the job went to his family and Ibrahim paid for them to quit Brunei and return to wherever they came from. He didn't encourage them to stay. A widowed woman with children had to find some way to earn money to feed her kids, and he wouldn't stand for moral corruption among his crew.

Seafaring tribe. Yes. He felt there was no better way to describe it, as he stood in the stern of one of the American fast boats, watching the rib boats they had just launched fanning out ahead of him. Five rib boats, with five men in each, led by his second in command, Kamito. Five more in each of the Mark V motherships, with himself commanding the hard shell boats with their Gatling guns.

Ibrahim had learned in the navy, the more people involved in an operation, the simpler you have to keep the plan. The simplicity of the plan for this operation was helped by the fact he had negotiated a fat upfront fee for this job and didn't need to hijack either of the White Star Ships, just *sink* one of them.

He reached for the radio handset and flipped the radio on. "Kamito, come in." All ten boats were sailing in a loose group, about twenty yards apart. Lim hadn't lied. These Mark Vs were just as fast as a rib boat.

Kamito's voice came over the radio. "Yeah, boss?"

"Fifteen miles. Get ready for the split."

"No worries, boss. Out." Both Kamito's and Ibrahim's boats had X-band Marine recreational radars raised on a t-bar at their rear. With these, they could easily track the big ships ahead of them from twenty miles away. To power the radar, Ibrahim's boat was carrying a five-kilowatt-hour power cell which also provided power to the radio transmitter that was key to their assault.

The biggest threat to the success of Ibrahim's simple plan was that damned helicopter gunship. An *armed* helicopter? Seriously?

He'd faced unmanned reconnaissance drones before and even a drone armed with a sonic disruptor. His response? Through a contact in Macau, he'd found a source who could provide him with man-portable Chinese-made Flying Crossbow missile systems. They could knock down anything flying lower than 20,000 feet and were pretty much idiot-proof – just point, lock, shoot. But they cost $30,000 each, which was more than some jobs netted him, which was why he'd had to lean on their benefactor again, Mr. Lim, to sponsor their use. He'd persuaded Lim to cough up $100,000 for two missiles, so even if Ibrahim burned them both, he'd be able to replace them and still come out $40,000 ahead, but he found it all very disheartening.

What was the world coming to, when a simple seafarer had to arm himself with damn *missiles* just to get a job done?

"What is the world coming to, when a woman gets shot,

kills her attacker to save her own life, is threatened with imprisonment and then forced back to work to help protect her jailers?" Bunny was asking Ginger as they made their way, one stair at a time, up to the bridge, after checking in with the ship's surgeon again. "And a doctor won't even give her a damn painkiller?"

"He said painkillers can dull your reflexes and cause nausea," Ginger told her. He was carrying her helmet because she needed both hands on the stair rails to steady herself against the constant roll of the ship.

"Morphine then. One lousy shot of morphine."

"You want to take that helo into action with *morphine* in your system?"

Her head throbbed, and she still felt like a white-hot poker was sticking out of her back. "Yeah, Ginger, that's *exactly* what I want."

"No one is going to sign off on that."

She could hear voices on the bridge as she neared the entrance door. They sounded reassuringly calm, considering what was probably about to go down. She knew it wasn't the first time they'd faced a militia assault while underway, but from the little Bose had told her, it seemed this one was on a scale they hadn't faced before.

As she walked onto the bridge, the voices stopped. Pedersen had been looking at a radar plot with one of his men and turned to face her. Bose was standing at another console behind him, his face unreadable. Bunny squared up to Pedersen as best she could, ready for whatever was coming and prepared to give as good as she was about to get.

"Welcome to the bridge, Pilot O'Hare," Pedersen said. "I'm glad to see you are alive. I've been told by my medico your injuries are only light. But he also said something about a possible concussion, so I have to ask you directly; are you mission capable?"

The business-like welcome took Bunny aback. "As far as someone under arrest can be mission capable, yes, Captain."

"Law of the sea is law of the sea, O'Hare," he told her. "I didn't write it. You fired on my vessel, and you killed a man. You are under arrest and will be handed over to US authorities who will investigate your actions. Can I offer some advice?"

"Do I have an option?"

Pedersen gave a tight smile. "No. My advice is that it would be in your interests for the Captain of this vessel to be disposed to provide you with his full and unreserved support during that investigation. Currently, he is. Do you wish to change that?"

O'Hare counted to three and let the chip fall from her shoulder. "No, Captain. It would be appreciated."

"Good. Now sit down before you fall down," he said, indicating a chair fixed to the floor at the rear of the bridge that resembled a large gamer's swivel chair. Ginger handed her her helmet. "Chief Mate, please brief Ms. O'Hare. The rest of you, back to your work."

Bose waited until she was settled and then walked behind the rest of the watch crew to stand in front of her. "My turn. Are you well enough to physically pilot that aircraft?"

Was she? *Was she hell.* She had taken a 9mm slug in the back. She had a blinding headache. She'd been arrested for murder. She had a grudge against the world big enough you could ski off it. But there wasn't exactly anyone else on the boat who could fly that Vapor. "I can do it."

He didn't look convinced. "What you did before, piloting it remotely. Would that be a better option?" He waited.

"Not for a hot engagement like we're facing," she told him. "Look, I won't be alone up there. I'll hand off as much as I can to the AI, and I'll play it safe."

"What if you collapse in the cockpit?"

"Same as you saw before. If it doesn't get command inputs, Vapor flies itself home."

He nodded. "Good enough. We have repaired, refueled and rearmed the aircraft, including its midsection-mounted minigun."

She thought about what he'd just told her. "The AI can fly

the aircraft if I can't, but it would be good to have someone on that mini-gun to give us more engagement options. Do you have anyone on the crew who…"

There was a cough from beside her. "Uh, hello?" Ginger was standing with a finger in the air. "Trained on the M134 when I was in His Majesty's Navy, remember? A long time ago, but the beastie on that Vapor looks pretty much identical."

Bose shook his head. "You'll be needed on comms, Mr. McIntyre."

Ginger tapped his ear again. "And like I said, comms is wherever I am. It's not limited to my radio room. I can patch into the systems on the aircraft and run comms from there. In fact, I'll have a better overview of the engagement from up in the air than I would locked inside my broom cupboard on *Andromeda*."

Bose thought about it. He turned to Bunny. "Is it really necessary to have a door gunner for this engagement?"

"In a target-rich environment like we'll be facing, yes, Chief Mate," she told him. Bunny winked at Ginger. "But if he falls into the sea or something, I can run your comms for you."

Bose nearly smiled. "Well, that's good to know. Mr. McIntyre, report to the helipad immediately and board the aircraft."

"Now?"

"How soon can you get airborne?" Bose asked Bunny.

"Ten minutes, if your maintenance crew has done their job properly."

"*Now*, Mr. McIntyre."

"How soon can you get airborne again?" The lieutenant commander of Mischief Reef PLAN air base was asking Li Chen.

She'd made it down with thirteen of her sixteen pilots. The Americans had claimed two of her pilots, shot down, and another had been forced to bail out of his aircraft due to engine failure. It was a miracle more of her squadron had not been lost to mechanical failure, given the violence of the storm they had just weathered. Of Mischief Reef's twenty J-10 fighters, only six had made it back. Search and rescue teams, including patrol boats dispatched an hour earlier, were tracking eight GPS beacons from downed pilots. Only eight of seventeen downed pilots had survived to trigger their beacons, but there was no guarantee they were still alive. The beacons could also be activated automatically by contact with sea water. Their pilots could be dead, paralyzed, or shark bait by now.

Their unconfirmed kill tally was twenty-five, but according to Chen's AI – which she trusted more than the inflated reports of Mischief Reef's pilots – the real number was *eleven*. And not a single US pilot.

"Comrade Commander, it would take our plane captains on the carrier *Liaoning* at least thirty minutes to turn those aircraft around," she said. "And they are completely familiar with the J-16. Your ground crews are not. I would estimate forty to forty-five minutes, at least."

"We do not have forty-five minutes," the man said, eyes boring into her. "Radar has detected another US drone wave forming up over the Philippines. It is less than thirty minutes until they reach standoff missile range."

"They would not attack us here," Chen insisted. "They said publicly they are restricting their attack to the air and sea around Pagasa!"

"And you trust them?" the Lieutenant Commander asked. "I do not." On his wall was a flat-screen display with a map of the Operations Area and he walked to it, pointing at a group of icons. "This is the *Yushen*, helicopter landing ship, and its escort. The task force is still two days' sailing from Pagasa. There are 2,000 Marines and 30 helicopters embarked on the *Yushen*. They cannot enter the American exclusion zone and land their troops unless we have complete control of the air over Pagasa."

"Of course. What reinforcements are we expecting?"

Chen knew that in addition to her J-16 squadron, the carrier *Liaoning* had 12 FC-31 Gyrfalcon fighters available. But they would usually be kept back for carrier defense – she did not expect them to be released for the conflict over Pagasa. The other two Chinese carriers were not within range of the Spratly Archipelago, but land-based aircraft from China's Southern Command would be able to base out of Mischief and Fiery Cross reefs. It was precisely for this kind of action that China had established air bases on those two very remote reefs.

"Between Mischief and Fiery Cross reefs, we have enough fuel to sustain 72 aircraft in combat operations for two days. Third Air Division at Lingshui will be sending replacements for the J-10s we lost, and two squadrons of J-11 Flankers. They will send another two squadrons of J-11s to Fiery Cross Reef to supplement their J-10s and keep us supplied if we take more losses…"

Chen did a quick bit of math. Three squadrons at each base was equivalent to a regiment of 28 aircraft each, or about 56 aircraft. With her 13 J-16s, that gave them around 70 aircraft. But… "Sir, the J-11 is a thirty-year-old third-generation relic, and you've seen what the American drones did to your J-10s! Our aircraft will be chewed up and spat out."

"You show disturbing lack of faith in Air Force doctrine, Comrade," the Lieutenant Commander warned her. "We destroyed 25 American aircraft, and our losses were negligible…"

We did not destroy 25 aircraft, and the loss of 17 pilots is not negligible, Chen thought, but was politically astute enough not to say it aloud.

The officer continued. "The main enemy thinks it has a technological advantage, but as we showed in Korea, it cannot match our numerical advantage. For every missile it fires at our aircraft, we will fire four at theirs. Every time they shoot down one of our planes, we will replace it with another. Every time they withdraw from our airspace to return to their bases, we will take to the skies over Subi Reef to reclaim them. America has neither the aircraft, nor the political will, to enter into a sustained conflict with the People's Republic Army Naval Air Force."

Chen nodded politely, but inside she was seething. He sounded like a newsreader on State television, but you could not shoot down unmanned enemy stealth fighters with propaganda.

As far as she could see, there was only one chance of winning this battle, and it would not be won by operational commanders like the man standing in front of her. She needed a regimental-level battlefield commission, even if only temporarily, and she had about thirty minutes in which to convince her commanding officer on the carrier *Liaoning* to help her secure it.

Dying time

Pagasa Island, Spratly Archipelago, 0800, January 10

Captain Heraldo Bezerra of the PN Seabees was wondering how the propaganda unit of the Philippine Marines would deal with the scene in front of him. In the airconditioned back room of the Pagasa village clinic, he was looking at bodies, stacked floor to shoulder height. On the right, Filipino soldiers, or what could be found of them. It was a bit hard to estimate due to the lack of congruity between limbs and torsos, but he estimated about fifteen. There were at least that many out in the clinic and lying on beds in nearby houses, with wounds of varying seriousness. On the left side of the cold room, ten Chinese commandos in their black uniforms. Give or take.

Saddest of all, six villagers, two or three who had died in the cruise missile strike, and another two or three who had died in the naval barrage. Unlike the soldiers, the civilians had been laid out individually, their bodies covered in bedsheets. He lifted one and looked at the face of the woman beneath it.

She looked much calmer than when he had last seen her. Serene even. In that face, he could see something of the girl she must once have been. A pretty, bright girl, he imagined. Strong-willed. Tough. She had to have been tough to be eking out a life on an island like Pagasa.

What was the name of her husband? It seemed like a lifetime ago, the last time he'd seen her, in the school hall. Distraught. Angry.

A lifetime ago. Well, yes. For her, it was.

Ah, that was it. Gonzales Maat.

He made a sign of the cross. Rest in peace, Mrs. Maat.

Crab cakes. Why is it always crab cakes, Lewis thought to herself as she surveyed the buffet on the sideboard in the White House

Situation Room that she and the other members of ExCom had barely left during the day. It was 9 p.m. and they'd somehow missed supper, but Abdor had organized some warm food for them.

Right now, she was bunkered down with President Fenner, his Chief of Staff, Abdor, and Defense Secretary Kahn. Of the other ExComm members, Victoria Porter had gone to her office at State, General Cavoli to the Pentagon, and NSA Director Kyle Sandiland had gone to the Homeland Security Office on the other side of the basement to make some calls. The Vice President was taking donor meetings the President had been forced to excuse himself from.

"Ah, crab cakes!" Fenner said, sounding delighted as he stepped up beside her. "I love these guys."

She was about to tell him crab cakes, mac and cheese was no meal for a grown man when NSA Director Sandiland walked back in, cell phone to his ear, and snapped his fingers to get their attention. "…yeah, I'm back there now. Send it through to a screen."

"Developments on the cyber front?" Lewis asked, putting her plate down again. They were already dealing with a tenfold increase in cyber-attacks on strategic infrastructure and commerce sourced to China since news of the US attack on the Chinese base had reached Beijing.

"And some," Sandiland said and walked to a wall of screens as one of them changed to show a rolling feed of social media posts.

"Is this live?" Lewis asked.

"Is what live?" Fenner interjected, trying to follow the scrolling feed.

"It *was* live streamed but this is a recording," Sandiland confirmed.

"That's a sideshow," Kahn said with a dismissive wave.

"*What* is a sideshow, dammit?" Fenner demanded.

"It's a Chinese misinformation campaign, sir," Abdor told him. "An adjunct to their covert cyber-attacks. It was anticipated. They use bots to create tens of thousands of fake accounts and then flood social media with posts created by AIs…"

Fenner stepped up to the screen. "Wait, that's *me*."

Embedded in a social media post was a video of President Fenner standing at the podium in the White House press briefing room. It looked exactly like the briefing he had held the day before announcing the start of *Operation Fencepost*. But the live captions at the bottom of the video told everyone it wasn't. The text matched his facial expressions and mouth movement, but they were not his words.

…and therefore I am resigning immediately…

"Deepfake," Abdor said. "It's a deepfake."

"I don't care what it is," Fenner said. "Bring up the sound and play it from the start."

The deepfake video was as near to perfect as modern technology allowed. After a rash of deepfaked videos in the early 2020s, the White House and other governments around the world, not to mention pop and movie stars, had agreed on a common standard for authenticating online materials and guaranteeing the veracity of their posts. The same internet standards authority that issued worldwide web addresses produced randomly generated one-time codes that were applied to any official image or video. They appeared as a small series of digits and numbers in the bottom right corner of the image. Any media or government organization with a license could type the digits into a search engine and confirm whether the image or video was genuine or not.

The problem was humans. Most were lazy, and took what they saw at face value without doing the lookup before they liked, commented on, or reposted a fake image. The problem was exacerbated when the account liking, sharing or commenting on a deepfake was itself a fake, operated by an AI bot. Within hours of posting, a deepfaked video could have hundreds of thousands of comments or reposts. Within a day, that could be millions.

So for all intents and purposes, it was the President of the United States standing at the podium right on the screen, dabbing his brow and looking shattered, before he grasped the podium in both hands and leaned into the microphone. The real-world participants in the White House Situation Room stood in silence as the volume was turned up on the video in the post – which had more than 108,000 comments or shares already:

Thank you for coming. I have some terrible news to relay, and then, well ... then I have an announcement. I will not be taking questions.

This morning at 0400 Washington time, I received the news that our aircraft carrier, USS Doris Miller, which was sailing in the East Philippine Sea, was destroyed by missiles fired by ... we suspect ... a Chinese submarine.

The deepfake Fenner mopped his brow again.

At this time ... at this time we believe Doris Miller was lost with all hands. I repeat. We have not and do not expect to recover any survivors.

Abdor turned to Fenner. "I'll get out a denial immediately."

"Yes, go," Fenner told him, biting his lip. His alter ego onscreen continued. The pattern of speech also mimicked Fenner faithfully. He had never been good at off-the-cuff speeches, and his pauses and repetition had been reproduced to enhance the image of a man under pressure and out of his depth. *Our thoughts go of course ... they go to the families of these men and women. Now to ... I have ... I have an announcement.*

I was against this war. I only agreed to it on the advice of my Cabinet, and especially based on the advice of our Joint Chiefs of the military, who guaranteed me they could keep our losses to a minimum. Clearly, they were wrong. China's military is more powerful than ... more than we imagined.

The deepfake Fenner lifted his kerchief to cover his face and sobbed, openly. After more than a minute, he straightened up, wiped his eyes and continued.

All of these young men and women ... I cannot ... and ... and therefore, I am resigning immediately as Commander in Chief and President of the United States. Vice President Tyler will be sworn in immediately after ... well, immediately, effective now.

Thank you and God … God Bless the United States of America.

The last sentence was said in a hoarse whisper, and after a short, shocked silence, there were shouted questions from the media as the apparently broken President Fenner left the room with a stumbling gait.

"Turn it off," Fenner said quietly. When no one moved immediately, he turned to the aide and snarled. "I said turn that damn feed off!"

"Don't worry about it, Mr. President," Kahn tried to calm him. "People are so used to these things now, even the late-night shows are doing them. No serious media is going to run with that, they'll check the code and can it."

Blood was rising on Fenner's throat. "People seeing a clip on a late-night show where I'm telling a knock knock joke is one thing." He pointed at the screen, finger stabbing at the air. "No one follows serious media anymore except you, Phil. That damn travesty has already gone around the world and back, picking up a million reposts in the time we were watching it. My God, the families of our sailors aboard the *Doris Miller*, they're probably going out of their minds."

Carmine wasn't analyzing the emotional impact of the message, she was too busy already analyzing the content. "That was a seriously high-quality production. It wasn't some back-street Shanghai hacker. Let's assume it was a Chinese State-authorized deepfake," she said. "What does it tell us?"

Fenner ran a hand across his face. He picked up his crab cakes again, and a can of pop. He moved toward the conference table. "I don't know, Carmine, what does it tell us?" he said with barely disguised sarcasm.

She kept rolling. "First. They named the *Doris Miller*. Either a good guess, or they know where we are launching those aircraft from. No surprise there, but it confirms they have tasked satellites to follow our strike group and nothing we launch from that bearing is going to surprise them from here on in. If they know that, they know about Clark Base too."

Secretary Kahn nodded. "Fits with what Space Command is

reporting."

Carmine continued. "Then there's the psych warfare angle. Fake POTUS just said he didn't agree with his Cabinet but got talked into *Fencepost*. He referred to discussions around minimizing casualties. Someone has told them Cabinet is split on this operation. This social media campaign is supposed to fan those flames."

"Someone, who?" Fenner growled. "Someone in *this* room?"

Carmine held up a flat palm. "Stop that thought right there, Mr. President," she said. "The people in this room are probably the *real* target for that deepfake. We're supposed to be looking at each other right now, wondering … has someone been indiscreet? Or worse? Is someone in this room feeding China with intelligence on our deliberations?"

Kahn raised a hand. "Guilty." He saw shocked looks. "Not of talking with China, dammit. Of wondering if maybe someone had. We have had some pretty … robust … discussions around *Operation Fencepost*." He looked apologetically at Carmine. "As I watched that video, I was thinking *damn*, someone here has been spilling Cabinet secrets."

"Which is what they want you to be wondering," Carmine said immediately. "We see this video, it's referring to Cabinet splits, *Doris Miller*, minimizing casualties … we're supposed to start looking for a leak inside Cabinet. The President has Secret Service check everyone's phone records and suddenly everyone in this room is looking over their shoulders."

"Madam Director, that is an evil mind you have there," Kahn said with fake admiration. "But now you mention it … we *have* built our strategy around using autonomous aircraft only, with an iron-clad principle that we will do all we can to minimize US military casualties… how could they…" He stopped and laughed. "Dammit, that's one deep rabbit hole."

Carmine nodded. "Any competent AI could have deduced that, based on our tactics in the theatre to date, and previous public statements and actions by this administration. This is a psych warfare street fight, Mr. Secretary. And it is only going to intensify."

Abdor re-entered the room and saw everyone look at him. "Press Secretary will issue an immediate denial and reassure the families of the *Doris Miller* that ... what? What are you all looking at?"

"It's Chuck, don't you think?" Fenner turned to Carmine with feigned subtlety.

"Definitely," she smiled. "Chinese Deep Throat if ever I saw one."

Abdor looked confused and while Fenner put him out of his misery, letting him in on the joke, Carmine sat back and thought hard. The deepfake had been very culturally adept, knowing that causing panic among the thousands of family members of the *Doris Miller*'s crew would guarantee the video post got traction and, at worst, cause confusion, at best, strike a blow to morale inside Navy and Navy families. It was also technically adept ... the dabbing of the brow with the kerchief, the wracking sobs, the awkward pauses of Deepfake Fenner had been nothing short of completely convincing. But if the real purpose of China's misinformation campaign was to sow dissent among the members of the Fenner Cabinet, they had misjudged their target audience.

Washington could be a snake pit; she was the first to admit that. There had been passionate arguments over the administration's China strategy over the last few years and months and not a few shifting alliances inside and outside Cabinet. But on the final decision to confront China by building up the Philippine base on Pagasa Island, and standing up to Chinese diplomatic or military action in the wake of that decision, the President's inner Cabinet was rock solid.

Wasn't it?

She looked around the room at Fenner, blowing off tension by joking with Kahn and Abdor. Then remembered that Victoria Porter wasn't present.

Chinese military politics is a snake pit, Li Chen was thinking. She was standing in the office of the Commander of the PLA Navy air brigade based on Mischief and Fiery Cross reefs, trying to make clear to him that subordinating his brigade to her meant he would need to follow *her* orders for deploying his air assets. It seemed that simple reality was beyond his ability, or willingness, to understand.

"With respect, you are looking at this conflict wrongly, Comrade Commander. You see it as a game of pure numbers. I see it as a question of competing technologies. We are fighting unmanned stealth fighters with piloted aircraft two generations older," Li Chen was explaining. "We cannot fight them on their own terms."

"And what are 'their terms', Comrade *Acting* Commander?" Mischief Reef's Lieutenant Commander asked. Li Chen had persuaded Rear Admiral Li Bing, Commander of Southern Fleet and her commanding officer aboard the *Liaoning*, to order the man opposite to subordinate himself and his aircraft to Li Chen until further notice. He was not happy about handing his baton to a junior officer and was not afraid to show it with his sarcastic emphasis on her rank.

"Patrolling stubbornly over Subi Reef and Pagasa, while American drones track and engage us from a hundred miles away, Comrade Commander," she replied without rancor. "As you have been doing. It will only lead to further slaughter."

"Then what do you propose?"

Li Chen had a map in front of her. "We pull our aircraft back. Cover Mischief Reef and Fiery Cross with continuous standing air patrols but do not engage American aircraft unless these bases are threatened."

"That is the action of a coward!" he exclaimed, his eye muscle twitching with barely controlled anger. "You would be surrendering control of the air to our enemy. Our troops on Subi Reef would be unprotected."

"For now, yes. Subi Reef is already out of commission. Our wounded have been evacuated and remaining troops are dug in.

A response to the American aggression is being prepared by Southern Command Fleet Base. Until then, you will not deploy your fighters for anything other than combat air patrols to protect our airfields."

"What kind of strategy is it, Comrade, that requires me to order my pilots to *hide* from their enemy and leave Subi Reef, our largest base in the Spratly Islands, unprotected?" he asked bitterly. "I will not comply with such defeatism."

She could take his insolence no longer. To Li Chen, this balding, sweating officer with a paunch and a sneer represented all that was wrong with the PLA Naval Air Force. He made a virtue out of mindlessly following the doctrines he had been trained in twenty years earlier. Was unable to think an inch outside the box that was his comfort zone. And considered any new idea to be not just insubordinate, but dangerous.

"Commander, you are the kind of fool who would stand outside his house in a storm and wave his fist at the clouds, instead of moving his family to high ground. You are relieved of your command and will be placed under arrest."

He stood gaping at her as she walked to the door and signaled to a Lieutenant in the outer office. "You. By the authority of Rear Admiral Li Bing, I have placed the Commander under arrest. Please have him escorted to his quarters and post a guard to ensure he remains there." The Lieutenant also stood gaping at her. "*Now*, Lieutenant!"

The man hurried past her, saluted his now former CO, and waited uncertainly to see what the man would do. The Commander picked up his cap from the table beside him, put it firmly on his head and made to walk out past Li Cheng. As he drew level, he stopped. "You will fail, and your actions today will see you tried for dereliction, if not treason. I look forward to witnessing at your trial."

Li Chen stood in the door of his office and watched as the Lieutenant organized for an Ensign to take the man to his quarters. When that was done, he returned to Li Chen, saluted and stood in front of her, waiting.

"Thank you, Lieutenant," she said. "That was regrettable but necessary. Tell me, is the Commander popular with the personnel?"

The man appeared taken aback by the question. "I do not understand, Comrade Commander."

She looked directly into his eyes. "I am asking you whether the other officers will respect the commission granted me by Rear Admiral Li Bing, or whether they will mutiny." She smiled. "A simple question."

She saw the man's Adam's apple working as he weighed his answer. "To answer the Comrade Commander's first question, the Commander was not a popular leader."

"I thought not. Please gather the pilots in the ready room for a briefing. Immediately. And get me the CO at Fiery Cross Reef on comms. We have no time to waste."

The strategy she had just laid out was one she had agreed with Admiral Li Bing and his staff on the *Liaoning*. The Americans plainly wanted a war of attrition over Subi Reef and Pagasa Island. Pagasa and Subi were meat grinders and the enemy expected her to keep feeding it meat, cut by cut, aircraft by aircraft. She would not oblige. She would hold her aircraft back, doing what she could to protect China's other bases in the Spratlys from any expansion of American aggression.

Meanwhile, Admiral Li Bing would secure the forces needed to drive the Americans out of the skies over the South China Sea and enable China to bring its assault ship in and put enough troops and air defense batteries ashore at Pagasa to ensure it remained, *forever*, Chinese.

Li Chen walked back into the office and looked out of the former Lieutenant Commander's window at rows of fighters lined up on the Mischief Reef runway like they were awaiting inspection. The first thing she would do was get combat air patrols set up over the base and put those damn aircraft into revetments and underground hangars.

The US President had said he didn't want a war with the Chinese people, but was she not Chinese? Had the Americans not just waged war on her and her pilots?

Chen felt a strange sense of betrayal. She had completed post-grad engineering in California and hadn't for a minute of her time in the USA felt anything but welcome. She'd even taken her NBA-obsessed younger brother to a Golden Bears game when her family came to visit and he'd left the stadium with a bright yellow sweatshirt he wore day and night for the next two years. That night, after they left the game, she snuck him into a blues club where he'd fallen in love with the blues and broken his thumb in a fight defending her from the advances of a drunken Chinese patron.

Now the same nation that had given her an education and given her brother an obsession with blues guitar was trying to kill her.

The Lieutenant stuck his head through the doorway and pointed to the handset on the desk. "Comrade Commander, the CO of Fiery Cross base is on comms for you."

Chen turned away from the window. *Back to work. This is going to be interesting*, she told herself as she sat down.

"This is going to be interesting," Bunny O'Hare said quietly as she eased the Vapor off the deck and set it up to climb rapidly to high altitude for its engagement with the militia boats. She had conducted numerous hostile engagements in her RAAF F-35 stealth fighter over Syria, and with unmanned aircraft in US government service, most frequently the X-47B Fantom. But never after a punch in the ribs from a 9mm slug and never with a gunner. She looked over her shoulder 'through' the bulkhead at Ginger – if there ever was a more unlikely door gunner in the history of air combat, she'd like to meet them.

It did not help that in addition to her bruised back, her head was still throbbing from being clubbed by her would-be assassin.

Bunny had checked in with Leclerc after reaching the bridge, giving her an update on what had happened since they spoke.

"I'm so sorry," Leclerc had said, sounding like she meant it. "It was my fault he slipped through."

"Yeah, well. All's well that ends ... well, in a pool of someone *else's* blood. Pirates are hiring assassins now?" Bunny asked.

"No. But nations who hire pirates are hiring assassins, apparently," Leclerc told her. "China desperately wants that convoy stopped. Please, be careful up there, mon amie."

Which was nice. Someone apart from herself worrying about her.

"Sorry, did you just say, 'this is going to be interesting'?" Ginger asked on comms. He was wearing a crew helmet that allowed a second crew member aboard the Vapor to talk with the pilot or the ground, and, through a heads-up display in the visor, to see the same tactical view screen Bunny was looking at.

"Did I say that out loud?"

"Yeah, you did. And it doesn't exactly inspire confidence, O'Hare," Ginger told her. Ginger was strapped into a seat in the payload bay. He did not appear to be enjoying the ride.

"I meant interesting as in ... exciting, you know," Bunny told him. "But not bad exciting. Good exciting. As in, you have nothing to worry about but, still, interesting kind of thing."

"Still not inspiring confidence."

Bose broke in over comms. "Vapor, *Andromeda*, I am showing data handshake. Radar telemetry from the Vapor is supplementing our surface radar. We are now seeing *ten* targets. Five larger, patrol boat-sized, five smaller, look like cigarette boats or rib boats."

Bunny checked her instruments. "Roger, *Andromeda*. I'm passing ten thousand for fifteen. When I reach safe altitude, I'll begin imaging the targets for you. What range do you consider them a threat?"

"Anything inside two miles, Vapor," Bose told her.

"Good copy, *Andromeda*. Out." She was also seeing a good

data link between the air-sea radar on her Vapor, the surface radar on *Andromeda* and the surface radar on *Orion*. Looking at the White Star convoy via camera out of the windows of the Vapor, she couldn't imagine any pirate crew being able to take the two ships on. The *Andromeda* was sailing with engines full ahead, kicking up a huge bow wave. The *Orion* looked massive, even from the altitude she was viewing it from. "Ginger, we're coming up to 20,000 feet. You can unbuckle now and put on the gunner harness."

"Aye."

"Make sure you've got your tether line fixed to a hardpoint and plug in your oxygen mask. I don't want you falling out if I make a radical maneuver, and I don't want you passing out from lack of oxygen if I have to climb suddenly."

"Don't fall out, don't pass out, got it," he said drily. "Any other tips?"

"Sure, since you ask," Bunny said. "There are ballistic vests in a locker against the forward bulkhead. Pull one on. Make sure that damn mini-gun is loaded and powered up *before* we need it." The Vapor's mini-gun was fed by a belt of ammunition and required electrical power to spin its six barrels. The gun on the Vapor was limited to 2,000 rounds a minute, fed by a 5,000-round belt. Watching Ginger fumble with his tether as he tried to hook himself up beside the sliding door, she sincerely hoped they would not have to use it.

No sign of that damn gunship yet, Ibrahim thought.

His Marine radar showed they were about ten miles out from the two White Star ships. He'd expected to see the big black aircraft appear by now, if only to inspect them visually. Could it be that Lim had actually delivered on his promise to try to deal with the aircraft through other means? That would certainly make Ibrahim's job easier.

He checked the radar plot again. It was time. He got on the radio. "Kamito, we are going to split in five minutes. Your group hangs back, we move up alongside. Understood?"

"Understood, boss, splitting the boats in five."

"You'll see when we've been successful. Wait until the target falls away and then attack, one pair at a time. Once we start our attack, you won't be able to contact us, so if you got questions, now is the time."

"Just like we practiced, boss. Don't worry, we got it."

Ibrahim worried. It was his job to worry. Sure, they'd trained. But these weren't proper navy sailors. His crew were amateurs: some hadn't even gone to sea in boats before they joined him. If they'd passed the weapons and boat handling tests Kamito had put them through, he'd taken them anyway, because he needed a constant supply of brave men. There was one extra test Ibrahim insisted on, though. He had no time for drunks or drug users, and for that reason, he preferred practicing Muslims – not radicals, just solid family men he recruited through the Seta Ali mosque – but such men weren't easy to come by. So every man on his crew was drug tested before he joined and if Ibrahim or Kamito caught wind that one of his crew had begun using drugs on the sly, they were out. Same for men who couldn't handle their liquor. No interrogation, no hard feelings, but no second chances either.

He looked at his watch, then back at the wake from the twin water jets at the back of the boat. They were not only fast, they were quiet. Not something he needed for the coming assault, but might be useful some other time, like approaching a target quietly, at night. They had a ramp at the back that the rib boats were stored and launched off, which took a bit of practice, as did driving the damn things, because they didn't have a wheel like a normal boat, they had joysticks and throttles like an airplane. But his younger guys were right at home up front in the airplane-like cockpit; it was like playing a computer game for them.

Two minutes … one … *mark*! "Kamito, split!"

Two of the Mark Vs and all of the rib boats peeled away to starboard with Kamito's Mark V, headed for the rear of the

White Star convoy. Ibrahim's Mark V and one other kept plowing ahead, on a parallel course to the White Star convoy that would put them abreast, about five miles out. He didn't need to get any closer for what he had planned.

Ibrahim checked his men were in position. He had two up front in the cockpit, one driving, the other as a reserve in case their driver was incapacitated during the attack. There was another man standing by the boat's mini-gun, hanging onto its twin firing grips, knees bent as he rode the bucking deck over the waves. At his feet was the long tube of a Flying Crossbow missile launcher. Ibrahim turned to the man beside him in the rear of the boat, just under the camouflage overhang, and pointed at a radio transmitter sitting on a wooden palette on the deck of the boat. A thick cable ran from the transmitter to an antenna fixed to the overhang. "Fire it up, Salvador."

The man pulled a pot from under a seat, put it on his head and grinned sheepishly. "You want one, I brought a spare, boss."

"What the hell, Salvador?"

"This thing could fry your brain, Kamito told me," the man explained. "How close we are to it." The man on the gun was listening intently and started to look worried.

"You want to worry about your nuts, not your brain," Ibrahim told him. "You can forget having kids after this."

The man frowned. "You serious?"

Ibrahim shook his head. "No, you idiot. Neither was Kamito. Take that pot off your head and turn that thing on, now."

'That thing' was another gift from the generous Mr. Lim. It was a US-made 180 lb. man-portable Communication Emitter Sensing and Attack System II (CESAS II). Ibrahim had to wonder how Lim had managed to get a hold of all this surplus US equipment, but where there were means, there were ways. CESAS had originally been developed to protect US troop convoys from remotely triggered roadside bombs but had evolved considerably since then. CESAS II had a twenty-mile range and could jam all of the most commonly used radio frequencies.

Like the frequencies used by the automated identification system (AIS) aboard the White Star *Andromeda* that communicated its position to the world. Or the frequency it might use to send out a mayday once it came under attack.

And the frequency it used to control the propulsion and steerage systems of its unmanned trailing utility ship, the White Star *Orion*.

"What the hell?" Bunny had just lost her connection to *Andromeda*'s data stream. All other systems were still nominal, but the link to the *Andromeda* was down.

"Vapor, run a systems integrity check, please," she said. "*Andromeda*, Vapor, come back, please … *Andromeda*, Vapor…" She waited. Nothing. OK, weird. "Ginger, I've lost our link to the *Andromeda*, radio is down too, can you do anything to…"

She looked over her shoulder. Ginger was staring into the bulkhead-mounted camera that she used to view the personnel module in the payload bay and tapping his helmet by the ear. He was also indicating that *his* comms were down. His mouth was moving, but she couldn't hear him over internal comms either.

Of course not. The helmets were connected by Bluetooth. If the ship's comm system was down, it was possible the Bluetooth system was down too. Reaching into a compartment beside her chair, she rummaged around until she found what she was looking for … a thin fiber optic cable. She showed it to Ginger as she plugged one end into her helmet, and the other into the panel between her seat and the empty copilot seat. Turning to the camera in her own compartment, she held it up so he could see it, and waved it at him. Eventually he got the message and started searching the personnel compartment for a cable like it. After a couple of minutes, he found one and connected his helmet to a wall socket near the mini-gun mount.

"…you hear me?"

"I hear you, Ginger."

"What's going on? I lost my link to the ship."

"*We* lost our link to the ship," she told him. "And our internal Bluetooth system. I'm running a system integrity check." Several painful seconds went by.

System integrity checks complete. All systems nominal, the AI reported.

"Vapor, I have lost radio communication with the *Andromeda*. Are we receiving any radio signals from the ship?"

No, pilot.

"But the radio is working?"

All communication systems are fully operational.

A thought began to niggle at the back of Bunny's mind. "Vapor, please scan all radio frequencies for traffic and tune to the first transmitter you find."

Scanning… One transmitter was found.

"Only one? Vapor, put it on speaker, please."

The noise that came through her earphones was a high-pitched squeal that warbled up and down. She had heard that kind of signal once before. Over Syria.

"Ginger, we are being jammed."

"Jammed? By who?"

"Three guesses."

"I have never heard of militia boats carrying heavy-duty jamming equipment before."

"They had a Chinese-made drone following us. A Chinese J-15 fighter stopped me from shooting it down. The US has just started a shooting war with China, and we are headed straight into the conflict zone. I'm guessing they're getting a little help?"

"Oh my God," Ginger said.

"It's not that bad," Bunny reassured him. "It's not strong enough to affect our avionics. We are still…"

He had his nose pressed to the armored viewing glass in the side door panel. "No. The *Orion*. The transmitter jamming us is also jamming the signal controlling the *Orion*."

Bunny tilted the Vapor on its port wing and looked down at the sea below. They were making a wide circle around the convoy below as they clawed higher in the sky, and she looked down at the big freight ship. She couldn't see anything amiss.

"Looks normal to me."

"No, look at her wake," Ginger said, horrified. "She's programmed to go into collision avoidance mode if she loses contact with her mothership."

"Well, that's probably good, right?" Bunny asked.

"No. *Not* good. She's lost her comms link, and she's lost her radar. She'll drop her speed to five knots and use optical guidance for collision avoidance, which means she'll try to avoid *Andromeda*. You can see from her wake. See! She's slowing and turning!"

Bunny checked her own radar screen. It was just showing static. But looking out her port window, now that she was approaching 20,000 feet, she didn't need radar to see the threat anymore.

On the glittering sea below, about five miles behind the *Orion* and closing, was a group of boats. Another was about five miles abeam of the *Andromeda* and holding parallel. As she watched, the *Andromeda* started turning towards them. She could imagine the scene on *Andromeda*'s bridge right now as they realized they had not just lost comms, they had lost control of the *Orion*. It would not be pretty. "Pedersen has decided those boats off his beam are the threat. He's trying to put himself between them and the *Orion*," she decided.

"His radar will be down. He won't be able to see the ones behind her," Ginger pointed out.

As Bunny turned to check on them visually, two of the smaller boats broke from the pack and started sprinting toward the *Orion*. In the ideal world, she'd try to take out the boat doing the jamming first, deal with the others after the *Orion* was back under *Andromeda*'s command. But which damn pirate boat was doing the jamming?

"Crap," Bunny said. "Ginger, hold bloody tight."

Hauling the Vapor around on a wingtip, ribs aching in protest, she pushed her throttle to the gate, lit her tail and pointed her nose at the *Orion*.

Ibrahim could no longer contact Kamito on the other group of boats, but that was a good sign. It meant the American-made jammer was working.

"It's slowing," the man on the mini-gun called out, pointing at the *Orion*. "Starting to turn. And the lead ship is coming around toward us."

From up front, the man in the starboard cockpit seat yelled too. "Boss! An airplane, starboard side, high!"

Ibrahim's head snapped around. A small black dot, dropping from the sky towards Kamito's boats at the rear of the freighter. He scrabbled over and grabbed the missile launcher from the mini-gunner's feet. Whipping it to his shoulder and powering the launcher on, he looked through the targeting scope and tried to find the gunship, but he was waving it around uselessly without getting any targeting lock tone. He took his eye away from the scope and looked up in the sky again. The airplane was still falling toward the sea, but it was either too far away or too high still for him to get an infrared hit off it.

He lowered the launcher again. The client had supplied them with two Flying Crossbow missiles, and Kamito had the other. He just had to hope Kamito had seen the gunship too.

Bunny knew from her run over the militia base that they had some heavy firepower on their boats, so she wasn't taking any chances. She aimed the Vapor at the sea well ahead of the bow of the *Orion*, aiming to put the big ship between her and at least two-thirds of the militia boats.

The maneuver meant she had to get from above 20,000 feet to under 500 feet before she reached the *Orion*, which meant a

241

nearly *vertical* dive. The tiltrotor propellers at the end of her wingtips had folded themselves back and tucked themselves into the engine nacelles. The machine was being pushed by its two rear turbofan engines and she watched the airspeed in her visor carefully, pulling back on her throttle as her airspeed rocketed through 200 miles an hour ... two fifty ... three hundred ... *three fifty*...

The Vapor was rated for a maximum speed of three eighty miles an hour, and she winced as she pulled her throttle all the way back and her airspeed indicator clocked over three eighty ... three *ninety* ... the sea was rushing up toward them from horizon to horizon. She could see no sky, only sea, the Vapor shaking like it was trying to tear itself apart, and the AI started warbling in her ears as she dropped below 10,000 feet, still pointed straight at the waves...

Collision warning, pull up. AI assistance is recommended. Collision warning, pull up. AI assistance is recommended.

"Shut up, Vapor! Bring up guns."

20mm guns armed.

A targeting reticle appeared in the front of her helmet visor. From the back, she could hear Ginger moaning.

Four hundred miles an hour. Five thousand feet. She pulled all the way back on the flight stick in her right hand and got nothing! The aircraft didn't react. Four thousand five. Now it was responding, the nose coming up a little. Four thousand ... eight five ... three ... nose still below the horizon ... speed 410 ... *come on, you big black beauty* ... three five ... three... two five ... still diving ... speed 390 ... The Vapor had no airbrakes, and if she deployed her flaps now, they would probably tear out. But she had no choice. Flipping a switch with her left hand, she applied half-flaps and the aircraft buffeting got worse, but her nose started coming up faster ... altitude two thousand feet ... *Orion* right ahead of them ... speed 350 ... throttle forward again ... retract flaps ... 500 feet, three eighty miles an hour...

She twitched her flight stick to send the Vapor down the

starboard side of the *Orion*, its massive flanks looming over them as they screamed over the water. There, ahead of them, she could see the militia boats, small dark shapes rushing toward her. Two boats were going down the left side of the *Orion*, two down the right, a larger one further back; and the two on the right were coming right at her.

She put the targeting reticle on the left-most boat and as it turned from white to green, she jabbed her thumb on the 20mm cannon firing button, held it for two beats, and then tapped her right rudder pedal.

Kamito had done it exactly like they'd practiced. They'd pulled in behind the freighter, riding its wake like jet skiers, with knees bent and faces to the wind. A couple of the boys in the Mark V with him had started whooping, and Kamito let them. He needed their blood up.

Their radios were down, but he signaled to the rib boats and they had sprinted forward, two left, two right, aiming for either side of the *Orion*; up front were two men holding telescopic poles with the magnetic mines at the end of them, armed and ready to swing at the hull of the ship. All they had to do was get in close alongside, swing the mines down to the waterline, let the magnetic clamps stick them to the hull, and then get the hell out of there. The idea was to get them as close together as possible, to try to blow one large hole in the side of the ship instead of two smaller ones, but holes were holes. *Orion* wasn't a double-hulled warship.

Kamito watched with satisfaction as the rib boats powered away ahead of them, leaving him, another Mark V, and one rib boat trailing in reserve.

But then he saw another boat appear from behind the *Orion*. Small, dark, and coming at them *fast*. No, not a boat! A bloody airplane, skimming across the water.

"Gunner!" he yelled, pointing. The man was crouched behind their mini-gun and swung it around, but since the

243

approaching aircraft was right off their bow, his traverse was blocked by the wheelhouse cockpit structure. Kamito ducked his head under the overhang and yelled at his driver. "Turn! Hard starboard!"

Where was their bloody missile? He'd put it up the back, out of the way while they were launching their rib boat. He'd figured they'd see the big gunship in plenty of time to grab and arm it.

He'd figured wrong.

Bunny watched her shells slam into the rib boat right in front of her and then spray right as the aircraft responded to her tap on the rudder. A line of 20mm explosions danced across the water and intersected with the second rib boat. A heartbeat later she was flashing past them, caught a glimpse of men throwing themselves into the water, past the bigger boats further back, and pulling her machine into a high-speed climb away from the militia guns.

Kamito's gunners on the three Mark Vs started hammering away at the retreating aircraft, but their boats were bucking up and down on the wake from the *Orion*, so their streams of shells just sprayed wildly across the sky. Kamito turned to look back at his rib boats. Two were hit, half-submerged, men bobbing in the water around them and desperately trying to climb back aboard. They wouldn't sink, not completely, because the fiberglass bottom was lined with compartmented air cells inside its rubberized ribs. Kamito knew if there was blood in the water, his men would be terrified of sharks.

His other two boats were approaching the *Orion* now, bouncing over its stern wake and preparing their run down its port side. Kamito could see men from *Orion*'s security crew hanging over the railing and pulled some binos off his shoulders to see what they were doing. They were running along the portside railing, probably triggering anti-boarding foam, a thick, slippery layer of gel that prevented boarders from getting a purchase on the hull if they managed to use magnetic grapples to hook onto the ship.

He looked down at the waterline. As expected, they'd also deployed prop fouling nets to try to keep the rib boats from getting too close. But that was the point of the telescopic poles they'd mounted the magnetic mines on. Each was 20 feet long, so they could stick them to the hull of the ship without getting in close. They still had to be careful, though, and he could see them bobbing in the ship's bow wave now, poles waving in the air as the rib boat drivers edged closer and closer to the massive freighter.

The men topside couldn't see them because of the curve of the ship's hull, or they'd surely be firing on them by now.

Come on, move it! Kamito willed his men. He turned to his gunner, who had run an entire belt of ammunition through his minigun and was reloading as it cooled off. "Forget that thing. Get the bloody missile ready in case it comes back."

Bunny leveled out at 10,000 feet and five miles out from the boats she'd just attacked. Not an altitude she liked, because if those militia were carrying anti-air missiles as Pedersen had warned, she was probably in range and she'd now lost the element of surprise.

"They're alongside now," Ginger called out. "But I can't see what they're doing."

The larger gunboat-sized vessels were still holding their distance from the *Orion*, two of them five miles to starboard and holding parallel, three more behind the freighter. The radio jammer was probably on one of those. She still had to deal with those rib boats, though, and she weighed up her options. There was one option that gave her a slim chance of regaining the advantage.

"Get ready on the port side, Ginger," she told McIntyre

over the internal intercom.

"The mini-gun is on the starboard mount," Ginger pointed out.

"So, dismount it, move it portside," Bunny told him.

"It weighs 40 lbs.," he complained. "Plus the ammo…"

"You have five minutes before I need you on that gun, portside door open, gun swung out, ready to engage."

"Ah, ya mangled *fud*," he cursed, but started uncoupling the gun from its starboard mount.

Her vision was starting to blur. She blinked and it cleared again. That probably wasn't a good sign. She'd turned her oxygen to 'rich', which had helped clear her headache, though.

She had no idea what Ginger's curse meant and didn't exactly have time to look it up. She put the Vapor into a gentle climbing turn that would enable Ginger to keep his feet and give him time to move his weapon, while it brought her Vapor up and around to the front of the *Orion*.

Every second he took was a second they didn't have, but even Bunny O'Hare knew yelling at him right now wouldn't make him move faster.

The black gunship was still pulling away from them, moving higher and ahead of the White Star ships. Kamito frowned. Perhaps it had used all of its ammunition? Or maybe it was going after Ibrahim. They were passing the sunken rib boats now, the men clinging to their punctured sides yelling for help. Kamito sent a hand signal to one of the other Mark Vs to stop and pull the survivors out of the water, while he, the other Mark V in his group and their reserve rib boat kept trailing the freighter.

The aircraft was a distraction. He should be focused on the two rib boats trying to plant their mines, deciding whether to send his reserve boat in to get the job done. He peered through his binos. It had seemed a lot easier when they practiced against a fishing trawler that Ibrahim had hired. Kamito could see the huge bow wave from the *Orion*, plus the anti-piracy fouling nets the ship had deployed, were making life difficult for the men in the rib boats. They'd ease in, waving their poles, get to within ten yards of the hull with the mines on the end of their poles, and then a bow wave would knock them away again.

Finally, one of the boat drivers saw his chance, darted in, and his polemen slammed their mines onto *Orion*'s hull. Both rib boats pulled away now, their drivers afraid of getting caught in the blast. The mines were set to trigger 20 seconds after they were planted.

He held his breath, and then with a bright orange and yellow flash, the mines detonated. The men around Kamito cheered. He brought up his binos.

High, dammit all!

They had to be planted down by the waterline, but the explosions he'd just seen were at least ten feet above it. Their rib boat must have been rising on a bow wave when they stuck the mines. Another thing they hadn't experienced when they'd been practicing on the smaller fishing trawler.

He still had two boats. He motioned to his reserve boat, waving it to come in closer so he could yell to the driver.

Leaning over the side, he cupped his hands over his mouth. "Go in with the other boat. Don't plant your mines so high. Low, down by the waterline! Low! Got it?"

The man nodded and pushed his throttle forward, spearing into the waves ahead of Kamito's Mark V as the rib boat that had successfully, but impotently, planted its charges made its way back toward them.

Alright. Where is that damn gunship?

'That damn gunship' was coming around ahead of *Orion* and pointing its nose at the sea again. But a little more gently this time, since they were only coming down from ten thousand, not twenty. And also because Ginger now had the left side crew compartment door wide open, the mini-gun swung out, and was standing in the doorway with legs bent, riding the bumps as the Vapor dropped lower and lower, like he was a circus acrobat standing on a galloping horse. A large, red-headed, wide-eyed, freckle-faced circus acrobat.

Bunny was keeping the bulk of the ship between her and the rib boats she assumed were still trying to get in close to *Orion*'s port side. Perhaps they were preparing to board it … even she could see it was slowing down now. She dropped the Vapor down to wavetop height and came at it from its front starboard quarter.

"Ginger, I'm going to swing around the bow in front of the *Orion* and down the port side. You'll have about five seconds to spray your mini-gun at any bad guys you see down there, before I break hard right. Our egress is going to enable me to put guns on the boats about five miles abreast of the *Orion*, but it's going to get hairy. They will see us coming."

"Aye, I'm ready."

She rolled their machine into a right-hand bank, flashed in front of the *Orion* and then rolled the other way, hauled back on the stick and lined the Vapor up to fly right down the portside flank of the ship. Ahead and to her left, she saw two rib boats jockeying to get alongside it. She had no chance of getting her nose guns on them, but that's why she had Ginger with her – to give them a broadside as she zoomed past. She had no real hope he would actually hit anything, but he might just scare them off.

Five miles out from the *Orion*, Ibrahim had watched the black gunship make a suicide dive toward the sea, flatten out, and then disappear behind the ship. When it reappeared, it rose into the air in what seemed, from a distance, to be a slow gentle climb.

He saw tracer fire from the guns aboard Kamito's Mark Vs follow it up into the sky, but with no apparent effect. And there was no missile launch from Kamito's boat. The aircraft had taken him by surprise.

With some satisfaction, though, he watched through his binos as two of Kamito's rib boats approached the *Orion*, sailed up under its overhanging sides and, after about five minutes of jockeying in and out, managed to stick a couple of mines to *Orion*'s sides. Not that he could see that much detail, but he could surmise it from the way the rib boat drivers suddenly peeled away from the ship at speed, as though it was radioactive.

From five miles away, the explosions that followed seemed incredibly small on such a massive vessel, and like Kamito, he could see they were too high. But he was better placed than Kamito to see the damage they caused and saw with some satisfaction that each charge had opened a hole in the side of the ship about the size of a car tire. A couple more, down at the waterline, and the *Orion* would be in deep trouble. Perhaps the rib boats on the other side had had better luck, if the aircraft hadn't scared them off.

Jammed, his communications technician had told him the *Andromeda* would not be able to control the freighter trailing it. The fact it was slowing down below ten knots now was a bonus he hadn't allowed for, but of course it made sense. You couldn't have a 50,000-ton vessel barreling through the water at speed with no one steering it. *Much safer for everyone if it was at the bottom of the sea*, he reflected wryly. Lim had told him that putting the *Orion* on the bottom was a key objective, but even forcing it back to port, crippled, would earn him fifty percent of the contracted fee. Together with the hardware he'd been given, even at fifty percent fulfillment, he'd return to Brunei a happy man.

Now Kamito sent another boat forward, the boat that had successfully attacked dropped back, and two rib boats again started jockeying to get up alongside the big ship. If they weren't successful, the engagement wasn't over. He had more poles and magnetic mines aboard his own craft. Using his own boat to attack the *Orion* was not part of the plan, but a man always needed a plan B, didn't he? Or C.

Scanning the sky, he saw the black aircraft wing over in the distance and start descending toward the sea again, but ahead of the *Orion* this time. What was it playing at?

No matter, whatever it was doing, if it kept coming around, it might get within range of his Flying Crossbow this time. He lifted the missile to his shoulder and checked the seeker unit was still powered up.

Bunny hammered down the port side of the *Orion* at 300 miles an hour and about a hundred feet off the water.

Ginger saw the two rib boats skidding around in the lee of its hull, bumping up and down on its bow wave, and he opened fire before he reached them, judging his aim by watching the splash of his shells into the water. Just like the time he was in a car crash, time seemed to dilate around him. He saw the splash of his shells between the Vapor and the targets, adjusted his aim to put the tracer fire further out, closer to the ship itself ... *too close*! ... then they were on the rib boats and his shells stitched across them from left to right, pouring straight into the inflated pontoon of one and sawing with horrifying effect across the bodies of the men inside the other, before O'Hare banked hard right and Ginger quickly lifted his thumb off the mini-gun's firing switch.

He didn't have time to think about what he'd just done, as Bunny hauled the Vapor around into a tight banking right turn and pointed it at the other group of militia boats.

Ibrahim saw the gunship flash down the side of the *Orion*, heard its door gunner open up on his rib boats, and kept his missile launcher pointed impotently at it as its targeting box blinked red in the viewfinder. The action was five miles away and his Flying Crossbow missile had a range of two and a half. But then the aircraft banked and he saw with grim satisfaction that it was coming around, to *point right at him*.

He yelled over his shoulder to the man on the mini-gun on his boat, and the crew on the other Mark V. "Come around! Open fire on that bloody gunship!"

As Bunny hauled the Vapor around on its axis and pointed it at the militia boats off *Orion*'s beam, something tore in her left shoulder and she screamed. Letting go of the stick, she clutched at her back.

Who had she been kidding? She wasn't fit to fly.

But she just had to get through the next thirty seconds. After that, she could order the Vapor to take itself home. She put the targeting reticle for her 20mm guns onto the nearest of the larger boats, figuring it had to be one of them doing the jamming, given how they were riding out here, away from the action astern.

Then tracer fire started lancing out from both of the gunboats, white fingers of death slowly twirling towards her, then accelerating until they whipped past at light speed. The gunners on the boats weren't professionals, that much she registered in the first second as the tracer fire sprayed either high or wide.

Her vision was starting to blur again, and she blinked furiously, trying to clear her sight. She had to hit those boats. Unless she knocked out the jamming, the White Star convoy was doomed, she was sure of it. She waited for her reticle to turn from white to green, her thumb hovering over the firing stud.

Ibrahim stood with guns hammering beside and behind him, his entire focus on the small white box in his viewfinder. *Come on, you big ugly pig of a plane!*

He saw muzzle flashes on the nose of the gunship, saw cannon shells start chewing through the water toward him.

None of it mattered. His entire universe was that little white box.

It started blinking and then turned dark red. *Fire!*

As the missile left his shoulder launcher with a thundering whoosh, the shells from the gunship finally reached him, chewing through his gunner, his deck and the boat behind in a double line of explosions that cut both boats in two and sent Ibrahim flying through the air and into the sea.

Bunny had time to see the launch of the missile. Pulled desperately back on her stick as the Vapor pumped out missile decoys and automatically kicked in hard right rudder to try to spin itself away from the source of the threat.

It wasn't going to be enough.

Ginger had been flung to the deck of the crew compartment when Bunny had banked hard toward the militia boats and lay there gasping, staring up at the grey ceiling. He heard O'Hare scream, then saw tracer fire flash past the still open door to the compartment as the Vapor put its nose down and kept rushing onward. If he hadn't been tethered to a hardpoint, he'd have been flung around like a rag doll and probably broken his neck.

Then with a mighty heave, his stomach fell to his feet as the Vapor pitched up, clawing at the sky, and he was sliding again, this time toward the rear of the machine. His tether cable pulled him up just before he slammed into the rear bulkhead.

His relief was short-lived. At that moment, the Chinese-made Flying Crossbow missile struck the Vapor. Its impact-fused warhead hit right between Ginger's feet, about a yard from his groin.

Trying to get some relief from the pressure cooker atmosphere inside the Situation Room, Fenner and Lewis were taking a turn around the White House Rose Garden.

Fenner was scratching his head. "You ever worry there's too

many moving parts?" he asked. "Air war over Pagasa, submarines offshore, missile systems on a convoy headed north, a Philippine Marine battalion cooling its heels at Clark Air Base waiting to load aboard the C17s…"

She smiled. "I've been to children's birthday parties with more moving parts," she told him.

He laughed. "Wish I had your ability to put things in perspective, Carmine."

"No, I mean it," she said. "You been to a five-year-old's birthday party lately, Mr. President? There's clowns, ponies, pinatas, DJs, Vegan Korean BBQ and Banh Mi stations, VR Olympics…"

"*Vegan* Korean BBQ?"

"I know, right? Kids used to be happy with hot dogs or sushi. Not these days."

As he nodded sagely, Carmine's cell phone buzzed. Her mother?

"Sorry, sir, it's my mom," she said, picking up the call but putting her hand over the microphone.

He gave her an understanding wave. "Say hi from me. I'll go back down."

She waited until he had gotten a few steps away and then put the phone to her ear. "Mom?"

A man's voice replied. "No, Madame Director. And I apologize for the subterfuge, I felt it necessary for both our sakes."

She checked the number. The address link on her screen definitely said 'Mom'. Whoever was calling her had commandeered her mother's cell number. She immediately pressed a number combination on her phone to start a traceback and record the call.

"Uh … do we know each other?"

"In fact, we do; you and I met at the Trilateral Negotiations in Delhi. If you recall, I spilled a cup of tea on your shoes, it was most embarrassing."

Her blood went cold. It was an innocuous incident, but one

she would of course never forget. During a break in the US–China–Russia negotiations over Korean reunification in 2031, a Chinese official walking past her had tripped and spilled a cup of tea at her feet. He'd made a small fuss over it and later sent her a pair of shoes through diplomatic channels in apology. She remembered it clearly, since the man had not been a minor Chinese functionary but was none other than her counterpart in China's Politburo, a Vice Premier of the Chinese Communist Party and Director of China's Central Analysis Commission – General Jack Chunhua. A long-time Party member with impeccable political connections, he'd completed a master's degree in data analytics at Boston's MIT as a student before entering the military and beginning his meteoric rise.

The incident on the sidelines of the Trilateral conference was the only direct contact she had ever had with the man, but now she wondered if he had engineered it specifically so that he could refer to it later, if the need ever arose. "I … do remember something of that nature … General."

"Then we are 'on the same page' as you Americans say," the man said, not correcting her use of his rank. "Madam Director, I want to pass on a message."

"Then I suggest you call the State Department, General," Lewis said carefully. "They have a 24-hour public number."

He gave a slight chuckle. "No, Madam Director, this message is for your ears only. I need to speak to the woman who has President Fenner's complete confidence, and that is not Victoria Porter."

Lewis was impervious to flattery, especially from her enemies. The comment also had the feeling of another blunt attempt to cause division in Fenner's Cabinet. She thought about hanging up there and then but was more than a little intrigued. "Please, get to the point."

"Ah yes, I am sorry. You must be very busy right now. As a show of goodwill, to establish my bona fides, and at great personal risk, let me provide you with some information. I assume you are recording this call, so I will speak quickly. In your role as Director of National Security, have you come across any reporting on the Chinese HSU-003 unmanned autonomous submersible?"

She had, of course. First paraded through the streets of Beijing in the mid-2020s, the HSU-003 was China's largest operational unmanned submarine. Fitted with a low acoustic signature propulsion system, powered by hydrogen fuel cells, pulling its fuel from the seawater around it through electrolysis, it was a stealth submarine with a virtually unlimited range. The latest reports she had read said the HSU-003c version of the sub had been fitted with modular payload bays that allowed it to deploy either torpedoes or mines.

Both China and the US were signatories to the 2029 Bern Convention on the use of AI in warfare, which prohibited the deployment of any nuclear-capable military platform under AI-only control, without a 'human in the loop'. But no one inside the current US administration seriously believed that if pressed, China would resist the temptation to put nukes in its fleet of HSU-003s and sail them into US naval bases waiting for a strike command. For exactly that reason, all major US military and civilian ports had seen their seabed sonar detection sensors upgraded to be able to detect submersibles like the HSU-003.

"No, General," she lied. "I have not. Why don't you tell me about it?"

He chuckled lightly, indicating he realized she was dissembling. "As you would know, these are our most advanced long-range underwater drones, capable of navigating themselves to any point on the globe with pinpoint accuracy. Right now, there are ten HSU-003s positioned above your West Coast undersea internet cable nodes."

The hair rose on the back of her neck. "I'm sorry, *what*?"

"Cable nodes. I'm sure you have people who can tell you more about it, but I am given to understand that more than 95 percent of the internet traffic going into and coming out of the US West Coast is carried by undersea cables which terminate in fewer than 12 nodes on the seafloor off California, Oregon and

Washington State. Ten of those are what you might call 'critical', and two of those … excuse me, I have written them down … uh, Morro Bay and Hillsboro, are dedicated to traffic between the USA, Hawaii and Guam. I am sure you can imagine what it would mean if those cable nodes were destroyed."

She didn't have to imagine. In preparing for *Fencepost*, NSA and CyberComm had wargamed a Chinese cyber-attack on the US East and West Coast internet infrastructure, especially the cable gateways that connected the USA to the world. They had identified several possible vulnerabilities and hardened the gateway's defenses against cyber-attack. She knew for a stone-cold terrifying fact they had no defense in place to protect the nodes against a *physical* attack. What would such an attack mean? It would mean all the data currently flowing across the Pacific to Asia would have to be rerouted through the East Coast. Websites across the country would crash. Cash machines and retail registers would be unable to process payments. E-commerce and financial transactions would be throttled. More importantly, as soon as it became obvious what had happened, a US tech stock crash of cataclysmic proportions was inevitable.

Lewis found her blood rising. "General, is this a threat?"

"No, it is the opposite. It is a warning, Madam Director. These assets, and others like them in the undersea and space domains, have already been moved into place. But to date, I and other like-minded individuals on the Politburo have successfully argued against their use. I am afraid, though, that if you continue your aggression in the South China Sea, I am not sure how long we can prevail."

She could not contain her anger. "General, the United States is China's superior in *all* domains, whether above or under the sea, in space, on land, sea, air, or cyberspace. We are not one of the minor Asian powers you are used to bullying. There is not a move you can make in any domain that has not been anticipated and you will soon find that Newton's Law applies –

every action on your part will provoke an equal and opposite reaction."

"I disagree with your opening premise, of course, Madam Director, but your argument is a version of the one I used myself. I can sense neither of us is a fan of war – cold or hot, conventional, cyber or nuclear. I see nothing but mutually assured destruction if we continue down this road."

Carmine took stock. Her priority right now was to get off this call and relay the intelligence about the potential attack to the Joint Chiefs for action. "General, you said you had a personal message you wanted me to pass on to President Fenner?"

"Yes. It is important you understand what I am about to tell you. I fear you may see Pagasa as a limited conflict about Philippine sovereignty over a small island in the Pacific, with the added bonus that it gives you the chance to 'give China a bloody nose' as you are fond of saying. But in Beijing, we see control of the South China Sea as a strategic pillar in the 100 Years' War."

"The hundred years' war?" Carmine frowned. It was a concept she had not come across.

"Ah, I had assumed you would be aware of the phrase. No matter. Since 1949, China has been striving to regain its place as a world power. Several years ago, at a closed Politburo meeting, our Premier declared his expectation that by 2059, that ambition would be realized. And he laid out four pillars that would signify we had won this 'hundred years' war'. The first and second pillars are full sovereignty over the provinces of Hong Kong and Taiwan. The fourth is China executing the first manned landing on Mars."

"The third pillar involves Pagasa?" Carmine couldn't help but sound dubious.

"Indirectly. The third pillar is effective Chinese control of the Three Seas: the Yellow Sea, East China and South China Seas. China has no ambition to 'dominate the Pacific', as you so often assert. But any meaningful military threat to China's future existence would require an invading army to cross one of the Three Seas to attack us. China will *never* be completely safe until we control the Three Seas."

Carmine had heard all of the various theories about China's quest for dominance in the South China Sea, from oil and gas resources, to fishing rights and national security. The way the Chinese General described it, it was an unquestionable strategic necessity. As essential to China as control of its borders with Mexico and Canada was to the USA. The only problem with that logic, Carmine knew, was that it was not shared by the other nations that bordered the 'Three Seas'.

"Let me make sure I understand," she said. "Boiling it down, you are saying China is going to make a stand over Pagasa and is already considering escalating this conflict into a major war."

"You have it, Madam Director. We did not think our small intervention on Pagasa Island would provoke the United States in the way it has. I and my allies on the Politburo have succeeded so far in influencing our leader to show restraint in the face of your aggression, but I do not know for how long that restraint will hold. Is a small rock in the South China Sea so important to US interests that it is willing to risk Total War with China?"

"Ah, but it is not just a small rock in the South China Sea, is it, General?" Carmine responded. "You just made clear it is control of that Sea itself at issue here, and China will not be satisfied until it can unilaterally decide who can and cannot sail in the waters of that Sea. You know very well that is a situation the USA could never entertain. You say you are against war, but you offer only threats, not a way out of this conflict."

The January DC air was as cold as the atmosphere on the call, but the Chinese General was not easy to dissuade.

"There *is* a way, Madam Director. The US has long recognized that Taiwan is a part of the People's Republic of China while maintaining 'unofficial' relations with that rogue State. I believe I could persuade my Politburo comrades to accede to a similar 'policy of ambiguity' over the South China Sea. The US could recognize the Republic of China's claims to certain territorial features in the South China Sea already inhabited by China, without surrendering the right to freedom of navigation in those waters, and in return, China would make certain … concessions."

She thought about this. "Are you saying that if we recognized your Spratly Islands bases, China would be happy to recognize Philippine possessions and allow US carrier strike groups to sail through the South China Sea?"

"Happy, no. Willing to negotiate a compromise, perhaps."

She had to get off the call. "I can tell you this, General. Our treaty with the Philippines is not ambiguous. The International Permanent Court of Arbitration has affirmed Pagasa Island as Philippine territory. Our defense treaty with the Philippines obliges us to come to the defense of the Philippines if its territory comes under attack, as Pagasa clearly did when you attacked it with cruise missiles and landed special forces soldiers. There can be no 'policy of ambiguity' about Pagasa."

"I can convey that message to our Premier, unofficially," the General said. "Will you similarly test the idea with your President?"

"Alright, but I'm not optimistic, General. We currently control the airspace over Pagasa and the sea around it and could land troops on that island at any time we so chose," she said, with more confidence than she felt. "In a very short period of time, Pagasa Island will be unassailable. My President is not likely to see this as a situation in which he should make any concessions, at all."

Of that, Lewis was sure. She had been standing beside Fenner when he signed the Executive Order to initiate the attack on Subi Reef base. After signing, he had put down his pen, pushed his chair back from the Resolute Desk and muttered to himself, "No more red lines. Screw you, China."

"It won't surprise you, then, that for rather different reasons, my Premier sees the situation in much the same way.

Nonetheless, if we are to avoid a world-shattering war, we must try to find a middle way."

In the air over the South China Sea, Bunny felt the Flying Crossbow missile strike and expected the bulkhead behind her to explode forward, crushing her and bathing her in fire. The Vapor bucked, but it settled back into normal flight quickly and she pushed its nose down, leveling out and swinging away from the boats below.

"Vapor, system integrity report."

All systems nominal.

"Nominal my furry red arse," a panicked Scottish voice said in Bunny's helmet.

Bunny swung her head around. The cameras inside the crew compartment showed Ginger McIntyre still lying spread-eagled on the floor of the fuselage, the nose and shaft of a Flying Crossbow missile sticking up about a foot from his groin as he began flailing his legs, trying to get away from the warhead but unable to because she had the Vapor in a powered climb.

"Bloody hell, Ginger," she said. "Be careful! You kick it, you could set it off."

"No shit, O'Hare," he said, still crabbing backward. "I got an idea, girlie. You come back here and mind the bollicking great warhead in the crew compartment, I'll fly the bluidy airplane."

She couldn't fault him for panicking. He was sharing an enclosed space with 10 lbs. of high explosive that by all rights should already have vaporized him and broken the plane's back. And it had been her near-suicidal attack run that had put it there. But the modular construction of the Vapor's payload bay meant there was no hatch between the cockpit and the crew compartment. She couldn't even bring him into the cockpit with her.

She checked her systems again, looked at the sky around her, scanned the sea below with her external cameras. She'd cut the two militia boats in two, men were flailing in the water around them. She was a little short on sympathy for them right at that moment. She had radar and comms back, could hear *Andromeda* hailing her. That meant *Andromeda* should have control of *Orion* again. They could look after themselves for the next few minutes.

"Ginger, just stop moving!" she said. She was worried his panicked backward scramble would dislodge something inside the crew compartment, with catastrophic results.

"O'Hare, you can kiss my..."

"Do you *want* to die?!" she asked, calmly and firmly.

He finally stopped flailing his legs and set his feet securely on the deck. "Och, alright. Now what?"

"Push yourself *slowly* back. The locker where you got your ballistic vest, can you get inside it? Put the other vests between you and that warhead?"

He looked over his shoulder. "Maybe ye could fit in there, ye bloody dwarf. But not me. Not in a million years."

"Then you've got one option. Take out every vest in that locker, wrap them around yourself and find a corner as far away from that missile as you can."

"I've got a better idea," he said through gritted teeth. "Tell me where I can find a parachute and I'll jump into the sea."

"Wish I could," she said. "But rotary-winged aircraft don't pack chutes. Usually fly too low to use them, plus, if things go wrong, our rotors are our parachutes."

"A lot of useless information, not helpful, O'Hare," he said. He had pushed himself backward and was sitting with his back up against the forward bulkhead, glaring balefully at the missile. "Assuming we make it back to *Andromeda*, how are we to land this freaking machine with that wee beastie sticking out of our belly?"

Bunny had already been thinking about that. Her radar showed the militia boats trailing behind the *Orion* had now started falling further back. The jamming had definitely been broken. It seemed the attack was ebbing out.

"I don't want to put the Vapor down on *Andromeda*'s helipad with the chance that thing could cook off. I'm not saying it's likely, but if it happened, apart from killing us, it could put *Andromeda* out of action too. I mean, it probably won't happen. But it could."

"Okay, was that your version of a pep talk?"

"Just running scenarios, Ginger," she told him. "The better option, I'm thinking, is we radio *Andromeda* and get her to lower a boat. I hover off their stern, we jump out with life vests, they pull us out of the water."

"*We* jump out?"

"Yes. You think I want to stay aboard this machine any more than you do?"

"And the Vapor?"

"I'll order her to land herself on *Orion* before I jump. *Orion* has three helipads, each of them rated to take much heavier aircraft than *Andromeda*'s helipad. Even if that missile cooks off as she lands, it won't put the *Orion* out of action."

Bunny saw Ginger stand up and start pulling ballistic vests out of the locker and then stand there, trying to work out how to wrap them around his legs, arms and head. "This is absolutely the last bloody time I fly with you, Bunny O'Hare," he muttered.

With the adrenaline of the engagement starting to wear off, her throbbing headache and the pain in her ribs came flooding back. She looked beyond Ginger at the warhead sticking up through the floor and her vision began to blur again. "It may well be, Ginger. It may well be."

"Find the source," Commander Daniel Okafor of the *USS Congress* was telling his Electronic Warfare, or EW, officer. "I want to know who is sending out that jamming signal, and I want them found yesterday."

Aboard the *USS Congress*, Okafor was leaning over the shoulder of his EW officer down in the ship's comms room.

His crew didn't love him for it, but he wasn't a man for standing on the bridge relaying orders and waiting for a response when the action was elsewhere. The mysterious jamming signal had appeared on the *Congress*'s sensors about thirty minutes earlier. It was too weak to disturb the frigate's sensors, and it was too weak to get a good bearing on it, but it was strong enough for them to pick it up.

That told Okafor it was military. Which he did not like.

Congress was patched into Space Command data on the Operations Area for his mission, and while it wasn't anything like real-time, it was current enough to tell him there should have been no naval traffic of consequence along the bearing of that jamming signal. No civilian traffic either, for that matter. Not the kind that would be radiating a jamming signal strong enough for *Congress* to pick up.

"Range estimate?"

"Uh, hard to say without knowing what's emitting the signal, but I'd like to say it's in the low single-digit kilowatt range, so ... lowball twenty, highball fifty-mile range?" the man said.

What had made Okafor leave the bridge and come down to talk with his EW officer was the fact they were supposed to check in with their target convoy when they hit fifty miles separation, and they'd done so.

But they'd gotten no response. And about fifteen minutes later, his EW officer had reported he was picking up radio signals consistent with military spec jamming equipment. Frustratingly, their own powerful surface radar, which would have been able to burn through the jamming, would be occluded by the large Philippine Bugsuk Island for at least the next twenty minutes.

He patted the officer on the shoulder. "Send that bearing to the CIC." Okafor watched the man work his keyboard, then reached for the button mike on his throat. "ACO, Captain."

"Air Control Officer, aye Captain."

"ACO, you should have received bearings on a radio interference signal. I want an MQ-20 in the air and flying down the bearing to that signal," he said. "Report back to me on any shipping or other activity."

"Aye, aye, sir."

The MQ-20 was a vertical takeoff and landing drone that could be deployed by any ship with twenty square yards of free deck space. It was hybrid-electrically powered, fitted with auditory-optical-infrared sensors and could lift and deploy a 300 lb. payload of sonar buoys or GPS locators. It could extend the eyes and ears of the *Congress* to points over the horizon in situations where its radar was blinded.

"Jamming signal down, sir," his EW officer said suddenly. "I've lost it. It's like it just shut down."

That should be good news, but Okafor was not happy. On the other side of Bugsuk Island was his mission objective, the White Star convoy. He should have met them and escorted them from Singapore Harbor. But *Fencepost* had kicked off 24 hours early and so he was still steaming through the Sulu Sea, two hours from the new rendezvous point.

Dammit, all they had to do was head up the coast of Malaysia and Brunei into Philippine waters without getting into trouble. What could possibly have gone wrong?

Kamito was looking at the wreckage in the water with his binos as his Mark V SOC craft powered towards Ibrahim's position. They'd gotten their radio signals back – which he took as a bad sign – but he couldn't raise Ibrahim. Another bad sign. What could possibly have gone wrong?

Alright, he'd seen that damn gunship fly down the port side of the huge freighter and fill his rib boats, and their crews, full of holes. He'd wasted precious time fishing the survivors out of the water before he and the two other Mark Vs had been able to head for Ibrahim's pair of two Mark Vs.

He had the drivers power the boats flat out. He had to reach Ibrahim before that damn leading vessel did. The *Andromeda*, wasn't that its name? As soon as the *Orion* had its control umbilical cut, that *Andromeda* had made a beeline for Ibrahim's boats, like it *knew* where the jamming was coming from. He guessed that if it got close to Ibrahim it would at the very least deploy its damn acoustic cannons. Those things could deafen a man for life. Rib boats were so fast they could get in under the bluff bows of a freighter and hide there where an acoustic cannon couldn't affect them, but the big Mark V patrol boats would be easy meat for the approaching feeder ship.

Fifteen hundred yards, he guessed, judging the distance to the *Andromeda*. They had maybe ten minutes before it was on them.

"There!" he yelled, pointing his boat driver at men splashing in the water, waving to try and get attention.

They eased up alongside the wreckage of the other watercraft, his men hauling their crewmates desperately aboard. Those who flopped into the bottom of the boat coughed seawater out of their lungs and then set about hauling other men aboard.

Kamito was scanning the water desperately for Ibrahim. He'd seen the black gunship flying low across the sea toward Ibrahim's element, seen both the aircraft and the ships open up on each other, the missile shooting out from Ibrahim's ship seeming to smack the aircraft amidships. He'd expected it to explode, but instead it had pulled up and away, as though fleeing from the battle. His men had let out a throaty cheer, but Kamito hadn't felt like joining them. He'd ordered his three Mark Vs to head for Ibrahim's boats at flank speed.

"Portside!" he yelled. A man was floating face down in the water there. *Ibrahim!* Five pairs of hands reached outboard and hauled him in, and he fell onto the bottom of the boat like a landed tuna. A man rolled him onto his back and started trying to resuscitate him, but Kamito didn't need to be a doctor to see it was going to be of no use.

Two minutes more and the three boats had pulled all the men out of the water that they could find. Most were alive, a lot weren't.

The lead ship, *Andromeda*, was closing now. Two hundred

yards off.

"Get moving," Kamito told his driver.

"Where to?" the man asked.

Kamito surveyed the damage around him. They had one rib boat left, three of five Mark V SOC craft. But no more mines. Their spare mines and poles had been aboard Ibrahim's boat, and that had been smashed, along with the jamming radio. He looked over at Ibrahim, the man who had been working on him climbing off now, defeated. Given the violence of the gunship's attack, he'd probably been dead before he hit the water.

"Maura terminal," Kamito said. "This job is a bust."

It wasn't a job Li Chen had wished on herself. The men in the command center around her probably didn't realize that. She tried to see the situation through their eyes. They had seen her march into their CO's office, claiming she had the authority of Rear Admiral Li Bing, and then what probably seemed like moments later saw their CO marching out, under arrest.

But if that was the most confusing thing that happened to them in this war – and Li Chen was under no misapprehensions, this 'limited maritime conflict' was indeed a war – then they were lucky.

Li Chen had not felt so lucky. She was a commander of a test pilot squadron. She was a combat pilot. She lived to push experimental aircraft to their limits, risking her life and the life of her pilots so that thousands of others would not have to. She had qualified the FC-31 *Gyrfalcon* stealth fighter for carrier operations on China's three new aircraft carriers. She had volunteered her unit to test the AI backseater for the J-16, even as rumors were spreading throughout the PLAN Air Force that the aircraft was cursed and its 'ghost' backseater had been responsible for the deaths of five pilots.

It was true, there were teething problems with the autonomous flight capabilities of the backseater AI. It proved capable in early testing of managing avionics, weapons, sensor and navigation systems, but it could not pilot the J-16 through basic fighter maneuvers or dogfights. Twice – not five times – it had flown its pilots into the dirt during mock dogfights.

Chen and her pilots had ironed out those bugs. They had learned to fly the machine within the limitations of its AI, and then use its capabilities to the maximum. Staying high, well out of visual range, they let the AI manage the aircraft while they managed the battlesphere, allocating targets, launching missiles, engaging enemy ground and air targets like they were Gods of the Air.

It was Li Chen's J-16 pilots who had informally renamed their unit from Special Aircraft Squadron to Ao Yin, named for the white bull demon with four horns that was always looking for victims to feed himself with. Their AI was never satisfied. No sooner had it locked and dispatched one target than it was looking for another, and another. They had horned bull motifs painted on the noses of their aircraft.

And that was where she belonged, up there with her pilots. Not down here on Mischief Reef, dealing with a million questions, large and small.

"Comrade Commander," the man standing in front of her said for the third time, trying to get her attention. Unsure of her exact rank, they had taken to calling her Commander, since she clearly carried an Admiral's imprimatur, which put her above the Lieutenant Commander she had replaced, even though she only carried Captain's stars on her lapels. "We have six aircraft on readiness, six on CAP, six inbound. You wanted to alter the standing order?"

Chen looked up from the summary of fuel, ordnance and provisions that she had asked to be prepared. "Yes, Lieutenant. Double the number on readiness, maintain five on combat air patrol at all times. I want those on readiness to be truly on readiness, able to be airborne within three minutes if I order it, is that clear? And pass the same order to Fiery Cross Reef base."

"Yes, Comrade Commander!" he said, and ducked out of

her office again.

Chen had just hung up from a call with the Admiral.

"Comrade Chen, were you absent from officer's school on the day our cadets were taught that your job is to make your superior officers' lives easier, not harder?" the Admiral had asked after greeting her.

Chen had smiled. The sixty-eight-year-old Li Bing had been like a grandfather to her; the mentor, benefactor and counsel that every young officer needed – no, dreamed of. She had no idea what had caught his eye but from the moment she had appeared in front of him to receive a decoration for her first combat action – during a brief and ill-judged conflict over Okinawa – he had made clear to her superiors that she had his favor, and should be awarded every opportunity to prove herself worthy of it.

"I may have been sick that day, Comrade Admiral," she told him. "I apologize if I have caused the Admiral any embarrassment."

"No more than usual, Chen," he said mildly. "Though it is not usual practice when assuming a new posting to place the commanding officer under arrest."

"He would not recognize your authority. Comrade Admiral," she said, moving on to the issue topmost on her mind. "Sir, I have adjusted our patrol posture to avoid the US engagement zone but retain the capability to respond instantly if we detect Philippine ships or aircraft trying to reinforce Pagasa. Can I request you send an officer more suited to this command than myself? I firmly believe I should be back with my pilots and…"

Li Bing's voice lost its warmth. "Commander Chen. Your beliefs, and your wishes, are irrelevant at this time. You were right to recommend we pull our air assets back from Pagasa and Subi Reef. I trust, therefore, that you are now doing what is needed to ensure the safety of our bases at Mischief and Fiery Cross reefs if the Americans should choose to expand this conflict."

"Yes, Comrade Admiral!"

His voice softened again. "Commander, I will share with you details I would not normally share with an officer of the line. I expect you to treat this confidence with respect."

Chen swallowed. "Of course, Comrade Admiral."

"From the moment of the attack on our forces on Subi Reef, the Americans' intentions were clear. And their perfidy was not unexpected. We have been preparing for this day for many years. How well do you know the history of the South China Sea, Commander?"

"My ancestors were traders in these seas, Admiral."

There was a respectful silence on the line before the man reacted. "I was not aware of that. That you find yourself in that place, at this time, would seem to be your karma, Commander."

"Yes, Comrade Admiral."

"And so, you would be aware that in reclaiming our position as masters of the South China Sea, we are merely reinstating the natural order that existed in that region since the Han Dynasty, for nearly one thousand years."

Chen had done well enough in history at school. "Against the western usurpers who have only made their claims in the last 100 years, yes, Comrade Admiral."

"In Beijing, they are referring to this conflict as the 100 Years' War, did you know that?" Li Bing asked. "It mattered not whether the trigger was Pagasa, another reef, another island ... a war with the West was inevitable. We have been preparing for it since 1 October 1949."

A war one hundred years in the making? The idea sent a shiver down her spine. But of course, it was true. It had been building from the moment China won the second Sino-Japanese war in 1945 and began to reclaim its former position in the world order.

"I will serve the People's Republic in any way I can, Comrade Admiral."

"I know you will, Chen. As I said, we have prepared for this day. From the moment American bombs struck *Chinese* troops on *Chinese* soil, we have been readying an air and sea offensive that will humble our main enemy. When the time comes to launch that offensive, you and your pilots will be the tip of the spear that drives into the Americans' hearts. Until then, you will do what is needed to keep our bases in the Spratly Archipelago safe."

"Yes, Comrade Admiral!"

As she had cut the call, she had returned to the boring work of reviewing the disposition of assets and logistics on Mischief and Fiery Cross reefs with new energy.

Tip of the spear in the 100 Years' War? She felt almost drunk with the thought. She was but a mote in the eye of the giant that was Chinese history, but she was about to earn her place in it.

White House Situation Room, January 10

Carmine Lewis felt like pouring herself a strong drink. A double bourbon on the rocks would do nicely right now. And maybe the same for the others in the room, even though it was only just past lunchtime.

Kahn and Abdor had started a shouting match and the rest of the participants in the meeting were trying to calm them both down. Except for Victoria Porter, who was regarding the debate with undisguised scorn. The room had dissolved into acrimony over the realization China was, once again, not playing by the *Fencepost* rule book. It was supposed to be bringing its air force into the theatre to oppose the US exclusion zone. It was not. It was holding them back, which meant that there was no chance of flying in Philippine reinforcements to shore up the troops on Pagasa. It also meant the PLA Navy air force was still a threat to the approaching White Star convoy, and the Chinese assault ship task force was getting closer by the hour.

The word 'cluster' had been used more than once.

Carmine Lewis had decided not to intervene, since if they were blowing steam at each other, they weren't blowing it at her, and she needed to focus. One of the screens in the Situation Room was showing a video feed so boring that everyone else had stopped watching it, except Lewis and Chairman of the Joint Chiefs, General Cavoli. Looking at her watch, and checking the feed, she leaned over to him. "Think we should bring that up on the main screen now and put the comms feed on loudspeaker?"

General Cavoli looked in the direction of the argument and motioned to an aide. "Should have done it long ago."

President Fenner slapped a hand down on the table. "Phil, Chuck, back the hell up," he said loudly. The room went suddenly quiet. "Now, I want you people to stop telling me how bad our situation is, and start giving me options…"

The room fell quiet and Carmine took the opportunity to insert herself. "Gentlemen, Madam Secretary. The US Navy Poseidon is approaching the Morro Bay cable node."

That got their attention, and they shuffled back to the table and sat down. As soon as Lewis had passed on the intelligence from her mystery Chinese contact, Cavoli had ordered his Navy counterpart to despatch an aircraft or ship to investigate whether it was true that China had parked unmanned submersibles over America's vulnerable cable nodes. That mission package had turned out to be a P8 Poseidon submarine hunter-killer aircraft.

Cavoli was listening to the communication between the pilot and his crew, and his commander at Naval Station Halsey Field in San Diego. Cavoli had a headset that could connect him to both the pilot and Halsey Field if needed, but for now he simply translated the rapid-fire, jargon-heavy communications for the people in the room.

"He's making a pass over the node and deploying scanning laser," Cavoli said. "Seafloor there is inside its 600-foot penetration range. If there is a Chinese sub over or near that node, we'll find it." The newly deployed blue-green laser system on the Poseidon could only penetrate about as far as sunlight under the surface of the water, but it had one big advantage over traditional sonar buoys that used sound waves to detect their targets – unlike the ping of a sonar buoy, the laser scanner was undetectable by the submarine below. It meant that a submarine hiding at depth would not know it had been spotted until the Poseidon dropped a homing torpedo right on top of it.

"He finds anything, he's not to attack, is that clear, General?" Fenner said. "At this stage, we just want to know what's down there. If anything."

"This whole thing could be a bluff, trying to take us off task," Kahn muttered.

"The mission is reconnaissance only, Mr. President," Cavoli confirmed. "That Poseidon is carrying ordnance, but I would need to authorize an attack."

Like most missions of its kind Lewis had monitored inside the White House Situation Room, watching and listening to the live feed was a combination of frustration at the fact that, for most of the time, nothing was happening, and fear that at any moment, something would.

Cavoli put a hand to his ear, listening to a rapid-fire discussion on the loudspeaker. "Contact…" he said. "It's picked up a large submerged object holding two hundred feet down, directly over the node. They're refining the contact, trying to identify it. Size and shape should be enough for confirmation."

"The bastards," Kahn swore, turning to Lewis. "Your source wasn't lying."

There was more dialogue on the comms, and Cavoli pulled off his headset, looking grave. "It's a match, sir. High probability the object is a Chinese HSU-003 submersible drone. Your orders?"

Fenner didn't hesitate. "Pull that aircraft out and get Navy, Coast Guard and divers out checking the damn seafloor up and down the East and West coasts and inside every harbor. If there's anything bigger than a dolphin out there, I want it tagged and flagged in case the situation goes south."

Lewis thought fast. The Chinese General had not lied. But he had mentioned China moving assets into place both under the sea *and* in space. "Any news from Space Command, General?"

Cavoli shook his head. "No new threats detected. But that doesn't mean they haven't repositioned either their kill-vehicle capable or satellite warfare satellites. Their new jamming sats aren't much bigger than a damn lunchbox and they've deployed near a hundred of them. We can't guarantee perfect information on their positions at all times."

"They cut those cables and take out our Pacific satellites, our communications with our forces on either Pearl Harbor or Guam are seriously compromised, correct, General?" Porter asked.

"Yes, Madam Secretary," Cavoli replied. "More than compromised. It will be like shouting into tin cans joined together by string, across the width of the Pacific."

"But a logical first move if the Chinese intention was to isolate our forces in the Pacific before a major attack?"

"Yes, ma'am. But we can't defend 5,000 miles of cable, and we shouldn't overestimate Chinese anti-satellite capabilities. The likelihood they'll take down our satcoms with Pearl and Guam is minimal."

"But not zero, General."

General Cavoli was massaging his temples. "No. The warning they gave to Director Lewis was pretty clear. They have submersibles in position to conduct similar attacks on other coastal US targets … maybe worse. And we may not be looking at conventional warheads, we could be looking at nukes."

Lewis started. "General, I disagree. I was the one who took that call. The Chinese General, if that is who it was, was warning us we are on the brink of a major war – one China is apparently prepared to fight. But no one was threatening us with nuclear weapons."

Cavoli leaned forward. "I have the transcript here, Madam Director. Let me quote: *I see nothing but mutually assured destruction if we continue down this road* ... The threat seems pretty clear to me."

Porter was nodding. "I agree with the General. The question, therefore, is whether we continue with *Fencepost*, ignoring the threat over our heads and under our seas as the Madam Director seems to suggest, or act now to de-escalate. We have been offered a diplomatic exit from this situation in which all parties can save face."

Carmine was being wedged. It was a classic Porter strategy. Position your adversary in a corner with arguments of their own making and then isolate them by allying yourself with an opposing view. The problem for Porter, and it was the reason she would never supplant Lewis in Fenner's circle, was that Carmine didn't play by that book.

"The Secretary of State is right," Lewis said. "Those *are* the options. Continue with our plan to fortify Pagasa and halt the Chinese expansion into the South China Sea, risking escalation to Total War, or back down and negotiate a deal handing China de facto control."

Porter wasn't done. She went to her fallback response when counterattacked. "What, then, do you suggest, Madam Director? Or is your contribution limited to summing up the obvious?"

Lewis sat back. To respond to the barb now would be to lower herself to Porter's level. Fenner would either have her back now, or he would not. Both she and Porter waited to see.

In fact, it was Vice President Tyler who smoothly interceded. "It seems to me, the deal offered by our backchannel Chinese friend is a win-win," he said. "For China. It would effectively cede control of the South China Sea to China and simultaneously destroy our relations with just about every nation in the region."

"Mr. Vice President, I do not agree," Porter said. "China agrees to keep its hands off Philippine territories in the Spratly Archipelago, and we get freedom of navigation in the South China Sea…"

"In defined sea lanes," Defense Secretary Kahn scoffed. "Some freedom."

"In mutually agreed sea lanes, Phil," Porter followed up. "In return, we recognize Chinese territorial possession of a few rocks and shoals in the South China Sea which, de facto, are already Chinese. I haven't heard anyone here saying they want to expand this war to try to push China off the bases it has already built?" She looked around the room and waited, but no one spoke up. "I thought not. So why not make the best of a geopolitical reality that already exists?"

Around the table, all eyes turned to Fenner. He leaned back in his chair and stared at the ceiling. Then he leaned forward, placing his hands on the table in front of him and staring at some point on the wall in the back of the room. "I don't like it. It has shades of Munich 1939. But neither do I like the idea of starting an all-out war with China. So, I'll think about it while you all earn your pay and do everything in your power to ensure that damn convoy gets to Pagasa in one piece."

"Captain, you have more than earned your pay today," the *Congress*'s Captain Okafor told his opposite number in the White Star convoy.

They had just managed to make radio contact with the ships they were to escort, and Okafor had listened in horror to the Captain's retelling of the events of the last few hours. *Congress* had launched a surveillance drone but it was still about thirty minutes out, so he had no vision of the convoy yet.

"You are sure the *Orion* is still seaworthy?" Okafor asked, dubiously. It sounded like the ship had been hit hard in the last militia attack.

"Yes, we put men over the side before we got her in control

and underway again. There are two holes in her portside hull, but both are a few feet above the waterline. We have sealed the cargo compartments near the holes and jury-rigged some patches. Any water that enters through the breaches in the hull can be contained." Pedersen sighed. "There was no damage to the cargo. *Orion* is still, as you say in your navy, mission capable."

Okafor looked at a plot on the screen in front of him. "We will come alongside in the next hour. From there it is still six hours to Pagasa Island."

"What is the situation around Pagasa, Captain?" Pedersen asked Okafor. "We have only been able to pick up scattered news on longwave radio since the jamming was lifted. Our satellite internet capability is not up and running yet."

Okafor considered carefully what he could, and couldn't, share with the civilian captain. Given what the man and his crews had already been through, he decided to err on the side of oversharing. "Philippine troops still hold Pagasa and show no sign of caving. China's naval and air base at Subi Reef has been rendered inoperative by US strikes, probably for at least the next 72 hours. We have air superiority over the Operations Area, but that isn't as good as it sounds, because China appears to have pulled its aircraft out."

"But not its troops?"

"No. They've reinforced nearby bases. No sign they're pulling any boots out." Okafor couldn't hide his own misgivings. "I hate to say it, but it looks like China isn't backing down as we'd hoped."

The civilian surprised Okafor with his response. "I don't give a damn about geopolitics, Captain. My orders are to get your cargo and vital humanitarian relief to Pagasa Island. That's why I signed on for this voyage, and that's what I'm telling my crews when they ask me why we are still sailing north, into a conflict zone."

Okafor nodded. He liked the man's simple perspective on events. He had a sailor's sensibility. *Don't worry about the storm approaching, sail the sea that lies off your bow.* "Understood, Captain Pedersen. You said your satellite comms are still down?"

Okafor heard muffled conversation in the background before Pedersen returned to him. "Yes, Captain. As I explained, we have weathered two pirate attacks. They were driven off by our helicopter, but it took damage and our helicopter crew is currently floating in the sea about a mile astern. One of them is my communications officer. We are in the middle of rescuing them, but until then, I have no communications technicians aboard."

"Wait. You lost your aircraft?" Okafor frowned. He'd studied the White Star convoy ship specs and was aware it had sailed with a vertical takeoff rotor aircraft. He wasn't aware it had the capability to drive off pirates, which he assumed meant it must have been armed or carried crew who were, but that was a conversation for a later time.

"No, it piloted itself back and landed on *Orion*."

Okafor looked in surprise at his executive officer, who was also listening in on the exchange. "I'm sorry, it landed *itself*?"

"Captain, I can give you a full report when *Congress* is alongside. It has been an eventful 24 hours."

The man sounded pained, on the edge of control. Okafor decided to let him go about his business. He checked his radar plot. "Very well, Captain. We are closing on your position. Is there anything I can do for you? I saw that both of your ships have helipads. I could fly a comms technician out to you."

"Thank you, but we hope to have our comms technician back aboard soon," the other man said. "But if you have an unexploded-ordnance disposal team aboard your ship, we could use them on the *Orion*. It seems our aircraft has a rather large missile sticking through its belly which could do with removing."

There had not been much left of former assistant comms technician and would-be assassin, Lawrence Winter, after he had been shredded by Bunny O'Hare. Not much that was recognizable, anyway.

But the surly bucket crew that O'Hare had passed on her way up to the bridge after being rescued had recovered several important items from the blood-steeped deck. Winter's pistol, his cell phone, and two intact thumbs. The hardware they handed to the Chief Mate, Bose, who locked it away for use in evidence, and the thumbs they double bagged with the rest of the body and placed in cold storage.

Which was lucky because his telephone was, of course, thumbprint locked. At the request of and, after he declined in revulsion, the rather forceful insistence of White Star Risk Group, Ginger McIntyre used the surplus thumbs of his former assistant to unlock his telephone and digitally clone it.

Their crucial role in *Operation Fencepost* meant Sylvie Leclerc's team was not alone in supporting the White Star convoy. She had access to the full resources of US Naval Intelligence and the security apparatus behind it. The digital clone of Winter's cell phone was sent for examination by the US National Security Agency.

On the cell phone they found the app Winter had been using to contact his Chinese handler. It was hidden inside a common brick-busting mobile game that required the user to log on. Looking behind it, they were unable to recover or read the encrypted messages Winter had been exchanging, but they could see several important details.

He had contacted his handler every day at 2300 hours local, following an incoming message. He responded by attaching and sending an encrypted text file. And of course, being dead, he had missed his last check-ins. The NSA cyber warfare expert who relayed the information to Leclerc told her in his experience, if an agent missed a scheduled contact, the cyber link to their handler would be considered burned and would go silent.

But they'd copied the app to a burner phone for her, just in case.

Inside the White Star Risk Group office she waited until 2300 hours and then opened the app. Once through the game welcome screen a popup appeared: *ENTER BONUS VOUCHER #...*

As she watched, the NSA AI working behind the app took over and started running pass phrases through the input field faster than she could possibly follow. She had no idea what algorithms lay behind it, but guessed from what she was seeing that NSA was quite familiar with the Chinese app. In seconds, it stopped churning and settled on a ten digit alphanumeric pass phrase it was happy with.

Here goes nothing, she thought, knowing she probably wouldn't get a second chance. She hit 'enter'.

A blank black screen with a blinking cursor appeared. And stayed blank. She tapped a key and saw it was accepting her input. Was she supposed to write something? She had agreed a strategy with the NSA and she followed it. It was pretty straightforward advice: 'try to provoke a response'.

She typed quickly.

>*The pilot is alive because your weapon misfired. Urgently need new instructions.*

The screen remained blank. Was the message even received?

Then it blinked.

>*Upload report*

They had decided that uploading anything at all would be sure to prompt suspicion. Because they had no examples of previous uploads, whatever they uploaded now would be so different from what had been uploaded before that it would only result in contact being severed. Also, according to NSA, it was unlikely Winter's Ministry of State Security handler was at the other end of the telephone. It would be a data clearing warehouse, a mailbox where a Chinese cyber warfare analyst would log the contact, validate it and then send any intelligence up through the system. She needed to get to Winter's MSS handler, not some random data processing flunky.

>*No. I am unclear how to proceed.*
>*Upload report*

Was she dealing with a dumb AI bot that had only one canned response? Or was there a human at the other side of the black screen? Leclerc decided that less was more.

>*No. Orders?*

She hit return and waited. She was about to give up when the cursor started blinking again and text flowed across the screen. It was definitely not a bot at the other end now.

>*Instructions follow. Prepare to destroy communications equipment and evacuate ship. Acknowledge.*

She frowned at the screen. No questions, just a simple order. Destroy the ship's comms equipment and get off it? How had Winter been planning to do that? Why were they ordering him to quit? No … there was a more important question.

>*How long do I have?*

The cursor on the black screen remained stubbornly static. After two long minutes, it moved.

>*Unknown.*

She swore out loud, causing a couple of people in the office to look her way. What did that mean? Was another attack on the convoy imminent or not?

>*If I act too soon they will be suspicious. I need a time frame.*

She tried to imagine the discussion at the other end of the line. Perhaps they really didn't know. It wouldn't be unusual for information regarding an imminent military action to be compartmentalized, shared only with those who needed to know.

>*You will receive a 30 minute warning. Prepare to act. END*

The messaging screen disappeared and she was dumped into the game app again.

She reached for her laptop. She had to get a message to the convoy. There was no way to interpret the conversation except that another attack was being planned. Destroying the comms equipment on the *Andromeda* would sever its links to both its escort, the *USS Congress*, and the *Orion*. It was an act from which there would be no way back for Winter, since he or McIntyre would be the only persons aboard capable of doing so. He would be 'burned' and China would be losing what was probably its key intelligence asset. They would surely only do so if a dramatic intervention was planned.

An air strike? No. More likely a submarine – invisible, deniable.

As she typed up her report she crossed her legs and saw she had a jagged run on her stockings.

Ah, the dangers of living a life of international intrigue.

The Chinese soldier had found a jagged splinter of metal in his thigh. Eugenio had watched, fascinated, as he sat up against a wall, strapped a tourniquet on his upper thigh, then worked the splinter out, fresh blood gushing out like a cork had been pulled. The man had nearly fainted, and Eugenio had rushed over to prop him up, certain he was going to die.

The bleeding had slowed, and Eugenio had gone and got a bedsheet, helping the man tear it up to make a pad and bandage it over the wound. It was soaked in an hour and had to be replaced, but the next one seemed to work better. The soldier ordered Eugenio to go with Diwa to pee in a bucket, and then tied her up again himself. She wouldn't eat and she wasn't saying much. Eugenio was worried about her.

Now he was alone with Eugenio in one of the front rooms, sitting with his head up against the wall, eyes closed, pistol on his lap, breathing faster now than he had been before. He was also starting to sweat, even though it was relatively cool inside the bunker. He suddenly opened his eyes and looked around, focusing on Eugenio after a moment.

"Do you have antibiotics?" he asked.

"What, sorry?"

"Pills, like for infection?"

"Maybe at the clinic," Eugenio told him. "I could go and…"

"No. You would bring soldiers."

"No, I wouldn't, I…" Yes, he would. That was exactly what he was thinking.

"Yes, you would. I would." He closed his eyes again. Maybe if he fell asleep, Eugenio could cut Diwa free and they could run for it. He stared at the soldier's right arm. More particularly, the scars on his right arm he'd seen when he was fixing the guy's bandages. The commando had thick round scars on the inside of both forearms, from his wrists to his elbows.

"What are you looking at?" the man asked. Eugenio saw with a start his eyes were open again. "These?" He held out his right arm so Eugenio could see. "Cigarette lighter burns," he told him.

That was pretty scary. "Is that part of your training?"

The man let out a short laugh. "No. Do your parents ever argue or fight?"

"Sometimes."

"Mine used to fight really bad. When I was younger, I couldn't get the words out to tell them to stop." He looked at his arm, touching one of the scars. "When they saw me doing this, then they would stop."

Eugenio reached out without really thinking about it and touched the man's arm. He didn't pull it away. "They must have fought a lot."

"Yeah," he said. "Then I joined the commandos and my parents were the least of my worries." He adjusted the pistol in his lap, putting his hand over it. Then he set an alarm on his watch. "I'm going to sleep thirty minutes now. You should stay still and not wake me, or I might get confused and shoot you.

Stay where I can see you. Got that?"

"OK."

"OK. When I wake up, we are going to wait until it is dark, and you are going to help me down the hill, to the beach."

"Why?"

"You ask too many questions," the man said. He picked up the pistol and waved it at Eugenio. "You help me, and you and your girlfriend go free. OK?"

"OK."

Ruan watched the kid slide back against a wall through half-closed eyes. He was a good kid. Ruan wasn't a kid person, but this one seemed almost human. He cried a bit, but he didn't whine and complain all the time. And this place, well ... he and his little girlfriend had really done a good job cleaning it out and stocking it up. That showed a lot of get up and go too, the two of them up here, making believe the world had ended and they were the only two left alive.

Which, actually, wasn't too far from the truth of it, far as Ruan could see. Their ambush and the cruise missile attack were supposed to persuade the Filipinos to get off Pagasa. Instead, they'd counterattacked. So, he'd called down a rain of high explosive on them, but that had gone wrong too. What had Liu been thinking, calling artillery down on their own position? He stopped himself, heard his mother saying ... *don't speak badly of the dead, Ruan.*

So why are you alive, Ruan? Damn good question, Ma. He touched the locket on a small silver chain around his neck that his mother had given him when he'd made radio technician. No, it couldn't be that simple. His Ma had given him the expensive chain and locket because she'd been so glad he wasn't going to be a rifleman, and Ruan hadn't had the heart to tell her that a radio operator had twice the chances of getting shot as a rifleman, because his radio antenna made him a sniper magnet. Also, it weighed nearly 30 lbs., which meant he had to swim, wade through the surf and go into combat with at least 15 lbs. more weighing him down than the other guys.

Still, there was some reason he'd made it through. Maybe it would become apparent. Just do the next thing, Ruan, and then the thing after that – worry about tomorrow tomorrow.

He realized his mind was wandering. Thinking about a conversation he had with Liu before they dropped off the side of the patrol boat and climbed onto their UDVs. He'd patted his throat under his wetsuit for about the tenth time, checking the locket his Ma had given him was there.

"What the hell is with the fidgeting, Ruan?" Liu had asked.

"Nothing, Lieutenant," he'd told Liu. But he didn't look convinced. "My neck chain," he admitted. "My Ma told me to wear it for luck, but it itches. I'm thinking I should take it off."

Liu had shaken his head, pulling his face mask up and getting ready to jump into the sea. "You wear it. We're going to need all the luck we can get."

Ruan had worn it. But a lot of luck it had brought them. Sure, he was alive, but everyone else in his unit had either been taken out during the retreat or killed by the artillery strike *he* had called down on them. And now, it seemed, it had all been for nothing.

Sepsis. Septic shock. That was what he was worried about right now. The shell splinter he had pulled from his leg had been small, but it had gone in deep and left a jagged wound. He had nothing to sterilize it with. He'd lost a lot of blood before he recognized the wound was more than just a torn muscle. Low blood pressure. Accelerated breathing. Fever. Yeah, definitely septic shock setting in.

An ordinary person would probably feel disheartened at that thought. Or distraught at the thought his entire team was either dead, wounded or prisoners of the Filipino Seabees. But Ruan was not an ordinary person. Ruan was the first one in his family to have applied to try out for the brutal training regimen of Jiaolong Commandos precisely *because* he was not ordinary. In fact, he inhabited a very special place on the autism spectrum that gave him an ability to focus on whatever he had been told to do, to the exclusion of petty distractions such as pain, fatigue, confusion or wasted emotion. His passing out report had said as much.

Corporal Ruan has stamina and endurance beyond anything I have seen in a Jiaolong Commandos candidate before, the sergeant responsible for his training had written in his confidential report. *He has a tendency to question orders which to him do not make sense, and lacks the wit not to ask the same question twice if he doesn't like the answer. But if I was tasked to put together a list of personnel able to penetrate deep behind enemy lines, execute their orders and fight their way out surviving on nothing but typhoid ridden water and the blood of the leeches they pulled from their nether regions, Corporal Ruan would be at the top of that list.*

Ruan was not dismayed. He knew what his situation was, and he knew what he had to do about it. He'd eaten, now he had to sleep, build up some energy. Then he had to get down to the coast where they'd moored their small underwater delivery vehicles, contact the patrol boat offshore, and get himself extracted. His head nodded and he caught himself, looking through hooded eyelids at the kid. He showed no sign of making a run for it. Good kid. Loyal to his little girlfriend. He wouldn't do anything stupid.

Ruan closed his eyes. He felt bad and it was hard to sleep with a bad conscience. He couldn't let the two kids go free, or the Filipino Seabees could send their little gunboat after him and capture him before he made it a mile offshore. There was just no way.

Captain Heraldo Bezerra narrowed his eyes, looking up. He heard aircraft, high overhead. Looking up, he saw the deltoid shapes of two American drones that had become a regular sight in the skies over Pagasa. At first, the sight had caused his troops to cheer, but as every hour went past without word they were being reinforced, the cheers had subsided. He hadn't the heart to tell his men what he'd been told by the 2nd Marines forward base at Puerto Princesa. There were no Philippine reinforcements on the way: their ancient troop transports would be too vulnerable to attack by PLA Navy aircraft, even with US air support. The American convoy, protected by its powerful escort, was their best, their only hope.

Well, at least the American convoy was still on its way. So, he had to be ready.

He turned and surveyed the damaged deep-water pier. Two long sections of planking had been destroyed in the cruise missile and naval artillery bombardments. And the ramp up from the pier was still missing fifteen yards. He had every single available man working on it. It was going to be touch and go. He'd been told the convoy had helicopters that could shuttle some personnel back and forth, but it was the medium landing ship that would be ferrying the bulk of the troops, radar, missiles and their launchers from the transport ship that would anchor out in deeper waters.

The floating dock wouldn't be able to withstand a tropical cyclone but as long as it didn't take a direct hit from a 2,000 lb. bomb, it would be more than sufficient for landing a platoon-sized detachment of US Marines, their supplies, and ordnance. Heraldo had been let into the plan for Pagasa to the extent his superiors felt was necessary for him to do his job. The White Star Lines *Orion* and *Andromeda* transport ships and frigate *USS Congress* would be arriving offshore in the next 48 hours. A US Marine rifle squad would be flown off the *Congress* first, as soon as the convoy got within helicopter range. The feeder vessel *Andromeda* would then offload the rest of the US troops plus naval and air defense missiles and launchers on Pagasa. Last of all, the construction materials they needed to fully repair the runway and harbor.

He watched his men laboring in the sun. Water. He'd get cold water brought over from the village, give them a break. A short break. But that was a Seabee's life, wasn't it? From their first day in boot camp, they learned that they'd be spending a lot more of their time in uniform with a shovel or ax in their hands than a rifle.

Li Chen had just finished discussing the new revetments that she'd ordered the air base engineers to construct to protect her precious aircraft. The reason the base's previous CO had his aircraft parked up in rows like he was expecting an inspection was because the base was not designed for extended support of so many aircraft. He had nearly 36 aircraft on the base now, and only 12 hardened concrete revetments that could park two aircraft each. That had left a full squadron of aircraft, not surprisingly her own J-16s, parked out in the open.

The Lieutenant in charge of the engineers had tried at first to complain that they didn't have enough sand and concrete to build the twenty-foot-high protective walls around the now widely dispersed fighters that she'd demanded. So, they'd agreed to a compromise: they would slope the floor of the shelters downward and use the sand they dug out to build the walls up to at least ten feet on three sides. That would put her fighters inside packed earth, reinforced berms at least six feet higher than their cockpits, two aircraft to one revetment. The berms wouldn't be enough to stop a direct hit from an American bomb or cruise missile, but they'd absorb and redirect any blast damage or shrapnel from a near miss. And with canvas stretched over the top of them, American satellites wouldn't find it easy to count her airframes or identify their aircraft type.

It was a compromise. The aircraft would have to be manually towed out of their shelters instead of being able to taxi out themselves, loading them with fuel and ordnance would take more time, but an aircraft that had to be towed out in order to arm, refuel and take off was better than one that lay in a smoking pyre because a stray enemy bomb landing a hundred yards away had shredded it.

The Lieutenant had estimated 48 hours to complete the six

additional revetments. She wanted them *yesterday*, but she'd given him 30.

She had a cup of cold jasmine tea on her desk and sipped it thoughtfully as she looked out across the air base. Eighty percent of the aircraft were now housed in the makeshift revetments. Within 24 hours, they all would be.

And she would be ready.

At 0400 that morning, she'd taken a call from Admiral Li Bing. "Comrade Commander," he'd said, using her temporary title. "I have good news."

Her mood had lightened at that. She needed some good news. She'd just finished reading a report from her intelligence unit about Chinese losses in the Pagasa conflict to date. Two Coast Guard *Jiangwei* class frigates sunk. Seventeen aircraft destroyed, eleven pilots lost over Pagasa, before she had persuaded the Admiral to stop wasting them defending Subi Reef and pull them back. In the attacks on Subi Reef, another ten aircraft, fixed and rotary winged, and thirteen personnel killed or wounded. The American attacks on Subi Reef had been brutal, and indiscriminate. What kind of enemy was this?

A ruthless one, Chen, she told herself. *Don't forget that.* She turned her mind back to the Admiral's last comment. "What good news, Comrade Rear Admiral?"

"We will have the air assets in place to support the planned assault on Pagasa within 36 hours. Our task force has slowed to ensure it does not reach the American exclusion zone before then, but that has enabled us to supplement the task force with a *Renhai* class cruiser, the *Dalian*."

Chen nodded. The *Renhai* class was China's most advanced stealth destroyer, similar in capability to the American *Ticonderoga* class. She could manage any role, from anti-air to anti-ship or shore attack, but her real power lay in her ability to close on enemy surface combatants before they realized she was there, and then from a hundred nautical miles away decimate them with the unstoppable power of an electromagnetic rail gun that could fling its shells through the sky at seven and a half times the speed of sound.

In company with the two anti-air destroyers already in the task force, it made for a fleet more powerful than anything the Americans could bring to play in the Operations Area within that timeframe, unless they decided to commit a carrier strike group, and there was no sign so far of that.

"That is good news, Comrade Admiral. I have reordered the combat patrol roster to ensure we always have a squadron airborne, one on readiness and one recycling, both here and on Fiery Cross. And I have taken the precaution of ordering the engineers to ensure all parked aircraft are protected from blast damage. Thirty-six hours will be more than enough time for them to complete their work."

"Excellent. We still do not expect the Americans to widen this conflict to include our bases on Mischief or Fiery Cross reefs, but it always pays to expect the worst. Have you had to put down any more mutinies?"

She'd smiled. "No, Comrade Rear Admiral. The Commander on Fiery Cross had been updated on events here and has been most respectful in his communications."

"Good. You will be pleased to know I plan to replace you before we renew air operations over the Spratlys. Lieutenant Commander Choy will be flying in tomorrow morning and the man you have under arrest will be returned to Dalian for a disciplinary hearing."

Another officer might have felt wounded pride at the news her temporary field promotion was already being revoked. But Li Bing knew his mentee well. Chen felt only relief. She was best suited – both in age and in temperament – to lead from the front, in her cockpit, not from behind a desk. "Yes, thank you, Comrade Rear Admiral. Sir, with your permission, I have identified a weakness in the American strategy and would like to exploit it when we re-engage."

"I would hope my planning staff has already identified it, Captain, but I am interested to hear it."

"Sir, the American stealth aircraft are launching self-guided missiles at us from outside fighter radar range and our ground radars at Mischief and Fiery Cross reefs are having trouble picking them up. But they have an Airborne Warning aircraft supporting them over Luzon, probably flown off their carrier. It is feeding targeting data to their fighters."

"Yes, that seems to be their strategy. We have explored the option of targeting the American carrier with ballistic missiles or submarines, but that would be an escalation Beijing is not willing to consider, yet."

"Of course, sir. But if we can just bring down that Airborne Warning aircraft, it could force them to close to where we have a better chance of engaging them."

"It is no doubt flying over Philippine airspace, behind their fighter screen."

"Yes, sir. But still, I believe an attack would be possible."

There was a pause as Li Bing weighed her argument. "We have not considered operations over the Philippines yet, Captain, because we do not want to legitimize the basis for this conflict by declaring war on either the US or its Philippine vassal. If the Philippines tried to invade Pagasa with ground troops, that might change. But for now, the conflict is contained, and very soon, it will be decided."

Contained? Two Coast Guard frigates sunk; seventeen aircraft shot down!? She kept the thought to herself.

"Sir, I can carry out the attack on that aircraft personally, with a single aircraft," she said. "If needed, you could denounce it as the action of a rogue pilot."

She could almost hear the cogs turning inside the Admiral's head. "I will put your suggestion to my staff," he said. "In the meantime, plan to resume area denial operations over Pagasa from 0200 hours, January 11."

"Yes, Comrade Rear Admiral!"

Point of the spear. She and her pilots would be ready.

Where the metal hits the meat

White Star Risk Group offices, Singapore Marina Center, January 11

Sylvie Leclerc was ready too. She'd been ready for a night and half the day. Sitting in her office at White Star Risk Group as one shift of her *Fencepost* team checked out, and another shift checked in.

She'd pulled two chairs together and used them as a makeshift bed, feet up, head lolling on her chest as she dozed, her cell phone in her lap. Somewhere in Virginia, USA, there was a cyber warrior doing the exact same thing as her, with another clone of the Chinese app. She'd been told she could stand down, the app would be monitored 24/7.

She didn't care. She'd made the mistake of leaving the background check on Winter to others to follow up, and that had nearly cost the Australian pilot her life. She wasn't going to let something like that happen again, even if it meant sitting here staring at a silent cell phone for hours.

Not that she had much more to do right now, beyond routine White Star duties. Since the US Navy frigate had joined up with the convoy, her role as go between had become redundant, with the *Congress* taking over the job of shepherd, and bringing its own superior intelligence gathering resources into play.

One of her Risk Group analysts had kindly offered to bring her noodles, and she'd gratefully accepted. She was sitting twirling her fork in the bowl and inhaling the delicious spicy aromas when the cell phone on the table suddenly buzzed.

She dropped her fork and grabbed the phone, opening the Chinese app with an oyster-sauce-stained fingertip. In the message field was a single two-word sentence.

Act now.

She jumped to her feet and walked quickly to the door of her office. "Someone, get me an encrypted line to US Naval

Intelligence!"

300 miles SE Pagasa Island, Philippine territorial waters, January 11

"Contact! Bearing zero zero niner, depth 150, range ten miles."

"What have you got?" the *USS Congress*'s Tactical Action Officer, or TAO, asked his sonarman.

"Subsurface object ahead, sir. No propulsion sounds on passive arrays, it's dead in the water and dead ahead of us."

On the bridge, Commander Okafor was monitoring the exchange. Thirty minutes earlier they'd received a direct communication from the Office of Naval Intelligence that another attack on the convoy was imminent, and the threat vector was probably military. Possibly an air or missile attack, more probably subsurface. How the hell they had gotten that intel he had not bothered to ask, and probably did not want to know. He'd immediately ordered the ship to general quarters.

It wasn't unusual to come across a submerged object at some point on a long voyage. Containers were lost off container ships all the time and didn't always sink straight away. It could also be a capsized fishing boat, or a dead whale for that matter. Only laser sounding or active sonar could tell him exactly what they were dealing with, but everyone on the bridge was thinking the same thing.

Submarine.

His XO, "Knuckles" Diavolo, put Okafor's thoughts into action without him needing to give an order. "TAO, Bridge, send the Firescout drone to prosecute that contact." When his order was confirmed, he turned to the Comms watch. "Contact Pedersen on *Andromeda*. Tell him to prepare to turn port ten degrees inside the next five miles."

Okafor realized he was gripping the console in front of him

with white knuckles, and told himself to calm the hell down. A submerged container. It was probably just a submerged container.

The *Congress* had met up with *Orion* and *Andromeda* just off Banggi Island and the convoy was proceeding line astern up the coast of the Philippine island of Palawan, inside Philippine economic territory waters. They'd planned to hold their current course for another fifty miles before turning northwest toward Pagasa, a dogleg track made necessary by the shallow and dangerous waters of the Spratly Archipelago. But also, one that kept them as far from the Chinese base at Mischief Reef as possible, for as long as possible.

Okafor had sent an ordnance disposal team over to the *Orion* as requested. When the Petty Officer leading the team had told Okafor he'd 'never seen anything quite like it', Okafor had asked him to send images back. Sticking diagonally through the floor of the White Star tiltrotor was a Flying Crossbow missile, its warhead protruding two feet up into the crew compartment. He had seriously considered ordering Pedersen to get his pilot to fly the machine off the *Orion* and ditch it in the sea, but he had a nagging feeling they might need the tiltrotor. The Vapor looked like an advanced version of the Bell V-280 tiltrotors he was more familiar with, and if so, it would prove very useful ferrying men and materiel to Pagasa when they got within range. It had taken four nerve-wracking hours, but his men had gotten the warhead off the missile and then cut the body of it out of the floor of the tiltrotor without blowing holes in themselves, or the landing pad on the *Orion*.

The two ships' crews had been through hell in the first two days of their voyage. Not least the tiltrotor's pilot. While his ordnance team had been working on her aircraft, he had her brought across to the *Congress* to give Okafor and his Master at Arms a fulsome explanation of how it was she had come to be shot, regain consciousness, launch the tiltrotor and hose *Andromeda*'s deck with cannon fire, with fatal consequences for *Andromeda*'s comms assistant, before passing out again.

His first impression had not been promising. He'd checked her record and though it was not spotless – not even close to – he'd expected someone more ... *squared away.*

Instead, the woman standing before him reminded him less of a former combat pilot and more like a roadie for a heavy metal band. She was about five foot six, with cropped, dyed platinum hair, and wore a leather flight jacket over a torn black t-shirt through which he could see no skin, only tattoos. She had two nose rings, a stud in her lip, another in her eyebrow. After being shown into Okafor's stateroom by his Master at Arms, she stood in a very relaxed 'at ease' stance, but also with a look of open hostility.

Okafor tried to disarm her. "Lieutenant O'Hare, welcome, please sit down. This is an informal discussion, nothing you say here will be used in evidence in any legal proceedings."

"Not a Lieutenant anymore, Captain," O'Hare told him, not moving to sit. "That was several lives ago."

Okafor tapped a tablet on the table in front of him with a callused finger. "From the White Star dossier that Captain Pedersen forwarded to us, and his account of your defense of his convoy, it seems you can take the girl out of the Air Force, but you can't take the Air Force out of the girl, Lieutenant."

Now the pilot sat, wincing as she took off her jacket and slung it over the back of the chair. "Does that mean I'm not under arrest?"

He shook his head. "I'm sorry, that's not something I can decide. When we make port again in Guam, you'll be met by officers of the Fleet Master at Arms and have to explain yourself to them. Despite the extenuating circumstances, a man *has* died by your hand."

She seemed to be weighing her words before she replied. "Actually, sir, by my count somewhere between ten and twenty men died by my hand over the last few days." She fixed him with a hard gaze. "Since you're counting."

"That, Lieutenant, is why you are sitting here right now, having this friendly conversation," Okafor's Master at Arms said. "And not being led to the *Congress*'s brig."

She frowned. "Not following."

Okafor spread his hands on the table. "How familiar are you with developments on Pagasa Island in the last 48 hours?"

She shrugged. "Not very, to be honest. All I know about Pagasa is we are supposed to be delivering a few hundred tons of building materials, medical supplies, fuel and ammunition to Pagasa to the Seabees there, on behalf of the Philippine government, and it's *your* job to get us there in one piece," O'Hare said, not letting him know how much she really knew, since she wasn't supposed to know it. "Which, since we're being all friendly, I have to say, the US Navy has not been doing a terrific job of so far. Sir."

Okafor let the remark slide. "Getting shot up by a few pirates is nothing compared to the hell those Philippine troops and civilians have been going through over the last week, Lieutenant," Okafor said, his eyes narrowing. "They have been hammered by cruise missiles and naval artillery, and attacked by a force of Chinese commandos inserted by submarine. In their defense, one of our aircraft took out two Chinese Coast Guard frigates, and *USS Doris Miller* has knocked their Subi Reef base out of commission, but those Philippine Seabees are only hanging on by the skin of their teeth."

"I'm guessing the shooting isn't over yet," O'Hare said.

"Not even close. My read on this is that we hoped that if we got in behind the Philippines, China would back off. Instead, they antéd up." He turned on his tablet and pulled up a database, showing O'Hare an image of a ship. A *massive* ship. "The *Yushen*. Currently inbound Pagasa in the company of two destroyers and a cruiser, with up to 2,000 Chinese Marines embarked. We are doing our utmost to arrive in theatre before it does, but it will be close."

Bunny wasn't fazed. "So, sink it."

Okafor smiled. "Would it were that simple, Lieutenant."

She shrugged. "World's most powerful navy, you telling me you can't sink a little assault ship? I thought you just said you sunk two Chinese Navy frigates?"

"*Coast Guard* frigates. And maybe it will come to that, but we are trying to prevent a full-scale war, not start one." He paged forward to an overhead image of helicopters lined up on the *Yushen*'s deck. "We expect that as soon as the *Yushen* gets inside helicopter range, about 150 miles out, they will load troops onto these Z-20 choppers and move on Pagasa. They could theoretically put 600 combat troops ashore inside three hours."

"So, your aircraft can shoot them down before they hit the beach."

"They're ready to do so, but they can't engage until the Chinese units get inside 20 miles and China will probably throw every fighter it has on Mischief and Fiery Cross reefs into the fray to protect them. Too many would get through."

Bunny looked at the photographs. The big Chinese helicopters looked like copies of the American Blackhawk, and probably were. She quickly grasped the tactical situation. "I was briefed that you are carrying a Marine rifle company?"

"Closer to a platoon. Forty men. But most importantly, every squad is armed with MANPAD missiles that *can* deal with any Chinese choppers that make it through."

"Assuming you can get them to Pagasa first. Why aren't the Philippine armed forces flying their own troops in already?"

"They don't have the airlift capacity, and even if they did, China has more than enough air power in the theatre to cause significant casualties. We didn't expect this mission to be a footrace and when we planned it, we expected to be able to call on US transport aircraft out of Clark Base to fly in the Phillipine troops after we got to Pagasa. Pentagon won't risk those machines at this time."

"My Vapor can carry 15 troops and their equipment. It is big and ugly, but stealth coated. We go in tonight, three trips, I could have your men ashore by daylight. What protection can you give me?"

Right on cue, there was the sound of jet fighters circling overhead. They all looked up. "Our friends have arrived,"

Okafor told her. "We will have a minimum of six Fantoms overhead for the rest of this voyage. We also have standing combat air patrols over Pagasa. And this ship can cover you out to 200 miles with its anti-air missiles, while *Doris Miller*'s pilots can cover the LZ. A single aircraft could get through."

"I don't know the *Doris Miller*," Bunny admitted. "It has electronic warfare aircraft?"

"Electronic warfare configured Sentinel drones."

"If they have a spare, I want one riding shotgun," she said. "That Vapor is not so hot at dodging missiles. Better we don't get spotted."

Okafor remembered her wincing as she took off her jacket. "I have to ask. How bad were your injuries?"

She reached up and felt her shoulder. "The Andromeda has a good doctor: he said I escaped with mild concussion, maybe a fractured rib. He said the bullet hit just below my left sub-something artery but stopped before doing too much damage, due to my awe-inspiring musculature." She paused. "I'm paraphrasing but I know that's what he meant, though he did say the carbon nanotube mesh in my flight jacket also helped." She frowned. "There is one medical risk I should raise, though."

Okafor leaned forward. "What's that?"

"I have been spending a lot of time in close proximity to a very red-headed Scotsman," she said. "I have no idea what the side effects of that might be."

Okafor thought about the exchange and looked quickly at the monitor to his right that showed activity on the aft helipad. O'Hare had flown the tiltrotor over and it was in the process of being loaded with the Marines' ordnance. He was not completely comfortable with putting his Marines' lives in the hands of the unknown and unorthodox Australian pilot, but none of his own aviators were qualified to fly the experimental tiltrotor and there was no time to have a suitable machine and pilot fly in from the *Doris Miller*, 1,300 miles away.

He tuned back in to the audio feed from his CIC. "Firescout

sounding report. Object displacement is estimated at 7,000 tons. Length ... three-sixty feet. Beam 36 feet. Request permission to deploy sonar buoy."

Seven thousand tons! *Not* a damn container, then. And not a dead whale. Okafor knew his sonar team would be running the data from the laser sounder aboard the Firescout through their AI, but he was already willing to make a bet.

Chinese Type 95 nuclear attack submarine. Lying in wait.

Diavolo looked a question at Okafor and he gave a terse nod. His XO took the microphone. "CIC, Bridge. Deploy buoy and ready ASROC with dummy charges."

The Firescout drone could drop a sonar buoy right on top of the contact. Even though the Type 95 had an anechoic sonar-absorbing coating, at a depth of 150 feet they should be able to get a solid return. Dropping the buoy so close would also tell the Chinese submarine's Captain he had been spotted.

What happened next was up to him. Diavolo had ordered his subsurface weapons officer to prepare to engage the contact with anti-submarine rocket or ASROC dummy charges, a standard procedure in peacetime to either scare away a potential threat or force it to the surface to identify itself. They would only be used if the contact made a threatening move, like opening a missile or torpedo launch tube.

"Buoy deployed; contact confirmed. Classifying ... Chinese Type 93 or 95."

Okafor had been right. He turned to his XO. "Announce battle stations. Helm, port ten degrees, ahead full. Alert *Andromeda*."

As his orders were relayed, in the feed from the CIC, Okafor heard a voice on the edge of panic. "*Cavitation*. Contact is moving. Updated acoustic classification, Type 95 ... torpedo doors opening! I have acoustic launch indications."

"ASROC, fire dummy charge. Deploy countermeasures." Seconds later, from vertical launch cells behind the superstructure, two anti-submarine rockets shot into the air toward the contact's location. At the same time, a sonar jamming pod dropped from the stern of the *Congress* and began trailing through the water behind it, to both jam and decoy any incoming torpedo. At this point, the anti-submarine defense crew did not know whether the noise of launch tubes opening on the Chinese submarine meant a conventional torpedo or a missile launch, so they also deployed a Nulka anti-missile decoy – a drone that shot from its launcher to hover off the stern of the *Congress* and draw enemy missiles to itself.

"Contact is turning to heading one two four, depth 160, range 14 thousand six, speed six knots climbing. ASROC splashdown ... charges ..."

The small dummy charges on the rockets were set to detonate almost immediately on splashdown so that the risk of damage to a submarine below would be minimal and their intended effect, as warning shots, would be obvious.

"... charges ... detonation ... contact cavitation increasing, it's going deep, depth 180, 190 ... *torpedoes*! Torpedoes in the water!"

Okafor gripped the console desk in front of him and stared fiercely out ahead of his ship as though his gaze alone could stop the Chinese torpedoes. His calm voice belied the tension in his gut. "ASROC, load Mark 54, bracket the contact, shoot when ready. Alert *Andromeda*."

Diavolo relayed his order and after a short delay, two more anti-submarine missiles blasted out of the *Congress*'s vertical launch tubes, arcing overhead toward their starboard forequarter. This time they were not fitted with dummy charges but with Mark 54 homing torpedoes.

Okafor watched the plot showing his outgoing missiles and the incoming torpedoes. Fewer than eight minutes had passed since the Chinese submarine had first been identified by the *Congress*, and within the next eight minutes, one or both of the two ships could be dead.

Bunny O'Hare grabbed for a support column in the crew

compartment of the Vapor as the *Congress* heeled hard over to port. Bunny had been acting as impromptu loadmaster as members of the *Congress*'s crew had begun stacking crates of small arms ammunition, grenades and anti-air missiles into the rear of the crew module. There was bucket seating for sixteen in the compartment, and they even had to lay missile crates under the seats in order to get the ordnance of a full squad of Marine riflemen stowed away. Bunny wasn't worried about the weight – her Vapor was rated to lift a 10,000 lb. Howitzer if needed – but the machine wasn't armored, as Ginger had discovered to his lasting horror. Even a heavy-caliber rifle round through the floor of the payload module could touch off one of those missiles and…

Tonight's problem. Right now, she needed to see why the *Congress* was trying to imitate a jet ski swerving between angry surfers. Luckily the Vapor was securely tied down.

At that moment, the Battle Stations klaxon sounded and the men around her aircraft started running with intent in every direction. As she climbed out, she saw two missiles blast out of the rear vertical launch tubes, and a decoy rocket began hovering behind them in a cloud of smoke. By the missile's trajectories, she could see they were ASROCs. There was a hostile submarine out there somewhere.

Not. Good.

"O'Hare, what's going on?" a Scottish voice from the *Andromeda* said in the earbud which Ginger had given her. "I just spilled me tea we turned so sudden."

Bunny looked around her. She'd only been aboard a warship in a combat zone once before in her life, and that had been during an attack by a hostile submarine. What she was seeing looked worryingly familiar.

"China finishing what those pirates started is my guess," she said. "You near a lifejacket? Put it on."

"Oh hell, I'm not splashing about in the bluidy water again," he moaned. "Go down with the ship, I will."

"You do that, Ginger," she told him. "I'm not. Got to go."

She had run around to the cockpit of the Vapor and grabbed her helmet. If the *Congress* took a torpedo in the guts, and she was guessing by the chaos around her that it was about to, she did not plan to be aboard as it went down. She jammed the helmet on and powered it up. "Vapor, begin emergency startup sequence."

Emergency startup initiated.

As the systems inside the machine whined into life, Bunny ran around her machine, pulling off the rotor tie-downs. She couldn't release the high-tensile cables holding the undercarriage in place, not with the ship currently tilted at a ten-degree angle as it leaned hard to port, but she ran over to the cable release, ready to pull it at the first sign they were in trouble.

"Vapor, rotate to idle."

Rotating.

The heavy rotor blades on the ends of the wings began turning, slowly at first, then faster and faster until they settled into a gentle thudding rhythm. Propwash blasted across the deck, nearly taking her off her feet. Even at an idle, the Vapor generated a strong downdraft.

Bunny ducked involuntarily as two more missiles punched out of the *Congress*'s vertical launchers and arced out in front of them.

Sooo. Not. Good.

"Torpedoes running deep. *Congress* is not the target," Okafor's sonar technician down in the CIC declared. "Heading is one seven niner. Target projection … target is *Orion*. One minute to impact."

Okafor spun around, looking at the panoramic view aft of his ship on the large flat wall panel behind him.

Of course. China didn't know or didn't care about the small complement of Marines aboard *USS Congress* or the frigate's admittedly limited warfighting capabilities. She was, after all, one lone frigate. But China cared deeply about the missile systems the US planned to install on Pagasa. Those pirate attacks, this submarine attack, they were all intended to do one thing. Stop the *Orion*. With a turning circle of about a half mile, the big ship was a guaranteed kill for any advanced homing torpedo.

"*Andromeda* is coming around," Diavolo said, pointing at the faster lead vessel. "Pedersen is putting himself between that submarine and the *Orion*!"

"ASROC torpedoes tracking, thirty seconds to impact on hostile contact," his sonarman announced. Okafor had nearly forgotten about their own attack. For a millisecond before launching it, he had hesitated. Attack a Chinese submarine outside the US exclusion zone, at the height of an international crisis? It could be one of the last orders he ever gave as *Congress*'s Captain. But he was authorized to engage a hostile target if the convoy was threatened.

That, he had done.

"Twenty seconds to enemy torpedo impact on *Orion*," the sonarman said.

Okafor was barely listening to him. His entire focus was on the screen spanning the back wall, and the vision it showed of a merchant ship, about to die.

Bunny felt the angle of the *Congress*'s deck ease a little and the throb of its engines settle. Looking out over the fantail of the helicopter deck she could see *Andromeda*, about a half-mile astern, and *Orion*, another half-mile behind that. The ship was leaning out as she turned, hard, cutting across the *Congress*'s foaming wake. *Oh, hell, Pedersen was going kamikaze.*

She held a hand up to her ear. "Ginger!" she yelled into her earbud over the noise of her rotors. "Brace for impact, mate!"

Whether he heard her or not, she didn't know. At that moment a massive spout of water suddenly appeared below *Andromeda's* waterline and the report of an explosion boomed across the waves. The *Andromeda* stopped dead.

And then it began listing heavily to port.

Bunny could clearly see it leaning over, the cranes on its starboard side dipping toward the water. She could see men jumping into the sea off its foredeck. Then a second torpedo hit, and the entire ship disappeared in a ball of fuel and flame.

She saw an Ensign running past her and grabbed him by the arm. "You. Get some men, gather as many life jackets as you can and load them and yourself aboard this aircraft!"

He looked at her, startled and puzzled. "Ma'am?"

"Don't *ma'am* me, my name is Lieutenant Karen O'Hare and you will do as I say or I will bloody heave you over the side, is that clear?!"

"Aye, ma'am!" He snapped to attention and saluted before running off. *Congress*'s deck was approaching level again as it completed its turn and started making speed for the stricken *Andromeda*. Bunny heaved on the release holding the Vapor's undercarriage cable ties and they whipped back down into the deck. She slammed down the visor on her helmet and ran for the cockpit. "Vapor, do you have a position on the *Andromeda*?"

I have a position that is three minutes twenty seconds old. Its AIS beacon has stopped broadcasting.

"Create a waypoint on *Andromeda*, 100 feet altitude, last known position. Prepare for takeoff."

Creating navigation waypoint. Preparing for takeoff.

She frantically checked instrument and system readouts. Out of her window she saw the Ensign and three seamen running toward her, arms ringed with life jackets. She jumped out of the cockpit and pulled open the crew compartment door, waving them in. "Get in!"

This time they didn't stop to question her. The four men threw themselves and the life jackets they were carrying into the crew compartment and she locked the door open. Then she jumped in behind them, piled into a chair and started buckling up. The four crewmen took her lead and did the same.

"Vapor, takeoff and move to waypoint, best speed."

Moving to waypoint, setting altitude for 100, best speed.

The Vapor leaped off the deck and into the air with a stomach-dropping lurch. As they cleared the deck, Bunny saw a spout of water rise in the air several miles off their forward quarter. Hits on an enemy submarine? She certainly hoped so.

The man beside Bunny was the Ensign she had buttonholed out on the flight deck and he looked nervously over at her. "Ma'am ... uh ... who is flying this thing?"

"Don't worry. I am. With this," Bunny said, tapping her flight helmet. Then she thought again. "Unless you see me jump into the sea. In which case you have permission to worry, Ensign."

Mischief Reef, Spratly Archipelago, January 11

Li Chen had spent the last several hours in a state of nervous anxiety. Precious hours wasted, cooling her heels as China marshaled the greatest air armada of any nation since the Americans had put 1,800 aircraft into the air over Iraq for their *Operation Desert Storm*. But that total had been over 40 days. For the coming storm over the South China Sea, China had assembled more than 700 fighters and was sending them all into the Operations Area *on a single day*.

The bulk of the force was older J-7s and J-10s, but nearly 200 were 4th-generation J-11s and J-16s, plus more than 50 J-20 Mighty Dragon and FC-31 Gyrfalcon stealth fighters flying off the carriers *Liaoning* and *Shandong*.

They were not going to hit the Operations Area simultaneously. But they were phased to allow China to put waves of over 100 aircraft at a time into the airspace over the South China Sea and sustain that strength for up to 48 hours. The first wave of aircraft would move in at 0400 hours, as the assault ship, *Yushen*, reached helicopter launch range. The task force itself brought an awe-inspiring anti-air capability to the battle, its four escort vessels able to identify, track and launch missiles at up to 150 enemy air targets at a time, at ranges out to 200 miles.

As the eastern horizon began to lighten, the first troops from the *Yushen* would start going ashore on Pagasa Island. Within five hours three full companies of troops would have been landed, and the *Yushen* task force would be moving in to dock on the island, with China's position in the South China Sea unassailable.

The largest number of aircraft the Americans had put into the Operations Area during the early attacks on Subi Reef had been thirty. With only one aircraft carrier group apparently dedicated to the conflict, flying its aircraft in and out of Clark Base 500 miles east on Luzon, Chen could not see that the Americans would be able to do any more than make nuisance attacks against the massive Chinese fighter force.

More worrying was the undersea threat to the *Yushen*. A week earlier, she would not have considered it possible the Americans would even *think* of sinking a Chinese warship. But they had shown no compunction at all about dispatching the two Coast Guard frigates patrolling Pagasa. The *Yushen*'s picket of advanced destroyers and anti-submarine rotary-winged aircraft should be capable of defending it against American submarines or submarine-launched missiles, but that belief had never been tested in combat against the main enemy, and privately she had her doubts that any navy had yet solved the problem of how to defend ships against hypersonic sea-skimming missiles traveling at five times the speed of sound. Still, it was one thing to attack near helpless Coast Guard ships, another to take on some of the most modern ships in the Chinese fleet. She doubted the Americans would dare take this conflict so far.

As her lone aircraft took to the sky from Mischief Reef, and Chen looked down to see the mass of men, women and machines on the move on the ground below her, she felt an uncontrollable sense of pride wash through her.

Nearly a hundred years of preparation had culminated in this day. A hundred years of sacrifice, of social, economic and military progress, of single-minded determination to return China to its rightful place in the world order after the humiliations of the late nineteenth and twentieth centuries. Today, here in the South China Sea, it would test itself against its most powerful foe.

It was a test it could not afford to fail.

As Li Chen took off from Mischief Reef and climbed out, Bunny O'Hare was just 200 miles away hovering at 100 feet near a sea of oil and flame.

"Vapor, forward, fifty yards!" she yelled. Below them, men were swimming desperately away from the *Andromeda* or clinging exhausted to floating flotsam. They were the lucky ones. She had seen several bodies, burned and blackened, that had not made it out of the flaming oil.

Andromeda had broken in two after the second torpedo strike. Her stern, the cargo space loaded with heavy building supplies, had gone straight to the bottom. Her bow section and superstructure had canted over, flipped upside down and then filled with water so that only the top ten feet of the bow was still above the waves. Anyone who managed to get out and swim to the surface was emerging into a thick, cloying layer of fuel oil, much of which was burning as it drifted away from the wreckage.

Bunny had two of the sailors handing life jackets to her and two more standing by the Vapor's open payload bay doors, and as fast as they could hand them forward, Bunny and the others were throwing the life jackets toward the swimmers below. Inside a few minutes, there was a small raft of jackets floating on the water with exhausted men clinging to them.

Congress had dropped two fast rib boats and they would be on the *Andromeda* in a few minutes, but Bunny could see that some of the burned and blackened men below would struggle to survive even that long. The tiltrotor gave the swimmers something to swim *towards*, at least, and the downwash from its propeller blades also served to hold the oil and flame at bay.

Bunny reached behind her. "JACKET!" she yelled, clutching at empty air.

"None left, ma'am!" the Ensign behind her replied.

There was no more they could do. The two rib boats from the *Congress* were starting to move through the oil slick now, pulling men from the water as the *Congress* itself closed on the wreckage. Of the Chinese submarine, there was no sign. It must have gone straight to the bottom. Without the *Andromeda* to control it, *Orion* had slowed to a crawl. Bunny assumed the *Congress* would have to take it under tow somehow.

"Vapor, return to *USS Congress*," Bunny said to the AI. As the aircraft spun in midair and pointed itself back at the *Congress*, she looked down at the *Andromeda*.

Returning to USS Congress. I am no longer able to locate White Star Andromeda. Do you wish to designate US Navy frigate USS Congress as new home base?"

Bunny hung from the door, scanning the swimmers in the sea below as the Vapor pulled away. She hadn't seen any who looked like a misanthropic Scotsman.

Li Chen was going to be firing the first shot of the coming air battle. Admiral Li Bing had been true to his word and had put her proposed attack on the American Airborne Warning aircraft to his planning staff.

It had been quickly approved.

Li Bing had done her the honor of giving her the news himself. "You will be flying alone, so that we can disavow your actions if needed," Li Bing said. "We cannot allow your mission, as bold as it is, to be an excuse for the Americans to declare full-scale war against China or vice versa. That declaration may come, but it is not our intention for it to come today."

"I understand, Comrade Admiral," she said. "Can I ask … no, forgive me. I will prepare for my mission."

The Admiral's voice softened. "Ask what, Li Chen?"

"How far do we think the Americans will go?" she asked. "We can protect our ships from the sky, but would the Americans go as far as to attack the *Yushen* by submarine?" She was already thinking ahead to the moment she returned from her first sortie and would have to be ready for her next. Not worried for herself but wondering how many Chinese sailors and pilots would survive the coming days.

She could hear the hesitation in his voice. "Events are … on a knife edge, Captain. Both our navies and our air forces are engaged. Losses on both sides have been painful. But for China, bearable."

"Nevertheless, Admiral. They used hypersonic missiles against our frigates patrolling Pagasa. If they…"

"Courage, Captain. They dare not attack the *Yushen*. The Americans have been shown that our warfighting capabilities go beyond what we have in this small theatre," he said. "By now, they have realized that if they attack *our* ships in *our* home seas, we will take this war to the seas surrounding the USA and the sky above it. And even if they respond to the mobilization of our Southern Command air forces with every aircraft they have within range of Pagasa, we will still outnumber them three to one."

He spoke with understated certainty, and she wanted to believe him. But she could not believe the Americans had gone to war in the South China Sea without being prepared to match China machine for machine, missile for missile, and ship for ship.

The J-16 was not a stealth aircraft. To make matters worse, as Li Chen took off from Mischief Reef, she had six PL-21 long-range air-to-air missiles hanging off hardpoints under her wings, and six short-range PL-10s which added twenty percent to her radar cross-section. If the American airborne early warning aircraft was as effective as their propaganda claimed, she could be detected before she got within the 120-mile range of her PL-21 missiles. If she got too close to the American Clark Air Base and its ground radar operators were alert, she could also be detected by the defenses at the American base and find herself on the receiving end of a volley of Patriot missiles. If the Americans had an *Aegis* anti-air warfare destroyer patrolling the seas off the west coast of the Philippines…

The list of 'ifs' was long, so to reduce the risk of detection, Li Chen turned east and dropped her machine down below 'minimum safe altitude' – using the J-16's terrain-following radar to skim her over the wavetops at 100 feet. She would burn a lot of fuel with such a tactic, but hers would hopefully be a straight-in, straight-out attack where endurance was not her primary concern.

Because of the high risk of detection, Admiral Li Bing's planners had allocated her a very precious support system. A single Skyhawk stealth drone. The Skyhawk had first been photographed during flight testing in the early 2020s and early unarmed prototypes had been deployed to the carrier *Liaoning*, on which Chen had served. She had been one of the test pilots exploring how it could be used in 'teaming' scenarios, flying as an automated wingman beside manned aircraft, while other pilots based on the carrier itself explored its use for reconnaissance and even anti-ship, anti-submarine warfare.

Only twenty full production Skyhawk drones had been deployed to date, so Chen felt a swell of pride as she looked over her port wing at the dark, dart-like aircraft holding formation with her. It was far superior to the American X-47B Fantoms they had faced over Pagasa in the initial days of the conflict. For a start, it had 'supercruise' capability, able to fly at greater than the speed of sound without using afterburner. Like the Fantom, it had active phased-array radar, but was also equipped with AI-supplemented passive sensor arrays that could detect enemy stealth aircraft by looking for 'holes in the sky', triangulating multiple ground and air radar sources to find gaps in the background radiation that could be stealth aircraft.

But most critically for Li Chen's upcoming mission, it had a unique 'missile slingshot' capability. Even though it did not carry missiles of its own, it could connect to long-range missiles fired by other aircraft, and then guide them to their targets so that the missiles did not give themselves away by using their own onboard radar until the last possible moment. Teaming a stealthy Skyhawk with a PL-21 missile increased the chances of a successful long-range missile intercept tenfold.

As she got within fifty miles of her planned missile release point, Chen sent the Skyhawk zooming into the sky ahead of her to supercruise altitude, and sent it straight towards the sector over the northern Philippine island of Luzon where the US airborne warning aircraft had been most frequently seen. The twin-turboprop US Hawkeye was big, slow and vulnerable, but it would not be alone. It would have at least two American fighters protecting it, perhaps more. She and her Skyhawk would have to find a gap in the Americans' defenses and pierce it with their slingshot missiles.

She put her machine into a low and slow figure-eight holding pattern and handed off flight control to her AI 'backseater' so that she could concentrate on the coming engagement. She had a multifunction display panel in front of her that showed the position of the Skyhawk, and the display was slowly filling with other contacts over Philippine airspace as the Skyhawk mapped, classified and tracked every aircraft it found. Most were commercial passenger or freight aircraft and for a moment, Chen felt a sense of apprehension as there were two commercial passenger flights from Bangkok to Luzon Clark International that were between her and a straight-line missile shot toward the American Hawkeye patrol sector. Deliberate? The Americans hiding their military aircraft among civilian air traffic to reduce the chances of an engagement? She would not put it past them.

Damn it. She ran a few calculations and then moved her Skyhawk twenty miles north of the commercial air corridor. She would have to fire her missiles toward the drone in max endurance mode, hand off control once they had cleared the flight corridor, and then have the Skyhawk 'bend' the missiles back towards their targets.

But first, the Skyhawk had to find the Hawkeye.

Alert, unidentified aircraft!

The AI voice in Chen's helmet had been infused with urgency to grab her attention and an icon appeared on her helmet visor with an aircraft ID underneath it. Not picked up by the Skyhawk but by her own infrared sensors ... which meant it was *close*. And now another icon appeared, two American Fantoms! She flicked a new display window onto the console in front of her, glad for now that her backseater was doing the flying so that she could focus on the suddenly complex tactical environment. The American drones were twenty miles north of her, flying a straight line east to west from Luzon on a bearing for the airspace over Pagasa. They were climbing, pushing through 20,000 feet, so they might have just taken off from Clark Base. They could be pickets, protecting the Hawkeye at a distance. Or a combat air patrol headed for Pagasa. She took control and gently oriented her aircraft toward them as they passed abeam of her, occluding her engines to minimize the risk they'd pick up her heat signature. They continued flying straight, heading up through 26,000 feet now.

They had not seen her.

A new alert from the Skyhawk flashed up on her visor, demanding her attention. *More* Fantoms! She watched for a moment. They were already at altitude, 25,000 feet, range ... sixty miles. Curving through the sky right over the middle of Luzon, right where they had previously identified the Hawkeye. Good. It was probably there, or enroute! She could wait for the two Fantoms to move south, slingshot her missiles out to the Skyhawk and in toward the Hawkeye and still have fuel to spare. But first, she had to...

A new icon appeared, blinking insistently. Her heart leaped at reading the label underneath it. *E2E Hawkeye*. She could see now why it had taken so long to identify. It was coming in from the east, no doubt just starting its patrol.

Keeping a close eye on the Fantoms disappearing behind her, she handed flight control to her backseater again and began setting up her shot. She had to time it so that it would reach the Skyhawk as the target's close-in escorts were moving away from it. The math was not complicated but took precious seconds. She set a countdown timer to tell her when to fire.

Missiles armed. Waypoints ... set. Targeting handshake from Skyhawk, green. Slingshot mode, confirmed. Thirty seconds to optimal release point.

She made one last check of the skies around the target. Commercial flights to the south, nothing bigger than a low-flying light aircraft between the targets and her Skyhawk.

Ten seconds to optimal release point.

Four ... three... two ... one! She blinked twice and, in staggered sequence, two PL-21s dropped from their hardpoints and boosted into the sky ahead of her.

Twenty miles east and thirty thousand feet above her, the two Fantoms of Gremlin flight, bound for Pagasa, were being controlled by pilots sitting at stations two armored decks below the *Doris Miller*'s superstructure. Their enclosed trailer-like stations were essentially like walk-in cockpits, with the same flight and systems controls as a conventional fighter, but with much larger wraparound screens that simulated a 360-degree view around their aircraft, inlaid with tactical and instrument displays. At just under the speed of light, commands from their flight sticks, throttles and pedals were relayed through the ship's antennas to satellites above and bounced back down to their aircraft, so that, for all intents and purposes, their pilots were 'flying' their Fantoms in real time.

There were advantages to not sitting in a cramped cockpit 30,000 feet over the South China Sea, and as he reached for the lukewarm cup of coffee at his elbow, the pilot of Gremlin one considered that while being able to sip on a brew during a mission was great, best of *all* was the ability to make a quick trip to the heads if things were quiet, like they were now, hundreds of miles out from their patrol sector...

"Gremlin two, Gremlin one, putting my machine into formation keeping mode for five," he said.

"Last night's chili coming back to haunt you, Lieutenant?" his wingman asked.

"You know it, Gremlin two, burning ring of fire..." he grunted. He set his machine to hold formation with the other aircraft, engaged its flight assist mode, and stood, pushing away the head and eye tracking rig that was positioned over his head when he was in the chair. He had two comms buds in his ears that had to stay there even when he was using the head, and he hadn't taken a full step away from the cockpit when one of them began chiming.

Missile alert!

Freaking typical. He spun back around and dropped back into his seat. "What have we got, Two?" he called, pulling the head tracking rig back into place over his head, eyes scanning the screens around him.

"Missile launch detected on infrared, sir, bearing ninety-eight degrees, altitude below five thousand, track is east ... away from us."

"Follow me around," Gremlin one said, pulling his Fantom into a banking turn to orient it back toward the east. "Ground to air, you think? Chinese ship?"

"Maybe. Two ... I have *two* contrails on visual."

Both pilots could see what the other was 'looking' at and there, ahead and below, he saw two white contrails against the green sea. He followed their track back from west to east, looking for the ship that might have fired them, but saw nothing. No aircraft either. "Call it in to Air Ops," he told the other pilot. "Try to get a heading on those missiles. I'm engaging phased array, let's see what's down there."

In the cockpit of Chen's J-16, a radar warning receiver alert sounded as soon as the American pilot began searching for her. High, rear aspect, targeting radar. *Those damn Fantoms.* She had missiles outbound, needed to ride out the contact until she got a signal from the Skyhawk that it had taken control – she could not hide, could not run. One minute.

Sixty long seconds.

Plenty of time in which to die. Even as she thought it, the radar warning receiver tone changed from 'active search' to 'locked' mode. The Americans had found her.

But technically, she was in international airspace, outside the US no-fly zone. Had they seen her launch? She had to brazen it out. She did not need to be pointed at the Skyhawk to control it or the missiles she had sent toward it, so she took control of her aircraft again, pulled her machine around in a tight banking turn, lit its tail and pointed its nose at the sky.

Straight at the American fighters.

As she did so, she engaged her own targeting radar and switched her radio to the International Guard emergency channel. In calm, Californian-accented English – she had done her undergraduate studies at Berkeley – she hailed the American fighters. "Ah, US aircraft on my six, this is Philippine Air Force Golden Eagle T-50 of 730 Combat Group, Clark Base. Kindly shut down your targeting radar, you just made my wizzo wet his diaper."

It was a brazen bluff, but one she'd rehearsed for just this moment. The PAF T-50 was a twin-seat fighter, like her J-16. Smaller, but that wouldn't be obvious on radar, and if the Fantom pilots closed to within visual range, the resemblance might just fool them for a few precious seconds.

The American aircraft stayed locked on, but they didn't fire. An agitated American voice came back at her. "PAF T-50, we saw missiles fired near your position, we aren't reading an IFF beacon and you are broadcasting in the clear. Hold your position as we close to visual range. And turn off your own damn targeting radar, thank you."

Twenty seconds.

"Live fire exercise, don't worry. You're on the *Doris Miller*, right, pilot?" Chen asked casually. "I was attached to VFA-2 for six months about two years ago. Is the chow still as bad now as it was back then?"

Ten seconds.

"Attached to VFA-2 my ass," the US Lieutenant muttered, any doubt that the aircraft below was Chinese now dispelled. Anyone who had served on the *USS Doris Miller* knew that no one actually called it by its full and clumsy name. The World War 2 US sailor and Navy Cross recipient it had been named after had been known by the nickname 'Dorie' and that's what its crew called their carrier – 'Dorie M' for short, or if they were being formal, 'The Dorie Miller'.

And their mission briefing had not included information about no damn PAF live fire exercise. The Lieutenant ignored the unidentified pilot's banter. "Gremlin two, you got a lock on those missiles?"

"Roger, One, I have two missiles outbound the contact, heading zero three eight and climbing. But I've got nothing down that bearing. Looks like they shot at empty sky. Could be an exercise like they said."

The Lieutenant checked his tac screen. It showed the position of all known friendly and civilian aircraft in the sector, and there was *nothing* in front of the flying missiles. He had two commercial passenger jets fifty miles to the east, a couple of Stingray refuelling drones, circling lazily over Luzon nearly eighty miles away … and further east of the Philippine mainland, another flight of Fantoms escorting the incoming Hawkeye controlling the air over the Northern Philippines and the South China Sea.

It made no damn sense! Could he even engage a Chinese fighter this far outside the no-fly zone? He dialed in the frequency for the Hawkeye. "Air Ops, Gremlin leader. I am in contact with an unidentified, possible Chinese aircraft, bearing zero four eight degrees, altitude under 1,000 feet, speed 680 knots, range twenty miles and closing. The contact just launched missiles at an unknown target northeast then hailed us on Guard claiming it is a PAF T-50 conducting live fire exercises. We are moving in to get a visual on the contact. Patching data through, your orders, AO?"

The operations team aboard the *Doris Miller* had been monitoring the contact and replied immediately. "Good copy, Gremlin. Obtain visual ID and report, we'll get onto PAF Luzon and confirm."

"Roger, wilco, Air Ops," he said, and switched comms to his wingman. "I'll get eyeballs on this joker, Gremlin two, you swing around and set up on his six. Stay sharp, I never saw a Chinese fighter traveling alone. He'll have friends somewhere."

Chen cursed. The two Fantoms were staying high but separating, one headed toward her, the other west; pointed away from her for now, but she had no doubt they were setting up to bracket her. They had not responded to her hail, which made her even more suspicious. Nothing she had seen in the last few days gave her reason to believe the Americans would respect the safety and neutrality of international airspace. But then again, neither had she.

Her missiles were seconds away from the Skyhawk's control zone. But she had to decide *now*. Prosecute the contact moving west, or the one moving north? Neither were close, and pursuing one would be a signal to the other to set up to attack her.

Handshake. Before she could decide, a chime in her helmet indicated her missiles had transitioned to slingshot mode.

Automatically, the Skyhawk to her east took control of them, gave them the coordinates for the American Hawkeye, and ordered the missiles onto a new course.

It needed no more help from her. Bringing up her weapons screen with a simple blink, Chen armed her remaining missiles.

"Uh, Lieutenant, those two outbound missiles just changed course," his wingman's voice in Gremlin one's helmet told him.

"Homing on something up there we can't see," the Lieutenant acknowledged. "Stay cool, Gremlin two, start to come around as soon as…"

"No. I mean *radically* changed course, sir," the man said. "New heading south-southeast; they're headed straight for our Hawkeye!"

He couldn't assume the Hawkeye could see them. Blood going cold, the Lieutenant flipped his radio frequency back to the Hawkeye controller. "AO, Gremlin two, warning, you have…"

Before he could complete his sentence, his world exploded into a cacophony of visual and auditory warnings. *Missile alert! Incoming.* He pulled his stick right to roll his Fantom onto its back and then back, to send it screaming toward the sea. His wingman did the same, reacting to missiles fired at him. The Chinese fighter had engaged them both, simultaneously. If he had been in the cockpit of his aircraft, he would probably have blacked out at worst, or be panting heavily with exertion at best, but sitting in his seat on the *Doris Miller*, he lost no composure at all. He didn't even spill his coffee. "Gremlin two, evade and re-engage."

"Copy, Gremlin one, engaging."

Chen watched her radar screen as it showed the American fighters diving for the sea, far to the west. But her mind was already with her missiles in the east again, watching as they ignited their second-stage boost and started accelerating toward the American Hawkeye at more than *four times* the speed of sound. They would take about thirty seconds to cover the last twenty miles to their target, engaging their own homing radars for the final seconds of their flight to ensure they did not miss.

The Hawkeye was showing no sign that its human pilots realized a fiery death was headed their way.

Her backseater automatically began blasting radar and radio-wave energy at one of the American fighters to try to blind it. Once the Hawkeye was down, she could call her Skyhawk back and she would no longer be outnumbered. It had no conventional weapons itself, but the Americans would not know that.

Locking up the American that was the target of her jamming suite, she fired again.

"Can't... I got no missile lock, One," the Lieutenant's wingman said. "I'm being jammed!" He'd evaded the Chinese fighter's first shot and tried to get a firing solution on him, to no avail.

His flight leader had come up against Chinese jamming in his second sortie over Pagasa, several days earlier. Few of the Chinese aircraft were electronic warfare capable. This one apparently was. That made it a J-16. The J-16 was extremely maneuverable, known to be an excellent knife fighter. The Fantom was no slouch, but the millisecond delay in reaction time between when the Lieutenant twitched his stick and when his Fantom several hundred miles away responded could be the difference between life and death in a dogfight with a competent opponent. The Lieutenant knew better than to even try.

"Sending Gremlin one autonomous," the Lieutenant announced, tapping a button on his flight stick with his forefinger. Immediately, the stick vibrated to indicate the aircraft's own combat AI had taken control, and it spun on its axis, orienting itself at the Chinese fighter zooming up towards it. Target locked, weapons free, it sent a homing radar missile downrange.

His wingman did not have time to respond. He had not been able to see the Chinese missile arrowing toward his aircraft on his scrambled threat display and, without warning, every screen and instrument on his multifunction displays went dead. "Gremlin two is down," he reported. "Gremlin two is down."

Chen saw the American missile closing on her, and though she didn't know it, she did exactly the same as the American pilot, blinking at an icon to give flight control to her backseater, lifting her hand away from her flight stick and taking hold of the handgrips at each side of her seat, steeling herself. The main difference between the two of them was that the American was entrusting his aircraft to his AI from the safety of a trailer aboard the *Doris Miller*. Chen was putting her very life in the silicon hands of her AI.

A more arrogant pilot, or one from an earlier generation, might have refused, not trusting her life to a bunch of computer chips. Li Chen was not one of these. She knew the box of transistors in the fuselage behind her was more than just a computer. It was a networked intelligence that was connected not just to a satellite above, but, through it, to every other aircraft, ship and ground radar within hundreds of miles. It didn't just see the missile coming toward it, it knew exactly how to respond to it, having learned the lessons of not just one pilot, but thousands of pilots, over tens of thousands of real and simulated engagements.

It also knew, with quantum certainty, exactly what Chen's J-16 was capable of. Not the capabilities of a generic J-16, but of *her* J-16. It felt the flow of rushing air over every surface, knew exactly how fluid that air was, at what temperatures, altitudes and angles of attack. It monitored the strain on the airframe, and the vital signs of its pilot, as it flung the machine around the sky, flying the fighter and the human inside it not *near* the edge of the envelope, but right on it.

With a roll that nearly tore her arms out of her shoulder sockets, the J-16 snapped onto a wingtip and, punching out flares and chaff, reversed direction with a thrust-vectored turn that slammed Chen's helmet back into her headrest with a force that made her see stars.

The American missile speared into the sea behind her, and before she could even blink the red mist from her eyes, her AI launched another missile at the remaining American.

Gremlin one was vaguely aware that his wingman had rushed into the cabin behind him and thrown himself into the observer's chair there, but the man was smart enough to say nothing, because he could see his flight leader was also in trouble.

The Lieutenant's muscled jaw was knotted and though he was experiencing none of the G-forces his machine was experiencing as it corkscrewed through the sky over the South China Sea, he was pale. And for now, relegated to the status of observer, just like his wingman.

If he'd been in the cockpit of his unmanned fighter, that wingman would probably have been dead. At best, he'd be hanging from a silk shroud, watching the sea below rush up toward him. Instead, he watched as his flight leader's aircraft evaded yet another missile fired by the Chinese fighter and flipped level, throwing itself into a screaming, skidding turn that would point it back at the enemy so it could try to get a new solution on it.

With a sound that sent his stomach to the floor, the young pilot saw a new icon appear on Gremlin one's radar warning screen. A second Chinese fighter, its targeting radar locked on the remaining Fantom, moving in from fifty miles away, just off the coast of Luzon!

With dread certainty, Gremlin one waited for the warning that would tell him more missiles were on their way, but it never came. With only one American fighter left in the fight, the two Chinese aircraft both fixed all of their jamming energy on their enemy.

And the screens in front of the Americans dissolved into pixelated snow. The Fantom's systems were supposed to be hardened against jamming. Guess China hadn't read that memo.

"I'm out," the Lieutenant said as his stick went dead. "She's on her own now."

Li Chen had no sign whether the jamming energy her J-16 and the fast-approaching Skyhawk were blasting at the American fighter was successful or not. All she knew was that, for now, there were no new missiles coming at her. For the first time in several long minutes she was able to check her tac display.

The Hawkeye aircraft was gone.

The US Fantom, however, wasn't. It or its pilot had apparently decided that the best solution to burn through her jamming radiation was to close on the last known position of the Chinese fighter jamming it. It had swung around and was coming right at Li Chen. *Fast.*

She left her Skyhawk high and kept it in active jamming mode, angled toward the approaching Fantom so that it could keep its electronic warfare antennae directing energy at the American. Meanwhile, she took back control of her J-16 and pointed it west, toward Mischief Reef. About two minutes later, the Fantom passed overhead, about ten thousand feet above her and going hell for leather for the position she had just vacated.

She drew a deep breath and, as her separation increased to twenty, then thirty and finally fifty miles, she let it out. She ordered her Skyhawk to disengage, move to supercruise altitude, and trail her home. Then shook her head in wonder. *Two* kills. She sent a silent message of praise to the AI engineers of the Shenyang Aircraft Corporation. She was a damn good pilot, but there was no way in the Seven Heavens she could have managed that engagement on her own and come out of it alive, let alone with two kills.

For the first time since the Americans had wiped Subi Reef air base off the surface of the South China Sea, she dared to hope.

After an early morning meeting of the full National Security Council, members had dispersed to attend to their responsibilities and President Fenner retired to his private study next to the White House Oval Office for an early lunch.

Joining him were Abdor and Lewis – while the corridors buzzed with the several dozen staff working around the clock in the White House keeping the machinery of government turning over while its political masters were distracted by events a half world away.

Fenner had asked for coffee and sandwiches to be sent in and then dismissed his personal assistant. He sat down on a sofa with a heavy sigh.

"Hell of a day," he said, pouring Lewis and Abdor a coffee. While they had been meeting, word had come that a Chinese submarine had attacked the White Star convoy and sunk the *Andromeda* with significant loss of life. In response to questions from the media, China was denying responsibility for the attack – claiming that it was most likely the result of mines placed by Brunei-based pirates – which was a double-edged sword. On the one hand, it gave China a convenient cover story that fit the events earlier in the convoy's passage. On the other hand, it meant that China could not protest the destruction of its submarine at the hands of the *USS Congress*.

Most importantly, though, it had delayed the *Congress* for several hours as it completed the rescue of survivors from the

Andromeda, and with the help of White Star software engineers, established a wireless link to the *Orion* so that it could command the huge semi-autonomous 'trailing ship' to follow it. The delay had meant that, at best, the convoy would arrive in Pagasa waters just hours before the Chinese *Yushen* assault ship task force. And it made the mission to land *Congress*'s Marines even more time-critical.

Fenner continued. "How many lives lost on that ship?"

"Early estimates, at least twenty," Abdor told him.

"It's like China wants a full-scale war," Fenner said. Abdor nodded.

"Or they think *we* do…" Lewis said. The two men looked at her with surprise. "Why wouldn't they, the way this has played out? Their cyber-espionage operation in Manila told them we plan to fortify Pagasa. They don't like that, try to stage a small-scale blockade, we respond with a major air offensive and destroy their biggest base in the Spratlys, but we both lose dozens of aircraft. They try to sneak a few commandos onto the island under cover of a cruise missile strike, get the Philippine troops to surrender, which they don't, and we sink two of their Coast Guard frigates. Meanwhile they're paying pirates to try to stop our convoy deniably, and when that doesn't work, they try to sink it outright and lose a nuclear attack submarine…"

"I'm not about to walk a mile in China's shoes, if that's what this is, Madam Director," Abdor told her.

"Just stay with me … a faction inside the Communist Party Politburo reaches out to us, tries to make a deal and to show us they're on the level, lifts the cover on a covert economic warfare operation to blank half our international internet bandwidth … or worse…"

"Or that call was part of a psy-ops mind game," Abdor interjected. "As you yourself said."

"Or it *wasn't*," Lewis replied. "And we're ignoring a chance to exit gracefully from this. Meanwhile, every time we act, China reacts, we're sinking each other's ships and we're just inches from a death spiral toward a catastrophic conflict."

"You're saying we should *take* their deal now?" Abdor asked. "I can't keep up with all this pivoting, sorry."

Lewis laughed. "That's a fair call, Chuck. No, I'm not saying that. I'm saying we need to find a way to short-circuit this tit for tat escalation. Putting a few Marines on Pagasa and shooting Stinger missiles at their incoming helicopters isn't it. That just puts off the real fight to another day." She shrugged her shoulders. "But I have to admit, I'm stumped right now."

"Who are you, and what have you done with the Carmine Lewis who always finds the back way out of the party as the police are coming through the front door?" Fenner asked.

Abdor's cell phone buzzed and he took the call. "Yes, General … uh, huh. Yes, he's here." He arched his eyebrows as he listened. "I see. You better tell him yourself."

"That doesn't sound good," Carmine said as Abdor leaned forward and put his cell phone on the table between them, tapping the key to put it on loudspeaker.

Abdor looked grave. "General, you're on speaker," he said. "The President and Director Lewis are here with me."

The usually gruff bass voice sounded inappropriately small and tinny in the large office. "Mr. President, Madam Director, there has been another development."

"Go ahead, General," Fenner said.

"Sir, Space Command has just reported that satellite intelligence indicates China's Southern Command has started putting everything it has into the air and is moving it to bases in Guangzhou and Hainan Island. DIA also has new human-source intel indicating that China is mobilizing upward of ten fighter brigades."

Fenner frowned. "Brigades, how many aircraft is that?"

"More than 500, sir," the Chairman of the Joint Chiefs said. "Their assault ship task force is continuing toward our exclusion zone. Our aircraft patrolling over Pagasa will soon be within anti-air missile range of the assault ship's escorts. My people believe that before that ship hits helicopter launch range, China will surge its aircraft and they *will* achieve air domination over the Spratly Archipelago sufficient to get their troops ashore, Marines or no Marines. That island will fall, Mr. President."

Fenner's face fell. "So, it's game over." He looked to Abdor, but found no succor.

"None of us believed China would take it this far, this fast," Abdor said, shaking his head. "Cyberwar, yes. A limited kinetic conflict, definitely. But unmanned undersea bombs off our coast, nuclear subs attacking civilian ships? A 500 fighter *armada*? No one foresaw this."

Fenner straightened. "I guess … I guess I'll call Victoria, while Carmine can see if she can reach that Chinese General, set up some kind of deal before this hits, so we can save some face."

"No, Mr. President."

Both men stared at Carmine Lewis, their faces a mixture of despair and hope. "No? Why not?" Fenner asked.

"General Cavoli, can you stay on the line?" Carmine asked. She looked at Fenner with a calm smile. "That backdoor out of the party? China just showed us where it is."

Someone else than Bunny O'Hare might have felt despair after the attack on the White Star convoy. Grief even. But she was not someone else. So, when the *Congress*'s rescue crew came back with the burned body of the late Angus McIntyre in the bottom of their boat, she didn't weep. Sure, she'd just started thinking to herself that, of all the characters in the world to strike up a friendship with, a cat-loving, mankind-hating, red-headed Scotsman was probably the least likely. But the combat pilot in O'Hare tended to divide the world into two kinds of people. Dangerous, and not dangerous.

Angus had been starting to look like one of the not-dangerous kind.

There had only been a few of those in Bunny's adult life. A

US Navy Lieutenant Commander called Alicia Rodriguez. A Marine Gunnery Sergeant called James Jensen. A hundred-year-old Japanese nurse. A crippled British pilot with robotic legs. She was beginning to think maybe Ginger Misanthrope McIntyre could be the fifth.

And the fecker had gone and died on her and she knew exactly who was to blame.

What had been a geopolitical conflict had just become intensely personal. So, as she marched up grey-painted stairs to the bridge of the *Congress*, she was in no doubt what her main priorities in life were right there and then. First, defeat China. Second?

Mourn a radio operator called Ginger McIntyre. And a Chief Mate called Kapil Bose. And Captain Jorgen Pedersen.

But first things first. As she approached the bridge, a young Lieutenant JG stepped out, took in a woman in filthy civilian clothes, flight helmet in one hand, and as she made to push past him, he put up a hand to stop her. "Ah, you can't go in there, ma'am. We're still at general…"

Bunny put her helmet on his chest, pushed him bodily against the wall and kept going.

The bridge was a scene of organized chaos. Men and women were quietly and efficiently going about their business, but no one seemed the least bit calm. O'Hare had enough sense not to bother Okafor, but she saw Diavolo, his XO, and made straight for him.

"Lieutenant, my machine is fully loaded, fueled, armed and ready for takeoff, why isn't it full of bloody Marines?"

Diavolo, who had been talking with the *Congress*'s helmsman, turned and frowned. "Sorry, what?"

"I said," Bunny continued with poorly disguised impatience, "I was under the impression there was some bloody urgency about getting your Marines and their MANPAD missiles onto Pagasa Island. Dusk is approaching. Conditions couldn't be better, so why the hell…"

Diavolo looked at her, and no doubt saw a woman on the

edge. He didn't snap, bark or bite back at her. "Come," he said simply.

He led her over to a flat tabletop LCD, punched a couple of icons and brought up a screen showing the Operations Area. On the right, the Philippine Palawan Islands, the icons that were the *Congress* and *Orion* tracking northeast, hugging the coastline. Two hundred and fifty miles northwest, Pagasa Island. Between them, the dotted outlines of a dozen rocks, reefs, and shoals through which they would have to thread themselves.

"Alright, pilot," the XO said. "Sitrep. Try to keep up. In about a half-hour we will start to turn northwest, heading through this obstacle course to Pagasa. It will be three and a half hours before *Congress* is close enough to that island for us to cover it with our anti-air missiles." He pointed to a cluster of icons north of Pagasa. "Chinese task force. Any advantage we had in getting to that island first, we lost following that submarine engagement and rescue. The *Yushen* and its escorts are the same distance from Pagasa as us, and because we have that goliath in tow now, we are both making the same speed – about 20 knots."

Bunny interrupted. "So, I can launch now. That Vapor flies twice the speed of any Chinese transport helo. I can get one squad onto the island and be back here, loading the second and on my way before that Chinese assault ship can…"

"No question," Diavolo said. "But there is this." He punched an icon that Bunny immediately saw overlaid a plot of air contacts onto the map.

"There's something wrong with your data feed," Bunny said. The air north and west of Pagasa was speckled with red Chinese aircraft icons. Not tens, not dozens … hundreds. Over Pagasa and to the southeast were between twenty and thirty lonely blue American icons.

"Nothing wrong," Diavolo said. "We lost our airborne warning aircraft a couple hours ago, so we don't have 20/20 vision, but we have enough Fantoms and Sentinels in the air to be confident that what you see is what is up there, and then some." He swept a hand across the red swarm on the plot. "We are not sending you, or our men, into that shit storm. You won't possibly make it through."

Bunny bent over the screen, weighing up the situation. "There are too many aircraft for China to be basing them locally. If those Chinese fighters are flying from the mainland, they won't have more than a couple hours endurance. They'll have to pull back soon. When they do, we can…"

"Navy Intelligence says what we are looking at there is just one-third of the total force China is putting into the air today. They're keeping the bulk of the force back until *Yushen* gets in helo launch range, and then they'll surge. Our Fantoms will engage, but they'll be outnumbered three to one. And for every Chinese machine we take down, there are two to take its place. We're flying as many Fantoms in from Guam via the *Doris Miller* as we can, even got some coming up from Darwin and down from Okinawa, but they won't turn a tide like that."

A heat built in Bunny's chest. "So, we're going to let them just walk in? After everything that happened today, *that's* the plan?"

Diavolo reached over and put a hand lightly on her shoulder. She was going to knock his hand away, but he was old enough and ugly enough he could get away with it. "Easy there. No. That *ain't* the plan." He turned, looking over at Okafor. "Right now, I don't know what the plan is, exactly. But something is brewing. Why we haven't unloaded your machine is, you're still going in."

Finally, something Bunny could hold on to. "When?"

"I have no freaking idea, Lieutenant O'Hare, but get down to your machine and be ready to load up and light out within five minutes of me sending word, alright?"

"You got it," she said and turned to go, but he was still holding her shoulder and held her back.

"You've got a few minutes, O'Hare. You probably want a shower and change of clothes," he said gently. He nodded toward the men nearby, a couple of whom were looking at them sideways. Holding out the hand that had been resting on her shoulder, he showed her his fingertips were black with the oil she'd covered herself in, helping unload bodies recovered from the Andromeda. "You're starting to scare the locals."

Li Chen had returned from her mission taking down the Hawkeye and walked straight into a briefing with her pilots. After the PLA Navy Intelligence Officer was finished with his briefing of the strategic environment, mission parameters and expected enemy force disposition, Chen had addressed them, looking each of her pilots in the eye as she spoke.

"You are the pilots of Ao Yin Squadron, the four-horned bulls. You will roam the skies like the bull demon, seeking out targets and dispatching them without mercy. No pilot in the sky or skulking below the decks of an American carrier comes even close to the skills of you and your *Zhi Sheng* backseaters – I have just proven this!" She spoke without pride or arrogance. "I took my J-16 deep into enemy airspace, handed control of it to my *Zhi Sheng* and he not only shot down two American aircraft, he evaded the missiles the enemy fired, jammed their radar to blind them, and flew me safely home." She pointed at a man she knew lacked full trust in the AI. "Your *Zhi Sheng* can fly better than you. It can manage your systems better than you. But it cannot think for you. Let your backseater do the flying and fighting, while you tell it where to go and what to attack. You must trust in its power, the power of Ao Yin. Is that clear?"

They had roared their agreement.

She had led half of her unit into the sky for the first phase of the attack. The other half would be scrambled when the *Yushen* started launching its helos. The six aircraft were spread out either side of her with two miles separation, systems dark for now, cruising at 20,000 feet toward Pagasa airspace and the American fighters there. Though the American Fantoms were stealth aircraft, Li Chen's pilots would not be going in blind.

Ahead of her, a squadron of Chinese J-20 stealth aircraft paved the way for her and her pilots. Sliding through the air as invisibly as the Americans, scanning the skies with their passive sensors and seeking out the telltale gaps in background radiation, the errant radio and radar signals that leaked from their enemies' aircraft into the ether around them, they began plotting the American patrols' positions and mapping them onto the J-16 pilots' screens.

It was, as they said in the Hollywood movies one of her pilots was enamored with, a 'target-rich environment'. Enemy icons filled her targeting display. "Ao Yin pilots, Ao Yin leader," she called. "Engage *Zhi Sheng*. Confirm targets and attack."

On pylons under their wings hung eight PL-21 ramjet missiles. As they got within a hundred miles of Pagasa, their AIs locked up the targets the J-20s had identified, shared them between the six aircraft, and their pilots confirmed them.

Within moments, four missiles had dropped from beneath Li Chen's wings and were speeding through the sky ahead of her, trailing thin white smoke. They would not engage their ramjets and go beyond Mach 2, or engage their own sensors, until the terminal phase of their attack. For now, they took their guidance from the invisible J-20s and, with luck, the Americans over Pagasa would not even know their aircraft were already under attack.

To her north and south, she saw the ancient J-7 fighters flying decoy maneuvers, as planned. Copies of cold war Mig-21s, they had no chance of surviving an engagement with modern warplanes like the Fantom, so they were being used as bait. Flying in large formations, easily detected, drawing the Americans away from Pagasa toward what they thought would be easy kills.

Meat shields, her pilots had irreverently called them before she put a stop to that kind of language. They were heroes, the young boys who flew the J-7s, fresh out of fighter training. Li

Chen nodded with satisfaction as she saw on her tactical screen that the decoy was working. Dozens of American aircraft were breaking north and south to attack the swarming J-7s.

Many of their brave pilots would not be alive, minutes from now.

But neither would the American aircraft. Because even as they turned to engage the massed Chinese squadrons at a range from which the J-7s could not return fire, the missiles of Chen's Ao Yin Squadron were turning to follow them.

Two decks down on the *USS Doris Miller*, inside his Fantom control station, Lieutenant JG Bruno Forcetti adjusted his seat and focused on the scene playing out across his multiple screens. This war was days old, but he'd yet to fire a missile in anger. He'd only been sent on patrol over Pagasa after the Chinese had pulled their aircraft back, and so the few missions he had flown so far had been relatively boring patrols out of Clark Base, over the exclusion zone where the most excitement he'd had was occasionally picking up a Chinese aircraft orbiting a hundred miles south-east at Mischief Reef or the same distance away at Fiery Cross Reef.

That was all going to change today! His flight had been vectored north of Pagasa, to intercept a host of Chinese aircraft that ground radar back at Clark Base had detected moving in from the near mainland Chinese island of Hainan.

Thirty plus bandits! And they would not be waiting for them to break Pagasa air identification zone airspace before engaging. The kid gloves were off now. He worked his radar and targeting screen as his machine closed on the enemy. One forty miles … one twenty … he got an electronic signature ID on the enemy aircraft now. J-7s? *Are you kidding me? This is what China is bringing to this fight?* He felt almost sorry for the pilots of the piles of junk in his crosshairs. They carried only short-range missiles, they would not even be able to get close to Forcetti's Fantom before he and his fellow pilots started swatting them from the sky. Probably couldn't even *see* the drones stalking them.

A literal turkey shoot.

One hundred miles. Optimal range for the six Peregrine missiles in his Fantom's weapons bay. He tapped each of the targets on his targeting radar screen and tightened his hand on his flight stick as he got a missile launch tone in his ears. On inter-pilot comms he heard the four pilots of his flight announce almost simultaneously.

"Fox three, fox three..."

One by one, he punched all six missiles out of the belly of his Fantom and prepared to turn it back toward Clark Base. Their orders were to engage at long range, deliver their full payload and hurry back down to reload and refuel. They'd been told China would be sending fighters against them in waves, and right now, as the Chinese aircraft scattered in front of his missiles, he saw the briefing wasn't an exaggeration. Holy. What a...

Missile warning! An alert in his ears, an icon appeared on his heads-up display monocle. Missiles on his *six*? He rolled the Fantom onto its wingtip and pulled back on the stick, sending it zooming toward the source of the attack, desperately trying to create an impossible intercept angle for the incoming missile. Missile-decoying chaff and flares punched into his wake.

His machine almost made it. The first Chinese PL-21 missile fired by the Ao Yin pilots was spoofed by the decoys and flew into a cloud of metal foil before exploding two hundred yards behind Forcetti's Fantom. The second was not so easily fooled. It locked onto the white-hot gas plume streaming through the Fantom's engine baffles and, at four times the speed of sound, buried itself in the Fantom's exhaust and exploded behind its engine.

Painfully for Forcetti, the blast sent his machine flipping through the air, tail over nose, and shredded the Fantom's control surfaces, but it did not lose its link to the satellite above and it kept streaming data and vision to his control station.

All the way down to the sea.

Not all of the Fantoms fell to the J-16s' missiles. Two managed to evade the attack and, side by side, they curved around and began hunting their attackers. With missiles hanging off her hardpoints, Li Chen's radar cross-section was relatively large and it took no time at all before her radar warning receiver showed the Americans' radar sweeping across her machine in search mode, and then switching to targeting mode as they locked her and her pilots up.

She was too far away for effective jamming, but she didn't intend to let the Fantoms have it all their way.

She switched frequencies to the J-20 stealth aircraft out ahead of her as her backseater locked up the two remaining Fantoms. "Knife squadron, Ao Yin leader. Enemy has found us; your assistance would be appreciated."

Missiles inbound! Chen dropped her arms, gripped the seat below her butt as her straps automatically tightened and the aircraft began to maneuver to avoid the incoming American missiles. Not before it had dispatched two missiles of its own, though. Chen gritted her teeth and closed her eyes, her flight suit explosively inflating to help push blood away from her extremities and back to her core. Despite the hard turn the J-16 was in, she felt her missiles drop from her rails and punch into the sky, but where they were going and where the enemy missiles were now, she had no idea. That was not her problem right now. All of her focus was on her breathing, on clenching the muscles in her legs to keep blood flowing to her head as her machine inverted and changed direction in a radical, high-g U-turn in the sky.

Her head started lolling on her shoulders. Her hands went slack on the seat grips. She felt consciousness slipping away, then the J-16 righted itself. Shaking her head to clear her vision, she looked at the sky around her, down at her threat display. What had happened?

"Ao Yin leader, Knife leader," the J-20 squadron commander's voice said in her ears. "We took care of those Fantoms for you. Sorry for your pilot. Knife out."

Sorry for your pilot? "Ao Yin pilots, report in!" she commanded. One by one her pilots called in, but the calls stopped at four. She checked her tac screen, spooled the data backward urgently, replaying the engagement. Ao Yin three was down, struck by two American missiles. No emergency beacon deployed. He hadn't ejected.

The man she had told to trust his *Zhi Sheng* AI. Had she been wrong? Or had he ignored her, tried to evade the American missiles without AI help? In the past, it was a question she might never have gotten an answer to, but with every second of his engagement reported to the *Zhi Sheng* cloud AI so that it could learn from its mistakes, she would eventually be able to pull the data from his engagement and see what had gone wrong.

If she made it back herself.

The ExComm subset of the US National Security Council were gathered in the underground Situation Room as events began playing out over Pagasa. It was coming up to nightfall in the South China Sea, dawn in DC. None of the people in the room had slept during the night.

As they'd feared, their Fantoms were being overwhelmed by the Chinese fighter armada. The US drones' kill-to-loss ratio was about two to one, but it wasn't near enough to make a dent in the mass of red dots in the sky. The Chinese mainland fighters were engaging the US aircraft from the north and west, while their fighters flying out of Mischief Reef and Fiery Cross Reef in the south-east and south-west were cutting off the American aircraft during ingress and egress from the combat zone.

The only thing that made it slightly less horrifying was that they had not lost a single human pilot since the crew of the

Hawkeye earlier that day.

"What's the news out of Guam?" Fenner asked.

"Twenty Fantoms and four Sentinel electronic warfare aircraft took off four hours ago, sir. They're on the ground at Clark, being made ready," Cavoli said. "And we have a new Hawkeye from the *Doris Miller* inbound. It should be on station inside the half-hour."

"No, the other assets."

Cavoli pointed at a screen that showed a satellite map of the Operations Area, centered on the airspace between Guam and Pagasa, with the Philippine island of Palawan dead center. Six white icons were approaching Palawan's east coast. "They're here now. They'll hold over the island until we see the Chinese commit their main force. We don't want to show our hand early."

Porter shook her head. "Six aircraft. Hard to believe after all that's happened, it comes down to six aircraft."

"If it helps, think of it this way, Madam Secretary," Abdor told her, without taking his eyes of the screen, "it's 4.8 *billion* dollars on the wing right there, and that's not counting the cost of their ordnance."

"What helps," Lewis reminded them, "is to think of the Chinese surge as an opportunity, not a threat."

"They have us right where we want them, is what you mean," Fenner smiled.

Porter chewed her lip thoughtfully. "I hope you are both right."

As they emerged from the bunker, Ruan had one arm around the boy and the other holding on to the shoulder of the girl. He had the pistol in the harness on his leg, on the side away from the boy. He didn't want to give him ideas. In the top pocket of his tunic he had the scope from a rifle that one of the others had left behind.

He'd slept longer than he'd wanted, but when he'd woken

with a start, the two kids were right where he'd left them. He'd dragged the radio to the wall where the antenna cable ran, attached two leads to it and tried calling the patrol boat offshore.

No answer. Maybe it had been hit at the same time as those frigates? He tried again. Whatever had happened to it, it was gone. His mind was wooly, but it still worked. His UDV. He had to get back to his underwater delivery vehicle. It had a range of about thirty miles. They'd only used five getting ashore the other day. What day was that? Yesterday? Day before? He couldn't remember. Anyway, it should still have twenty-five miles endurance. Subi Reef base was 16 miles south-west. He could do it with a few miles to spare. It would be an uncomfortable journey, but if he did it on the surface, he wouldn't need a tank.

His leg had stiffened up as he'd rested, and standing on it now, it felt like he was dragging a lump of wood. A hot, throbbing lump of wood. He looked out at the sky. A grey dusk was settling over the island, and a cool sea breeze blowing in. He lifted the rifle scope, flipped it to infrared and scanned the hillside below and to the sides. No movement, no telltale green glow indicating a human body crouched in the undergrowth.

The sea had a slight swell, but the skies were clear, with no sign of a storm. No moon either. So, the patrol boat wasn't there; everything else was lining up in his favor, right?

"Please?" the girl asked. "I want to go *home*."

"OK," he told the kids. "We go down to the beach and then left, there are some rocks just offshore, you know them?"

The boy nodded. "Yeah. We get you there, and then you let us go, right?"

He put the scope back in his pocket and his arm around the boy's shoulder again. "Sure," Ruan lied. "We're all going home."

He heard the sound of jets overhead, looked up, but couldn't see anything. From far away, an explosion? Wherever that fight was, it wasn't *his* worry.

Captain Heraldo Bezerra knew exactly what was happening overhead. The US Navy was getting its ass handed to it by the Chinese, was what.

He'd been on the radio to Puerto Princesa to report to them that his men had finished the pier and were ready for the convoy's arrival. It wasn't pretty; in fact, it was downright ugly, but he was sure it would hold the twenty or thirty tons he'd been told it would need to hold. They'd taken a sounding out at the end of the pier and found the water was forty-six feet deep – deep enough for that freighter to come alongside and unload right onto the dock, if it came and left at high tide.

He had to be honest, though. He had little hope he would ever see a ship pulling in alongside his long ugly dock. Not an American ship anyway. He didn't need Puerta Princesa to tell him there was a massive air battle raging overhead and that could mean only one thing.

Chinese troops were on the way.

As he stood looking out over his pier, he sensed someone walk up behind him and turned.

"Would be a nice night, except for, you know, the war," Mayor Reyes said.

"Except for that, yes," Bezerra agreed. He swiveled and looked east, at the small rise in the middle of the island that was Pinya Hill, and the landing strip to the right. They heard a sonic boom overhead.

"The Chinese are coming again, aren't they?" Reyes asked.

"Yes."

"In boats?"

"Not the first wave," Bezerra told him. "They'll come in on helicopters, try to land at different points around the island." He pointed. "But mostly there, on the airstrip, because it's the only place to get a lot of men down in a short amount of time." He looked up at the summit of the hill, where his men were rigging some lights.

"You going to take your men up there?" Reyes asked. "Try to hold on as long as you can?"

Bezerra shook his head. "No, that's a decoy. Hoping they'll waste some rockets or missiles on it." He nodded at the treeline north of the east–west runway. "I'm taking a leaf from their own book. We'll let the first wave land, then attack them from the treeline as they try to move out. But there's only about thirty of us combat capable now. Won't take them long to work around us and fence us in. And then it's game over."

"We'll stay in the village as you suggested. I got people making white flags to hang from the windows."

"Best idea."

"You could just surrender too," Reyes suggested. "If it's a fight you can't win."

Bezerra thought seriously about that. It was true. After all, what could his thirty combat engineers do against a couple of hundred Chinese Marines? Or a thousand? Not to mention the fact the clinic was overflowing with wounded soldiers and civilians. Maybe a quick surrender would get them the help they needed.

A man came running up to him with a mobile radio on his back. "Captain, Puerta Princesa for you."

He took the handset. "Bezerra."

He recognized the voice at the other end. It was his PN Seabees CO. "Captain, I have news. The Americans are going on the offensive overhead, going to try to push the Chinese aircraft back. If it works, they're going to fly four squads of US Marines in to Pagasa by tiltrotor, near a full platoon. Tell your men. The Chinese don't have tiltrotors so, for God's sake, if you see one coming in to land, don't shoot at it."

"When, sir?" Bezerra asked.

"Could be any time, so dig in, and stay alert."

"Yes, sir," he said wearily, handing the handset back to the man carrying the radio. The brigade intel officer had not long ago told him the Americans were on the back foot, and to prepare for an assault by Chinese troops. Now they were counterattacking and he should prepare for US reinforcements?

He reached down and picked up a shovel by his feet. Either way, there was one part of his orders that would be the same no matter how events turned out. He handed the shovel to the man with the radio. "Join the others by the airstrip and start digging, son."

The Vapor sat on the aft helo deck of the *Congress*, ticking in the late afternoon sun as the heat of the day left the metal of its airframe and escaped into the air. In its cockpit, Bunny O'Hare went through her pre-start checklist for the third time, purely out of habit, since in reality it was the aircraft's AI who would flip the switches and check the instrument readouts.

Swinging her head around, her helmet allowing her to see 'through' the bulkhead behind her, Bunny checked the 14 men buckled into the bucket seats of the Vapor's crew compartment. Because of the ordnance packed in around their seats, they sat with their feet at seat level and knees just about at waist level. It was not going to be a comfortable ride, but she guessed it was going to be a whole lot more comfortable than what awaited them if they managed to make it to Pagasa.

Which, to Bunny O'Hare, was a very, *very* big if. She'd been given a sitrep by Diavolo before heading to her machine, and it had not been good. The Chinese 'surge' was underway. The US had thrown another 20 fighters into the fray and accounted for close to 50 Chinese aircraft, but they'd lost nearly every Fantom they'd committed to the fight, several of them to anti-aircraft missiles fired by the Chinese escort ships now entering the Operations Area. The Chinese clearly saw the battle going their way, and their third and largest wave of aircraft was moving in from the mainland to supplement the nearly 100 fighters that were already covering Pagasa.

Within a few minutes, China would own the skies over the island.

At that time, they would start launching their helicopter

transports from the deck of the *Yushen*.

That was also when Bunny O'Hare would take off from the *Congress* and make her thirty-minute low-level run into Pagasa with her load of Marines, because according to Diavolo, at that point in time, "China's pilots are going to have a lot more to worry about than your little machine."

Six aircraft. As the US Secretary of State had observed, it didn't sound like much.

Except that the aircraft the US had put in the skies over Palawan were probably the most powerful air interceptor aircraft that had ever flown, which was certainly not what their designers had imagined when the early prototypes first took to the air.

They had been asked to design a replacement for the venerable B-2 Spirit strategic bomber, a billion-dollar behemoth that could circle the globe if needed, and, with its 60,000 lb. payload bay, deliver everything from cruise missiles to nuclear gravity bombs. To replace it, Northrop Grumman came up with a smaller but more deadly machine, the B-21 Raider. Smaller, because it could carry 'only' 30,000 lbs. of ordnance; deadlier, because its smaller radar cross-section made it much harder for an enemy to detect.

The machine could fly manned or unmanned. Unmanned missions were the norm, but any mission in which the B-21 deployed with nuclear weapons on board required a 'man in the loop' – human pilots as a meatware failsafe.

The Raiders over Palawan were unmanned. And they were carrying weapons their original designers had not foreseen, on a mission which never in their most sleepless nights could they have anticipated their machines would be called on to execute. But fortunately for planners of *Operation Fencepost*, the modification of the Raider to perform as a stealth interceptor of incalculable power had been green-lighted several years earlier, and Carmine Lewis had remembered seeing it named in one of the several 'what if' documents that had preceded the approval of their final operational plan.

As one, the six jet-black flying wings turned west, away from Palawan and Philippine territory, toward Pagasa Island and the hundreds of Chinese aircraft, and now helicopters, flying over the Spratly Islands across a fifty-mile front. Though they had accounted for nearly a hundred Chinese fighters over the last several hours, no American fighters were left to oppose them.

That is, no fighters in the traditional sense. There were still six American combat aircraft flying, though they were invisible to the Chinese aircraft in the South China Sea, and the anti-aircraft missile destroyers sailing across it.

As the Raiders of Ironsides flight hit the Palawan coast and went 'feet-wet', their pilots – based on Guam – ran through their weapons arming and launch sequence.

It took a few minutes because, in their payload bays, each of the B-21 Raiders carried no fewer than two hundred AIM-260 Joint Advanced Tactical Missiles. That gave the six Raiders the ability to fire *one thousand, two hundred missiles.*

As they readied their weapons, China surged four hundred aircraft into the target area.

The AIM-260 long-range anti-air missile didn't need target data, though it was much more accurate if it was given it before launch. It was a true 'fire and forget' weapon that could be launched down a bearing or toward a GPS coordinate and, once in the designated combat area, start looking for targets with its multimode radar, infrared and optical seekers. More like tiny near-invisible kamikaze drones, AIM-260 missiles flew in swarms, sharing data with each other so that if one of them spotted a group of targets, it shared the data with other missiles nearby and called them in to join the attack. And if they did not find a target, they would loiter until their fuel ran out, just in case a target happened past. They would attack anything that did not have a civilian or allied IFF, Identify Friend or Foe, transponder.

"Ironsides leader to Ironsides flight, report weapons state," the Captain in command of the flight requested, even though on the screens inside his control station, he had perfect information on the weapons and system state of every one of the Raiders in the flight.

"Ironsides two, weapons armed, systems nominal."

"Ironsides three, weapons armed, systems nominal."

One by one, the other pilots reported in. The B-2 Spirit that the Raider had replaced had required two crewmen, and the B-21 still flew with two when it was carrying nuclear weapons. Only a single remotely located pilot was needed to fly a Raider in uncrewed, conventional weapons mode.

The Captain of Ironsides one called through to the new Hawkeye early warning aircraft now circling cautiously twenty miles east of Palawan. It was tracking a couple of hundred contacts, mostly third- and fourth-generation Chinese fighters, and uploading its data to the Raiders to give them bearings down which to fire. Once the updated data was downloaded, the mission Commander got on the radio to his flight again.

"Ironsides flight, mission is go. Synching targeting data. Set fire to salvo, five-zero units, launch salvo one on my mark."

He watched as green lights lit up across one of his screens, indicating each aircraft had downloaded the latest target data and fed it to the missiles in their weapons bays.

"Ironsides one, opening bay doors…" If the Raiders had a vulnerable moment, it was now, during the launch of their missiles, when their radar cross-section would briefly spike. "*Fox three*, missiles away…"

In bundles of five, the AIM-260 missiles dropped out of the belly of each Raider. Their mission's orders called for an opening salvo of fifty, for a total of *300 missiles* in the first salvo. The Hawkeye would register strikes against the aircraft it could see (it might not, for example, be able to see Chinese stealth aircraft) and then extrapolate this kill rate to the estimated total number of aircraft over the target. If more salvos were needed, and it was expected they would be, the Hawkeye would order them.

The Raider captain 'looked' across at another Raider flying two miles off his starboard wing, his wraparound screens showing him a view similar to, but better than, one he might get out of the windows of the cockpit if he had been sitting in the machine himself. He had conducted air-to-air engagements before in simulations, and in exercises. But nothing had prepared him for the feeling right now as he watched missile after missile drop from the belly of the aircraft beside him, fall slightly behind as each one ignited the first stage of its two-stage motor, and then accelerate away from its mothership. In front of his own aircraft, he saw a mass of contrails as missiles literally *filled* the sky ahead of him.

He wasn't sure what he'd expected to feel. After all, he was a professional, and this was just another day at the office.

Except it wasn't. It was war. And what he felt, looking at the blizzard of missiles he'd just unleashed, was ... *horror*.

Li Chen looked across the sky and into the heads-up display on her helmet visor with a feeling of pure delight.

It showed ... nothing.

No enemy targets, at all. Which was just as well. Of the six aircraft she had left Mischief Reef with, only two were still flying off her wing. She had lost three pilots, one definitely killed, one she saw eject with her own eyes, and another whose beacon she saw activate as he hit the water. She had no way of knowing what the total cost of the day's engagements had been, but her tactical display showed all known friendly aircraft, and with the surge of aircraft from the mainland that had arrived in the last half hour, there were more aircraft over the South China Sea now than there had been at the height of the battle.

If she applied her own losses to the number of aircraft she knew had been sortied for the first phase of the battle – a very unscientific method – then China had lost nearly a hundred pilots in the last few hours. Still, only a fraction of those it had committed.

Of her own victories, she had not kept count. Three? Perhaps four. Most were not her victories after all. They belonged to her *Zhi Sheng* AI. The combination of J-20 stealth aircraft as spotters and *Zhi Sheng* J-16s and surface warships as snipers had proven a formidable one, even against the super maneuverable and hard to detect American drones. More than once she had seen a contact reported by a pilot, only to have it destroyed by a missile from a ship a hundred miles behind them. It had been an awe-inspiring demonstration of the power of combined arms and battlesphere data integration.

Now, about fifty miles behind her, she could see on her tactical screen the icons for rotary-winged Z-20 assault helicopters taking off from the assault ship *Yushen* and forming up so that they could hit the beachhead at Pagasa in strength.

Fuel warning. Approaching bingo fuel.

The voice in her ears forced her eyes down to her system's status screen again. Yes, it was time to turn her flight back to Mischief Reef. They had done their job today. Others could seal the victory.

Contact. Unidentified aircraft bearing one two zero, altitude 500, range 22, speed 340, heading zero zero.

What? It was a single, low-flying contact. Slow. Probably not a fighter. And too fast to be a helicopter. A civilian aircraft, perhaps, that had stumbled into the middle of a war zone? It would not be unheard of.

"Ao Yin pilots, this is Ao Yin leader – return to base. I will check out this contact and follow."

Her pilots acknowledged, and she was not surprised to hear the relief in their voices. She checked her weapons stores. One PL-21 and one short-range PL-9 were all she had left. Plus guns, of course.

She had no desire to attack an unarmed civilian aircraft, but it seemed to be on a heading for Pagasa and if it was determined to reach that island, she might have to.

Bunny had anything but perfect information on the battle overhead. She felt like someone sheltering under an umbrella as they ran through a hailstorm trying to reach cover. Somewhere north-east of her, if all had gone to plan, a swarm of self-guided missiles was streaking toward Pagasa. Directly ahead of her, though, just about the whole damn PLA Southern Command Army and Navy Air Force was circling.

Ten minutes. She was just ten minutes out of Pagasa.

She had no phased-array radar of her own and had shut her rudimentary flight radar down so as not to attract unwanted attention. She couldn't pull data from any other allied aircraft. Her stealth airframe coating and low flight profile had protected her this far, but for the first time in her life, flying into a hot combat zone, she felt totally naked. All she had was a simple radar warning receiver which for now was...

Oh hell, no.

Blinking at her, as a chime sounded in her ears. A fighter radar had locked onto her. Should she light up her own radar and try to locate it?

No, Bunny. Don't make yourself interesting. You aren't alone up here.

She reached for her internal comms. "Gentlemen, check your harnesses. We have company." Then she flipped to the *USS Congress*'s frequency. "*Congress*, Vapor, I have an admirer. Bearing two eight four. Range, about twenty. Can I get an assist?"

Okafor had given his CIC orders to relay to him any contact at all from the Vapor. Getting the Marines ashore wasn't *Congress*'s primary mission – landing the missile defense systems on the island was – but he saw the two as interconnected. *Congress* had not been able to assist with anti-air support during the early phase of the Chinese surge; she was too far away. But she was within missile range of Pagasa airspace now, and he had let his air defense crew know they were to stay ready to support allied aircraft on request.

Hearing O'Hare's voice over the bridge loudspeakers, he turned to Diavolo. "Help the lady, would you, XO?"

Diavolo reached for a mike. "CIC, Bridge. Did you copy the transmission from the Vapor?"

"Bridge, CIC, roger that. We have a possible contact down that bearing. Working up a firing solution."

Okafor nodded at Diavolo.

"CIC, Bridge. You are clear to engage. Advise the Vapor."

Moments later a single missile blasted from the vertical cells behind *Congress*'s superstructure and arced into the air.

Surface radar! Li Chen's *Zhi Sheng* sent the warning directly to her visor, with a range and bearing. It was too far from shore to be ground-based. There must be a hostile ship out there.

In the time it took her to process the information, the radar went from search to targeting mode and a new alert flashed in her visor. *Missile launch!*

All autonomy was taken from her as her backseater went defensive and prepared to evade the enemy missile. It didn't deem the small unidentified contact as sufficient a threat to dedicate resources to dealing with it yet. A possible error, Chen realized. There would have been no harm in sending a missile at that contact and *then* evading the incoming threat.

No matter, it could wait.

Bunny O'Hare had no intention of waiting to see what happened to the hostile fighter. As word came from USS *Congress* that it was engaging the Chinese aircraft, she lit up her own radar, got a bounce off the enemy fighter and quickly studied the data.

Nineteen miles, fifteen thousand feet, closing at 600 knots ... probably busy evading *Congress*'s missile right now, which was why it had not fired on her yet. Her Vapor was a sitting duck if the Chinese fighter was allowed to engage beyond visual range. Every instinct in her body told her to turn toward the enemy, close the gap to guns range and try to engage the Chinese fighter. When your alternative was hopeless, a hopeless strategy didn't seem quite so insane.

Bunny weighed the lives of the 14 men in the seats behind her in her mind. The way she saw it, if *Congress*'s missile didn't strike home, they were all about to die. If she took on the Chinese fighter head to head, they would probably die too, but they'd die *fighting*. When she brought her thoughts back to reality, she realized her fighter-pilot reflexes had already made the decision for her. While her mind had been deliberating, her body had turned her machine toward the Chinese fighter, pushed the throttle forward and was closing on it at full thrust.

Unless it bugged out completely, they'd be on each other inside a minute.

Chen had her jaw clenched as her machine rolled through the sky and reversed again. She'd gotten used to the feeling of being a passenger in her own fighter, but it didn't make the sensation any easier to process. The sense of helplessness was barely balanced by the feeling of trust she'd developed for her silicon backseater. But it wasn't infallible, as three of her pilots had found out. Whenever g-forces allowed, she turned her eyes back to her situation display and…

The light aircraft was turning *toward* her?!

Suddenly, her ears started filling with screams. The cool and professional background murmur of inter-squadron communications that she'd been listening to as her fellow pilots coordinated their movements through the airspace over the South China Sea had turned to a hysterical babble. What the…

Chinese aircraft icons on her display started winking out of existence. Aircraft by aircraft, the cloud of dots on her tactical display started inexplicably thinning out. A dread fear gripped her gut.

She heard the panicked voice of one of her own pilots. "Ao

Yin leader! I have a missile alert. Engaging *Zhi Sheng. There's no time! I can't…"*

The voice went silent, his aircraft disappearing from her radar. But the screams and warnings of other pilots continued.

She barely even noticed as the enemy missile she was dodging herself speared down out of the sky and buried itself in the waves behind her. Her backseater had taken her down to one thousand feet, and the dark sky of the South China Sea filled her cockpit windows from horizon to horizon. In the post-dusk twilight, it was impossible for her to tell what was sea and what was sky. For the first time in her life, she found herself paralyzed. *She should … she …*

Her backseater decided for her. Straightening up, it drew a box around the small aircraft coming straight towards it.

Arm guns and engage? It asked her. All she had to do was blink.

Bunny put her targeting reticle on the dark shape rushing toward her. Thanks to the *Congress* it hadn't fired on her yet, but as she watched *Congress*'s missile fly wide and strike the sea, she realized that advantage had already passed.

"Vapor, autofire when in range," she ordered, not trusting her own reflexes at such crazy closing speeds.

Target locked, autofire mode engaged.

All she had to do was keep the dark blur inside her targeting reticle for the next second. It really wasn't that hard if you thought about it.

And neither is dying, O'Hare.

Another of Li Chen's pilots cried out in terror. Across the width of her tactical display, aircraft icons were disappearing like fireflies in a rainstorm. They were being slaughtered – not in the tens, or dozens, but in the *hundreds.*

How? Mind-numbing terror filled her soul. She lifted her

hands up toward her face, felt them blocked by her helmet.

Arm guns and engage? The text flashed insistently in her visor. All she had to do was double blink.

But she was frozen with fear. A small black shape lifted itself from the dark background of the sea below. Twin streams of red tracer flashed from its nose.

Li Chen took a 20mm round right in the chest and was dead long before her J-16 exploded and slammed into the South China Sea.

No freaking *way*, Bunny thought, hauling her machine around and pointing it back at Pagasa Island. How had she survived that? The Chinese fighter was coming down at her from altitude and had her dead to rights. It should at least have gotten a shot away.

Well, that was air combat, she reflected. *Some days you ate the bear, and other days the bear ate you.*

She flipped on the inter-plane comms. "Sorry about the rough ride back there, we had company, but it's not going to trouble us now. We are ten minutes from the LZ."

Reflexively, she ran her eyes over her instruments, checking fuel and engine states. Ammunition: on the *USS Congress* she had watched weapons loaders put a 2,000-round belt in each gun. Which gave her just 20 seconds of continuous fire. She'd just used six. She couldn't fault the AI's aim, but its profligacy with her ammunition was unforgivable. She'd fire her own guns from now on.

And suddenly, there it was. A dark on dark shape, low on the horizon, that she had wondered more than once if she would ever see.

Pagasa Island.

She opened the internal comms again. "Gentlemen, we are approaching our destination. I hope you have enjoyed flying Air *Andromeda*. As you prepare to depart the aircraft, we kindly request you check the seat and floor around you and ensure you do not leave anything highly explosive behind. We thank you for flying Air *Andromeda* and hope to see you aboard again one day soon."

She smiled to herself. Yeah, okay, she'd rehearsed that speech in her head. Air *Andromeda*. She thought probably Ginger would have enjoyed that part.

As they reached the beach, Eugenio and Diwa helped the Chinese soldier wade out into the shallow water. The rocks he'd spoken of were about twenty yards off the beach; about five yards out, the water got too deep for Diwa.

"I can't go any deeper!" she said.

He'd taken out his pistol, saying he didn't want to get it wet, and held it in the hand he had around Eugenio's shoulder.

"Alright, this is as far as you go," the soldier said.

He looked at Diwa with a sad expression on his face. Eugenio wondered if maybe he had a sister and was thinking about her. But then he pulled back the chamber on his pistol.

Above them, Eugenio heard two loud reports, and they all looked up. Two strange fireballs, high in the sky, were floating down toward the sea, getting faster as they got closer to the waves until at last they plunged into the water a few miles away, sending gouts of water into the air. Up in the sky, where they'd been, were more strange lights. Eugenio had seen a meteor shower once, and it looked a bit like that. Or shooting stars. Hundreds of them.

Except shooting stars didn't fall into the sea. Not usually.

He tore his eyes away from the sky and saw the soldier, holding his gun in front of him, looking at Diwa.

"Where's your boat?" Eugenio asked him.

The man looked at Eugenio like he'd forgotten he was there. He turned toward the rocks. "Over there, tethered to the bottom with a weight belt." A wave washed in and nearly unbalanced him. He was still very weak.

He worked the breech on the gun again and a bullet came

out. He handed it to Eugenio. "For you," he said. "A souvenir." He opened his shirt and Eugenio saw he had a locket around his neck. He moved it out of the way so he could put the pistol in an inner waterproof pocket and zipped the shirt shut again.

"You two can go," the soldier said. "Find your parents."

"My father is a Chinese prisoner," the boy reminded him.

"What? Oh, yes. Well, now you know what that feels like, I guess," the man said. He waved them away. "Go on, go."

Eugenio took Diwa's hand and helped her wade out of the water. When they got to the sand, they started running. Eugenio looked back over his shoulder, expecting to see the man watching them.

He was gone.

"We don't have to run," Eugenio said, realizing Diwa was panting. They slowed to a walk.

"My parents … are going to be … crazy worried," Diwa said.

"You're lucky," Eugenio said. "My Ma is totally going to kill me."

Bunny was totally unprepared for how small the island was. The size of a few football fields, someone had told her. Leclerc? It looked much smaller in the dark as she skimmed in over the waves toward it. About a mile out she pulled back on the stick, getting a little height so she could get her bearings, and saw the east–west runway she recognized from satellite images.

"Don't shoot, I'm one of the good guys," she muttered quietly to herself. She hoped the White Star logo on the black doors was visible from the beach.

The island looked deserted. She keyed the internal comms. "I don't see any sign of life. I don't like it. It's going to be a rolling touchdown. Suggest you get ready to fight your way out," she told the Marines in the crew module. They were already up and hanging on roof straps, carbines slung around their necks, small packs snuggled between their shoulder blades and in the small of their backs. "Green light means door is open, slide it left," she told them. "Heads down as you exit."

She pulled back on her throttle as the tiltrotors at the end of her wings moved from horizontal to vertical and the turbofans under her tail powered down. Spinning the cyclic wheel all the way down told Vapor she wanted to get on the ground, fast, and the AI managed the descent, dropping the landing gear in time for the Vapor to hit the sandy runway with a thud. Before they had even settled Bunny unlocked the rear door and the Marines started piling out. Bunny saw them fan out and throw themselves flat.

From the treeline, a single man emerged, waving a torch. As he got closer, Bunny recognized the uniform of a PN Marine Seabee. The US Marine platoon commander had ridden in with his first squad and rose from his prone position to exchange a few words. More Filipino soldiers emerged from the treeline. One of them approached a wary Marine and embraced him with a bear hug. Bunny didn't need to be a lip reader to understand what he was saying.

"Welcome to Pagasa."

The officer who had been the first to emerge from the trees was holding on to his hat and pushing his way through the tiltrotor's downdraft to approach the cockpit. Bunny dropped her cockpit side window and he leaned in. "Will you shut down or shall we just start unloading?"

"Just start unloading," Bunny told him. "I have two more runs to make, this is just the first."

The man stepped back and looked at her machine. "You came from the American convoy?"

"Yes."

"Can you take our wounded back with you?"

She nodded. "Of course, if you have a nurse or someone who can look after them during the flight."

"I will assign one of my medics. That's okay?"

"No worries."

He sent a man running away to pass on the word to start bringing ambulant wounded to the airstrip, and then went around to help unload her machine. Bunny set the engines to idle and locked the wheel brakes, then popped the cockpit door. "Guess I'm helping too."

Together with the Marines and Philippine Seabees, Heraldo Bezerra and the pilot started hauling crates out of the crew compartment of the tiltrotor and stacking them beside the runway.

Heraldo lifted the top of one of the crates labeled *FIM-92 Launcher*. Inside was a long green tube with a box hanging off the front and an antenna array folded around the muzzle. He stood looking down at it.

"You know how this works?" he asked the pilot, who was dumping a crate of 7.62mm ammunition on the ground.

She walked over. "Yeah, when a Stinger can ruin your working day, it pays to know a little about it." She pointed down into the box. "These have been preassembled and preloaded in case we came in hot. You just lift it to your shoulder, put the crosshairs over the target and then interrogate it."

"Interrogate?"

"Identify Friend or Foe challenge switch is in front of the handgrip. Press that, it tells you if you are pointing at a good guy or bad guy. Steady beeping is a bad guy. Pull the trigger, and fire." She frowned. "I thought you were a Filipino Marine."

"Seabee," he told her. "Rifles and pistols, yeah. Squad weapons, maybe. Shovels, definitely. Stinger missiles, not so much."

"I heard you did a pretty good job here so far, Captain," she told him.

He ignored the praise, looking at the piles of crates and then over at the treeline. He called the platoon leader over. "My men are dug in behind the treeline, Lieutenant. I suggest you take your ammunition there and store it in a trench." He pointed at Pinya Hill. "There's a sandbagged emplacement up there would be good for siting a Stinger team too, gives them an uninterrupted view over the whole island." He looked grim. "It survived the first cruise missile strike; our plan was to pull back there if we got pushed back from the airfield."

"I'll take a team up there with Stingers and comms," the Marine officer nodded. "Keep the rest down here with your men."

Heraldo nodded and turned back to the pilot. "Next time you come in, if the airstrip here is too hot to put down, you can land next to the solar generation plant. You'll see the panels from the air. We started clearing some ground there for new panels that never got built. It's surrounded by..." He looked up. "What the hell is that?"

A series of sonic booms rolled over the island and what looked like a dozen contrails were spearing down through the sky, aimed at the sea to the north.

"That, Captain, is someone ringing on your doorbell," Bunny told him. She spun around to face the Marine officer. "Lieutenant, you have incoming. Forget unloading the rest of that ordnance. Your men haul what missiles you can up that hill, get on the radio, and I'll call targets for you." With that she started running for the Vapor.

Bunny had the Vapor airborne inside two minutes. The contrails she had seen were the remainders of the second salvo of 120 AIM-260 missiles fired by the B-21 Raiders, which had arrived to find just seventy Chinese aircraft still over the target area, most of their pilots still shaken from having evaded the missiles of the first salvo. Although China's air defense destroyers were now well within range of Pagasa and could have engaged, and probably destroyed, any conventional enemy fighters threatening their aircraft, they had no chance at all of engaging the small 150 lb. missiles of the AIM-260 swarm.

The swarm went to work on the remaining Chinese fighters, and when it was done, the remaining missiles went into loiter mode, looking for lower-priority targets.

Such as Chinese Z-20 troop transport helicopters.

The twenty choppers of the *Yushen*'s first wave of troop transports bound for Pagasa could not have been unluckier. They arrived in the combat zone at the moment the last of their air cover was swatted from the sky, under a night sky full of predators still hungry for prey. The AIM-260 swarm quickly conferred with itself, decided which of its members was going to carry out the attack, and sent them spearing down from 20,000 feet at the slow, fat choppers laden with Chinese Marines.

This was the curtain of contrails the troops on Pagasa Island had seen. Humping crates of missiles up to the top of Pinya Hill, they missed the sight of dozens of fireballs exploding out to sea, but Bunny saw them from the cockpit of her Vapor as she swung around to the south side of the hill and hovered just above its crest, eyes locked on her radar screen.

The radar was reflecting a mass of noise from the decoy chaff foil fired off by the Chinese choppers, desperate to try to decoy the American missiles falling on them. Most of them had tried in vain, the size of their machines and the heat of their engines seen from above making irresistible targets for the Raiders' missiles.

But from the white blob of radar noise, Bunny saw single shapes emerge and start accelerating toward the island again.

One, two … three … five … six … *seven*. As they separated from the blur of radar noise, Bunny saw two more missiles scream down from on high, and two more fireballs fell into the sea.

But that was all.

She dialed in the Marines' radio frequency. "Lieutenant, Vapor here, you in position?"

The man was panting. "We're here, ma'am, what have you

got?"

"Five bogeys, coming in echelon formation low, ten miles out, north-north-west." She rechecked her radar screen. "You had a guardian angel up there, but it seems their bow is out of arrows."

"We'll be ready," the man said.

Heraldo stood with his hands on his thighs, bent double and feeling like puking after the run up Pinya Hill.

I am way too old for this shit, he decided, for about the hundredth time in the last few days. As he tried to draw breath, he watched the Americans go methodically about their work. Each Stinger launcher was served by two men. One lifted it onto his shoulder and powered it on, putting his eye to the scope. The other stood beside him with low-light binos, looking out in the direction of the incoming assault. The enemy choppers could only be a couple of miles away by now.

But it quickly became obvious to Heraldo something was wrong. No one was calling targets and firing.

Bunny O'Hare could see exactly what was wrong. She had climbed to 10,000 feet and was watching the incoming formation of helos on radar. The Chinese assault troops weren't suicidal, and their transport helicopters were not unprotected. They had left *Yushen* in the company of four Harbin Z-19E light strike helicopters and two had survived the last American loitering missile strike. Looking through a zoomed low-light camera, Bunny couldn't see exactly what type they were, but she knew attack helos when she saw them. Their narrow fuselage and underslung rocket launchers left no doubt about that.

As she watched, three of the incoming assault helicopters slowed to a hover about five miles offshore, while the two attack helos continued onward, one breaking north, the other south, being careful and staying low while circling the island, no doubt conducting a fast recon with infrared vision, trying to spot troop concentrations.

The attack choppers relied on their small size and low altitude to hide from overhead fighter patrols and were moving outside optimal Stinger missile range. These two seemed to be proceeding with bloody-minded intent to lay down a barrage of standoff missile fire to pave their way for the troops behind them, and were less worried about whether they might get jumped from above again. She had to acknowledge their bravery. But there was a short distance from bravery to stupidity.

"Vapor, guns up."

Arming 20mm guns.

She looked quickly at the ammunition counter in her helmet visor. Thirteen hundred rounds, about fifteen seconds of fire.

Better make it count, O'Hare, she thought grimly. Her first objective must be to even up the odds. She had altitude, she had twice the max speed of an attack helicopter, but she was also twice the size: nowhere near as nimble. She couldn't afford a long, close-quarters engagement in case they were carrying air-to-air missiles.

Bunny twitched her stick left, sending her machine onto a wingtip and bringing it around behind the southernmost Chinese helo, which was crabbing along the coast doing its recon. Pushing her throttle forward and putting her nose down, she lined up her target.

The Marines on the hill had seen the two attack helos now too.

Heraldo heard someone yell, "Target, two o'clock low!" Seconds later he ducked as with an explosive whoosh a missile shot out from a team a few yards away and curved toward a fast-moving shadow, about a mile offshore.

He could only see a vague shadow against the sea in the

distance, which seemed to skip sideways, and dazzlingly bright flares sprayed from behind it as it turned away. Decoyed by the high-intensity flares, the Stinger went wide and kept flying.

Miss!

Now the shadow was coming around again, and Heraldo frowned as the sky around it seemed to brighten, and streaks of light started converging on their position.

"Incoming!" the Marine Lieutenant yelled, pulling Heraldo heavily to the ground.

Precision strike missiles. From the corner of her eye, Bunny saw a Stinger go wide, saw the Chinese attack helo on the north side of the island launch a salvo of missiles at the summit of the hill. There was nothing she could do about it. She had her sights on the helo flying south of the island.

Two miles out. She had to get inside a mile before she fired.

Two fifty miles an hour, two eighty … 3,700 yards… three hundred miles an hour … 3,200 yards … come on, you big ugly mother!

From the treeline by the landing strip, a Stinger also lanced out, toward her target. But it was another Hail Mary shot, and skidding through the air, firing decoy flares into the sky, the Chinese helo in her sights also decoyed the American missile. All it had done was confirm the position of the island's defenders at the air base and the Chinese helo began rising into the air, getting ready to launch its missiles.

Three twenty miles an hour, two fifty … 2,800 hundred yards … damn! They had finally seen her now, abandoned their ground attack and started to curve away from the island, trying to increase separation to her at the same time as they brought their nose back around so they could get guns or missiles on her.

2,400 yards … 2,200 … Her thumb reached for the firing stud on her flight stick. At the moment the reticle in her visor went from white to green, she jabbed her thumb down and caught the Z-19 mid-turn with a full broadside, her 20mm shells stitching it from nose to tail and shoving the light helicopter bodily sideways before it started spinning uncontrollably and slammed into the sea.

Before the Chinese chopper had even hit the sea, Bunny had pulled back on her stick and turned her attention to her radar. The Chinese assault helos had decided they couldn't loiter any longer. Using the cover fire from their escorts to make a run at Pagasa, they were headed for the landing strip. "Lieutenant, Vapor, you have three fast assault helos moving in … Lieutenant?"

For what felt like the tenth time in just a few days, Heraldo was eating dirt. The attack helicopter's guided-missile fire had zeroed in on their position on top of the hill with fatal effect. Ears ringing, blood in his mouth, Heraldo lifted himself to his knees and then unsteadily to his feet. The four Marines, and their officer, were scattered around the emplacement. He found one dead, the other three dazed or wounded, including the officer who was waving at him weakly, trying to say something. The only thing that had saved Heraldo had been that because he wasn't involved in engaging the incoming helicopters, he'd been standing slightly downhill watching the US Marines go to work.

He dragged the wounded men into cover and propped them up against sandbags, next to the crates they had humped up the hill with them. Thankfully their injuries seemed light, but they weren't in any state to continue the fight right then.

He heard the crackle of the radio beside the dead man and knelt beside it, picking up the handset. "Captain Heraldo."

It was the pilot of the tiltrotor. "Captain! You have three assault helos about five hundred yards out. All three are making for your landing strip…"

Heraldo stood. "My men down in the treeline will have to deal with them. We got hit bad up here."

"Understood. Will see what I can do. Out."

What she could do? Heraldo could see her machine, dragging itself back up to altitude. She was out of position after engaging the attack helo south of the island. Looking north, Heraldo could see the incoming assault troop helicopters. Three dark shapes, rushing in from the north, one behind the other like horses on a trail.

He was sure his men and the remaining Marines down in the treeline would be on alert, but those enemy helos would come in with guns hot, raking the treeline with autocannon fire from their waist guns. Some of them would get their troops away, unless…

He turned quickly, checking the sky for the Chinese attack helo to the north. He couldn't see it. But next to the three wounded Marines was a case containing a loaded Stinger missile. He might not be able to get down to the treeline to help his men, but he could do something. He bent and lifted the unfamiliar weapon from its case. It was not light, must have weighed about 30 lbs. He fumbled with it in the dark. *Power it on. Where the hell was the power switch…*

Bunny had eleven seconds of ammunition left. Reaching the top of her climb, and before she lost too much energy, she leveled her machine out and checked her radar. The three assault helos were only a mile or two out. The Chinese attack helo was swinging around the east of the island, toward the airfield, which was the logical landing zone for the Chinese troops. Setting up to lay down more missile fire, no doubt.

"Pagasa, Vapor, you down there, Captain?" Looking out her cockpit window she could see the hilltop where the Marine Stinger crews had been attacked was shrouded in smoke. She got the feeling there would be no help coming from up there.

Think, Bunny! What is the biggest threat? That attack helo, or the incoming troop carriers? It was probably 50/50 but she figured that if she was crouched in a shallow trench armed with only a rifle and a few grenades, waiting for three assault helos to sweep into view and start disgorging Chinese assault troops, she'd vote for the troop carriers.

Swinging around, she lined up on the Z-20 transport helo that was at the front of the line of fat beetle-like shapes heading straight for the island. Her ingress would take her right over the top of the Chinese attack helo, but it would probably have its nose toward land, not along her line of attack.

Probably. Probably could put you six feet under, O'Hare. If they can find the pieces.

Her airspeed built as she dropped from ten, through nine, eight and then five thousand feet. The helos below were probably moving in under five hundred feet. She adjusted her trim. Four hundred knots! Black shadows became solid through the blur of rotors. They must see her now. They would have to break soon, they must see death coming right for them.

Only one of the helos deviated from its approach. Executing a sharp turn to starboard, the lead helicopter put itself broadside on to O'Hare's machine and reared up into a hover. Its side door was wide open and Bunny saw the silhouette of a gunner inside, trying to keep his feet and steady himself. The other two troop carriers broke left and kept heading for the landing strip.

Bunny yawed her machine left, kept the targeting reticle in her helmet focused right on the gunner in the middle of the helo and thumbed her gun trigger. Twin lines of red tracer streamed towards the almost stationary chopper and exploded inside its crew compartment. Releasing her pressure on the left rudder, she walked the tracer fire along the length of the helo's crew compartment and took her finger off the trigger when she saw the tail section break away and men tumble from the shattered machine as it spun towards the sea.

The action had taken her too far, too fast to be able to bring her guns around to bear on the other two troop carriers, but she tried, putting the Vapor into a flat, skidding starboard turn that threw her forward in her harness as the aircraft decelerated massively. The other two troop carriers flashed past under her nose, boring in on the landing strip, just 500 yards out now. She couldn't get guns on them, the desperate maneuver was no use.

And it had made her a sitting duck for the Chinese attack helo that had seen her flash overhead, swung its nose around to follow her, and now opened up with its 25mm cannon. Luckily for Bunny, her crazy skid through the sky had taken the Chinese gunner by surprise and his shells sprayed wide, falling behind her; but she was down low now, over the northern part of the island, and the turn had bled her energy away.

Her only option was to keep turning.

Into the still-firing 25mm cannon of the Chinese attack helo.

Ah, right. Heraldo found the power-up switch for the Stinger. He climbed out of the trench running around the hilltop emplacement and stood looking down on the airstrip. The first of two Chinese troop carriers was already flaring, just yards off the ground, getting ready to disgorge its troops. As he watched, a Stinger blasted out from the treeline below and speared into the hot engines of the chopper, sending it thumping into the earth in a ball of metal and fire.

Small arms fire from the treeline started pouring at the second chopper in line. His men, backed by the rest of the Marine squad, seemed to have the situation in hand. He heard the tearing sound of an autocannon firing nearby and turned to see one of the small Chinese attack choppers screaming around to the north, tracer from its under-nose-mounted swivel cannon pouring into the sky towards…

The big black tiltrotor.

Looking into the launcher's scope, he waved it around erratically until finally he caught the helo in the crosshairs of the scope. Interrogate the target? *Forget that. No time.* Slipping his finger into the trigger guard, he aimed the missile at the attack helo and squeezed the trigger.

If he hadn't been standing on the side of a hill, that might have been the end of Heraldo Bezerra, right there. Bunny had forgotten to tell him that just before firing the missile, he should elevate the muzzle by ten degrees to allow for the slight delay before the missile's boost phase kicked in after firing. But the missile sprung out of the launcher, dipped momentarily, and then swooped downhill before zooming upwards.

Straight into the engine and rotors of the Chinese attack helo.

Heraldo winced as it struck. A giant hand seemed to shove the machine downward, its rotor flew straight up, and its back broke down the middle. It went careening out to the ocean as the tiltrotor straightened out, coming right over the top of where Heraldo was standing.

Heraldo ducked his head involuntarily and felt suddenly very, very tired. Wiping more blood from his mouth, he dropped the empty Stinger launcher to the ground and then fell to his knees.

Corporal Ruan of the Jiaolong Commandos was no longer pushing through the waves off Pagasa on his UDV. He was floating on his back, looking at the stars. Letting go of the UDV and just sliding off the mini-submarine so that he could rest his aching leg had probably been one of the best decisions of his short life.

The sky over the South China Sea was simply breathtaking. There were several very bright stars and millions of lesser ones, clustered around what looked like a cloud of orange dust. Why had he never noticed that before? And then, as he'd been lying there, he'd seen what looked like a meteor shower, with fireballs as the meteors entered the atmosphere, burned up, and fell into the sea.

Ruan felt as though the display had been timed just for him. *Are you seeing this, great-grandfather?* he asked his ancestor. He imagined it must look even more spectacular viewed from the heavens, where the old bugler was watching.

He knew he should resume his journey back to Subi Reef, but there was no hurry. And this moment may never come again. Bobbing up and down on his back in the waves of the South China Sea, Corporal Ruan allowed himself a small moment of peace in what had been a distressing and violent couple of days. He floated with his arms out to his sides, the scars on his forearms like a map of the brightest of the stars above.

So beautiful.

Corporal Ruan did not deign to react at the ripsaw sound of 20mm gunfire overhead a short while later, and he didn't even flinch as the shadow of a stricken Z-19 helicopter spun over his head. It struck the water a hundred yards to his right, and the violence of its splashdown sent three-foot waves washing over him. But he didn't sputter or choke, he just rode out the waves and then continued floating, calm face and unseeing eyes still turned to the stars.

You bloody beautiful Marines!

Bunny had seen the Stinger scream down from the hilltop and the attack helo that was milliseconds from drilling her Vapor full of holes dissolve in an angry red and orange fireball as she blasted past it. Swiveling her head over her shoulder, she saw it crash into the waves and, miraculously, several men bobbed up from the foam around and started splashing towards the shore. They would be in no condition to fight, but it would be best if there was a reception committee on the beach to meet them.

She curved around the island, her starboard wing dipped so she could look at the ground below. Filipino troops and Marines were advancing cautiously toward wrecked choppers on the landing strip. She could see a few Chinese troops lying on the ground, either wounded or dead. And a couple standing, hands in the air.

Bunny quickly checked her radar. It was showing nothing near or approaching the island now, either by sea or air. Her radar couldn't reach out as far as the Chinese task force, probably still about a hundred miles out, but if it had launched a second wave of assault troops on helicopters, she would have expected to see them by now. She checked her remaining ammunition. She was down to a few hundred rounds, maybe two short bursts or one long one. She hoped desperately she wouldn't need it.

She got onto the radio. "Captain, Vapor, that last helo is down, but there are a few survivors swimming towards the northern beach. You should probably send a squad over there to…"

"Pilot, this is Lieutenant Harley, the Filipino Captain has headed back down to join his men," the US Marine officer said tonelessly. "I'll get a squad down to that beach."

A new alert chimed in her ears and she saw two aircraft icons on her radar screen … to the east? Chinese aircraft returning from a sortie, perhaps. She couldn't see the aircraft type but they appeared to be headed straight for Pagasa. *Damn.*

"Harley, Vapor. You better get your heads down again, looks like you have incoming, fast movers from the east."

Swinging the Vapor around she dropped it low, hovering behind the western crest of the low hill in the middle of the island … the only cover she could use to make it difficult for the incoming aircraft to pick her up.

It was hopeless, though. While they were still twenty miles out, a voice came over her radio.

"Unidentified aircraft over Pagasa, this is US Navy aviation. You are operating in a military exclusion zone. Identify yourself or you will be attacked."

US fighters? *Alright!* They were back in the game. "Navy, this is White Star Vapor N192PH, operating on behalf of US Department of Defense. It's nice to see you guys."

"Nice to see you too, pilot. *USS Congress* told us to keep an eye out for you. You have clear air, no Chinese aircraft inbound. We'll try to keep it that way."

"Appreciate it, Navy. Vapor out."

Clear air at last, but for how long? She had to get down to that airfield again, finish unloading the ordnance in her payload bay, and load up with wounded. Then get back to the *Congress* and do the same trip, at least two more times.

Even though the distance between the warship and the island was closing by the minute, it was going to be a long, long night.

In the White House Situation Room, Carmine Lewis's cell phone started flashing to let her know there was a message. When she had read it, she stood up quickly.

From: Mom > Please call at your convenience on this number

It was most definitely not a message her mother would send, so it could only be her tea-spilling Politburo friend. She immediately got an image of the man, half a world away but standing in exactly the same kind of room as her, watching the exact same data on multiple monitors. With the reports coming in following the attack by the B-21 Raiders, in the basement of the White House, the mood was hopeful. Preliminary estimates were between 320 and 410 Chinese aircraft destroyed during the first and second phases of the day's conflict. Given most of the pilots of the Chinese aircraft would have had to bail out over the sea, even a conservative estimate came to 160–205 Chinese pilots lost. Seventy-three US aircraft had been destroyed or damaged, but the US had lost only five aviators – the crew aboard the Hawkeye destroyed in the first minutes of the battle.

Most importantly, the Chinese task force had slowed to a crawl. It had not stopped, but it was no longer sailing full steam for Pagasa, and it had not launched more helicopter troop transports toward the island. Navy had sent new combat air patrols into the area without encountering any opposition.

As Carmine re-read the cell phone message, she hoped it

meant she was about to find out how the mood was in Beijing.

Fenner saw the look on her face. "Something we need to be worried about?"

"My Politburo friend. You want me to put him on speaker?" she asked.

"Why not?" Fenner said. "Go ahead."

"No, Mr. President," Chuck Abdor interjected, shaking his head vehemently. "If he thinks you are on the call, that changes the dynamics completely. He gets direct access to you, which is something he should have to bargain for, if he gets it at all. And it should be the damn Chinese Premier you are talking with, not some flunky."

Fenner sighed. "Hell, I just wanted to listen in, Chuck."

"I can record it," Lewis said. "I'll take it in the office next door."

Carmine went next door. She would soon know if the caller was genuine or not. No one but an absolute insider would have access to real-time intelligence about the air battle over Pagasa. The first item on her agenda was to test how much he knew.

She called up the message and hit the key to call the number that had sent it. When it started ringing, she pressed the key combination on her phone that started a traceback and recording of the call. The traceback had led them nowhere last time, but they could use the recording of the last call, and this one, to confirm the man's identity, if NSA or CIA had recordings of him speaking.

"Madam Director," the man said. "Thank you … thank you for calling." She could hear he was extricating himself from a meeting, walking out of a room full of voices. If he was who he said he was, it was possible NSA would already be able to pull some intel from the call … the discussion in the background sounded like it was a heated one. "I must be brief. The arrangement I discussed with you. Have you put it to your President or other colleagues?"

"General, if you have been following events over Pagasa, you would know that we have no reason at the moment to be looking for a negotiated solution to this issue." She knew the comment risked angering him, but she needed to know she was really dealing with a Politburo or military insider. *Show me you are worth talking to, whoever you are.*

He didn't sound angry, he sounded ... distraught. "Madam Director ... I ... we lost more pilots and aircraft today than we lost in *three years* during the Korean war. The mood in the Politburo is – I don't know how to say this any other way – it is extremely dangerous right now."

"What do you mean by dangerous?" Carmine asked, convinced now of his authenticity, as much by his tone of voice as by his understanding of the situation in the South China Sea.

"I mean, Madam Director, the sentiment in the room is currently in favor of declaring a State of War with the USA," he said. "And by that I mean, everything short of nuclear. Cyber, space, land, sea and air war, to secure our position in the South China Sea." He paused. "And Taiwan."

"*Taiwan*? How can this..."

"If we are at war, if we initiate a general mobilization, there will be no reason not to move on Taiwan now as well. It will force you to fight across a broad front in which China has all the advantages. You would take weeks to move sufficient forces into position, while we would take only days. You know this much."

Lewis kept a cool head. "General, if you lost half as many pilots and aircraft today as our estimates show, your air force is in no position whatsoever to support operations in both the South China Sea and the straits of Taiwan."

"Madam, I am afraid that kind of rational calculus is not prevailing in the discussions I have been part of in the last hour," he said. "Please. I need what you call 'a circuit breaker', something I can take back into the room with me to give our Premier an alternative to consider."

Lewis felt the pain in every word, and also knew that if she took his request back into the Situation Room with her, her Cabinet colleagues would enter into a furious debate that could take hours to resolve.

Carmine Lewis was about to make the judgment call of her life.

"General, you can tell your Premier that my President may be willing to enter into talks about a non-aggression pact in the South China Sea," she said.

"Non-aggression ... I don't understand."

She thought fast. "All of the topics you raised previously ... US neutrality regarding existing Chinese possessions in the South China Sea, freedom of navigation in recognized sea lanes, these would all be on the table. But there is one non-negotiable condition for this offer. China must recognize Philippine sovereignty over Pagasa Island."

"And your missile installation on the island? Do you plan to proceed with..."

"Also not negotiable – unless you plan to demilitarize your bases on Subi Reef, Mischief Reef and Fiery Cross Reef?"

"I could not even raise that suggestion," he admitted.

"Then you need to get your comrades on the Politburo to recognize they are not in a position to achieve anything other than an agreement to enter into bilateral negotiations on a non-aggression pact, and recognizing Philippine sovereignty is the price for that offer."

"I understand. Thank you. I will take your offer to my Premier."

"Good to hear, General. We may have found a way out of this for both of our nations. But the clock is ticking. I must tell you that if we do not hear back from you within the hour, we will assume your answer is no, and China and the USA are, de facto, in a State of War."

"Understood. Goodbye, Madam." The line went dead.

Lewis leaned her head against the wall behind her and closed her eyes. *What in the hell did you just do, Carmine? Are you insane?*

She looked down at her cell phone as though expecting it to explode in her hand. Like the Situation Room was about to do, the minute she walked back in there and told her Cabinet colleagues what she had just done.

Bunny O'Hare arrived back at the *USS Congress* to find the ship once again at general quarters. More than that, she saw an emergency response team preparing Mission-Oriented Protective Posture or MOPP gear on the flight deck. The sort of gear you broke out if you were anticipating a chemical, biological or nuclear weapons attack. She supervised the offloading of the wounded she had taken aboard on Pagasa and explained to the next load of Marines on the flight deck how to stow their ordnance and equipment, then sprinted up to the bridge level to find Diavolo. She ran into Okafor on the stairs, on his way down to check on something, with an Ensign in tow.

"O'Hare," he said, nodding at her, clearly preoccupied with other matters than getting Marines onto Pagasa Island. But he stopped as he drew level with her. "We just got word from Fleet that Indo Pacific Command has been moved to DEFCON 2. We've just picked up the Chinese naval task force on radar, but it appears to be making very slow headway, and we're not showing any aircraft launching."

"We lost one of your men on Pagasa, Captain," she informed him. "I'm sorry."

"So am I," Okafor replied. "No change to our mission orders, though. We are still proceeding to Pagasa with *Orion*, expect to be dockside in six hours."

"So, I'm still flying the Pagasa Express?" she asked.

"The threat of Chinese action has not diminished. I appreciate you are a civilian and your status is currently…"

She interrupted him. "My status, Captain, is pissed off and hungry for payback, so if you still need me to put Marines on Pagasa, then that is what I will do."

He put a hand on her shoulder. "How are you holding up?"

"Bone-headed *and* thick-skinned, sir," she told him, tapping her skull. "Though I will be sending White Star Lines a repair bill for the bullet hole in my nice flight jacket."

"You can send that bill to me," he told her. "And I'll do what I can for you regarding the investigation when we dock in Guam. You'll need someone in your corner now that Pedersen is…"

"Unavailable. Is the word you are looking for, sir," she told him.

"Yes. I need to get below. As you were," he said, then smiled. "Then again, you always are."

Bunny watched Okafor go. Then decided to go back down and head straight back to the flight deck. DEFCON 2? Okafor had given her all the briefing she needed for now.

Forty-five minutes had passed since Carmine Lewis had spoken with the Director of China's Central Analysis Commission – General Jack Chunhua. She was no longer in any doubt about the man's bona fides. His knowledge of the air war over Pagasa had been too current for him to be anyone else, and if that hadn't been enough to convince her, the near panic in his voice sealed it for her.

Surprisingly, Lewis's biggest ally in the storm that followed her explanation of what had happened on her back-channel call had not been President Fenner. It had been Victoria Porter. If she had ever been handed a moment in which to sit back and watch as Carmine crashed and burned, it was the moment when Carmine explained to ExCom that she had just committed President Fenner to a one-on-one meeting with the Chinese Premier to discuss a non-aggression pact.

The room had divided along the lines she more or less expected, with Secretary of Defense Kahn and Chairman of the Joint Chiefs on the side of 'are you freaking kidding we just kicked China's ass' and Fenner's Chief of Staff, Chuck Abdor, and the NSA Director, Kyle Sandiland, on the side of 'any deal that gets China to stand down and hand sovereignty of Pagasa to the Philippines is a win'. Lewis had made her case, which largely consisted of reminding them that if they chose to walk her offer back, they were facing a declaration of war with China, and might be anyway if the Chinese Premier would not accept the deal. Which left Vice President Tyler and Porter to break the deadlock.

Tyler had weighed in on Carmine's side. "The objectives of this military intervention were, with minimal loss of American lives, to show the world we stand behind our allies, and to check China's expansion in the South China Sea *without* starting a broader conflict. In the last several days we have shown the world that our word is our bond, and though at great material cost, we have dealt a blow to China's air forces which may take them years to recover from. If they agree to parlay on the basis they will recognize Philippine sovereignty over Pagasa, then I say we have achieved our every objective. Whether there is value in such a negotiation, I defer to Victoria."

All eyes turned to Porter. She took her reading glasses off her face and laid them on the table. "The Director has put us in a difficult position." *Oh, here we go*, thought Lewis. Then tried to hide the surprise on her face as Porter continued. "But I don't see she had a choice. If she had sent General Chunhua back into his party room without hope for some kind of deal, we would probably already be at war…"

"You don't know that we aren't," Kahn interrupted.

"Do *not* talk over me, Phil, I'm not one of your interns," Porter snapped. "As the Vice President said, we can come out of this with the victory we were seeking, and everything else China wants us to put on the table – neutrality over their existing bases in the South China Sea, an agreement on freedom of navigation – are all things we can walk away from if we don't like what China is offering." She picked up her glasses and put them back on. "I vote we deal."

Fenner didn't hum and haw. "And so do I. But we pray for peace and prepare for war. Our forces in the Indo Pacific are at DEFCON 2 and will stay that way. This can still go very wrong."

Kahn had opened his mouth to continue the argument, but Fenner held up a palm. "Phil, you've said your piece and I've said mine. Inside fifteen minutes we'll see which way this wind is blowing."

They had sat in relative silence, broken only by the occasional phone call to, or from, worried staffers. But they didn't have to wait fifteen minutes. They only had to wait five.

Carmine's telephone buzzed.

From: Mom > Your terms are agreed. Our air and naval forces will stand down at the first sign you are doing the same. My Premier awaits a call from your President.

Carmine read the message and if she expected jubilation to sweep the room, she was to be disappointed. There was a tired silence into which President Fenner stood. "General, please move our forces to DEFCON 3, and pull any aircraft we have in the air back to Clark Base. Chuck, please set up the call with China's Premier for tomorrow. In the meantime, organize a presser. Get the press secretary to announce that the island of Pagasa remains in Philippine hands thanks to US intervention and we have agreed to a cessation of hostilities with China. Nothing too inflammatory, 'more details tomorrow as the situation is still evolving', that kind of thing."

"Yes, sir." Abdor rose and made for the door.

Fenner turned to address the rest of the room. "Ladies and gentlemen, I plan to attend the 6 p.m. service at Saint Stephen's this evening and thank God this is over. You are all welcome to join me." As he walked from the room, his eyes lighted on Carmine, and he gave her a nearly imperceptible nod.

Epilogue: two weeks later

At the closed-door ceremony to celebrate the sacrifice of the pilots of the Battle of the South China Sea, Admiral Li Bing distressingly lost count of how many medals he had pinned on the chests of weeping fathers, mothers, brothers or sisters. But he had an aide behind him, whispering the name of each of the recipients as they walked up and took the small piece of metal and ribbon that would never replace the child they had lost.

He said the same to each of them, and he meant it each time. "They gave their life for China's future."

The PLA Coast Guard air-sea rescue services had been awarded medals the day before, for saving the lives of more than 70 downed pilots over the two days of combat. China had lost 326 aircraft, but most damagingly, 254 pilots. By contrast, the PLA Navy intelligence service estimated the USA had lost 124 aircraft, and only a handful of pilots. Li Bing knew from experience he should treat PLA intelligence estimates with caution, and the real number of US losses was sure to be lower than that. It was a conflict from which China would draw many lessons.

And not all were negative. The *Zhi Sheng* AI-modified J-16 had shown capabilities beyond anything its designers had imagined, in the hands of Li Chen's Ao Yin Squadron. Teamed with the Skyhawk drone, or working in tandem with J-20 stealth fighters, it had racked up a kill-to-loss ratio of 6:1, which was more than double its nearest competitor, the theoretically more advanced J-20. He would wait for the final analysis to be made, but it seemed to Li Bing that if the question was 'what will be more powerful in future air combat, AI or stealth', the answer now must be 'AI'. Of course, the fighter that successfully combined both might be unbeatable.

His aide stepped forward and whispered to him. "The brother of Li Chen."

He had been waiting for this moment. He watched as the

young man, in his late teens, came up the steps and along the stage. He showed no sign of awkwardness or embarrassment, despite the huge audience of family members and military officials in the auditorium. Walking quickly up to stand in front of Li Bing, he bowed stiffly and then waited.

Li Bing leaned forward slightly. "Comrade Chen. I knew your sister, personally. She served on my flagship. She was my bravest pilot, as fearless on the ground as in the air."

"Thank you, Comrade Admiral," the boy said.

"She told me you are also training to be a pilot."

"Yes, Comrade Admiral..." He hesitated and Li Bing sensed he wanted to say something.

"Go ahead."

"Sir, when I graduate, it is my wish to be posted to Ao Yin Squadron to honor my sister."

Li Bing reached out without thinking and put a hand on the boy's shoulder. "Your instructors will decide which unit you are best suited to. But I will ask them to keep me informed."

"Thank you, Comrade Admiral."

He pinned the medal on the boy's chest, took his bow and watched him walk quickly from the stage. He turned and spoke quietly to his aide. "Get me his name and date of birth tomorrow. And a summary of his most recent assessments."

"Yes, Comrade Admiral."

Li Bing saw the boy go down the stairs and lost him in the audience as the next family member was announced. China had increased its recruitment quota for fighter pilots fivefold since the Battle of the South China Sea. It had also fast-tracked projects that would allow it to counter the new American AIM-260 swarming air-to-air missile. The next time young men like Li Chen's brother were asked to take to the skies in a war against the USA, China would be ready.

That there would be a next time, Li Bing had no doubt.

Eugenio Maat was waiting on the new deep-water pier

jutting out from the harbor on Pagasa Island with Mayor Reyes and just about the entire village. The Philippine Navy patrol boat had appeared on the horizon to the south-west and was already growing larger by the minute.

An honor guard of US Marines was there too, in their black dress uniforms, white caps and white gloves, to welcome his father home. They had swords on their hips and everything. Further down the dock the Filipino Seabee officer with the crazy hair was standing with some of his men, waiting to tie up the incoming ship.

Eugenio had heard he had bought one of the empty houses at the north end of the village and was planning to move his family to Pagasa. Eugenio never heard of anyone moving *to* the island by choice, so he figured the man must have been hit in the head by a grenade or something.

He could see the bow wave on the approaching boat now. It had been three months since Eugenio had seen his father, Gonzales, and he was nervous. Not to meet him, of course not, but worried what the Chinese might have done to him in three months of prison on Subi Reef. Mayor Reyes had told him the Americans had traded ten Chinese prisoners just to get back his father, so he hoped they'd treated him alright, in case their own prisoners didn't get treated well.

And then suddenly the patrol boat was pulling up alongside the pier and his father was stepping out and looking bewildered at the crowd of people, and the Marines were standing at attention and lifting out their swords and holding them raised in the air like they were forming an arch, and his father was ducking under them because he'd spotted Eugenio and ran toward him and swept him up in his arms and swung him around.

"Whoa, you got heavy, boy," Gonzales said, putting him down and hugging him tightly.

"Ma is dead," Eugenio told him straight away. Worried he might not have heard. "I been living with Mr. and Mrs. Flores."

"They told me," his father said. "We'll talk about it later, okay? Not in front of all these people."

"Okay."

"Let me look at you." His father pushed him away and held him at arm's length. "They told me you and Diwa got taken prisoner too. By a Chinese commando?"

"It wasn't like that," Eugenio told him. "He was hurt. I looked after him."

"That's not what they told me. You did, huh?"

"Yeah. He was bleeding and couldn't walk. We fixed his bandages, I kept a watch for him while he slept, and then we helped him down to his boat."

His father frowned, and Eugenio couldn't tell if he was angry or sad. "You really did that, eh? Looked after a man some people would call our enemy?"

When he said it like that, Eugenio suddenly felt like he'd done something wrong. But his father pulled him in tight again. "I'm proud of you, son. You're twice the man I am, at half the age."

People were waiting to shake his hand, so he hugged Eugenio one more time and then winked at him. "Let's get this over with and go home and make us a big mess of adobo, eh? I'm starving."

The Macau Jewel casino was a known haunt of Chinese Ministry of State Security operatives. They cruised the tables and bars on the lookout for indiscreet Chinese government officials, gathered compromising information on the gambling and other habits of foreign politicians, businessmen and women, or simply laundered money at baccarat.

Sylvie Leclerc was fairly sure that was what she was looking at right now as she watched two gamblers at the table in front of her throw bet after bet on the table without reacting in the slightest whether they won or lost. They were dressed in nondescript suits, sat drinking what looked like iced tea, and gave the impression they were totally bored. There was no communication between them, but she noticed that they always bet opposite hands: if one bet on the player to win, the other would bet on the banker, and vice versa. In that way, one of the two almost always won. In the short time she had been watching they had placed at least ten thousand US dollars in bets, turning dirty money into clean chips they would cash in on their way out. They had probably been at it for days.

They'd said nothing, communicating only with nods and grunts, but by the poor quality of their suits and their half-starved frames, she'd be willing to bet they were North Korean. Her eyes roamed the room looking for more interesting prey.

She was not at the Macau Jewel to enjoy herself. She was here on business, to settle an account for her employer, White Star CEO Karl Sorensen. It was a tasking she had accepted gladly.

It had weighed heavily on Sylvie's conscience that despite the warning she had been able to relay to the White Star convoy, many, many men had died in the Chinese submarine attack. Not a single day went past where she didn't look back and find fault in her own actions. It was her lack of attention to detail that had allowed the Chinese agent, Winter, to be placed aboard the *Andromeda*. It was her fault he had been able to feed information to China and its pirate militia, making it easy for them to intercept and nearly cripple the *Orion*. Her fault Winter had nearly killed the Australian pilot, risking the loss of the convoy's most potent defensive asset, the Vapor. That he had no doubt also provided data on the convoy's position, speed and planned course to the Chinese submarine, right up to the moment of his death, allowing it to set up a near perfect ambush. Her fault she had not been able to prompt Winter's Chinese handlers for more precise information about the impending attack on the convoy. Yes, she had been able to give them a vague heads-up, and then a warning of 'danger close' … but that had not prevented the Chinese submarine attack. Was it realistic to think she could have done so? Yes: if she had identified Winter earlier, if she had been able to have him detained and interrogated before he was killed by O'Hare, who knows what information he might have shared.

If, if, if…

Her eyes swept the room again. Sorensen had paid a large sum of money for the information that had led her here. She trusted the source. But plans could change, even those of unwitting targets.

She turned at the sound of clapping and shouts of joy, saw a party celebrating a win at a roulette table, and beyond them saw…

Daniel Lim.

The digital fingerprints in Winter's cell phone had given them several leads which had led to cutouts and blinded middlemen, but with the resources of the world's 25th richest man and a motivated US military intelligence apparatus behind her, it was only a question of time. A human source had eventually provided them with the name of 'Daniel Lim', or, as he was otherwise known, Captain Yi Ming of the Ministry of State Security, Third Bureau.

She had been told where and when she could find him tonight, but as soon as she laid eyes on him she saw that he was not at the casino to gamble. He had walked into the room and was doing exactly the same as her; leaning casually against a wall, scanning it for a target.

There was a very real and worrying possibility that his target was Sylvie Leclerc. From what she had been told about him, she wouldn't put it past the MSS officer to be hunting his hunter. His eyes fell on the baccarat table where she was standing, and she leaned forward over one of the North

Korean's shoulders to place a bet, letting her hair fall across her face as she did so. When she straightened again, Lim's gaze had moved on, but that meant nothing.

The situation was not as straightforward as she'd hoped. To be honest, she'd hoped to find him at a table, inebriated and worried more about the bets in front of him than the room around him. He was anything but. And if he was here for work, not pleasure, then she would bet all the chips in her hand that he was not here alone.

It didn't matter. She had worked with single-minded dedication for weeks to get herself to this point and she was not about to let the opportunity pass. She waited to see how the cards fell, gathered up her modest winnings – which she took as an omen – and then made for the room's exit on a path that would take her past Lim.

If he was here for her, he was taking her approach rather calmly. She was wearing a high-throated, long-sleeved black blouse, black ankle-length trousers and plain shoes with a low heel. Subtle makeup, simple jewelry. An outfit designed to make her blend into the wallpaper, not stand out. As she got within a few steps of Lim, he turned his head and looked the other way.

Now.

She reached for the ring on her right middle finger. The simple silver band had also cost her employer a small fortune. She pressed a small zirconium stone set into the band and a needle sprung out of it on the palm side of her hand. She flattened the hand, holding it down by her side. As she drew level with Lim she stumbled as though drunk, and grabbed his arm. He pulled back in surprise as she straightened.

"Sorry, sorry," Leclerc slurred, looking right into his eyes and letting her gaze linger just long enough to get a feeling for the man, but not long enough that he should become suspicious. Of course she was biased, but the feeling she got looking into his eyes was ... *eel*.

She gave him a small smile and then continued walking, half expecting him to follow, maybe try to stop her. But she reached the door and, turning her head slightly, saw him still standing there, watching her with a puzzled expression on his face.

She and Sorensen had thought long and hard about how to fashion a fitting end for the man who had worked so hard to send so many men to their deaths in the flaming, oil-covered waters of the South China Sea. A simple neurotoxin would have been obvious, giving him a quick, choking death.

Too quick.

Instead, the tiny poppy seed-sized bead of polonium-210 she had just injected under his skin would work its way into his bloodstream, concentrating in his red blood cells before spreading its deadly radiation to his kidneys, liver and bone marrow.

As she approached the casino exit, she took the ring from her finger, closed the needle, wrapped the now harmless object in a tissue and dropped it into a waste basket.

Daniel Lim was already dead, but Karl Sorensen and Sylvie Leclerc had just ensured his death would be a long and agonizing affair taking weeks, perhaps even months. She would be sure to keep tabs on him. At some time in the near future, as he lay in a hospital bed somewhere, tubes running in and out of his body as a heartbeat monitor counted down the remaining beats to the moment of his death, she would appear at his bedside and take a selfie.

She had promised Bunny O'Hare that.

The place where Ginger McIntyre had told his mother he wanted his ashes to be interred if he passed before her was in the graveyard of Saint Giles Church, Northumberland, in a tiny village called Birtley, not far from the Scottish border. At his service, she admitted she had not the vaguest idea why, since the family had no connections to the place.

It was a very small service, just the priest, a few members of McIntyre's family and Bunny O'Hare. Bunny couldn't help thinking she'd never seen such a concentration of ginger-haired men and women. It made her wonder if there was a collective noun for Gingers. A shout of Gingers? A brave?

After the service, Bunny went and found Angus's mother. She was a small woman with silver-streaked auburn hair and green eyes. "I think I can solve your mystery," Bunny told her.

Mrs. McIntyre was in her eighties, neither able to see nor hear too well, and she blinked uncomprehendingly at Bunny. "I'm sorry, what?"

"Saint Giles," Bunny said. "I looked him up. He was known as the hermit saint. Detested people, lived in a forest his whole life. Only friend was a deer."

"Ah," she nodded. "Aye. That's the sort of thing he'd think was amusing. Did you know him, then?"

"Not really," Bunny admitted. "I served on *Andromeda* with him. He saved a lot of lives."

Her eyes brightened. "He did? *My* Angus?"

"Yes."

Mrs. McIntyre put her soft hand on Bunny's and clenched it tight. "We're having a few drams back at the house. It's a good hour from here, but you'll come, will you not? I'd like to hear more about my Angus."

"Sure."

She squeezed Bunny's hand again and walked off. Bunny watched her go a few steps, then turn around and come back.

"You don't have the address, do you?"

"No."

"Or a car."

"No. I hitched here from Edinburgh."

She held out her arm. "You'd better come with me then,

lass. I must say you look a wee bit puggled."

/end

*Read on for Author Notes and a preview of
DMZ: Future War Volume 7!*

Author Notes

As I was writing PAGASA, it began to look frighteningly like reality could overtake fiction. In late 2020 China began sending hundreds of aircraft into Taiwan's self-declared 'air defense zone', either to provoke a response, to add military muscle to its diplomatic efforts, or just to test Taiwan's air defenses.

At the same time, it was revealed that China had tested a new hypersonic missile, possibly as part of a Fractional Orbital Bombardment System (FOBS) similar to the nuclear-armed missiles that Soviet Russia had flying around the planet at the height of the Cold War. Russia eventually abandoned FOBS because it was more effective to put nuclear missiles on submarines parked off an enemy's coast than to constantly fire them into a fractional orbit, but also because it was expensive, relatively easy to intercept for new anti-ballistic missile defense systems, and not particularly accurate. Whether China's hypersonic missile technology makes the concept suddenly attractive again, or whether it is simply part of China's massive effort to update its military technologies across all domains, remains to be seen.

Such developments were already a concern to the Quadrilateral Security Dialogue nations of India, Japan, the US and Australia. The Quad nations began conducting military exercises together in 2020 and in late 2021 the US, UK and Australia announced a new military alliance – AUKUS – squarely aimed at countering China's growing power in Asia and the Pacific. At the same time, Australia announced the purchase of nuclear submarines and related technologies from the US and UK.

As I wrote PAGASA, the wagons were beginning to circle around China and I was strongly reminded of the western efforts to contain the growing military and economic power of Japan in the 1940s through a series of economic embargoes and diplomatic initiatives intended to isolate and strangle Japan.

China has not ignored these new alliances and has been busy forging new alliances of its own. In October 2021 it conducted its first joint fleet exercises with Russia's Pacific Fleet. No formal treaties with Russia had been announced at the time of writing but that does not mean promises of mutual assistance have not been exchanged between the Russian President and Chinese Premier.

The Pentagon's military chiefs have been warning about Chinese military advances for several years, and it has now supplanted Russia as the 'main enemy' of US defense planners. While I was finalizing PAGASA, outgoing Chairman of the Joint Chiefs of Staff, Gen. Mark Milley, positioned China as "the biggest geostrategic challenge to the United States," while Deputy Defense Secretary, Kathleen Hicks, stated about China's military advances: "China is the one who is setting the measuring stick for how advanced (a) capability is and how large a challenge it is for us to overcome."

While there is an element of budgetary positioning in these claims, there is also a large measure of objective reality.

China is now one of only three nations with 5th-generation stealth fighter aircraft in its inventory, and it has not just one – the J-20 – but *two*, with a carrier-based stealth fighter known as the FC-31 Gyrfalcon now in flight testing.

Stealth may not be their greatest advantages. China has been acknowledged by US security experts as the world leader in AI development. On a recent visit to Beijing I saw evidence of this myself, joining a Chinese colleague for a visit to the 'doctor'. We went to a closed booth on a street corner like a public toilet cubicle: he entered his details into the screen inside and an AI chatbot led him through a discussion of his health, compared the details to the information in its database, matched its conclusion against his known medical and medication history and renewed his prescription on the spot. With no human intervention.

Now, imagine a world in which every lesson a fighter pilot

learns, including his or her actions in the moments before they are killed, are uploaded to a neural network that can study and *learn*, and then apply those lessons the next time it goes into combat.

If the *Zhi Sheng* (Intelligence Victory) backseater in the Chinese J-16 fighter sounds like fanciful future fiction to you, it isn't. The prototype, first rumored in 2020, has been photographed on exercises numerous times since. China's leader has set his AI engineers the task of leading the world in military and civilian AI applications by 2030 and has allocated billions of dollars in funding to support the ambition. *Zhi Sheng* is simply one possible application.

A military conflict fought by one side (in this case, the USA) almost exclusively using unmanned weapons systems might also sound fanciful. But imagine its appeal to politicians and military planners. Warfare half a world away, without a human cost to your own side? What's not to love about that? At the pace of current developments, this prospect will be reality within ten years. Already in development and close to being fielded by *every* major military power are unmanned ground combat vehicles, unmanned air combat vehicles, and perhaps most worrying of all, unmanned undersea vehicles. The Chinese HSU Large Displacement Unmanned Undersea Vehicle was first paraded through the streets of Beijing in 2019, but Indonesian fishermen have been pulling Chinese undersea drones out of the waters of the Java Sea since 2015. The US has a similar system, the Orca, in development (featured in the Future War novel, OKINAWA).

There is absolutely nothing stopping China or another nuclear power from putting nuclear weapons on these vehicles and positioning them offshore from major coastal cities across the globe. In fact, whether you live in New York, St Petersburg or London, there could be a nuclear-armed autonomous submersible sitting on the bottom of a harbor or riverbed in your city, right now.

The point of including this system in PAGASA, as part of

the Chinese response to US military action on the other side of the globe, was to highlight that as politically attractive as it might seem, using autonomous weapons in a major conflict as a way of limiting human casualties to your own side will not protect you from retaliation, either conventional or nuclear. There is no such thing as a war against a major power that can be limited to a far-off foreign sea or sky when that enemy has cyber, space and undersea warfare options that can immediately take the war to your own shores, without resort to the use of ballistic missiles.

The next-generation US B-21 Raider is early in its development and may not be in production by 2035. The US Air Force says of the Raider, "The B-21 Raider will be a component of a larger family of systems for conventional Long-Range Strike, including Intelligence, Surveillance and Reconnaissance, electronic attack, communication and other capabilities. It will be nuclear capable and designed to accommodate manned or unmanned operations. Additionally, it will be able to employ a broad mix of stand-off and direct-attack munitions. The B-21 is being designed with open systems architecture to reduce integration risk and enable competition for future modernization efforts to allow for the aircraft to evolve as the threat environment changes." From this it is clear that Air Force intends for the Raider to be able to be adapted to deliver any payload, anywhere in the world, in either piloted or autonomous configurations. The Pentagon has said that in any mission involving nuclear weapons, at least two human pilots would be in the cockpit.

In PAGASA, I speculate about the inclusion of America's future long-range air-to-air missile, the AIM-260, in the payload of the B-21 Raider. Not in a self-defense capacity, though of course that might also be valuable, but as a self-guided standoff weapon like all others, fired from a range of hundreds of miles to overwhelm enemy air forces through sheer weight of numbers. The US is already exploring the concept of such 'missile trucks', with the purchase of the F-15EX fighter which can carry up to 22 air to air missiles at a time, and trials of the Long Range Anti-Ship Missile (LRASM) on its P-8 Poseidon maritime patrol aircraft.

The autonomous trailing utility ship, White Star *Orion*, was patterned after the US Navy Hunter Continuous Trail Unmanned Vessel, but testing of civilian unmanned vessels is already well advanced. In Finland, trials are underway for "a fully autonomous ferry on a voyage between Parainen and Nauvo, Finland. The ferry navigates both in fully autonomous mode and under remote control operation." Meanwhile in Scotland, an Uncrewed Offshore Vessel has been sailing off the coast of Aberdeen, controlled by operators sitting in San Diego, USA. The Japanese Nippon Foundation has several projects in train, all of which are intended to provide ships with the ability to navigate themselves around the globe with little need for a crew. China's Shanghai Maritime University too is looking at the application of AI to future Marine Autonomous Surface Ships (MASS) and has already started designing new education and training courses – in cloud computing, big data, automation, remote control, satellite communication, and remote fault diagnosis – for 'maritime crews' who may never actually put to sea.

Finally, a note on the fraught geopolitics of the Spratly Islands. I offer no opinion on which nation's claim to islands in the archipelago is valid or not, but I have taken current events and projected them into a possible future. The opening scene in PAGASA is based on an actual event. In 2019 a large Chinese fishing vessel rammed and partially sank a wooden Filipino fishing boat, the F/B Gem-Ver 1, in the Spratly Archipelago. After the incident, according to Philippine authorities, the Chinese vessel turned off its navigation lights and sailed away, leaving the Filipino survivors in the water. China has denied this version of events, calling it 'a normal maritime accident'.

While several nations claim ownership of the various reefs, islands and shoals of the Spratly Islands, China has been the most assertive, building ports and air bases across the archipelago. Diplomatic protests about its actions have been ineffectual and toothless. China now has a fleet of several hundred fishing vessels operating in the South China Sea, protected by its naval air force, navy and coast guard ships, and by radar, anti-ship and anti-air missile emplacements throughout the Spratly Islands. In 2018, a Chinese warship narrowly avoided colliding with the US warship *USS Decatur* in the Spratly Islands, coming within 45 yards of its stern. In April 2020 the *USS Mustin* was forced to maneuver to avoid contact with a picket destroyer from China's *Liaoning* carrier strike group in the South China Sea. Western navies sailing through international waters are regularly warned against approaching 'Chinese territory' – the same applies to aircraft flying near Chinese military installations – and though they ignore these warnings for the most part, many observers see it as just a matter of time before a more serious scenario, such as the one in this novel, develops.

This writer, for one, hopes that never happens.

FX Holden, December 2021, Copenhagen.

Preview: DMZ

Future War Volume 7
Coming summer 2022

Over the Yellow Sea, July 27, 2036

Twenty-two-year-old Son Hee-chan was about to kill a man for the first time.

He'd known when he'd gotten his wings as a fighter pilot in the Republic of Korea Air Force that it was a possibility. An occupational necessity, his instructors had told him. If that reality isn't compatible with your religion, your personal values, or your conscience, ask for a transfer to Air Mobility and become a transport driver.

He'd stayed with the fighter program. He was at peace with his role flying heavily armed fast jets, and the responsibilities that came with it.

But Son had always expected that if it happened, if he pulled the trigger to send one of his missiles downrange at another pilot, it would occur in the heat of battle. At war, with a North Korean or Chinese enemy doing his best to kill Son Hee-chan or his fellow pilots.

Not like this. Not in cold blood. Not an *ally*.

As he'd climbed into the cockpit of his shiny new KF-21 Boromae fighter at South Korea's Jungwon Air Base, he'd dropped two of the tablets the North Korean agent had given him. He'd been curious what the small blue tablets were, and looked them up on the internet. *Selective norepinephrine reuptake inhibitors.* Used to treat depression and ADHD. Not exactly a common chemical enhancement for use by fighter pilots going into combat.

"You're going to need nerves of ice up there," the man had said, handing over a small plastic bag and clapping him on the shoulder. "And a steel will. These will help."

As he'd settled into formation behind his flight leader 5,000 feet over the Yellow Sea, 38 miles west of Seoul, he'd monitored his emotions with interest. Nerves of ice? Steel will? If the tablets were having any effect at all, it was to make him feel like he was a spectator in his own cockpit. He felt ... detached. His autopilot AI was doing most of the real work for now, keeping his aircraft faithfully in formation a hundred feet below and a hundred feet behind his flight leader. With a hundred feet separation to his right and left, the four other Boromae fighters of his fellow pilots bobbed up and down, ensuring they would present a perfect 'arrowhead' formation to viewers on the ground.

He looked at the helmeted heads of his comrades through his armored glass cockpit bubble. How many would still be alive thirty minutes from now? By habit, he checked the systems status indicators in the heads-up display of his helmet, ran his eye over the corresponding data on the wraparound single panel instrument display in front of his stick, and pulled up a tactical display, centering it on the screen. *Ah yes, here they come.*

His flight leader had been watching the same display. "Baem flight, Baem leader. DPRK aircraft bearing 358 degrees, altitude 10,000, range 40, speed 600, crossing the DMZ now and entering ROK airspace. Maintain heading and keep formation, Baem pilots."

It felt so wrong. But the tablets were working, because the wrongness didn't cause him to be nervous, or anxious. He just watched with growing interest as the six North Korean Mig-29 fighters flew unmolested into South Korean airspace. His display showed they had adopted an identical formation to the South Korean KF-21s and their arrowhead was pointing directly into the path of Son's flight. But he wasn't nervous, because it had all been in the official pre-flight briefing.

Even if the event hadn't been planned and scripted down to the last detail on both sides of the DMZ, even if he hadn't dropped two mood-killing tablets, Son wouldn't have been nervous. He was supremely confident in the capabilities of his new generation Boromae fighter. While not technically a stealth fighter, and still roughly the same size as a Mig-29, its Hanwae infrared sensors could 'see' the ancient Mig-29s at twice the range they could see his KF-21. Its active electronically scanned array radar could lock up to ten targets simultaneously, where the North Korean Mig-29 could at best target two. The six aircraft of Baem flight were constantly and instantaneously sharing data with each other as they flew, giving him the situational awareness of six pilots and their aircrafts' sensors. In contrast, a North Korean Mig pilot was alone in the sky with his own machine, and communicating with his fellow pilots at the speed of voice, rather than the speed of thought.

If they'd wanted, the South Korean Boromaes could have bracketed the Migs and launched a blizzard of missiles at the incoming North Koreans before they even realized they were being tracked. The battle would have been over before it began. But that thought belonged to another era.

"Weapons safe, maintain current heading and speed, stay cool, Baem pilots," his flight leader said as the North Korean fighters closed within ten miles. His high-pitched voice sounded anything but cool.

Son could see them now, the North Korean hawk-nosed twin-engined fighters banking slightly in the morning sun as they closed on the South Korean Boromaes, showing both their matt green upper skin and sky blue bellies. Perhaps the gentle banking turn was intended to show them that the North Korean fighters were also armed, just so there were no misconceptions. Which you could be forgiven for thinking was strange, given they were on a *peace* mission.

The first-ever joint patrol of DMZ airspace, by North and South Korean fighters.

To celebrate the signing at Panmunjom in about 25 minutes of the historic Peace Accord between the DPRK and ROK that would mark the end of a state of war that had existed since July

27, 1950. It was a moment both nations had been working toward since 2030, and the most important step in the pathway to eventual reunification, planned for 2040. There had been bumps along the way ... even the odd minor military skirmish ... but the day was finally here.

You'd think all the aircraft involved in a flight like this would be unarmed, carrying nothing more than, say, smoke pods, for the ceremonial fly-by over Panmunjom. But ironically it was the North Koreans who had insisted that all aircraft be armed: 'to show the power of restraint' or some such nonsense.

They'd come to regret that.

As the Mig flight slid in alongside them and manually matched speed and heading with them, he automatically looked at the missiles slung under their wings. Two Alamo medium-range, two Aphid short-range missiles. And something else. *OK, that's interesting.* He keyed his comms unit. "Baem leader, Baem four. I'm seeing Chinese Thunder Stone bombs on these Migs." The Chinese-made Thunder Stone was a 1,000 lb. GPS or laser-guided glide bomb and he'd never heard of North Korean fighters being armed with Thunder Stone bombs.

It was to be a day of many firsts, apparently.

"Acknowledged, Baem four. Must be trying to send some kind of message, but it's lost on me. Feet dry in two pilots. Keep it together."

A message? Well, the obvious message was 'we aren't alone up here, China is with us. See, they have sold us these bloody huge bombs, so you still need to take us seriously'. He looked back over his shoulder at the North Korean fighter that was flying in the rearmost starboard position of the arrowhead. He couldn't see the pilot through the flare of sunlight off his cockpit glass, but that was probably for the best.

His ocular infrared targeting system had automatically painted a box around the aircraft he was looking at, and with a tap of his middle finger on the multifunction button on his throttle grip, two IRIS-T infrared homing missiles were allocated to the target. His heads-up display flashed a warning.

"Missiles safed … missiles safed…"
Yes, I know, he told himself. *For now.*

DMZ, Chuk-tong Road, 14 miles north of Hwacheon, South Korea

Sergeant Kim Song Hye of North Korea's II Corp, 6th Infantry Division Border Force had killed a man before. In fact, she had killed two, and a woman.

But she didn't think of them as men or women. Not really.

Real men stayed with their families through thick and thin. Through famine, through sickness, through flood and fire. Real men did their duty to their State. Real women too; they cared for their elders, for the sick, for the children in their village, working in fields and factories to put food on the table, serving in the armed forces to protect their nation. So when she'd been standing in her border tower, legs braced, looking down the infrared sights of her Chogyok Pochong rifle at the men and women using the dead of night to try to sneak across the DMZ no man's land to the South, she didn't see anything but traitors: traitors to family, traitors to State.

And soon, 25 million North Koreans were going to join them. Traitors all.

The thought still dismayed her to the core. All she had been through, all she had suffered for the ideal that was the Democratic People's Republic of Korea, and it had come to *this*? She had wept for a week when Kim Jong-un had died suddenly, his brave heart worn out by the weight of carrying the burden of an entire nation within it. She had cried too when the People's Assembly had voted to appoint his sister, Kim Yo-jong, as Supreme Leader in his place. The first woman to lead their nation since its birth in the 1940s! Did this not prove how modern and right-thinking their leaders were? That was how she felt at the time.

She had been wrong. The Assembly had become a nest of weak-willed counter-revolutionaries. When Yo-jong had purged the Party Central Committee of several of its longest-serving members, Song had approved. It had showed the same force of will that her brother had shown. But when her first trip outside the DPRK was to South Korea, and not to Beijing, Song had begun to worry. Yo-jong had refused to even discuss nuclear disarmament on that trip, which had reassured Song somewhat, and she had returned with a promise of cross-border trade and a contract for winter fuel oil that had guaranteed no one in North Korea would freeze to death the following winter, which was more than Beijing could guarantee. So Song had given her new supreme leader the benefit of the doubt, even though the deal had damaged relations with their Chinese benefactors.

But then State TV began its reunification drumbeat. Not through a glorious military victory, but through *negotiation*. Every time Song saw the words 'negotiation' on a screen or in a newspaper, she heard 'subjugation'. She had felt physically ill that July in 2030, seeing Yo-jong on a podium with the South Korean President, announcing her 'Ten-Year Plan for Prosperity'. Prosperity based on dismantling the DPRK? That was no prosperity at all. Her grandfather had died in the war against imperialism in 1950, killed by American napalm. Her father had died in the sanction-induced famine of 2025. Her mother had delivered four children for the glory of the State, but had lost three more to stillbirth and starvation. Was this how their sacrifice should be honored? By dissolving their Supreme People's Assembly and merging it with that pale imitation to the South and calling it the Assembly of the Democratic Republic of Korea? By merging the DPRK and ROK armed forces and calling the Army that had secured North Korean independence for nearly a hundred years 'Northern Command'?

Recently, the regime had announced the creation of a new fifty-mile-wide scorched-earth DMZ on their *northern* border, facing their allies, China. The very thought brought bile up from her gut.

No. There was no place in the new Democratic Republic of Korea for Kim Song Hye. Nor for the comrades by her side. They had long ago decided they would rather die than see that humiliating day.

She watched with scorn as the soldiers of the South Korean DMZ Patrol climbed out of their jeep and approached the line across the road that marked the center of the DMZ. It was a line she'd only ever seen through her scope until recently, and never expected to be standing astride. Certainly, never waiting to greet the fat fools who were approaching in their mottled, grey-green camouflage American GI helmets, each mounted with a camera because their superiors could not trust them to carry out their orders.

She could already smell their cologne ... cheap and sickeningly sweet. What kind of soldier wore cologne? One trying to cover the stink of the garlic they ate with their pork every night, no doubt.

It was a weekly ritual they had encouraged for the last couple of months leading up to this day, luring the grinning fools into a sense of false security. Each Friday, they would meet at the dashed line across Chuk-tong Road, by the old border crossing. The ROK Lieutenant had already pulled the bottle of whisky out of his backpack and had shouldered his carbine, waving the bottle in the air above his head as though it was a truce flag.

"Stand at ease. Shoulder weapons," her own Lieutenant, Kwang Yong-il, said quietly. As she put her rifle strap over her shoulder, he pulled a large bottle of rice wine from his own pack and held it over his head, mimicking the approaching South Korean. Song looked at it in surprise. Until now, they had brought home-brewed liquor in large plastic containers with them, but she could see this one had been bought at a market. Premium Nongtaegi ... it had probably cost him a month's salary on a soldier's pay.

Until now, only the officers had drunk together and the

enlisted men and women had shared what was left after the South Koreans departed, Lieutenant Kwang turning a blind eye as long as they remained capable of marching and didn't drop their gear. But this time he also pulled a stack of tin cups from his backpack and instructed Song to hand them around.

"One sip. No more," Song told each soldier as she handed them a cup. "And look like you enjoy it. Got it?"

The South Korean Lieutenant was within hailing distance now, and as usual he shouted a puerile greeting.

"Hail, comrades of the future Democratic Republic!" he called out, waving his liquor bottle harder. He stepped up to Lieutenant Kwang and showed him the label. "A special day. I brought a bottle of Scottish whisky. Single malt!"

Song scowled. She was not naïve. It was a gesture intended to rub their noses in their own poverty, nothing more. But Kwang gave him a broad smile. "And for you, from my own hometown, our best Nongtaegi." He took the whisky and handed the North Korean liquor to the South Korean. Both stood nodding and reading the labels with ritual seriousness, showing appreciation for the others' generosity.

"I think today…" Kwang said, reaching out to Song for more tin cups, "… we should let the enlisted soldiers have a taste, what do you say?"

"Today, of all days," the South Korean Lieutenant agreed. "Yes…" He raised his voice as though addressing a parade ground and turned to his squad. "Today, we all drink. Soon we will be brothers and sisters under one flag. One Army!"

Song winced. One flag? But which? That was one of the many things that had yet to be decided before the new constitution of the united Korea could be signed.

Not while I am alive, Song thought.

Corporal Chang Myung Shin, 7th Infantry DMZ Patrol, didn't actually care which flag he served under. As he watched, Lieutenant Lee poured the heady North Korean brew into tin cups and handed it around. One Korea, two Koreas, six Koreas, he really didn't give a damn.

Two more years of service and it was *no* Koreas for him. He had a brother in San Jose who had his own tech firm providing IT consulting services to restaurants all over the Bay Area and Chang was going to help him expand into hardware imports. Quantum computing cores. South Korea had the highest concentration of quantum core producers in the world and Chang had a buddy who had mustered out a year ago and set up an IT hardware export company. He knew how to get the hard-to-source quantum cores at wholesale prices that guaranteed Chang and his brother couldn't lose money if they tried. They would set up a quantum river that flowed from the factories in Incheon and Kaesong to San Francisco and beyond.

As he reached for a cup of liquor, he looked around at the bare hillsides of the DMZ valley through which the Chuk-tong Road wound and said a mental goodbye. Raising the cup to his mouth, he sniffed the liquor inside. Spicy aroma. Actually quite nice. But he couldn't drink it until the two Lieutenants decided to toast. Lee would probably hold some kind of corny speech. The North Korean was a little more dignified, reserved. Chang had watched him with his people, and he seemed more like the kind of guy you'd want to go to war under. Lee was a loud-mouthed ignoramus.

He heard the scuff of a boot and saw the North Korean soldier standing nearest him, a woman with Sergeant stripes, lifting her rifle down from her shoulder and standing its butt on her boot, which was a bit weird but perhaps it was so she could manage her cup of whisky a little better, holding it in both hands and bowing her head as her Lieutenant poured for her. Yeah, see. That was a real army. Respect. Honor. Maybe some of that would rub off after the fusion of North and South.

The Sergeant looked up, saw Chang staring at her, and glared at him. He smiled back at her, holding his gaze in a way that dared her to look away. She didn't.

She was quite striking. Deep brown-green eyes, almond brown skin, jet black hair pulled back in a tight ponytail under her helmet. Underfed, like all North Koreans. Skin and bloody bone under her uniform … you wondered how they could carry an assault rifle, let alone all their other gear. He held his gaze on her a moment more, then raised his cup in salute and looked away, still smiling.

Let her win that one.

Yes, look away, fool, Song told herself. *You are yesterday, and I am tomorrow.*

It was something Lieutenant Kwang had told them as they prepared for their patrol. "Remember this. Yesterday does not exist. Now has already passed. There is only tomorrow, and how you will be remembered by those who follow."

The South Korean had been looking right at her and hadn't noticed that as she put her rifle butt first on the ground, she had used the action to pull back its cocking mechanism and set it to semi-automatic fire.

She feigned a sip of the Western whisky and watched carefully as the South Korean soldiers threw back the strong North Korean liquor with reckless abandon. *Yes, trust us*, Song thought, barely letting the whisky touch her lips. *Are we not your brothers and sisters?* She smiled, as though enjoying the moment, keeping her eyes on Kwang and waiting for his signal.

Chang had trouble taking his eyes off the Korean Sergeant, standing with her rifle resting on her boot as she sipped her whisky. She appeared so serene; at ease in a way her comrades were not. They were nervous, all ducking heads and averted gazes. She stood a little apart, listening, but not joining in, carefully watching everything. Typical bloody Sergeant, though, no matter whose army, they never missed a thing.

Sure enough, Lieutenant Lee raised a hand to get everyone's

attention. "My dear comrades," he said. "Quiet please, quiet."

Trying to be cool, Chang thought. Calling us 'comrades' as the North Koreans do. Like it's suddenly alright to talk like a communist.

Lee continued. "Today, in a few hours, our leaders will sign the peace accord in Panmunjom. Tomorrow, we will start the work of dismantling our guard posts along the DMZ, filling in the anti-tank trenches and rolling up the razor wire. By the end of the year, there will be no more DMZ!"

Chang's squad gave a throaty cheer, but the North Koreans remained unmoved. Lee didn't let the lack of response blunt his enthusiasm. He raised his tin cup. "I would like to make a toast to peace and prosperity!" He held out the liquor bottle he was holding to refill anyone who needed their drink topped up and indicated to the North Korean officer he should do the same.

Which was when Chang noticed that he really wasn't pouring anything into his soldier's cups. He was going through the motions, sure, but their cups were mostly full, it seemed, so he only made the shallowest of pours. Maybe they were just reluctant to drink in front of their officer, even though it had been agreed. But in their previous meetings, that North Korean officer had drained his cup like a desert soaking up rain. Today, he had barely even sipped, and though he made a show of topping up his glass, it was still full.

There was definitely something wrong. He saw several of the North Koreans casually, too casually, raise their hands to the straps of their rifles, as though adjusting them to be a little more comfortable. Looking at the woman near him, he saw she had shifted the grip of her right hand from the muzzle of her carbine down to the forestock, and she was holding it so tight the knuckles of her right hand were white. The thought struck him that there was only one reason to hold your rifle like that, or to have the butt of your carbine resting on your boot while drinking a toast.

If you were planning to bloody use it!

Taking a casual step to the side, Chang moved closer to the

South Korean soldier beside him, Private Park Min-jae. Leaning in and smiling as though sharing a joke under his breath, he spoke quietly to Park. "Something is wrong. Follow my lead."

"What?" The boy was the newest member of the squad and seemed to go through life with two default settings, either confusion or disappointment.

"Just follow me," Chang told him in a fierce whisper.

Lee raised his voice again. "OK, everyone has something to drink? Good, good, now raise your cups and…"

Chang stuck up his hand. "Lieutenant Lee, toilet break?"

Lee frowned at him. "What?"

"Before the big toast. Got to go behind a bush, Lieutenant!"

"Now? I'm making a toast here."

Their Sergeant, Kwon Shin-wook, glowered at Chang and opened his mouth to pull him into line.

"Thank you, sir," Chang said quickly, grabbing Park by the arm. "Two minutes, sir. Anyone else?" Chang looked around the squad, ignoring the glare of Sergeant Kwon. Another of the privates, Nam Bo-kyung, raised his hand meekly.

"Dammit, alright," Lee said. "Make it quick."

There was a low outcrop of rocks just behind them and Chang led the two privates over to it. What he would do when he got there he had no idea. But every nerve in his body was telling him to run, and that made so little sense he just had to listen to it. Looking over his shoulder, he saw the eyes of every North Korean were following them as they walked away.

They got behind the rocks, which only came up to chest height. Park still had a confused look on his face, but Nam shuffled in behind a rock, rested his rifle against it and started unbuttoning his flies. Chang slapped his hand away.

The man looked at him in surprise. "Corporal?"

"You aren't actually taking a piss, Nam, you are just making it look like you are while I think about this, alright?" Chang thumped Park's shoulder. "Look down at your boots, kid. You usually stand there gawping at the guy next to you while you piss?"

"Corporal, I don't understand…" Nam protested.

"The North Koreans aren't drinking," Chang told them, looking down at his own boots. "None of them. I think they're getting ready to jump us."

"What? Why?" Park asked. At least he was looking down now, playing along even if he didn't know why.

"Steal our weapons, take our damn wallets, I don't know. You see how skinny those bastards are? They'd probably just jump us for rations."

Nam looked over at the two squads and then back down again. "What do we do, Corporal?"

Yeah, what the hell are you going to do now, Chang? Didn't really think this all the way through, did you, comrade?

He looked quickly up and saw both officers looking over at them. Sergeant Kwon was pointing at the dirt beside him with an urgent gesture that made it clear they had better hurry up and rejoin the party.

But what would happen if they didn't?

Chang couldn't really see any other option than to find out. Lee had turned to the North Korean Lieutenant and started speaking with him, probably apologizing, Chang guessed. A few of the group of soldiers turned their eyes away from the rocks to watch and listen. Chang guessed they were thinking the exchange between the officers had the potential to be more entertaining than watching three guys piss on some rocks.

"Duck down," Chang said, turning his back to the rock and crouching as he pulled his assault rifle from his shoulder. Nam and Park were still standing, both looking at him like he'd lost his mind as he pulled at Park's trouser leg. "*Down* I said, Private!"

Song saw the three South Koreans by the rock disappear suddenly from view.

Lifting her leg quickly, she brought her rifle up and into her hands, dropping her whisky cup. "Lieutenant!" she barked.

Kwang looked over sharply, as did the South Korean Lieutenant. It was the last thing the South Korean officer did. Kwang acted instantly, pulling his sidearm from the holster against his hip and putting a bullet into the Lieutenant's surprised face.

It was a slaughter, and it was over in moments.

Song calmly and deliberately put two slugs into the chest of the South Korean Sergeant and then turned her fire on the private next to him. So did two of her comrades. Six South Korean soldiers' bodies jumped and bucked with the impact of the 5.45mm bullets spraying from the North Koreans' Chinese-made QTS rifles.

Before they even hit the ground, Song was running toward the rocks where she had last seen the fat-faced South Korean Corporal.

"Dammit!" Chang cursed at the sound of a pistol. As he rose from his crouch, there was an explosion of semi-automatic rifle fire and as he brought his rifle up and around, resting it on top of the rock behind him, he saw the female Sergeant with the long black ponytail running straight for him. She didn't look so pretty anymore. She was screaming something at the top of her lungs and firing from the hip as she ran.

Chang panicked. He pulled his trigger, realized with horror his K2 rifle was still safed and flipped it to full auto as he cocked it, then pulled the trigger again without even bothering to aim. His bullets chewed a line through the dirt in front of the North Korean and she veered off to the right, throwing herself down behind a bush.

Chang jumped as a rifle opened up beside him and looked over to see Nam had joined him in sending a volley of fire toward the North Koreans, who scattered like hens from a fox. Nam caught at least one of them flat-footed, and the man crumpled to the ground. The others found cover behind whatever nearby shrub, depression or small rock offered

403

protection and started directing fire toward Chang, Park and Nam.

A hell of a lot of fire. Chang ducked down, pulling Nam down with him, thinking quickly. Park was still crouched, a shocked look on his face. Hadn't even taken his rifle from his shoulder. Those rifles the North Koreans were carrying, weren't they QTS-11s? Those things could fire bloody airburst grenades, couldn't they?

As though to answer his question, Chang heard a loud crump, then the crack of a grenade in the air overhead as chips of rock flew around them. *Short.* It had exploded short.

The next one wouldn't. If he didn't get fragged in the next minute or two, he'd soon be flanked. There were at least nine North Korean soldiers still out there.

Twenty yards further away, he saw another outcrop of rock. Some kind of creek bed behind it maybe.

"I'm going to put down some cover fire. You see those rocks?" Chang grabbed Park by the sleeve and pointed. "Soon as I start firing, the two of you run for it, got it?"

The man nodded, and before he could think about it anymore, Chang rose out of his crouch and started firing wildly over the rocks in the rough direction of the North Koreans. He managed to raise a lot of dust around them, but then that damn woman started firing again from off to his left and he had to duck down again.

Nam and Park were zigging and zagging toward the cover of the rocks behind them.

Right, you.

With a last burst of fire which mostly went into the air over the North Koreans, Chang was off and running too. He heard the crack of another grenade above and behind him, something punched him in the shoulder, but he kept running. Reaching the next outcrop of rocks, he threw himself down behind them, landing on top of the prone Private Park. Nam once again had a little more presence of mind and rolled out from behind cover to send a tight volley of fire back toward the rocks they had just vacated, sending a couple of pursuing North Koreans back into cover behind them.

If there was a South Korean record for a 50-yard dash, Chang was pretty sure he had just broken it. He was gasping for air. Looking back behind them, he saw it *was* a dry creekbed he had spotted. A beautifully deep one.

Movement. Keep moving, that is your only hope. Don't let them fix you.

"Up!" he yelled at the others. "Remember your bloody rifles. After me!"

And with that, he bolted for the creek, not stopping to see if the two privates were following him.

Song had made it to the first group of rocks but then she had to duck behind them at the return fire that came from the South Koreans' new position.

Their squad had only one QTS-11 with a grenade launcher attachment, and only five defilade rounds for it. The man using it had already wasted two rounds. As he raised it to fire toward the rocks the South Korean soldiers were sheltering behind now, she put a hand on his arm. "Wait, Private. Take a breath. Make every shot count."

The man was wide-eyed and nodded. Settling the weapon against his shoulder, he sighted down the barrel, aiming it above the rocks 50 yards away. They were higher than the ones Song was sheltered behind, and they couldn't see the South Korean soldiers unless they stuck their heads out to fire.

We will have to flush them out, she decided. *We need to keep them busy. Flank.* She looked quickly behind her for Lieutenant Kwang and saw him crumpled in the dirt where they had been standing, knees drawn up into his belly, unmoving. But they still had numbers and a tactical advantage; she had to fix and flank the South Koreans while they were on the back foot.

She looked at the lay of the land between her and the South Koreans again. Bare ground. Scrub, stones and grass. *Speed and violence, that's our best tactic from here.*

Two more privates joined her at the rocks, and she turned to the man with the grenade launcher. "You send two rounds at those rocks a few seconds apart. You and you…" she said to the other privates, "…when he sends the first grenade, you go left and you, go right. Go wide. Hit the dirt if they start firing at us again and lay down cover fire. I'm going straight down the middle. Got it?"

"Yes, Comrade Sergeant!" The three soldiers shouted assent.

Song fixed the man with the grenade launcher with an intense look. "For heaven's sake, don't fire short this time, or you'll kill *me*."

"Yes, Comrade Sergeant!" he barked.

She checked her magazine quickly, reseated it and gathered herself. The South Koreans had stopped firing. It was now or not at all.

"Alright, go, go, go!" she yelled, bursting from behind the rocks and running straight for the South Korean position.

She heard the thump of the grenade launcher behind her and ducked involuntarily as the projectile sailed over her head and exploded near the rocks ahead of her. The private had aimed well this time, and most of the blast went down into the dirt behind the South Korean's cover.

That's going to hurt, she thought hopefully.

To her right, one of the men who had run out behind her had gone prone at the sound of the grenade detonating. He started firing at the rocks ahead. Not exactly as she had ordered, but good enough. She was doubling across the open ground, ready at any moment to throw herself to the dirt if she saw a South Korean point a rifle her way.

Thump. A second grenade sailed overhead, this time exploding further behind the rock outcrop in front of her, the man firing it being extra careful not to frag his Sergeant.

There was no reaction from the South Koreans. Dead or wounded? She hoped so. She reached the rocks and threw herself against them, back to the warm stone, her enemy just feet away on the other side. Should she go left, or right? Slow or fast? Did it matter? *Just get around there, Song.* She tensed herself. Creeping left, rifle across her chest, taking a step, looking quickly over her shoulder behind her to make sure she wasn't tackled from behind, then another step, another look, until she reached the end of the rock outcrop.

Now.

Rolling around as quietly as she could, she took two steps and rounded the outcrop, ready to shoot at…

Nothing.

She could see footprints in the dirt. They had been here. They were gone. She looked around. Probably that dry creek down there. She could see from the scrub along the lip of the creek bed that it went left and right a few hundred yards in each direction. Probably further. And it was deep. Following them in there would be suicide.

One of the privates joined her, panting from running hard.

"Get your breath," she told him. "We need to get back, check on the wounded."

"Then what, Comrade Sergeant?"

She put her rifle strap over her shoulder again, thinking about Lieutenant Kwang, curled in the dirt somewhere behind her. "And then we continue our mission," she told him.

Chang had stayed in the creek bed, rifle at the ready in case the North Koreans continued their pursuit. Not because he was particularly brave, but because the section of creek bed they had tumbled into was little more than a deep trench about twenty feet long, with rocks and scrub blocking both ends. He could see the creek bed extended further beyond the two blockages, but they couldn't make their way under the blockages, and to go over or around would mean exposing themselves to view again.

Private Park had finally recovered his wits, and when he got his breath, he rolled onto his stomach, rifle in front of him, and started to crawl back toward the lip of the creek bed, into a firing position. Nam was right beside him.

Chang put a hand out and stopped Park. "Let me." He belly-crawled back up the slope, gingerly sticking his head up and peering through the dead branches of a small bush.

Damn woman! She is relentless.

He saw the North Korean Sergeant standing behind the rocks they had vacated, looking around herself. She seemed to look straight at Chang and he froze, not even daring to breathe, but her gaze swept over him, left and right, and then another two North Korean soldiers arrived, and she turned her attention to them. After a minute or two, a short conversation and a last glance toward the creek bed, the three of them walked off, back toward the scene of the first attack.

"Corp, you're bleeding," Nam told him. He was back down the slope, lying on his back, rifle across his chest.

"What? Where?"

"Shoulder," Nam said, pointing at his own right shoulder. "Shoulder blade."

Chang vaguely remembered something punching him there while he was in full flight. That first damn grenade? Or the second one? He felt behind him and realized he couldn't feel the pressure of his fingers on his shoulder blade. It was completely numb. And his fingers came away wet with blood.

Crap.

"Get up here and keep an eye on those North Korean devils if you can," he told Nam. "We need to get out of this little ditch and into proper cover before they come looking for us." He started unbuttoning his shirt, fingers slipping on the buttons because of the blood. He realized he was shaking now and held his hands against his chest so the others wouldn't see. "Park, look at this shoulder and tell me if it needs to be plugged."

"Yes, Corp."

Chang rolled onto his stomach so the man could pull his shirt up around his neck, lying on his traitorous hands to stop their trembling.

"What in hell was that all about?" Nam asked softly. "One moment we're toasting reunification, the next, they're trying to kill us?"

Chang winced as Park pulled what felt like shredded cloth out of the mess that was his shoulder. Sharp pain was starting to penetrate the numbness already, as his adrenaline started to wear off. He gritted his teeth. "I don't know, Nam. But something tells me it was about more than our rations."

He needed to think. Their radio was back in their jeep. If the North Koreans weren't already in the act of stealing or destroying the vehicle, it was just a matter of time. So, calling for help was out.

"It's like you took a shotgun in the shoulder, Sergeant," Park told him. "It's pretty chewed up, but it doesn't look too deep and the bleeding isn't too bad." He pulled the shirt back down.

Chang's self-preservation instinct told him they should use the creek bed to exfiltrate; make their way five miles south, back to the South Korean demarcation line. Get safe. But his training told him he should try to find cover and observe what the hell the North Koreans were doing. Wait until they left, try to get back and check on Lee and the others, see if any were still alive.

His training won over his desire to just hide in a bush somewhere. He rolled onto his side and buttoned his shirt up again, wincing at the throb from his mangled shoulder.

The road wound through a valley lined with steep hills. In winter, it was covered in snow. In spring the creek bed they were lying in would flood with meltwater. Right now, everything was dead, dry and brown. If he stayed low… Looking over the lip of the creek bed to the hillside behind them, Chang made up his mind. "You two stay here in cover, watch they don't come this way. I'm going up a little higher, see what the hell they are up to."

Ungam-ni airfield, 10 miles west of Hwacheon, South Korea

"What the hell are they up to?"

Karen "Bunny" O'Hare jerked her chin up from her chest, coming instantly alert at the concerned note in the voice of the Boeing-Sikorsky Defiant's loadmaster, sitting back to back behind her.

They were only five minutes out of Ungam-ni airfield, and she'd only just folded her arms across her chest and closed her eyes.

All but three of the interior seats of the pilotless transport chopper had been removed and the load space had been packed with sensitive military research equipment to be freighted out of South Korea in advance of the merger of the North and South Korea armed forces. South Korea had been fertile territory in which to field-test equipment against an always alert adversary, but those days were drawing to a close, and the US had no desire for its most advanced weapons systems to fall into the lap of a still untested united Korean Republic.

The Defiant flew itself, but when in-flight the loadmaster on the Defiant had the job of monitoring comms, aircraft systems and confirming navigation waypoints. He had pushed up the heads-up display in his helmet so that he could focus on the fold-out console attached to his seat.

"What's up?" Bunny asked him. Her fellow DARPA colleague, Kevin Adair, was buckled into a seat beside her, looking anxiously at both of them.

"We're being painted by fighter attack radar," the Navy loadmaster said, a slight note of panic in his voice.

"Whose?"

"System says it's a North Korean Mig-29, but that can't be right. We're still in South Korean airspace."

"The Mig doesn't have to be," she pointed out. "We're only

ten miles from the DMZ. It could lock us up on radar from inside North Korea."

"But we're cleared to cross the DMZ," the loadmaster said. "I filed the flight plan myself. It's an approved cooperation corridor…"

Five years into the Reunification Transition process, new air corridors had been opened up to allow passage of civilian and approved military traffic across the airspace of the future Korean Republic. O'Hare and her payload were on their way from central South Korea to Hokkaido in Japan, on a track that would take them across the old DMZ and over a few hundred miles of what would soon be the *former* North Korea. A patch of air that for nearly a hundred years had been zealously guarded by the communist Democratic People's Republic of Korea Air Force.

And still was, apparently. At least for the next few hours, until the Peace Accord was signed.

"Should we be worried?" Adair asked.

"Chill," Bunny told him. "They're probably just making a point. Letting us know they're still in charge, for now."

"*You* can chill," the Navy loadmaster told her. "I'm authorizing air-to-air defense protocols."

She sighed. It might make him feel better, but it wouldn't make much difference if there really was an angry North Korean Mig out there that had them in its sights. The slow-moving Defiant was unarmed. It could skid around the sky firing anti-radar chaff or infrared-spoofing flares, but it was no match for a fourth-generation missile-armed fighter plane.

Now that he'd stirred her from her little catnap, though, Bunny picked up her helmet from the floor at her feet and jammed it on her head, pulling down its visor and turning on her own heads-up display. Not for protection in case they were attacked, but so that she could check on their baby. Adair had the job of monitoring its systems and position for the first couple of hours of their flight, but she preferred to check for herself.

She wasn't worried that the North Korean Mig posed a threat to it. The North Korean pilot should be completely unaware it even existed, and besides, the Gremlin drone mothership under Bunny's control was currently circling at wavetop height over the sea a hundred miles to the east, waiting for their chopper to go 'feet-wet' so that it could fall into formation with them and accompany them to Japan.

Where she would fly it into the sea.

Unfolding a flexible keyboard from a pouch on her khaki trousers, she called up a map of the Korean theatre that showed their flight plan, and the current position of the Gremlin, projecting both on the visor of her helmet.

Adair was watching her. He had his own helmet on and visor down monitoring the Gremlin's system state. "Gremlin's good," he told her. "They can't see it out there, right?"

"No chance." She rolled the keyboard up again and pushed it into her trouser pocket.

She wished her helmet was networked to the Defiant's avionics so that she could see the tactical map the loadmaster was looking at, but he was giving them a running commentary anyway.

"South Korean Air Defense is showing two Mig-29s on a parallel track just inside the DMZ, about ten miles back," he said. "It must be them."

"Pretty good bet," Bunny agreed. Despite the loadmaster's anxiety, she was tempted to return to her catnap. The reason she and all this tech were bugging out was that peace was finally breaking out across the Korean peninsula. And she would need to be fully rested for the mission that was awaiting them when they reached their rendezvous point in the Sea of Japan.

After all, it wasn't every day you had to land a nuclear-powered drone two hundred yards off the bow of an amphibious assault ship in one relatively intact piece so that it could be fished out of the water.

Then any thought of a sneaky nap disappeared as the loadmaster behind her yelled over the whine of the Defiant's turboprop engines.

"Missile! We've got incoming!"

Milliseconds later the chopper's defensive AI reacted, throwing the machine into a spiraling dive for the ground as the load space filled with the *thump thump thump* of missile decoys firing into their wake, and Bunny's webbing belt tightened automatically, jerking her back in her seat.

Earlier

"Alright, you evil bastard, what have you done?" Bunny O'Hare said to herself under her breath as she scrolled through screen after screen of computer code on the laptop perched on an oil barrel in the stifling heat of the huge metal hangar at Chu-dong airfield.

It had taken her and Defense Advanced Research Projects Agency (DARPA) software engineer, Kevin Adair, the best part of a week to get under the digital hood of the X-61C Gremlin drone mothership that had been carrying out operational certification patrols along the South Korean DMZ demarcation line.

Their job had not been made easier by the fact that the last software engineer on the program had lost his mind. Raving about 'nanobots in my bloodstream', he'd been carried away in an ambulance to Hwacheon Medical Clinic for urgent Stateside repatriation. But not before he'd locked the Gremlin into a figure-eight orbit at 60,000 feet over the sea off Busan in southeast South Korea and hidden its code behind about five layers of encryption.

Any other drone might have run out of fuel before Bunny O'Hare could be pulled out of the program she was working on at Peterson Air Force Base, Colorado, and flown halfway around the world to South Korea. But Gremlin was not any other drone. She was the final fruit of a program started ten years earlier to deliver a loitering drone mothership capable of both launching, recovering and recharging electrically powered micro-drones for either reconnaissance or swarming attacks. Gremlin was also the first and only US semi-autonomous airborne weapons platform fitted with the Seaborg Compact Molten Salt Reactor powerplant.

While the Gremlin program was publicly acknowledged by DARPA, the use of a Seaborg reactor as a power source was not. The South Korean public would probably not have reacted well to the idea of a pilotless nuclear-powered aircraft circling in the skies over 'the Land of Morning Calm'. But DARPA had never intended for them to know.

Gremlin was a familiar sight to air traffic controllers in South Korea and the cover story generated by DARPA was that she was simply a prototype loitering surveillance drone.

She was much, much more.

Her trashcan-sized 115-megawatt powerplant drove the two engines which kept her aloft, with enough reserve power to charge and recharge the 200 micro-drones docked to her four payload pylons. Each engine could put out nearly 1,600 horsepower – similar to the monster powerplants of the fastest World War 2 fighter aircraft – allowing it to reach speeds up to 450 miles an hour. With a fuselage that looked like a cross between a cruise missile and a stealth fighter, it would never outrun a supersonic fighter or anti-air missile, but it could twist and turn like a swallow in flight and was fitted with the same electronic warfare and air defense decoy suite used by the F-35 Panther fighter aircraft. It could fly anywhere from the nap of the earth up to 50,000 feet and had an effectively unlimited range.

Which was all well and good as long as it could be controlled and wasn't parked in orbit over Busan with its comms system locked down.

"Found it! Comms bypass code," Adair said at the laptop beside her.

"Can you isolate it?"

"Think so, give me five."

What else had the psycho done? Strangely, she wasn't so

worried about the nuclear power plant, unless the Gremlin was programmed to dive into a South Korean shopping mall. Its Seaborg reactor had been chosen precisely because its nuclear fuel was mixed into a molten fluoride salt which simply turned to solid rock if it came into contact with the atmosphere. It could never overheat and melt down.

Bunny was more worried about the drone's payload. The Gremlin had launched with a full payload of 40 recon and 160 swarming attack drones which its operator could launch and recover at will. If they could get into the weapons control system. Paging through the weapons system code modules, she couldn't see anything amiss. Navigation? Normal. Engine management and flight systems? Normal. Except ... wait.

"He's disabled the bloody landing gear."

"What?"

She leaned forward, paging back and forth through code to be sure. "Used a maintenance override to vent the landing gear hydraulics. We can send the command to lower and lock the gear, but it can't deploy. I can't land it."

Adair frowned. "Can't you, you know, just glide it in, land it on its belly or something, like they do on an airliner without landing gear?" He was a nice clean-cut kid, not long out of MIT, still a little overawed at the tech DARPA had given him to play with. He never cussed. He had no tattoos, visible or, Bunny was sure, otherwise. If he had a sweetheart, Bunny was willing to bet they met in high school. If there was a personality opposite of Bunny O'Hare, Kevin Adair was it.

Bunny laughed. "Sure, I *could* do that. I could dump the payload so that it didn't hit the dirt with 160 high-explosive micro-drones clinging to the fuselage..."

"Good."

"... but there is the little matter of that nuclear reactor."

"Ah. I thought it had all kinds of fail-safes?"

"It won't explode or melt down, no," she agreed. "But if it cracks open, it will leave a radioactive smear of molten rock along the runway about a hundred yards long. You want to volunteer to shovel it up?"

"Heck, no. I want to have kids one day," Adair said, turning back to his laptop. "And keep all my hair. What genius thought it would be a good idea to put a nuclear reactor on a flying drone?"

"I blame Russia. They decided to make a nuclear-powered cruise missile with unlimited range, and we had a President who said, 'well, if they can, why can't we?'. Luckily, we didn't go down that particular rabbit hole, but we still ended up here."

Adair had pulled up a map. "Ditch it at sea?"

Bunny nodded. "Ditch it at sea. Gently."

She was right. An urgent telecon with DARPA in Virginia, during which they got the Pentagon looped in, ended in the decision that Bunny would fly the Gremlin out. It had been designed to be flown either from a ground station, or from an airborne control center aboard a C130 gunship or similar. All she needed was a stable satellite uplink.

Bunny and Adair were told to pack up the ground station at Ungam-ni and transfer control of the Gremlin to an air-mobile console so that the drone mothership could be set to trail after her pilotless Defiant, three hundred miles from South Korea to the Sea of Japan, where the Landing Helicopter Dock, USS *Iwo Jima*, would be waiting to recover it.

Assuming Bunny could put it down on the water without breaking it into a hundred radioactive pieces.

They'd gotten to work quickly, tearing down the Gremlin's command trailer and supervising the crating of its sensitive equipment. In the end, Bunny was left standing on the side of the runway at Ungam-ni with the 100 lb. combined satellite transceiver and controller in a large duffel bag at her feet and the Gremlin circling safely fifty miles off the coast of South Korea. Like the loyal trooper he was, Adair was standing out in the sun with her and the rest of their gear, instead of being inside in the airconditioned hangar annex.

"You can go inside, it's bloody hot out here," she told him. "I'll get you, once I've loaded our stuff aboard and synched up the comms gear." Their ride was making a couple of pickups before it got to them. It wasn't likely to be on time.

A humid wind lifted off the concrete apron she was standing on. She'd always thought of Korea as a cold place and wished someone had told her that in July it could reach the high seventies. She'd left Colorado with her standard uniform of black khaki utility trousers, leather boots, torn black sweater, a few t-shirts and a toothbrush and was fast remembering black was not the right color for summer in Asia.

"No, that's alright. Anyway, it's coming now," he said, pointing at a small but growing black spot in the distance. So, she'd been wrong. It was on time. Soon the thump of the Defiant's twin rotors was audible. A few of the ground crew outside the main hangar stopped up to watch it come in. "Hey, can I ask you something personal?" Adair said.

Bunny frowned at him. "No."

"Cool, because I was wondering ... oh, you said no."

"No, Adair," Bunny repeated. "No offense, but I'm a 'need to know' sort of person, and you don't need."

"I get it, I was just wondering about the ... all the ..." He made a gesture at her face.

Bunny sighed. She guessed he was referring to her pierced nose. And eyebrow, lip, ears, and cheeks. Or the tattoos. "That's you asking me a personal question, right there."

"Right, sorry. But, did it hurt?"

She reached down, lifted up a duffel bag and handed it to him. "Mind on the mission, Kev."

"Right."

He looked like he was about to say something else, but the thud of the Defiant's rotors had increased in volume as it got closer, making conversation impossible.

That had been a couple of hours ago. Right now, Bunny was

waking to the smell of ozone. A smell she recognized. Fried electronics.

Where the hell was she? She looked around and decided she was upside down in a hell house of metal, glass and … blood? She could smell blood too.

Not her own. The blood was dripping from the young guy strapped into the chair beside her, the spear of a broken cargo restraint coming out the front of his chest. He was dead. Name, what was his name?

Adair.

Red Adair. Fred Adair. Like the movie star. No. His face looked so calm. *Dead* Adair.

Kevin. That was it.

She reached up to punch the clasp on the webbing across her chest and then realized that would be a dumb idea, because it would dump her on her head. And it seemed she had already taken a blow or two to the skull, her thinking as fuzzy as she was. She looked slowly and painfully around her. OK, another dead guy. The Navy loadmaster. She hadn't even had time to ask his name. She had no idea how long she'd been out, but hoped he'd died quickly. The angle of his neck and head suggested he had.

Reaching gingerly below her head with her hands, she felt a webbed baggage rack, empty. Saw some metal cases and smashed rolling pallets, like the kind every military everywhere loads into aircraft. Bottles of water, lying everywhere. Really? Their flight was supposed to be taking top secret ordnance out of South Korea and someone had decided they had room for a pallet of bottled water? Speaking of water … could she hear water outside?

Getting ready to take her weight on her right arm and hold onto her harness with her left, she hooked her feet into the chair supports by her ankles and punched the harness release on her chest. She dropped a few inches before her feet caught her fall and, crabbing at the baggage harness, she lowered herself down without breaking her neck. She was still wearing her helmet and thought about taking it off, but then decided it might just be keeping her skull together, and she could do it later.

She checked the Navy loadmaster for any sign of life, even though his neck was clearly snapped. He might have been paralyzed from the neck down, but alive. Luckily for him, he wasn't. Adair was well and truly gone too. She didn't even need to check for a pulse there.

There was a wedge of daylight at the rear of the payload bay and she crawled toward it. It led out to a rocky riverbank and a river in full flow just twenty yards away.

If you'd come down in that river, you'd have survived just long enough to drown, O'Hare.

She looked back at the upside-down Defiant. Her aviator's eye could see straight away why it had come down. Where its right turbine nacelle should have been was just a blackened hole and leaking engine fluid.

Missile. She remembered something about a missile. It must have homed on the hot engine. Of the push-prop tail rotor, there was no sign at all. It looked like the entire tail section had sheared off. That explained how she'd been able to get out so easily. Freight containers and pallets littered the ground behind the downed chopper.

There was something else trying to get her attention. A beeping noise in her ears. She blinked a few times, tilting her head to try and work out if the beep was coming from inside the chopper or outside it.

Stupid. It was the helmet. Her helmet was trying to tell her something. Her heads-up display visor had been pushed up during the crash landing and she pulled it down. Miraculously, it was still working, and connected to something inside the chopper. Oh, right, the Gremlin comms unit. Text was running across the bottom of a zoomed-out map of Korea.

Navigation deviation. Replot waypoints?

It was asking her whether she wanted to update the Gremlin's navigation waypoints to take into account her 'navigation deviation'. She laughed bitterly. Navigation deviation? That was one way to describe an uncontrolled crash landing. Outward from the rushing river, steep mountains covered in rocks and scrubby trees rose into the sky in every direction.

She slumped onto her backside and lay down on the cool, wet gravel of the riverbank, forearms up over her helmeted face.

What in the freaking hell kind of situation had she gotten into now?

DMZ: This is the Future of War will be out summer 2022

For news and announcements or to just hang out with author FX Holden visit:

https://www.facebook.com/hardcorethrillers/

Glossary

For simplicity, this glossary is common across all Future War novels and may refer to systems not in this novel. Please note, weapons or systems marked with an asterisk* are currently still under development. If there is no asterisk, then the system has already been deployed by at least one nation.

3D PRINTER: A printer which can recreate a 3D object based on a three-dimensional digital model, typically by laying down many thin layers of a material in succession

ADA*: All Domain Attack. An attack on an enemy in which all operational domains – space, cyber, ground, air and naval – are engaged either simultaneously or sequentially

AI: Artificial intelligence, as applied in aircraft to assist pilots, in intelligence to assist with intelligence analysis, or in ordnance such as drones and unmanned vehicles to allow semi-autonomous decision making

AIM-120D: US medium-range supersonic air-to-air missile

AIM-260* Joint Advanced Tactical Missile (JATM), proposed replacement for AIM-120, with twin-boost phase, launch and loiter capability. Swarming capability has been discussed.

AIS: Automated identification system, a system used by all ships to provide update data on their location to their owners and insurers. Civilian shipping is required to keep their transponder on at all times unless under threat from pirates; military ships transmit at their own discretion. Rogue nations often ignore the requirement in order to hide the location of ships with illicit cargoes or conducting illegal activities.

ALL DOMAIN KILL CHAIN*: Also known as Multi-Domain Kill Chain. An attack in which advanced AI allows high-speed assimilation of data from multiple sources (satellite, cyber, ground and air) to generate engagement solutions for military maneuver, precision fire support, artillery or combat air support.

AMD-65: Russian-made military assault rifle

AN/APG-81: The active electronically scanned array (AESA) radar system on the F-35 Panther that allows it to track and engage multiple air and ground targets simultaneously

ANGELS: Radio brevity code for 'thousands of feet'. Angels five is five thousand feet

AO YIN: Legendary Chinese four-horned bull with insatiable appetite for human flesh

APC: Armored personnel carrier; a wheeled or tracked lightly armored vehicle able to transport troops into combat and provide limited covering fire

ARMATA T-14: Next-generation Russian main battle tank

ASFN: Anti-screw fouling net. Traditionally, a net boom laid across the entrance of a harbor to hinder the entrance of ships or submarines. Can also be dropped from a fast boat, or fired from a subsea drone to foul the screws of a surface vessel.

ASRAAM: Advanced Short-Range Air-to-Air Missile (infrared only)

ASROC: Anti-submarine rocket-launched torpedo. Allows a torpedo to be fired at a submerged target from up to ten miles away, allowing the torpedo to enter the water close to the target and reducing the chances the target can evade the attack.

ASTUTE CLASS: Next-generation British nuclear-powered attack submarine (SSN) designed for stealth operation. Powered by a Rolls Royce reactor plant coupled to a pump-jet propulsion system. *HMS Astute* is the first of seven planned hulls, *HMS Agincourt* is the last. Can carry up to 38 torpedoes and cruise missiles, and is one of the first British submarines to be steered by a 'pilot' using a joystick.

ASW: Anti-Submarine Warfare

AWACS: Airborne Warning and Control System aircraft, otherwise known as AEW&C (Airborne Early Warning and Control). Aircraft with advanced radar and communication systems that can detect aircraft at ranges up to several hundred miles, and direct air operations over a combat theatre.

AXEHEAD: Russian long-range hypersonic air-to-air missile

B-21 RAIDER*: Replacement for the retiring US B-2 Stealth Bomber and B-52. The Raider is intended to provide a lower-cost, stealthier alternative to the B-2 with expanded weapons delivery capabilities to include hypersonic and beyond visual range air-to-air missiles.

BARRETT MRAD M22: Multirole adaptive design sniper rifle with replaceable barrels, capable of firing different ammunition types including anti-materiel rounds, accurate out to 1,500 meters or nearly one mile

BATS*: Boeing Airpower Teaming System, semi-autonomous unmanned combat aircraft. The BATS drone is designed to accompany 4th- and 5th-generation fighter aircraft on missions either in an air escort, recon or electronic warfare capacity.

BELLADONNA: A Russian-made mobile electronic warfare vehicle capable of jamming enemy airborne warning aircraft, ground radars, radio communications and radar-guided missiles

BESAT*: New 1,200-ton class of Iranian SSP (air-independent propulsion) submarine. Also known as Project Qaaem. Capable of launching mines, torpedoes or cruise missiles

BIG RED ONE: US 1st Infantry Division (see also BRO), aka the Bloody First

BINGO: Radio brevity code indicating that an aircraft has only enough fuel left for a return to base

BLOODY FIRST: US 1st Infantry Division, aka the Big Red One (BRO)

BOGEY: Unidentified aircraft detected by radar

BRADLEY UGCV*: US unmanned ground combat vehicle prototype based on a modified M3 Bradley combat fighting vehicle. A tracked vehicle with medium armor, it is intended to be controlled remotely by a crew in a vehicle, or ground troops, up to two miles away. Armed with 5kw blinding laser and autoloading TOW anti-tank missiles. See also HYPERION

BRO: Big Red One or Bloody First, nickname for US Army 1st Infantry Division

BTR-80: A Russian-made amphibious armored personnel carrier armed with a 30mm automatic cannon

BUG OUT: Withdraw from combat

BUK: Russian-made self-propelled anti-aircraft missile system designed to engage medium-range targets such as aircraft, smart bombs and cruise missiles

BUSTER: 100% throttle setting on an aircraft, or full military power

CAP: Combat air patrol; an offensive or defensive air patrol over an objective

CAS: Close air support; air action by rotary-winged or fixed-wing aircraft against hostile targets in close proximity to friendly forces. CAS operations are often directed by a joint terminal air controller, or JTAC, embedded with a military unit.

CASA CN-235: Turkish Air Force medium-range twin-engined transport aircraft

CBRN: Chemical, biological, radiological or nuclear (see also NBC SUIT)

CCP: Communist Party of China. Governed by a Politburo comprising the Chinese Premier and senior party ministers and officials.

CENTURION: US 20mm radar-guided close-in weapons system for protection of ground or naval assets against attack by artillery, rocket or missiles

CHAMP*: Counter-electronics High Power Microwave Advanced Missiles; a 'launch and loiter' cruise missile which attacks sensitive electronics with high power microwave bursts to damage electronics. Similar in effect to an electromagnetic pulse (EMP) weapon.

CIC: Combat Information Center. The 'nerve center' on an early warning aircraft, warship or submarine that functions as a tactical center and provides processed information for command and control of the near battlespace or area of operations. On a warship, acts on orders from and relays information to the bridge.

CO: Commanding Officer

COALITION: Coalition of Nations involved in *Operation Anatolia Screen*: Turkey, US, UK, Australia, Germany

COLT: Combat Observation Laser Team; a forward artillery observer team armed with a laser for designating targets for attack by precision-guided munitions

CONSTELLATION* class frigate: the result of the US FFG(X) program, a warship with advanced anti-air, anti-surface and anti-submarine capabilities capable of serving as a data integration and communication hub. The first ship in the class, *USS Constellation*, is expected to enter service mid-2020s. *USS Congress* will be the second ship in the class.

CONTROL ROOM: the compartment on a submarine from which weapons, sensors, propulsion and navigation commands are coordinated

COP: Combat Outpost (US)

C-RAM: Counter-rocket, artillery and mortar cannon, also abbreviated counter-RAM

CROWS: Common Remotely Operated Weapon Station, a weapon such as .50 caliber machine gun, mounted on a turret and controlled remotely by a soldier inside a vehicle, bunker or command post

CUDA*: Missile nickname (from barracuda) for the supersonic US short- to medium-range 'Small Advanced Capabilities Missile'. It has tri-mode (optical, active radar and infrared heat-seeking) sensors, thrust vectoring for extreme maneuverability and a hit-to-kill terminal attack

CYBERCOM: US Cyberspace combatant command responsible for cyber defense and warfare.

DARPA: US Defense Advanced Research Projects Agency, a research and development agency responsible for bringing new military technologies to the US armed forces

DAS: Distributed Aperture System; a 360-degree sensor system on the F-35 Panther allowing the pilot to track targets visually at greater than 'eyeball' range

DFDA: Australian armed forces Defense Forces Discipline Act

DFM: Australian armed forces Defense Force Magistrate

DIA: The US Defense Intelligence Agency

DIRECTOR OF NATIONAL CYBER SECURITY*. The NSA's Cyber Security Directorate is an organization that unifies NSA's foreign intelligence and cyber defense missions and is charged with preventing and eradicating threats to National Security Systems and the Defense Industrial Base. Various US government sources have mooted the elevation of the role of Director of Cyber Security to a Cabinet-level Director of National Cyber Security (on a level with the Director of National Intelligence), appointed by the US President to coordinate the activities of the many different agencies and military departments engaged in cyber warfare.

DRONE: Unmanned aerial vehicle, UCAV or UAV, used for combat, transport, refueling or reconnaissance

ECS: Engagement Control Station; the local control center for a HELLADS laser battery which tracks targets and directs anti-air defensive fire

EMP: Electromagnetic pulse. Nuclear weapons produce an EMP wave which can destroy unshielded electronic components. The major military powers have also been experimenting with non-nuclear weapons which can also produce an EMP pulse – see CHAMP missile

ETA: Estimated Time of Arrival

F-16 FALCON: US-made 4th-generation multirole fighter aircraft flown by Turkey

F-35: US 5th-generation fighter aircraft, known either as the Panther (pilot nickname) or Lightning II (manufacturer name). The Panther nickname was first coined by the 6th Weapons Squadron 'Panther Tamers'. There is much speculation about the capabilities of the Panther, just as there is about the Russian Su-57 Felon. Neither has been extensively combat tested.

F-47B (currently X-47) FANTOM*: A Northrop Grumman

demonstration unmanned combat aerial vehicle (UCAV) in trials with the US Navy and a part of the DARPA Joint UCAS program. See also MQ-25 STINGRAY

FAC: Forward air controller; an aviator embedded with a ground unit to direct close air support attacks. See also TAC(P) or JTAC

FAST MOVERS: Fighter jets

FATEH: Iranian SSK (diesel electric) submarine. At 500 tons, also considered a midget submarine. Capable of launching torpedoes, torpedo-launched cruise missiles and mines

FELON: Russian 5th-generation stealth fighter aircraft, the Sukhoi Su-57. There is much speculation about the capabilities of the Felon, just as there is about the US F-35 Panther. Neither has been extensively combat tested.

FINGER FOUR FORMATION: a fighter aircraft patrol formation in which four aircraft fly together in a pattern that resembles the tips of the four fingers of a hand. Four such formations can form a squadron of 12 aircraft.

FIRESCOUT: an unmanned autonomous scout helicopter for service on US warships, used for anti-ship and anti-submarine operations

FISTER: A member of a FiST (Fire Support Team)

FLANKER: Russian Sukhoi-30 or 35 attack aircraft; see also J-11 (China)

FOX (1, 2 or 3): Radio brevity code indicating a pilot has fired an air-to-air missile, either semi-active radar seeking (1), infrared (2) or active radar seeking (3)

GAL*: A natural language learning system (AI) used by Israel's Unit 8200 to conduct complex analytical research support

GAL-CLASS SUBMARINE: An upgraded *Dolphin II* class submarine, fitted with the GAL AI system, allowing it to be operated by a two-person crew

G/ATOR: Ground/Air Oriented Task Radar (GATOR); a radar specialized for the detection of incoming artillery fire, rockets or missiles. Also able to calculate the origin of attack for counterfire purposes.

GBU: Guided Bomb Unit

GPS: Global Positioning System, a network of civilian or military satellites used to provide accurate map reference and location data

GRAY WOLF*: US subsonic standoff air-launched cruise missile with swarming (horde) capabilities. The Gray Wolf is designed to launch from multiple aircraft, including the C-130, and defeat enemy air defenses by overwhelming them with large numbers. It will feature modular swap-out warheads.

GREYHOUND: Radio brevity code for the launch of an air-ground missile

GRU: Russian military intelligence service

H-20*: Xian Hong 20 stealth bomber with a range of 12,000 km or 7,500 miles and payload of 10 tons. Comparable to the US B-21.

HARM: Homing Anti-Radar Missile; a missile which homes on the signals produced by anti-air missile radars like that used by the BUK or PANTSIR

HAWKEYE: Northrop Grumman E2D airborne warning and control aircraft. Capable of launching from aircraft carriers and networking (sharing data) with compatible aircraft.

HE: High-explosive munitions; general purpose explosive warheads

HEAT: High-Explosive Anti-Tank munitions; shells specially designed to penetrate armor

HELLADS*: High Energy Liquid Laser Area Defense System; an alternative to missile or projectile-based air defense systems that attacks enemy missiles, rockets or bombs with high energy laser and/or microwave pulses. Currently being tested by US, Chinese, Russian and EU ground, air and naval forces.

HOLMES*: A natural language learning system (AI) used by the NSA to conduct sophisticated analytical research support. The NSA has publicly reported it is already using AI for cyber defense and exploring machine learning potential.

HORDE*: Drones, missiles or smart bombs with onboard AI and the ability to coordinate their actions with other drones while in flight, either autonomously or using preselected protocols. 'Horde' tactics differ from 'swarm' tactics in that they rely on large numbers to overwhelm enemy defenses. See also SWARM

HPM*: High Power Microwave; an untargeted local area defensive weapon which attacks sensitive electronics in missiles and guided bombs to damage electronics such as guidance systems

HSU-003*: Planned Chinese large unmanned underwater vehicle optimized for seabed warfare, i.e. piloting itself to a specific location on the sea floor (a harbor or shipping lane) and conducting reconnaissance or anti-shipping attacks. Comparable to the US Orca.

HYPERION*: Proposed lightly armored unmanned ground vehicle (UGCV). Can be fitted with turret-mounted 50kw laser for anti-air, anti-personnel defense and autoloading TOW missile launcher. See also BRADLEY UGCV

HYPERSONIC: Speeds greater than 5x the speed of sound

ICC: Information Coordination Center; command center for multiple air defense batteries such as PATRIOT or HELLADS

IED: Improvised explosive device, for example, a roadside bomb

IFF: Identify Friend or Foe transponder, a radio transponder that allows weapons systems to determine whether a target is an ally or enemy

IFV: Infantry fighting vehicle, a highly mobile, lightly armored, wheeled or tracked vehicle capable of carrying troops into a combat and providing fire support. See NAMER

IMA BK: The combat AI built into Russia's Su-57 Felon and Okhotnik fighter aircraft

IR: Infrared or heat-seeking system

ISIS: Self-proclaimed Islamic State of Iraq and Syria

J-7: Fishbed; 3rd-generation Chinese fighter, a copy of cold war Russian Mig-21

J-10: Vigorous Dragon; 3rd-generation Chinese fighter, comparable to US F-16

J-11: Flanker; 4th-generation Chinese fighter, copy of Russian Su-27

J-15: Flying Shark; 4th-generation PLA Navy, twin-engine twin-seat fighter, comparable to Russian Su-33 and a further development of the J-11. Currently the most common aircraft flown off China's aircraft carriers.

J-16*: *Zhi Sheng* (Intelligence Victory); 4th-generation, two-seater twin-engine multirole strike fighter. In 2019 it was announced a variant of the J-16 was being developed with *Zhi Sheng* Artificial Intelligence to replace the human 'backseater' or copilot.

J-20: 'Mighty Dragon'; 5th-generation single-seat, twin-engine Chinese stealth fighter, claimed to be comparable to the US F-35 or F-22, or Russian Su-57

JAGM: Joint air-ground missile. A US short-range anti-armor or anti-personnel missile fired from an aircraft. It can be laser or radar guided and has an 18 lb. warhead.

JASSM: AGM-158 Joint Air-to-Surface Standoff Missile; long-range subsonic stealth cruise missile

JDAM: Joint Direct Attack Munition; bombs guided by laser or GPS to their targets

JLTV*: US Joint Light Tactical Vehicle; planned replacement for the US ground forces Humvee multipurpose vehicle, to be available in recon/scout, infantry transport, heavy guns, close combat, command and control, or ambulance versions

JTAC: Joint terminal air controller. A member of a ground force – e.g., Marine unit – trained to direct the action of combat aircraft engaged in close air support and other offensive air operations from a forward position. See also CAS

K-77M*: Supersonic Russian-made medium-range active radar homing air-to-air missile with extreme maneuverability. It is being developed from the existing R-77 missile.

KALIBR: Russian-made anti-ship, anti-submarine and land

attack cruise missile with 500kg conventional or nuclear warhead. The Kalibr-M variant* will have an extended range of up to 4,500 km or 2,700 miles (the distance of, e.g., Iran to Paris).

KARAKURT CLASS: A Russian corvette class which first entered service in 2018. Armed with Pantsir close-in weapons systems, Sosna-R anti-air missile defense and Kalibr supersonic anti-ship missiles. An anti-submarine sensor/weapon loadout is planned but not yet deployed.

KC-135 STRATOTANKER: US airborne refueling aircraft

KRYPTON: Supersonic Russian air-launched anti-radar missile, it is also being adapted for use against ships and large aircraft

LAUNCH AND LOITER: The capability of a missile or drone to fly itself to a target area and wait at altitude for final targeting instructions

LCS: Littoral combat ship. In the US Navy it refers to the *Independence* or *Freedom* class; in Iran, the *Safineh* class; in other navies it may be considered equivalent to a frigate or corvette class. Has the capabilities of a small assault transport, including a flight deck and hangar for housing two SH-60 or MH-60 Seahawk helicopters, a stern ramp for operating small boats, and the cargo volume and payload to deliver a small assault force with fighting vehicles to a roll-on/roll-off port facility. Standard armaments include Mk 110 57mm guns and RIM-116 Rolling Airframe Missiles. Also equipped with autonomous air, surface and underwater vehicles. Possessing lower air defense and surface warfare capabilities than destroyers, the LCS concept emphasizes speed, flexible mission modules and a shallow draft.

LEOPARD: Main battle tank fielded by NATO forces including Turkey

LIAONING: China's first aircraft carrier, modified from the former Russian Navy aircraft cruiser, the *Varyag*. Since superseded by China's Type 002 (*Shandong*) and Type 003 carriers, the *Liaoning* is now used for testing new technologies for carrier use, such as the J-20 stealth fighter.

LOITERING MUNITION: A missile or bomb able to wait at altitude for final targeting instructions

LONG-RANGE HYPERSONIC WEAPONS (LRHW)*: A prototype US missile consisting of a rocket and glide vehicle, capable of being launched by submarine, from land or from aircraft

LS3*: Legged Squad Support System – a mechanized dog-like robot powered by hydrogen fuel cells and supported by a cloud-based AI. Currently being explored by DARPA and the US armed forces for logistical support or squad scouting and IED detection roles.

LTMV: Light Tactical Multirole Vehicle; a very long name for what is essentially a jeep

M1A2/3 ABRAMS*: US main battle tank. In 2016, the US Army and Marine Corps began testing out the Israeli Trophy active protection system to provide additional defense against incoming projectiles. Improvements planned for the M1A3 are to include a lighter 120mm gun, added road wheels with improved suspension, a more durable track, lighter-weight armor, long-range precision armaments, and infrared camera and laser detectors.

M22: See BARRETT MRAD M22 sniper rifle

M27: US-made military assault rifle

MAD: Magnetic Anomaly Detection, used by warships to detect large manmade objects under the surface of the sea, such as mines, or submarines

MAIN BATTLE TANK: See MBT

MASS: Marine Autonomous Surface Ship, or autonomous trailing vessel

MBT: Main battle tank; a heavily armored combat vehicle capable of direct fire and maneuver

MEFP: Multiple Explosive Formed Penetrators; a defensive weapon which uses small explosive charges to create and fire small metal slugs at an incoming projectile, thereby destroying it

MEMS: Micro-Electro-Mechanical System

METEOR: Long-range air-to-air missile with active radar seeker, but also able to be updated with target data in-flight by any suitably equipped allied unit

MIA: Missing in action

MIKE: Radio brevity code for minutes

MIL-25: Export version of the Mi-25 'Hind' Russian helicopter gunship

MOPP: Mission-Oriented Protective Posture protective gear; equipment worn to protect troops against CBRN weapons. See also NBC SUIT

MP: Military Police

MQ-25 STINGRAY: The MQ-25 Stingray is a Boeing-designed prototype unmanned US airborne refueling aircraft. See also X-47B Fantom

MSS: Ministry of State Security, Chinese umbrella intelligence organization responsible for counterespionage and counterterrorism, and foreign intelligence gathering. Equivalent to the US FBI, CIA and NSA.

NAMER: (Leopard) Israeli infantry fighting vehicle (IFV). More heavily armored than a Merkava IV main battle tank. According to the Israel Defense Forces, the Namer is the most heavily armored vehicle in the world of any type.

NATO: North Atlantic Treaty Organization

NAVAL STRIKE MISSILE (NSM): Supersonic anti-ship missile deployed by NATO navies

NBC SUIT: A protective suit issued to protect the wearer against Nuclear, Biological or Chemical weapons. Usually includes a lining to protect the user from radiation and either a gas mask or air recycling unit.

NORAD: The North American Aerospace Defense Command is a United States and Canadian bi-national organization charged with the missions of aerospace warning, aerospace control and maritime warning for North America. Aerospace warning includes the detection, validation and warning of attack against North America whether by aircraft, missiles or space vehicles, through mutual support arrangements with other commands.

NSA: US National Security Agency, cyber intelligence, cyber warfare and defense agency

OFSET*: Offensive Swarm Enabled Tactical drones. Proposed US anti-personnel, anti-armor drone system capable of swarming AI (see SWARM) and able to deploy small munitions against enemy troop or vehicles while moving.

OKHOTNIK*: 5th-generation Sukhoi S-70 unmanned stealth combat aircraft using avionics systems from the Su-57 Felon and fitted with two internal weapons bays, for 7,000kg of ordnance. Requires a pilot and systems officer, similar to current US unmanned combat aircraft. Can be paired with Su-57 aircraft and controlled by a pilot.

OMON: Otryad Mobil'nyy Osobogo Naznacheniya; the Russian National Guard mobile police force

ORCA*: Prototype US large displacement unmanned underwater vehicle with modular payload bay capable of anti-submarine, anti-ship or reconnaissance activities

OVOD: Subsonic Russian-made air-launched cruise missile capable of carrying high-explosive, submunition or fragmentation warheads

PANTHER: Pilot name for the F-35 Lightning II stealth fighter, first coined by the 6th Weapons Squadron 'Panther Tamers'. There is much speculation about the capabilities of the Panther, just as there is about the Russian Su-57 Felon. Neither has been extensively combat tested.

PANTSIR: Russian-made truck-mounted anti-aircraft system which is a further development of the PENSNE: 'Pince-nez' in English. A Russian-made autonomous ground-to-air missile currently being rolled out for the BUK anti-air defense system.

PARS: Turkish light armored vehicle

PATRIOT: An anti-aircraft, anti-missile missile defense system which uses its own radar to identify and engage airborne threats

PEACE EAGLE: Turkish Boeing 737 Airborne Early Warning and Control aircraft (see AWACS)

PENSNE: See PANTSIR

PERDIX*: Lightweight air-launched armed microdrone with swarming capability (see SWARM). Designed to be launched from underwing canisters or even from the flare/chaff launchers of existing aircraft. Can be used for recon, target identification or delivery of lightweight ordnance.

PEREGRINE*: US medium-range, multimode (infrared, radar, optical) seeker missile with short form body designed for use by stealth aircraft

PERSEUS*: A stealth, hypersonic, multiple warhead missile under development for the British Royal Navy and French Navy

PHASED-ARRAY RADAR: A radar which can steer a beam of radio waves quickly across the sky to detect planes and missiles

PL-15: Chinese medium-range radar-guided air-to-air missile, comparable to the US AIM-120D or UK Meteor

PL-21*: Chinese long-range multimode missile (radar, infrared, optical), comparable to US AIM-260

PLA: People's Liberation Army

PLA-AF (PLAAAF): People's Liberation Army Air Force, comparable to the US Air Force, with more than 400 3rd-generation fighter aircraft, 1,200 4th-generation, and nearly 200 5th-generation stealth aircraft

PLA-N (PLAN): People's Liberation Army Navy

PLA-N AF (PLANAF): People's Liberation Army Navy Air Force, comparable to the US Navy Air Force and Marine Corps Aviation, it performs coastal protection and aircraft carrier operations with more than 250 3rd-generation fighter aircraft, and 150 4th-generation fighter aircraft.

PODNOS: Russian-made portable 82mm mortar

PUMP-JET PROPULSION: A propulsion system comprising a jet of water and a nozzle to direct the flow of water for steering purposes. Used on some submarines due to a quieter acoustic signature than that generated by a screw. The most 'stealthy' submarines are regarded to be those powered by diesel electric engines and pump-jet propulsion, such as trialed on the Russian *Kilo* class and proposed for the Australian *Attack* class*.

QHS*: Quantum Harmonic Sensor; a sensor system for detecting stealth aircraft at long ranges by analyzing the electromagnetic disturbances they create in background radiation

RAAF: Royal Australian Air Force

RAF: Royal Air Force (UK)

ROE: Rules of Engagement; the rules laid down by military commanders under which a unit can or cannot engage in combat. For example, 'units may only engage a hostile force if fired upon first'.

RPG: Rocket-propelled grenade

RTB: Return to base

SAFINEH CLASS: Also known as *Mowj/Wave* class. An Iranian trimaran hulled high-speed missile vessel equivalent to the US LCS class, or the Russia *Karakurt*-class corvette

SAM: Surface-to-Air Missile; an anti-air missile (often shortened to SA) for engaging aircraft

SAR: See SYNTHETIC APERTURE RADAR

SCREW: The propeller used to drive a boat or ship is referred to as a screw (helical blade) propeller. Submarine propellers typically comprise five to seven blades. See also PUMP-JET PROPULSION

SEAD: Suppression of Enemy Air Defenses; an air attack intended to take down enemy anti-air defense systems; see also WILD WEASEL

SENTINEL*: Lockheed Martin RQ-170 Sentinel flying wing stealth reconnaissance drone

SIDEWINDER: Heat-seeking short-range air-to-air missile

SITREP: Situation Report

SKYHAWK*: Chinese drone designed to team with fighter aircraft to provide added sensor or weapons delivery capabilities. Comparable to the planned US Boeing Loyal Wingman or Kratos drones.

SKY THUNDER: Chinese 1,000 lb. stealth air-launched cruise missile with swappable payload modules

SLR: Single lens reflex camera, favored by photojournalists

SMERCH: Russian-made 300mm rocket launcher capable of firing high-explosive, submunition or chemical weapons warheads

SPACECOM: United States Space Command (*USS*PACECOM or SPACECOM) is a unified combatant command of the United States Department of Defense, responsible for military operations in outer space, specifically all operations above 100 km above mean sea level

SPEAR/SPEAR-EW*: UK/Europe Select Precision at Range air-to-ground standoff attack missile, with LAUNCH AND LOITER capabilities. Will utilize a modular 'swappable' warhead system featuring high-explosive, anti-armor, fragmentation or electronic warfare (EW) warheads.

SPETSNAZ: Russian Special Operations Forces

SPLASH: Radio brevity code indicating a target has been destroyed

SSBN: Strategic-level nuclear-powered (N) submarine platform for firing ballistic (B) missiles. Examples: UK *Vanguard* class, US *Ohio* class, Russia *Typhoon* class

SSC: Subsurface Contact Supervisor; supervises operations against subsurface contacts from within a ship's Combat Information Center (CIC)

SSGN: A guided missile (G) nuclear (N) submarine that carries and launches guided cruise missiles as its primary weapon. Examples: US *Ohio* class, Russia *Yasen* class

SSK: A diesel electric-powered submarine, quieter when submerged than a nuclear-powered submarine, but must rise to snorkel depth to run its diesel and recharge its batteries. Examples: Iranian *Fateh* class, Russian *Kilo* class, Israeli *Dolphin I* class

SSN: A general purpose attack submarine (SS) powered by a

nuclear reactor (N). Examples: HMS *Agincourt*, Russian *Akula* class

SSP: A diesel electric submarine with air-independent propulsion system able to recharge batteries without using atmospheric oxygen. Allows the submarine to stay submerged longer than a traditional SSK. Examples: Israeli *Dolphin II* class, Iranian *Besat** class

STANDOFF: Launched at long range

STINGER: US-made man-portable, low-level anti-air missile

STINGRAY*: The MQ-25 Stingray is a Boeing-designed prototype unmanned US airborne refueling aircraft

STORMBREAKER*: US air-launched, precision-guided glide bomb that can use millimeter radar, laser or infrared imaging to match and then prioritize targets when operating in semi-autonomous AI mode

SU-57: See FELON

SUBSONIC: Below the speed of sound (under 767 mph, 1,234 kph)

SUNBURN: Russian-made 220mm multiple rocket launcher capable of firing high-explosive, THERMOBARIC or penetrating warheads

SUPERSONIC: Faster than the speed of sound (over 767 mph, 1,234 kph); see also HYPERSONIC

SWARM: Drones, missiles or smart bombs with onboard AI and the ability to coordinate their actions with other drones while in flight, either autonomously or using preselected protocols. 'Swarm' tactics differ from 'horde' tactics in that swarms place more emphasis on coordinated action to defeat enemy defenses. See also HORDE

SYNTHETIC APERTURE RADAR (SAR): A form of radar that is used to create two-dimensional images or three-dimensional reconstructions of objects, such as landscapes. SAR uses the motion of the radar antenna over a target region to provide finer spatial resolution than conventional beam-scanning radars.

SYSOP: The systems operator inside the control station for a HELLADS battery, responsible for electronic and communications systems operation

T-14 ARMATA: Russian next-generation main battle tank or MBT. Designed as a 'universal combat platform' which can be adapted to infantry support, anti-armor or anti-armor configurations. First Russian MBT to be fitted with active electronically scanned array radar capable of identifying and engaging multiple air and ground targets simultaneously. Also the first Russian MBT to be fitted with a crew toilet. Used in combat in Syria from 2020.

T-90: Russian-made main battle tank

TAC(P): Tactical air controller, a specialist trained to direct close air support attacks. See also CAS; FAC; JTAC

TAO: Tactical action officer; officer in command of a ship's Combat Information Center (CIC)

TCA: Tactical control assistant, non-commissioned officer (NCO) in charge of identifying targets and directing fire for a single HELLADS or PATRIOT battery

TCO: Tactical control officer, officer in charge of a single HELLADS or PATRIOT missile battery

TD: Tactical Director; the officer directing multiple PATRIOT or HELLADS batteries

TEMPEST*: British/European 6th-generation stealth aircraft under development as a replacement for the RAF Tornado multirole fighter. It is planned to incorporate advanced combat AI to reduce pilot data overload, laser anti-missile defenses, and will team with swarming drones such as BATS. It may be developed in both manned and unmanned versions.

TERMINATOR: A Russian-made infantry fighting vehicle (see IFV) based on the chassis of the T-90 main battle tank, with 2x 30mm autocannons and 2x grenade or anti-tank missile launchers. Developed initially to support main battle tank operations, it has become popular for use in urban combat environments.

THERMOBARIC: Weapons, otherwise known as thermal or vacuum weapons, that use oxygen from the surrounding air to generate a high-temperature explosion and long-duration blast wave

THUNDER: Radio brevity code indicating one minute to weapons impact

TOW: US wire-guide anti-tank missile, fired either from a tripod launcher by ground troops or mounted on armored cavalry vehicles

TROPHY: Israeli-made anti-projectile defense system using explosively formed penetrators to defeat attacks on vehicles, high-value assets and aircraft. It is currently fitted to several Israeli and US armored vehicle types.

TUNGUSKA: A mobile Russian-made anti-aircraft vehicle incorporating both cannon and ground-to-air missiles

TYPE 95*: Planned Chinese 3rd-generation nuclear-powered attack submarine with vertical launch tubes and substantially reduced acoustic signature to current Chinese types

UAV: Unmanned aerial vehicle or drone, usually used for transport, refueling or reconnaissance

UCAS: Unmanned combat aerial support vehicle or drone

UCAV: Unmanned combat aerial vehicle; a fighter or attack aircraft

UDAR* UGV: Russian-made unmanned ground vehicle which integrates remotely operated turrets (30mm autocannon, Kornet anti-tank missile or anti-air missile) onto the chassis of a BMP-3 infantry fighting vehicle. The vehicle can be controlled at a range of up to 6 miles (10 km) by an operator with good line of sight, or via a tethered drone relay.

UDV: Underwater delivery vehicle. A small submersible transport used typically by naval commandos for covert insertion and recovery of troops.

UGV: Unmanned ground vehicle, also UGCV: Unmanned ground combat vehicle

UI: Un-Identified, as in 'UI contact'. See also BOGEY

UNIT 8200: Israel Defense Force cyber intelligence, cyber warfare and defense unit, aka the Israeli Signals Intelligence National Unit

URAGAN: Russian 220mm 16-tube rocket launcher, first fielded in the 1970s

U/S: Un-serviceable, out of commission, broken

USO: United Services Organizations; US military entertainment and personnel welfare services

V-22 OSPREY: Bell Boeing multi-mission tiltrotor aircraft capable of vertical takeoff and landing which resembles a conventional aircraft when in flight

V-280* VAPOR: Bell Boeing-proposed successor to the V-22, with higher speed, endurance, lift capacity and modular payload bay

V-290* VAPOR: Concept aircraft only. AI-enhanced V-280 with anti-radar reflective coating, added rear fuselage turbofan jet engines for additional speed, and forward-firing 20mm autocannons

VERBA: A Russian-made man-portable low-level anti-air missile with data networking capabilities, meaning it can use data from friendly ground or air radar systems to fly itself to a target

VIRGINIA CLASS SUBMARINE: e.g., *USS Idaho*, nuclear-powered, fast-attack submarines. Current capabilities include torpedo and cruise missiles. Planned capabilities include hypersonic missiles.

VYMPEL: Russian air-to-air missile manufacturer/type

WILD WEASEL: An air attack intended to take down enemy anti-air defense systems; see also SEAD

WINCHESTER: Radio brevity code for 'out of ordnance'

X-95: Israeli bullpup-style assault rifle. Bullpup-style rifles have their action behind the trigger, allowing for a more compact and maneuverable weapon. Commonly chambered for NATO 5.56mm ammunition.

YAKHONT: Also known as P-800 Onyx. Russian-made two-stage ramjet-propelled, terrain-following cruise missile.

Travels at subsonic speeds until close to its target where it is boosted to up to Mach 3. Can be fired from warships, submarines, aircraft or coastal batteries at sea or ground targets.

YPG: Kurdish People's Protection Unit militia (male)

YPJ: Kurdish Women's Protection Unit militia (female)

Z-9: Chinese attack helicopter, predecessor to Z-19

Z-19: Chinese light attack helicopter, comparable to US Viper

Z-20: Chinese medium-lift utility helicopter, comparable to US Blackhawk

Printed in Great Britain
by Amazon